LOOKING BOTH WAYS

LOOKING BOTH WAYS

Heritage and Identity of the Alutiiq People

Aron L. Crowell, Amy F. Steffian, and Gordon L. Pullar editors

A project of
The Arctic Studies Center, Department of Anthropology,
National Museum of Natural History, Smithsonian Institution
and
The Alutiiq Museum and Archaeological Repository

University of Alaska Press
Fairbanks

Elmer E. Rasmuson Library Cataloging-In-Publication Data:

Looking both ways : heritage and identity of the Alutiiq people / Aron L. Crowell, Amy F.
    Steffian, and Gordon L. Pullar, editors. — Fairbanks, Alaska : University of Alaska Press,
    c2001.
    xii, 265 p. : ill., maps ; 28 cm.
        Note: A project of The Arctic Studies Center, National Museum of Natural
    History, Smithsonian Institution and the Alutiiq Museum and Archaeological Repository.
        Includes bibliographical references (p. 247-254) and index.
    1. Pacific Gulf Yupik Eskimos--Alaska--History--Exhibitions. 2. Pacific Gulf Yupik
    Eskimos––Alaska--Ethnic identity--Exhibitions. 3. Pacific Gulf Yupik Eskimos--Material
    culture--Alaska–Exhibitions. 4. Pacific Gulf Yupik Eskimos--Alaska--Antiquities--
    Exhibitions. 5. Pacific Gulf Yupik Eskimos--Alaska--Religion--Exhibitions. 6. Pacific
    Gulf Yupik Eskimos--Alaska--Social life and customs--Exhibitions. I. Title. II. Crowell,
    Aron, 1952-. III. Steffian, Amy F. IV. Pullar, Gordon L.

    E99.E7 L665 2001

International Standard Book Number:
cloth, 1-889963-30-5
paper, 1-889963-31-3

Printed in Singapore by C & S Graphics

This publication was printed on acid-free paper which meets the minimum requirements for
American National Standard for Information Sciences—Permanence of Paper for Printed
Library Materials, ANSI Z39.48-1984.

PUBLICATION COORDINATION BY
    Pamela Odom, University of Alaska Press.

DESIGN AND PRODUCTION BY
    Dixon J. Jones, Rasmuson Library Graphics, University of Alaska Fairbanks.

OBJECT PHOTOGRAPHY BY
    Carl C. Hansen, Smithsonian Institution, unless otherwise noted.

ORTHOGRAPHY, PAGE X, COURTESY OF
    Jeff Leer, Alaska Native Language Center, University of Alaska Fairbanks.

FRONT COVER:
  • The village of Old Harbor, Kodiak Island, 1997. Photograph © Chris Arend/Alaska
    Stock.com
  • Lucille Antowak Davis lighting a seal oil lamp at the 1998 Alutiiq Elders and Youth
    Conference, Kodiak, Alaska.
    Photograph by Amy Steffian.
  • Painting from box lid, Karluk 1 site, Kodiak Island. Alutiiq Museum, Koniag, Inc.,
    collection. Photograph by Carl C. Hansen, Smithsonian Institution.

BACK COVER:
  • Kayakers from Nanwalek at the Tamamta Katuhluta heritage festival, Homer, Alaska,
    1997. Photograph by Lena Anderson.
  • Portrait carving, Uyak site, Kodiak Island. National Museum of Natural History,
    Smithsonian Institution. Photograph by Carl C. Hansen, Smithsonian Institution.

To all the new generations.
They will learn from this and keep it going.

Mary Peterson, Kodiak Island Elder

Contents

5 Súgucihpet—"Our Way of Living"

by Aron L. Crowell and April Laktonen

Orthography

The Alutiiq orthography used in this volume is the standard orthography currently employed at the Alaska Native Language Center, University of Alaska Fairbanks:

Stops:	*p, t, c, k, kw, q*
Voiceless fricatives:	*f, l̲, s, g, gw, h*
Voiced sonorants:	*l, r, y, w*
Voiced nasals:	*m, n, ng*
Voiceless nasals:	*m̲, n̲, ng̲*
Voiced vowels:	*a, e, i, u*
Voiceless vowel:	*e̲*

This orthography differs from the previous orthography in that it is strictly phonemic: it represents the sounds of the words rather than the underlying structures of the sounds. The main differences in the new orthography are

1. The letter *h* is used instead of *r* to represent the uvular fricative (which sounds much like French or German *r*), and the letter *r* is used to represent the "Russian r," which is now pronounced like English *r* by most speakers.

2. A voiceless sound is represented by underlining the corresponding voiced sound, if there is one: *l̲* is voiceless *l*, *m̲* is voiceless *m*, *n̲* is voiceless *n*, *ng̲* is voiceless *ng*, and *e̲* is voiceless *e*.

3. Double vowels (i.e., what is underlyingly a pair of identical vowels) are written by putting an accent over a single vowel; for example, old *aa* becomes *á*. (The reason for doing this is that double vowels are often very difficult to distinguish from single vowels.)

4. Double consonants are always written as a pair of identical consonants.

The one exception to the standard for spellings used in this volume is the spelling of the word, "Alutiiq," which follows the previous orthography. The old spelling has been retained instead of the new "Alu'utíq" because it is now in widespread use.

Alutiiq Elders

Participants in *Looking Both Ways* or quoted in catalog.

Name	Residence	Originally From	Dates
Ephraim Agnot		Akhiok	b. 1942; d. 1995
Virginia Aleck	Chignik Lake	Chignik Lagoon	b. 1944
Wilfred Alexanderoff	Old Harbor	Old Harbor	b. 1923
Lena Anderson	Eagle River	Chignik Lake	b. 1947
Clara Angasan	King Salmon	Iliamna	b. 1940
Ralph Angasan	King Salmon	Naknek	b. 1948
Vera Angasan	King Salmon	Ugashik	b. 1924
Katherine C. Brown	Anchorage	Naknek	b. 1944
Clyda Christiansen	Larsen Bay-Kodiak	Karluk	b. 1920
Johnny Christianson	Port Heiden	Port Heiden	b. 1939
Nida Chya	Old Harbor	Old Harbor	b. 1924
Irene Coyle	Kodiak	Akhiok	b. 1947
Lucille Antowak Davis	Anchorage	Karluk	b. 1924
Ierofei (Ralph) Demidoff		Afognak	b. 1909; d. 1964
Martha Demientieff	Nenana	Kanatak	b. 1933
Edward Gregorieff	Tatitlek	Ellamar	b. 1923
Carl Gronn	Kodiak	Naknek	b. 1937
Sven Haakanson, Sr.	Old Harbor	Ouzinkie-Olga Bay	b. 1934
Mary Haakanson	Old Harbor	Shearwater-Old Harbor	b. 1939
Nick Ignatin	Old Harbor	Woody Island	b. 1924
George Inga, Sr.	Old Harbor	Old Harbor	b. 1925
Innokenty Inga		Old Harbor	b. 1884; d. 1960
Julia Knagin	Kodiak	Karluk	b. 1928
Mary Kompkoff	Chenega Bay	Chenega	b. 1937
Evelyn Kosbruk	Perryville	Chignik	b. 1943
Ignatius Kosbruk		Perryville	b. 1917; d. 1998
Alberta B. Laktonen	Everett, WA	Karluk, Larsen Bay	b. 1930
Doris Lind	Chignik Lake	Pilot Point, Egegik	b. 1920
Matrona Macauly	Palmer	Ilnik-Chignik Lagoon	b. 1928
Roy Madsen	Kodiak	Kanatak	b. 1923
Larry Matfay		Akhiok	b. 1907; d. 1998
Martha (Naumoff) Matfay		Karluk	b. 1919; d. 1999
Mary Jane Nielsen	South Naknek	New Savonoski	b. 1945
Florence (Matfay) Pestrikoff	Kodiak	Akhiok-Old Harbor	b. 1937
John Pestrikoff	Port Lions	Ouzinkie-Afognak	b. 1910
Julia Pestrikoff	Port Lions	Afognak	b. 1916

continues on next page

Alutiiq Elders

Name	Residence	Originally From	Dates
Nick Pestrikoff, Sr.	Ouzinkie	Ouzinkie	b. 1935
Mary Peterson	Akhiok	Akhiok	b. 1927
Rena Peterson	Akhiok	Old Harbor	b. 1941
Lydia Robart		Port Graham	b. 1947; d. 2001
Mike Sam		Chignik	b. 1923; d. 1998
Olga Sam	Anchorage	Perryville	b. 1945
Feona Sawden	Port Graham	Port Graham	b. 1939
Roy Skonberg	Chignik Bay	Chignik Lagoon	b. 1931
Robert Stamp	Kodiak	Tatitlek	b. 1926
Joe Tanape		Seward-Nuchek	b. 1910; d. 1987
Mike Tunohun	Old Harbor	Eagle Harbor-Woody Island	b. 1912
Ivar A. Wallin	Kodiak	Chignik	b. 1915
Anakenti Zeedar		Old Harbor	b. 1918; d. 1996
Senafont Zeedar	Kodiak	Kaguyak	b. 1931
Jennie Zeedar	Kodiak	Karluk-Akhiok	b. 1930

LOOKING BOTH WAYS

1
LOOKING BOTH WAYS

Aron L. Crowell

You've got to look back and find out the past, and then you look forward.

—Sven Haakanson, Sr., Kodiak Island Elder, 1997[1]

LOOKING BOTH WAYS: HERITAGE AND IDENTITY OF THE *Alutiiq People* is a community-based exhibition from the Alutiiq people of southern Alaska. Its perspective and voice reflect the values of the people who shared in its creation. For Sven Haakanson, Sr., "looking both ways" means a commitment to examine and teach about the past so that Alutiiq culture and its ideals will be carried on through time. Educator Martha Demientieff speaks of a path of knowledge that connects generations and provides guidance for living: "I can only talk about what it means to me to be Alutiiq. And what it means to me

is that I have a path that I'm to follow, and I've been following that Alutiiq path all my life."[2]

In exploring what it means to be Alutiiq, *Looking Both Ways: Heritage and Identity of the Alutiiq People* retraces the turbulent history of an Alaska Native people and records the vital discourse of its contemporary culture. Alutiiq contributors to this catalog represent a range of life experiences and generations—Elders, scholars, community leaders, and young adults—with varied perspectives on the past, present, and future.

The project "looks both ways" in another sense, by bringing together internal and external views of the same cultural tradition. Archaeologists, anthropologists, historians, and linguists have worked for decades in Alutiiq communities and with Alutiiq materials in archives and museums. These researchers have sought to understand the origins and foundations of the culture, document its history, and interpret the rich variety of its social and artistic expression. Communities have supported and joined in these studies, yet there are inevitable differences between how Alutiiq people see themselves and how their way of life has been interpreted by others. Some respectfully disagree with specific findings or more generally question the attitudes, assumptions, and methods of Western science and scholarship. In this catalog, Alutiiq and non-Alutiiq authors share perceptions from all sides of this on-going dialogue and contribute to a process of collaborative discovery.

1   The village of Chignik Bay, Alaska Peninsula, 1996. *Left—* Margie Macauly-Waite, Council of Katmai Descendents, and her son Mikhail. *Right*—Lena Anderson, Elder advocate, daughter of Dora and John André.

Chignik Bay photograph © Chris Arend/AlaskaStock.com. Portraits by Carl C. Hansen, Smithsonian Institution.

3

Heritage and Identity

THE ALUTIIQ REGION INCLUDES THE ISLANDS AND coastal country of southern Alaska, from the Alaska Peninsula to Kodiak Island, the Kenai Peninsula, Cook Inlet, and Prince William Sound. Clear days along the often stormy coast reveal dazzling panoramas of ocean, mountains, glaciers, tundra, and forest. Today, more than 3100 Alutiit[3] live in villages, towns, and cities along this central portion of the Gulf of Alaska. Others now reside outside the region but look back with pride to these Alaska shores as their true homeland.

Archaeologists identify the earliest inhabitants of the region as Native peoples of Asiatic ancestry who arrived some 10,000 years ago. Alutiiq culture and society were shaped by hundreds of succeeding generations and enriched by wide-ranging relations with other Alaska Natives—Unangan (Aleutian Islanders), Yupiit, Dena'ina, Ahtna, Eyak, and Tlingit. The archaeological story of the Alutiiq past is introduced by Aron Crowell and Sonja Lührmann in chapter 2 and continued by Amy Steffian in chapter 4.

Historical literature from the early years of Russian-European contact in the eighteenth century A.D. recalls the complex social, artistic, and spiritual traditions of classical Alutiiq society, described in chapter 2. Two centuries of Russian and American colonial rule imposed serious threats to physical and cultural survival—decimation by smallpox, measles, and other new diseases; servitude and debt to fur-trading companies; forced acculturation and racial prejudice. New languages, religious practices, technologies, and political institutions were accommodated by a changing Native culture. Commercial fishing, gold prospecting, copper mining, logging, and the oil industry brought ecological destruction and the alienation of Alutiiq lands.

The name "Alutiiq" is itself a legacy of Western contact. The original self-designation was *Sugpiaq* ("real person"; plural *Sugpiat*). Eighteenth century Russian fur traders introduced a foreign term, *Aleut*, to refer to the *Sugpiat* and to several other linguistically and culturally

distinct indigenous populations in southern Alaska (see Jeff Leer's essay in chapter 2). This new name—pronounced as *Alutiiq* in the Sugpiaq language—was eventually accepted by Native people themselves. All three names—Alutiiq, Aleut, and Sugpiaq—are used for self reference today on Kodiak Island, the Alaska Peninsula, Cook Inlet, and Prince William Sound, according to local and personal preference. At the suggestion of our advisors and for the sake of simplicity, we have adopted *Alutiiq* (plural, *Alutiit*) for general use in the present project. The distinctive Unangan heritage of the Aleutian Island chain, where most people also refer to themselves as Aleuts, is not addressed in *Looking Both Ways*.

Throughout history, each generation of Alutiit has been compelled to renegotiate the core understandings that define both self and community. In chapter 3, Gordon Pullar examines contemporary identity from this perspective. Among the issues addressed by Pullar and other Alutiiq contributors are land rights, conflicting definitions of Native identity, language loss, relations with anthropologists, and the repatriation of human remains from museums. The writers touch on universal themes—spiritual ties to the land, the bonds of kinship and belief, respect for Elders and community, and the shared practices and meanings of subsistence life.

In chapter 5 Aron Crowell and April Laktonen describe the sustaining harvest of wild foods in Alutiiq communities, both past and present. Spiritual relationships with the natural world are still deeply a part of hunting, fishing, and gathering. This connection is expressed in traditional art and objects—from kayaks to weapons, clothing, and hunting hats.

2   The village of Tatitlek, Prince William Sound, 1990. *Right*—John F. C. Johnson, chairman, Chugach Heritage Foundation.

Tatitlek photograph © Henry Huntington/AlaskaStock.com. Portrait by Carl C. Hansen, Smithsonian Institution.

In chapter 6 Aron Crowell and Jeff Leer describe masked hunting ceremonies and traditional spiritual concepts as well as the heritage of Russian Orthodoxy, which has been part of Alutiiq culture for more than 200 years. Kodiak Island stories and dance songs, as transcribed by French linguist Alphonse Pinart in 1871–72 and recently interpreted by Dominique Desson, contribute to the discussion of continuity and change in Alutiiq spirituality.[4]

Alutiiq Elders have the final words in Alutiiq Paths (chapter 7). In their narratives and commentaries, Martha Demientieff, Olga Sam, Lucille Antowak Davis, Rena Peterson, Jennie Zeedar, the late Ignatius Kosbruk, Edward Gregorieff, the late Larry Matfay, and Roy Skonberg address values, recall the struggle to preserve Native language and culture, and recount through personal histories the events that shaped Alutiiq life in the twentieth century.

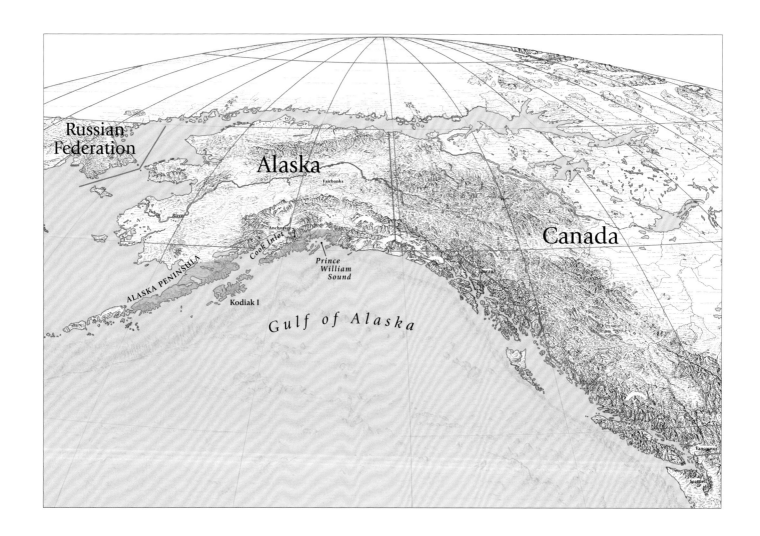

3   The Alutiiq region extends along the southern Alaska coast from Prince William Sound in the east to the Alaska Peninsula in the west, including the Kodiak Island group and parts of the Kenai Peninsula.

Map by Aron Crowell. Map projection courtesy of the U.S. Geological Survey.

4   Karluk village on the Karluk River, Kodiak Island, 1995. *Right*—Cindy Pennington, Alaska Native Heritage Center; advocate for Alaska Native women's rights.

Karluk photograph by Patrick Saltonstall. Portrait by Carl C. Hansen, Smithsonian Institution.

External Perspectives

IF ALUTIIQ CULTURE AND SELF-CONCEPTION HAVE changed over time, so have the perspectives—and prejudices—of outsiders. Early explorers and observers were influenced by European philosophies of the Enlightenment, which suggested that societies pass through stages of increasing rationality, from a primitive state of nature to civilization. Thus Gavriil Davydov, a Russian naval officer visiting Alaska in 1802–03, referred to the Alutiit as "savages." In studying Alutiiq culture, he sought to know the difference between a "man enlightened by science and one guided only by nature."[5] In 1877, William H. Dall wrote that the bottom levels of archaeological sites in the Aleutian Islands and Kodiak region represented the "lowest depths of barbarism," reflecting concepts of cultural evolution that prevailed in late nineteenth century anthropology.[6]

An understanding of the Alutiit and other Alaska Natives as "curious primitives" also motivated early museum collecting, and in the late nineteenth century, American and European museums intensified their efforts to gather materials from Native American cultures that were thought to be vanishing under the pressures of acculturation.[7] William J. Fisher, who purchased many of the Smithsonian objects in *Looking Both Ways*, reported in 1880 that the "race is dying out," making it all the more urgent to purchase objects of Alutiiq art and daily life.[8] Physical anthropologist Aleš Hrdlička collected the bones of hundreds of early Kodiak Island people from the Uyak Site during the 1930s, seeking clues to early migrations in the changing shape of human skulls.

Later anthropologists sought to understand Alutiiq culture in historic rather than evolutionary terms, through intensive study of oral traditions and cultural materials. Work in 1933 by Kaj Birket-Smith and Frederica de Laguna in Prince William Sound represents this important shift in intellectual tradition, as well as a new methodology that combined archaeological, historical, and ethnographic studies in a unified research effort. Another new direction was defined in the 1960s, when American anthropology and archaeology were influenced by theories of cultural ecology. Archaeological work was now combined with interdisciplinary studies in biology and geology, as in the Aleut-Konyag Prehistory and Ecology Project led by W. S. Laughlin and W. G. Reeder.[9] Over the next several decades, archaeology was practiced as a primarily scientific rather than historical discipline, with a strong emphasis on explaining human behavior in terms of adaptation to natural environments. Donald W. Clark conducted extensive research on the cultural sequence of the Kodiak Island archipelago, and Donald Dumond led a series of University of Oregon projects that sought to unravel cultural relationships on the Alaska Peninsula.[10] The social complexity of the Alutiit has became a focus of recent work, including investigations at Karluk led by the late Richard Jordan and by Richard Knecht.[11] The explicitly scientific approach of the "new archaeology" remains influential today, along with more historical and humanistic styles of research (see Crowell 1997 and Katharine Woodhouse-Beyer, this volume). Contemporary cultural studies include Lydia Black's research in Alutiiq ethnohistory, Joanne B. Mulcahy's documentation of women's healing traditions, and Patricia Partnow's work on oral traditions and ethnic identity on the Alaska Peninsula (see essays, this volume).

These changing attitudes and modes of thinking are reminders that all ways of looking at culture—from both the outside and the inside—may be influenced by personality, culture, intellectual fashion, and historical context. It is not possible to be totally objective, but checking ideas and results against the work of others can uncover biases. Equally important is seeking interpretative balance through cross-cultural discussion and review. In chapter 3, Sven Haakanson, Jr., considers the potential for an indigenous anthropology that joins interior and exterior perspectives and embraces just such a "new and more inclusive definition of collaboration."

Creating the Exhibition

THE PRESENT VOLUME IS OFFERED AS A COMPILATION of many voices, stories, and sources, in the spirit of sharing that produced the exhibition itself. *Looking Both Ways* was a broad collaborative effort involving a number of museums and communities. It was led by the Arctic Studies Center (National Museum of Natural History,

Smithsonian Institution) and the Alutiiq Museum and Archaeological Repository in Kodiak, Alaska, with assistance from the Anchorage Museum of History and Art. Planning and implementation of the project were supported by the National Endowment for the Humanities (NEH), the participating museums, Phillips Alaska, Inc., Koniag, Inc., and many other Alutiiq and Alaska organizations and sponsors (please see acknowledgements).

5   Boys with three-hole kayaks on the beach at Kiniklik, Prince William Sound, 1930s. A paddle leans against the covered boat. *Courtesy of the National Anthropological Archives, Smithsonian Institution (38, 108).*

Looking Both Ways was inspired in large part by community interest in seeing and learning from the Alutiiq objects that are held by the National Museum of Natural History in Washington, D.C. The Smithsonian materials, which include masks, clothing, and many other items of daily and ceremonial life, were purchased throughout the Alutiiq region in 1879–1894 by William J. Fisher, a German-born naturalist, museum collector, and commercial fur trader. After holding scientific positions with the California Academy of Sciences and the U.S. Fish Commission, Fisher came to Kodiak Island in 1879 as a tidal observer for the U.S. Coast and Geodetic Survey. He remarried locally and died in St. Paul (Kodiak) in 1903. Fisher's field catalogs and correspondence, which are stored at the Smithsonian Institution Archives, list almost 400 ethnological and archaeological objects that he purchased for the U.S. National Museum at the request of Smithsonian Secretary Spencer F. Baird. Alutiiq, Yup'ik, and Dena'ina items are included, many acquired by Fisher in St. Paul from local residents, visiting sea otter hunters, and fur company agents. Fisher also traveled to outlying villages on Kodiak Island and undertook a collecting trip along the southern shore of Bristol Bay in the summer of 1885, where he visited Ugashik, Egegik, Naknek, and Koggiung. He served as an Alaska Commercial Company station agent at Nuchek in Prince William Sound in 1889–90 and gathered additional materials there. Fisher's records at the Smithsonian list the items he purchased, the collecting locations, Native language terms, and brief ethnographic notes. These supporting materials have assisted in the interpretation of objects and provide a valuable record of Alutiiq life at the end of the nineteenth century.[12]

The idea for an exhibition grew out of discussions at the Kodiak Island Culture Heritage Conference in 1988 when Aron Crowell presented photographs and information about the Alutiiq objects in the Smithsonian's Fisher collection. At that time, Gordon Pullar was president of the Kodiak Area Native Association (KANA) and Richard Knecht was the director of KANA's Cultural Heritage Program. The vision was to combine the Smithsonian materials with extraordinary archaeological collections from Karluk and other sites on Kodiak Island which are now in the care of the Alutiiq Museum. Together with photographs, oral history, and contemporary objects, these museum collections could be used to explore links between contemporary culture and a heritage that extends into the deep past.

Serious work on *Looking Both Ways* began after the opening of the Alaska regional office of the Arctic Studies Center (ACS) in 1994 and the Alutiiq Museum in 1995. Established through a partnership with the Anchorage Museum of History and Art, the goal of the ASC is to develop cooperative projects with Alaska Native communities in cultural research, exhibitions, and education. Expertise at the Alutiiq Museum, in addition to its broad base of support from the regional and Alutiiq village corporations of Kodiak Island, presented an opportunity for ASC and the museum to cooperatively develop a community-based exhibition about the Alutiiq area.

After receiving support from NEH in 1995, an advisory panel of seventeen Elders, educators, and humanities scholars met to help shape and review the project. Their first recommendation was to involve more Alutiiq Elders and rural residents in the planning process. The advisors also suggested that the project encompass the entire Alutiiq region by engaging communities of the Alaska Peninsula, Cook Inlet, and Prince William Sound in addition to those on Kodiak Island.

In September 1997, a five-day Elders' Planning Conference held in Kodiak realized these goals. More than forty men and women from seventeen villages examined objects and photographs that represented traditional life. Working with curators, Alutiiq facilitators, and staff of the Arctic Studies Center and Alutiiq Museum, participants shared their thoughts about cultural identity, heritage, and the future. A large public audience joined in the discussions and social events at the conference. An Elders and youth conference held in 1998, organized by the Department of Alaska Native and Rural Development (College of Rural Alaska, University of Alaska Fairbanks), the Koniag Education Foundation, and the Arctic Studies Center, provided an additional opportunity to gather input and ideas for the project.

At these meetings, participants commented about objects and at the same time about larger issues, pointing to values, beliefs, and the ways in which cultural practice defines identity:

> If I see a basket that I think was used in the past for berry picking, that's not enough for me to know. What I do, which heals my spirit and makes my body healthy, is to go out and pick berries in a basket, knowing that for maybe ten thousand years my ancestors have been doing this. . . . And I hope that that kind of thing will come out as we look at these artifacts. And for the future, I'm bringing all my little grandchildren along to the berry patch and they're learning to say thank you to the land after we get our berries and treat the berries with big respect when we go home.

> —Martha Demientieff, 1997[13]

As described by Martha Demientieff, a berry basket is a useful object, a sign for an important subsistence activity, and a symbol of connection to ancestors and spiritual beliefs.[14] The contemporary significance of historical materials was illustrated time and again during interviews. While holding a *qayaq* (kayak) prow, the late Larry Matfay talked of his father's expertise as a sea otter hunter and about the ways in which the men and women of Akhiok village worked together to build the boats used in hunting and transport. The *qayaq* prow was for Larry Matfay and his listeners an evocative sign of the past, as well as a symbol of Alutiiq community. Stories about the "starring" ceremony held during the week after Russian Christmas were stimulated by photographs taken in the 1920s, and included an exchange about how this practice varies today among the villages. Wooden masks and human figurines inspired stories about shamans who were still active in some villages during the early decades of the twentieth century. Were shamans invariably dangerous or did some serve their communities and deserve respect because of their powers to heal? In addressing this topic, Elders sought

7   Augca'aq darts and targets

Kodiak Island
Alutiiq Museum, Kodiak Area Native Association Collection
(AM295:1-6) Length of darts 12 cm

Augca'aq is a traditional man's game based on sea mammal
hunting. It is played during the six weeks of Russian Orthodox Lent. Players kneel on the floor, as they would in a kayak,
and throw darts at a whale-shaped target that dangles from a
string. The players win points according to where a dart strikes
the target. Players and spectators gamble on the outcome. Elders recall times when clothing, guns, outboard motors, and
even houses were won and lost at *augca'aq* matches.

8   The late Ignatius Kosbruk of Perryville talks about the
whale-and-dart game called *augca'aq*. Photographed at the
Alutiiq Elders' Planning Conference for *Looking Both Ways*,
Kodiak, 1997. Left to right: Ed Gregorieff, George Inga, Sr.,
Ignatius Kosbruk, and Senafont Zeedar.

Photo by Maria Williams, Arctic Studies Center.

resolution of opposing views about these traditional
practitioners.[15]

While many objects in *Looking Both Ways* are familiar
to contemporary Elders, others were passing out of use
even in the 1880s when they were collected for the
Smithsonian. In large part, the social and spiritual iconography of ancestral materials is no longer a part of
daily communication. For this reason, information
about museum objects and the reconstructive work of
anthropologists and historians provide an important
complement to oral traditions and community-based
knowledge.

By developing their own museums and cultural centers and by asserting a broader role in the development

of exhibitions, Native American communities have achieved a new voice of self-representation that challenges the authority once assumed solely by anthropologists and curators.[16] As a result, exhibitions are being revitalized as an important medium of cross-cultural communication. In *Looking Both Ways*, the commitment has been to diversity of perspective, depth of inquiry, and genuine collaboration among scholars, Elders, and communities. Perhaps through so many eyes there can be a clear vision of Alutiiq culture in all of its complexity and depth.

9 Men with Russian Christmas star at the settlement of Tangihnaq (Woody Island) in about 1900. Village chief Kuzma is on the far left.

Courtesy of the Kodiak Historical Society. (P. 386-82 N).

Quyanásinaq—Many Thanks

SUPPORT FOR PROJECT PLANNING AND RESEARCH WAS provided by grants from the National Endowment for the Humanities (a federal agency) and the Smithsonian Institution (Special Exhibition Fund and Collections-Based Research Fund). Financial assistance for *Sugpiat Angnertat Katurtut, Elders' Planning Conference for Looking Both Ways: Heritage and Identity of the Alutiiq People* in 1997 was provided by the the Alutiiq Museum, Alaska Humanities Forum, Koniag, Inc., Afognak Native Corporation, Bristol Bay Native Corporation, Phillips Alaska, Inc., and Bristol Bay Native Association, with additional financial and in-kind support from the National Museum of the American Indian, First National Bank of Anchorage, Era Aviation, National Park Service, Kodiak Area Native Association, Alaska Development Corporation, Native Village of Perryville, Alaska Peninsula Corporation, Chignik Bay Village Council, Chugachmiut, Far West Corporation, Chugach Alaska Corporation, King Salmon Village Council, and Kodiak Historical Society. Special thanks as well to Vernon Chimegalrea, Irene Coyle, Mary Fajen, Joe Kelley, Mary Jane Nielsen, Cindy Pennington, Roberta Scheidler, Patrick Saltonstall, and Pat Thorne.

Support for Allriluukut "We Are One," the 1998 Alutiiq Elders and Youth Conference, was provided by the Afognak Native Corporation, Akhiok-Kaguyak, Inc., Alaska Airlines, Alaska State Council on the Arts, Alaska Humanities Forum, the Alutiiq Museum, Arctic Studies Center, Bristol Bay Native Corporation, Chugachmiut, Chugach Alaska Corporation, Era Aviation, Inc., Cook Inlet Region, Inc., the University of Alaska Fairbanks (Department of Alaska Native and Rural Development), Kenai Natives Association, Inc., Kodiak Area Native Association, Kodiak Inn, Kodiak Island Borough School District, Koniag Education Foundation, Koniag, Inc., Mary Patterson of KMXT Public Broadcasting, the National Endowment for the Humanities, Natives of Kodiak, Inc., Native Village of Afognak, Ninilchik Native Descendants, Old Harbor Native Corporation, St. Herman's Theological Seminary Archives, Woody Island Tribal Council, and the Alutiiq Cultural Association.

The production and tour of *Looking Both Ways* were made possible by a major implementation grant from the National Endowment for the Humanities and by matching funds from the National Museum of Natural History (Office of Public Programs), Phillips Alaska, Inc., Koniag, Inc., Alaska Humanities Forum, and the National Bank of Alaska. Funding from the Middlecott Foundation subsidized publication of the exhibition catalog by the University of Alaska Press. Sponsorships for Alutiiq student interns were provided by the Native American Internship program at the Smithsonian's Office of Fellowships and Grants. With shared pride and deepest humility, we recognize the very large circle of individuals gave generously of their time, knowledge, and expertise to create *Looking Both Ways*. We begin with thanks to the Alutiiq Elders who gave us access to their words and insights and who participated in the planning and discussion of the exhibition. Sadly, we note the passing of four individuals—Larry Matfay, Ignatius Kosbuk, Mike Sam, and Lydia Robart—who were important voices for their communities and contributors to *Looking Both Ways*. To all the Elders, we hope that we have done justice to your vision of the project.

Members of the advisory panel, who worked as a group and individually to guide our efforts, were: Lena Anderson (Alaska Peninsula), Lucille Antowak Davis (Kodiak Island), Martha Demientieff (Alaska Peninsula), John F. C. Johnson (Prince William Sound; Chugach Heritage Foundation); Margie Macauly-Waite (Alaska Peninsula; Council of Katmai Descendants); Donald Nielsen (Alaska Peninsula; Bristol Bay Native Association); Mary Jane Nielsen (Alaska Peninsula; Alaska Peninsula Corporation); Patricia Partnow (Alaska Native Heritage Center); Cindy Pennington (Kodiak Island; Alaska Native Heritage Center); Gordon Pullar (Kodiak Island; Department of Alaska Native and Rural Development, University of Alaska Fairbanks), Feona Sawden (Cook Inlet), and Marlane Shanigan (Alaska Peninsula). Humanities advisors on the panel were: William W. Fitzhugh (Arctic Studies Center, National Museum of Natural History); Nelson Graburn (University of California, Berkeley); Aldona Jonaitis (University of Alaska Museum); Molly Lee (University of Alaska Museum); and William Workman (University of Alaska Anchorage).

Our sincere appreciation as well to the administrative heads of organizations and bureaus that cooperated closely to make *Looking Both Ways* a reality: Robert Fri, director of the National Museum of Natural History (NMNH); Ruth Dawson, chair of the Alutiiq Heritage Foundation; Robert Sullivan, associate director for Public Programs at NMNH; Carolyn Rose, chair, and Daniel Rogers, deputy chair, of the Department of Anthropology, NMNH; William W. Fitzhugh, director of the Arctic Studies Center; Mike Headley, director of the Smithsonian's Office of Exhibits Central; and Patricia B. Wolf, director, and Suzi Jones, deputy director, of the Anchorage Museum of History and Art. All took a personal interest in seeing to the success of the project.

We salute the great work accomplished by staff, interns, specialists, and volunteers at participating organizations. Maria Williams joined the Arctic Studies Center staff as education coordinator in 1997–98 with funding from the National Museum of the American Indian and played an important role in implementing the 1997 and 1998 Elders conferences. Williams conducted a number of the videotaped interviews at the 1997 conference. Dee Hunt co-wrote successful funding proposals to NEH, the ARCO Foundation, and the Alaska Humanities Forum, helped to organize and implement the 1997 Elders' Planning Conference, researched historical photography for the catalog and exhibition, and contributed her research on clothing in the William J. Fisher collection.[17] Shirley Mae Springer Staten joined *Looking Both Ways* as project manager in 1999–2000 and ably handled the demands of coordinating a complex project with multiple priorities and funding sources. She worked with Elders to edit chapter 7 and helped to develop the exhibition film.

Mark Matson produced fine maps and illustrations for both the catalog and exhibition. Three undergraduate Alutiiq interns assisted at the Arctic Studies Center with research, meeting coordination, and production of the catalog and an educational CD-ROM: Jean Anderson (1997), Shauna Lukin (1998), and April Laktonen (1999). Undergraduate volunteer Emma Brown transcribed videotapes of the 1997 conference and compiled data on Alutiiq subsistence. Cindy Pennington transcribed the audiotapes on contract but also as a labor of love. Sonja Lührmann conducted research with Russian-American Company and Russian Orthodox church records for *Looking Both Ways* and for her Master's thesis, first as a volunteer in 1998 and then as a Smithsonian Fellow in 1999.[18] Volunteers Nicole Cain and Sarah Pearson assisted with final editing and compilation of the catalog manuscript. Jennifer McCarty aided in confirming Elders' permissions and in compiling material for the CD-ROM and website. In addition, the project received a steady stream of assistance and support from Anne Stone, Jack Mullaney, and Elisabeth Ward of ASC's Washington staff.

Special thanks to Judy Meidinger, Cindy Pennington, Xenia Gregorieff, Harry W. Kosbruk, Elizabeth Kosbruk, Freida Kosbruk, Sophie Larson, Florence Pestrikoff, Debbie Lukin, and Vivian Johnson for assistance with chapter 7.

In Kodiak, we extend our most sincere thanks to board members of the Alutiiq Heritage Foundation, who enthusiastically adopted this ambitious project from its inception. Throughout the planning and production of the exhibition they committed museum resources and gave their wholehearted support. We are grateful for the leadership of Nancy Anderson, Fred and Irene Coyle, Ruth Dawson, Sonja Delgado, Tonya Inga, Roger Malutin, Ole Olsen, Teri Schneider, Gwen Sargent, Clarence Selig, Rita Stevens, Linda Suydam, Jana Turvey, and Donene Tweten.

The staff of the Alutiiq Museum lent their energy and expertise at every stage of the project. Richard Knecht, the museum's first director, left Kodiak early in the project, but his valuable insights helped to formulate the exhibition. Knecht's archaeological research on Kodiak Island is represented throughout this catalog. Sven Haakanson, Jr., assumed the directorship of the museum in 2000, and gave his full support to the exhibition and to the planning of its Alaska tour. Christine Marasigan assisted with the organization of the 1997 Elders' Planning Conference and oversaw grant administration during the planning phase. Elizabeth Eufemio and Kathleen Skonberg assisted with object photography, negotiated loans, completed condition reports, and expertly packed objects for safe transport to Washington, D.C. Patrick Saltonstall, formerly the museum's assistant curator and later its curator, located contemporary photographs for the exhibition and generously shared images from his own collection. He also assisted with research and editing for both the exhibition script and this catalog and worked with project intern Sabrina Sutton to index, catalog, and transcribe Elder interviews from the museum's archives. Administrative support for the implementation phase was ably provided by Vickie Carmichael with assistance from Dayna Brockman, Darla Coyle, Trina Squarstoff, Jennifer Wooten, Angela McCormick, Jennifer Myrick, and Erica Guyer.

We also gratefully acknowledge organizations and individuals who contributed items for the exhibition. Father Piasius De Lucia, the students of St. Innocent's Academy, and Teacon Simeonoff made the beautiful Russian Orthodox Christmas star. The Diocese of Alaska Archive, St. Herman Theological Seminary, Kodiak, graciously donated a rare volume—an 1848 Gospel of St. Mathew in Alutiiq and Slavonic—with the assistance of Lydia T. Black. Artist Jerry Laktonen lent his "Joe Hazlewood" mask to the project, helping us to highlight contemporary arts. We were also able to include a bentwood hunting hat made by Jacob Simeonoff (from the permanent collection of the Alutiiq Museum) and thank the artist for his explanation of its designs. Some objects that are curated by the Alutiiq Museum and included in the exhibition are used with the generous permission of individual owners: Koniag, Inc., the Rice family, the Kodiak Area Native Association, the Afognak Native Corporation, the City of Larsen Bay, Jerry Laktonen, and the Alutiiq Heritage Foundation.

Joe Kelley of the Kodiak Area Native Association and Dave Norton (Arctic Sivunmun Ilisagvik College) co-led (with Aron Crowell) a University of Alaska Fairbanks museum studies field trip to Washington, D.C., in 1996 which provided an opportunity for additional study of the Fisher collection at the National Museum of Natural History. Kelley and Chris Cunningham of *Sea Kayaker* magazine provided expert analysis of the design features seen on Alutiiq boat models in the collection.

Skin sewers Susan Malutin and Grace Harrod participated in the 1996 research trip to Washington, D.C., and carried out detailed research on an Alutiiq ground squirrel parka in the William J. Fisher collection. Back in Kodiak, Harrod, and Malutin spent countless hours to create a replica of the garment for display in *Looking Both Ways*, including its complex ornamentation of embroidery, cloth, and caribou, mink, ermine, and sea otter furs. Support for this special project was provided by the Alaska State Museum's Grants-In-Aid program, the Alutiiq Cultural Association, and the Arctic Studies Center. A dedicated group of volunteers assisted the artists. We recognize Paul Dodge, Nona Campbell, Ella Moonin, Bobby Morrison, Christine Marasigan, Joy Marasigan, Elizabeth Eufemio, Eve McIntyre, Tracy Glaz, Hillary Van Daele, Jane Bernsten, and Vickie Carmichael. Mary Patterson Gertz skillfully captured the process on videotape. Roy Stoltenberg built the parka display case and shipping crates for exhibit objects.

Production and administration of the project in Washington, D.C., depended on the efforts of talented and dedicated staff at the Office of Exhibits Central (OEC) and the NMNH Department of Anthropology. Tina Lynch-Safreed created the exhibition design at OEC, and editor Rosemary Regan polished the exhibit script. As OEC project manager for *Looking Both Ways*, Rick Pelasara coordinated the efforts of a large fabrication and production team. We also thank Mary Dillon Bird, Eve Macintyre, and Richard Kilday for their advice and enthusiasm. Through the Department of Anthropology we received the benefit of Deborah Wood's skillful work as exhibition registrar; Catherine Magee's contributions as object conservator, and Deborah Hull-Walski's advice and assistance as collections manager. Greta Hansen and Edith Dietze gave us additional conservation advice about the Fisher materials. Special thanks as well to Zaborian Payne and Carole Lee Kin (Department of

Anthropology) and Keron Hopkins (Office of Sponsored Projects, Smithsonian Institution).

At the Anchorage Museum, registrar Judy Baletka provided advice on developing the exhibition tour, and will serve as the tour coordinator for *Looking Both Ways* in Alaska. Archivists Mina Jacobs and Diane Brenner provided invaluable help with research, references, and images. Alan Levy, who serves on the Anchorage Museum Association (AMA) board, assisted with our investigation of shipping options. Walt Hays, development director for the AMA, advised on funding strategies for the project.

Carl C. Hansen, chief of the NMNH Office of Imaging, Printing, and Photographic Services, photographed NMNH and Alutiiq Museum collections for the catalog. The Phase One Company donated the digital camera used for the project to the Center for Scientific Imaging and Photography at NMNH.

Jeff Leer of the Alaska Native Language Center (University of Alaska Fairbanks) provided invaluable assistance as linguistic consultant to the project. He transcribed Alutiiq language names from the Fisher field catalogs; provided Alutiiq place names from his original research for use in the exhibit and catalog; assisted in presentations at the 1997 Elders' Planning Conference; and contributed to the catalog as an author.

Patricia Partnow and Sue Pope developed the educational outreach program for the tour of *Looking Both Ways* through a contract with the Alaska Native Heritage Center in Anchorage. We thank the Alaska Native Heritage Center for a generous contribution of funds and expertise to enable the production of the exhibition's educational CD-ROM and web site. Research and development of the CD-ROM project were supported by the Smithsonian Institution and Chugach School District. Teri Schneider (Kodiak Island Borough School District), Terry P. Dickey (University of Alaska Museum), Edna Lamebull (Anchorage School District), Gale Parsons (Pratt Museum), and Martha Demientieff served as educational advisors and reviewers for teaching materials.

Film producer Francine Taylor, videographer Patrick Murphy, and sound recordist/editor Jonathan Butzke worked with us to record the 1997 Elders' Planning Conference on videotape and to produce the exhibition film. Marcia Lynn taped the audio record of the conference. Thanks also to the Subsistence Division of the Alaska Department of Fish and Game for assistance with photographs and data. Alaska Stock, Inc., of Anchorage provided contemporary images for the exhibition and catalog at a generous discount.

Finally, our thanks to editor Pamela Odom at the University of Alaska Press, designer Dixon J. Jones at Rasmuson Library Graphics, and to four anonymous reviewers who read the catalog manuscript and provided helpful comments and corrections. Special appreciation goes to Frederica de Laguna for her suggestions. William Fitzhugh, William Simeone, McKibben Jackinsky, Dee Hunt, Jim Fall, Ron Stanek, and Lisa Hutchinson-Scarbrough also read the manuscript, and William Workman provided a thorough review of the exhibition script. All opinions and remaining errors of fact and interpretation are the sole responsibility of the authors.

Chapter 1 notes

1 Alutiiq Elders' Planning Conference for *Looking Both Ways*, 1997. Audio and video recordings and written transcriptions of this conference are archived at the Alutiiq Museum and Archaeological Repository in Kodiak, Alaska and at the Anchorage office of the Arctic Studies Center. All quotes are used with permission.

2 Alutiiq Elders' Planning Conference for *Looking Both Ways*, 1997

3 "Alutiit" is the plural form of Alutiiq, meaning more than two people. Alternatively, people say "Alutiiqs."

4 Desson 1995.

5 Davydov 1977:104.

6 Dall 1877:56.

7 Cole 1985; Crowell 1992; Fitzhugh and Crowell 1988; Hinsley 1981; Jacobsen 1977; Krech 1989.

8 Fisher 1880.

9 Laughlin and Reeder 1966.

10 D. Clark 1966a, 1966b, 1970a, 1974a, 1974b, 1979; Dumond 1962, 1981; G. Clark 1977; Henn 1978.

11 See Crowell 1988; Steffian 1992b; Donta 1993; Fitzhugh 1996; Jordan and Knecht 1988.

12 For more detailed information about Fisher and his collecting activities for the Smithsonian and other museums, see Crowell 1992; Fisher 1880, 1882, 1883; and Hunt 2000. Fisher's field catalogs and correspondence with Spencer Baird and William H. Dall are in Smithsonian Institution Archives Record Unit 305 (United States National Museum, Registrar, 1834–1958. Accession Records 12209, 14024, 15687, 18490.

13 Alutiiq Elders' Planning Conference for *Looking Both Ways*, 1997.

14 Anthropological discussion about the "social life of objects" and their multiple contexts of meaning is reviewed by Susan M. Pearce in her *Museums, Objects, and Collections* (1992:15–35).

15 Attitudes toward shamanism and shamans' objects have been influenced by traditional teachings and experience (see Chapter 6) as well as by Russian Orthodoxy. Some early Orthodox missionaries were tolerant toward individual shamans and even regarded them as moral spiritual practitioners (Moussalimas 1990). Yet acceptance of the church went hand-in-hand with rejection of shamanism, according to Archimandrite Ioasaf in 1795: "They [Kodiak Islanders] take baptism so much to heart that they smash and burn all the magic charms given them by the shamans" (Pierce 1978:42). In 1885, William Fisher wrote that "Shamanism does not exist at present among the Ugashagamyutes [*Uggásahmiut*, Alutiiq people of Ugashik on the Alaska Peninsula] and Agliamyutes [*Agliamiut*, Yup'ik people of Naknek and Egegik], all of them being members of the Greek Catholic [Russian Orthodox] church. Specimens of Shamanism are extremely rare at present, the Russian priests making relentless war upon and destroying them whenever found" (Smithsonian Institution Archives, Record Unit 305). According to Elders at the 1997 conference, the Orthodox faith provides protection against personal harm from shamans.

16 Clifford 1991; Cruikshank 1998; Fienup-Riordan 1996.

17 Hunt 2000.

18 Lührmann 2000.

2

ALUTIIQ CULTURE

Views from Archaeology, Anthropology, and History

Aron L. Crowell and Sonja Lührmann

THE FIRST EUROPEAN EXPLORER TO REACH THE southern Alaska homeland of the Alutiit was Vitus Bering in 1741, then on his second voyage of discovery for the Russian crown. Earlier Russian expeditions, including Dezhnev in 1647 and Bering in 1728, had confirmed the presence of American land to the east of Siberia, but had not explored the coastline to the south.[1] Thus the Bering-Chirikoff expedition of 1741 and subsequent eighteenth century Russian, English, and Spanish voyages to the Gulf of Alaska probed a region that was new and extraordinary to Western understanding. Its indigenous peoples dwelt in large seaside villages, dressed in intricate clothing and headgear, and traveled in skin-covered boats of elegant design. Led by high-ranking chiefs, they were avid traders and warriors. Who were these Native Americans? Where had they come from?

10   Kodiak Islanders demonstrate the use of hunting weapons, 1818. Woven spruce root hats worn by the men are one of many indications that Alutiiq culture has been influenced by contacts with the Tlingit and other Northwest Coast Indian peoples.

Painting by Mikhail Tikhanov. Courtesy of the Scientific Research Museum of the Russian Academy of Arts.

It was natural to seek answers by comparing the Natives of southern Alaska to previously encountered northern peoples. Inuit (Eskimo) and Indian inhabitants of northeastern Canada were first mentioned in Viking sagas composed in the eleventh century A.D. Martin Frobisher, John Davis, James Hall, Henry Hudson, and other explorers met Inuit residents of Canada and Greenland during attempts to find a Northwest Passage across the Arctic. Captured Inuit were brought home for display in England and Denmark, stamping an image of arctic people on European consciousness. During the same era (sixteenth to eighteenth centuries A.D.), European explorers, fur traders, whalers, and fishermen became familiar with indigenous residents of Labrador, Newfoundland, and Quebec; Lutheran missionaries published scholarly studies about Greenlandic Inuit language and culture; and previously unknown Siberian peoples were absorbed into the expanding Russian empire.[2]

Georg W. Steller, a naturalist with Bering's second expedition and adjunct member of the Russian Academy of Sciences in St. Petersburg, was the first to speculate about the cultural identity of the Alutiit. During a brief visit to Kayak Island near Prince William Sound, Steller came across a Chugach Alutiiq camp and a subterranean storage cellar or house. The implements that he found there, along with objects discovered by Khitrov on nearby Wingham Island, convinced him that "most American inventions are identical to Kamchatkan or Asian ones" and that the people of southern Alaska must have

11 Bentwood boxes

Nuchek (*Núciq*), Prince William Sound, 1887–93 (left)
National Museum of Natural History, Smithsonian Institution
(NMNH 168637) Height 18 cm

Cook Inlet, before 1900 (right)
National Museum of Natural History, Smithsonian Institution
(NMNH 207747) Height 17 cm

Vessels shaped from thin planks of steam-bent wood held water
and food for kayak journeys or household storage. Hot rocks
could be added to bring the contents to a boil. Georg Steller,
naturalist with the Vitus Bering expedition in 1741, compared
Chugach Alutiiq boxes and other items found on Kayak and
Wingham islands near Prince William Sound to implements
used by indigenous peoples in eastern Siberia.

migrated eastward across the Aleutian Islands.[3] More evidence of connections across the North Pacific was acquired when the Bering expedition met a group of Unangan in the Shumagin Islands. Steller judged Unangan clothing to be like that of the Koryaks and Itelmen of eastern Siberia. Their kayaks resembled boats used in both Siberia and in Greenland, another indication that peoples of the Americas had migrated east from Asia. Davydov, Khlebnikov, Veniaminov, and other nineteenth century Russian students of Alaska Native cultures also held this view.[4]

English explorer James Cook visited Prince William Sound and Cook Inlet in 1778 and had the opportunity to meet Chugach Alutiit who came out to trade. Cook noted that kayaks, oil lamps, semisubterranean houses, and harpoons were used in both southern Alaska and in Greenland. Standing on the deck of the *Resolution* in Prince William Sound, Cook observed that Chugach "Canoes" (large, open skin boats called *angyat* in the Alutiiq language) were similar to boats described in Cranz's 1767 ethnography of Greenland. Because he had never personally met a "Greenlander or an Esquemaus," Cook reserved final judgment about the cultural identity of the Chugach. Nonetheless, their similarity to eastern arctic peoples gave rise to hope that the Atlantic and Pacific might be connected by the long-sought Northwest Passage. Cook's officers even debated whether glass beads worn by the Chugach indicated trade with

the Atlantic through the Northwest Passage or connections westward to Russian fur companies in Kamchatka.[5]

While Steller concluded that the Alutiit were of Siberian ancestry and Cook viewed them as probable Eskimos, Spanish explorers Arteaga (1779), López de Haro (1788), and Fidalgo (1790) referred to the Alutiit as "Indians."[6] This was at least partially a matter of prior experience. The Spanish had never been arctic explorers, although Basque whalers who were stationed in Newfoundland during the early 1600s may have introduced the word "Eskimo" into European usage.[7] Probably more significant was the fact that Spanish voyages proceeded north along the American coast from California to Alaska, so that resemblances between Alutiiq and Northwest Coast societies must have been very apparent to them. In both areas, people wore face paint, labrets (lip ornaments), nose pins, wooden body armor, and basketry hats that were woven from spruce root fibers. Among many types of implements used in both areas were wooden quivers, halibut hooks, and spoons carved from mountain goat and mountain sheep horns.

12 Chugach Alutiiq trading parties in kayaks and large open skin boats *(angyat)* meet James Cook's *Resolution* and *Discovery* at Snug Corner Cove in Prince William Sound, 1778. Etched from a drawing by John Webber.

Courtesy of the Anchorage Museum of History and Art (B86.94.10.45).

The Origins of Alutiiq Culture

EACH OF THESE IDEAS ABOUT ALUTIIQ ORIGINS comprehended only part of the story. Contemporary studies suggest that the Alutiit are actually related to many different North Pacific and arctic peoples. A combination of migration, descent, and cultural interchange among these groups explains how the eighteenth-century inhabitants of Kodiak Island, the Alaska Peninsula, Cook Inlet, and Prince William Sound could plausibly be compared to Siberians, Greenlandic Inuit, Aleutian Islanders, and Northwest Coast Indians. Archaeologists, anthropologists, and historians have sought to unravel this complex heritage. In the process they have come to appreciate both the originality of Alutiiq culture and the many sources that have enriched it. As in all fields of science and the humanities, however, important issues remain open to debate.

One part of this debate concerns the origins and spread of Inuit culture[8] and its relationship to the Alutiiq past. The area of Inuit occupation extends from the northeastern tip of Siberia across arctic Canada to Greenland and southward along the subarctic coasts of Alaska and Newfoundland. Six closely related languages, including Alutiiq, are spoken across this vast distance.[9] While some Inuit are interior hunters, most depend on sea mammals such as seals, walrus, and whales. All utilize a wide range of other resources including birds, fish, and plant foods. In the past, equipment for this northern way of life included stone lamps that burned sea mammal oil for heat and light, parkas and other tailored skin garments, waterproof clothing made from animal intestines, ground slate knives, kayaks, and many kinds of harpoons and other hunting weapons. Snow houses, popularly associated with Inuit life, were used mainly in the central Canadian Arctic and northern Greenland. Throughout Alaska, including its southern coast, winter dwellings were substantial structures made of stone, sod, wood, and whalebone. Related spiritual beliefs and oral traditions are still shared across the circumpolar world, and physical traits show that peoples who are culturally Inuit also share a high degree of genetic inheritance.[10]

Anthropological opinion generally recognizes a northeast Asian foundation for Inuit culture, as well as a critical period of development in the Bering Strait region that began about 2000 years ago. However, the earliest intensive maritime adaptations and the first appearance of a number of characteristically Inuit artifacts were actually far to the south, in the Alutiiq region and adjacent parts of the Gulf of Alaska.[11] It may be that this area, where larger numbers of people have always lived than along more northern coasts, played a critical role in nurturing the development of maritime-oriented Inuit cultures of the Bering Strait area, where new Asiatic cultural

13 "Woman of Prince William Sound." Painting by Cook expedition artist John Webber, 1778.
Courtesy of the Anchorage Museum of History and Art and Horden House Rare Books, Sydney.

14 **Nose ornament**

Alaska Peninsula, 1879–82
National Museum of Natural History, Smithsonian Institution (NMNH 72484) Length 12 cm

In classical Alutiiq society, a child's nose was pierced shortly after birth to accommodate a nose pin. The ornaments were made with beads, feathers, bone, dentalium shells, or sea lion whiskers. This example consists of glass beads strung on copper wire.

15 *Ulukaq*—Knife

Karluk 1 site, Kodiak Island, about A.D. 1400–1750
Alutiiq Museum, Koniag, Inc., Collection
(AM193.87:9250) Width 25 cm

*"My mom used to be handy with that thing, even the older people
and the men used that* ulukaq.*"*
            —Larry Matfay, Kodiak Island Elder, 1992

The ground slate *ulukaq* (or ulu) is a traditional tool of coastal
peoples throughout the Arctic. With its smooth, easily sharpened edge, it was perfect for splitting fish, cutting meat and
blubber, and preparing skins. People in the Alutiiq region began using these knives about 3400 years ago, at about the same
time they adopted nets for fishing. Modern versions are made
of steel.

elements and specific adaptations to sea ice and ice-edge
hunting were added.[12]

Human occupation of the Alutiiq region (see
chapter 4) began about 10,000 years ago during a warming period that followed the last (Pleistocene) ice age.
The people who came to live on this newly ice-free southern Alaska shore belonged to what archaeologists call
the "Paleoarctic" cultural tradition. Their Siberian ancestors had crossed into Alaska some 1500 years earlier,
gradually spreading throughout Alaska and southeast
into what is now British Columbia.[13] The Paleoarctic re-
orientation from inland to coastal life around the Gulf
of Alaska may have been the earliest such transition to
occur in the North Pacific, and one of the first in the
Americas.[14] Some archaeologists have suggested that the
transition took place even earlier along now-submerged
Pleistocene shorelines of the Bering land bridge, Gulf of
Alaska, and British Columbia, although direct evidence
for this hypothesis is lacking.[15]

By the first part of the Ocean Bay period (about 7500
to 3500 years ago), Paleoarctic descendants possessed
many specialized tools for coastal living. The Kachemak
tradition (about 3500 to 900 years ago) arose from
Ocean Bay, and was marked by larger and more permanent settlements, innovations in subsistence technology,
new ceremonial practices, and the artistic carving of bone
and stone. During late Kachemak times, the Alutiiq region seems to have been part of a great network of cross-
cultural communication that extended around the
northern Pacific Rim. Interchanges between Kachemak
and related cultures in the central Gulf of Alaska and
Norton Tradition populations on the Alaska Peninsula
were part of this trend. Through such contacts, coastal
ways of life similar to those practiced in the Gulf of
Alaska for thousands of years now spread to both sides
of the Bering Sea, including the Sea of Okhotsk where
the maritime Okhotsk and ancient Koryak cultures developed by the end of the first millennium A.D. New artifact types came into use over great distances around

this ocean arc, including ground slate tools and oil lamps from the Alutiiq area and eastern Aleutian Islands, toggling harpoons from Canada and northern Alaska, pottery from Siberia, and labrets from the Northwest Coast.[16] Archaeologists note that critical cultural developments took place in the Bering Strait region between 2000 to 1000 years ago. Peoples of the Old Bering Sea, Okvik, Punuk, Birnirk, and Thule traditions embraced new forms of art and ceremonialism, hunted whales and walrus, and conducted war using armor and a powerful new compound style of bow.[17] Thule people expanded rapidly across Canada to Greenland, replacing descendants of an earlier wave of migration known as the Arctic Small Tool tradition.

Northern Bering Sea artifact styles such as gravel-tempered pottery and triangular slate blades for hunting and fighting weapons also spread to the south, appearing in parts of the Alutiiq region after A.D. 1000. At this time, there are archaeological indications of intensified warfare in the Gulf of Alaska, including construction of settlements on inaccessible "refuge rocks."[18] Archaeologists have differed in their interpretations of these data. Don Dumond (see chapter 4) suggests that aspects of Thule culture appeared in the Gulf of Alaska as the result of "a very substantial influx of population" from the north,[19] while Donald W. Clark sees a more gradual, cumulative process of small-scale movements and cultural blending

16 Wooden labrets

Karluk 1 site, Kodiak Island, A.D. 1400–1750
Alutiiq Museum, Koniag, Inc., Collection
(UA85.193.3471) Length 11.5 cm (right)
(AM193.94:821) Length 6 cm (left)

Labrets were worn in piercings beneath the lower lip or through the cheek. The earliest use of labrets, about 4600 years ago, is documented by finds at archaeological sites in British Columbia and southeastern Alaska. Use of these facial ornaments spread north into the Alutiiq region about 1100 years later. Their use was discontinued in the early decades after Russian contact.

17 Barbed lance head with sheath

Ugashik (*Uggásaq*), Alaska Peninsula, 1885–86
National Museum of Natural History, Smithsonian Institution
(NMNH 127763) Length 50 cm

This barbed bone lance head is armed with a triangular blade of slate. It was mounted on the end of a long wooden shaft and used to kill beluga whales. The wooden sheath protected the sharp stone blade from accidental damage. Triangular slate blades, a Bering Sea invention, are found in Alutiiq region archaeological sites after about A.D. 1000.

18 Owl and human face masks

Karluk 1 site, Kodiak Island, A.D. 1400–1750
Alutiiq Museum, Koniag, Inc., Collection
(UA84.193:1044) Height 23.5 cm (left)
(AM193.87:9260) Height 22.5 cm (right)

Archaeological Alutiiq masks from upper layers of the Karluk 1 archaeological site on Kodiak Island bear stylistic resemblances to Yup'ik dance masks from farther north, one of many discoveries that suggest an historical link between Alutiiq and Yup'ik cultures. Holes around the edges of the masks anchored hoops that encircled them to represent levels of the cosmos. The owl, depicted by the mask on the left, was one of the spirit-helpers who assisted shamans. Birds appear on many Alutiiq masks and carvings and play a prominent role in oral traditions.

that did not overwhelm or displace the resident population of the region.[20] Richard Jordan and Richard Knecht suggest that artifacts from archaeological layers at the mouth of the Karluk River and at other sites on Kodiak Island show a relatively smooth transition from Kachemak to late precontact Alutiiq culture, without any evidence of Thule migration.[21] It is important to note that other new artifact types found in the upper layers of these sites, such as large splitting adzes, pebbles engraved with pictographs, and slate lance points, point to contacts east and west with the Northwest Coast and eastern Aleutian Islands.

The question of cultural relationships at this late stage of Alutiiq history can be considered with the aid of nonarchaeological evidence. For example, Alutiiq origin stories record the migration of people from the north (see chapter 4), and by one account these newcomers defeated and intermarried with Tlingit people who resided on Kodiak Island.[22] Although the period for these legendary events cannot be established, they may refer to cultural changes of 1000 years ago.

Linguists also note that the Alutiiq language (also called Sugpiaq, Sugcestun, or Aleut) is so closely related to central Alaska Yup'ik that it may very well have been carried south to the Gulf of Alaska coast in relatively recent times, displacing an unknown aboriginal language.[23] Comparative studies of Alutiiq art, tool and clothing design, beliefs, and oral traditions also suggest a very close relationship with Yup'ik culture, although Tlingit and Unangan characteristics are also well represented. These studies include Margaret Lantis' analyses of Alutiiq mythology and ceremonialism, joint work by Kaj Birket-Smith and Frederica de Laguna on Chugach ethnography and archaeology, and Lydia Black's interpretations of hunting hats and iconography.[24]

Biological anthropology provides other clues concerning Alutiiq origins, although the results are often contradictory. In varying degrees, the Alutiit appear to be genetically related to Inuit, Northwest Coast, and Unangan populations.[25] One recent study of teeth concludes that modern Alutiit are closest to Yup'ik people, while their ancestors of more than 1000 years ago were somewhat closer to the Tlingit and other Northwest Coast groups.[26]

Considering all of the available information, it seems likely that Bering Sea immigrants did arrive in the Alutiiq region at around the beginning of the last millennium. The size and reason for this hypothetical population movement are unknown, although shifts in territory have been common events in Alaska Native history. According to this reconstruction, the ancestral Yup'ik dialect spoken by the newcomers was adopted throughout the Alutiiq area, replacing an older non-Inuit language. Ceremonial practices and mythology from southwestern Alaska were blended with local traditions. Some new artifact styles were introduced, but close ties between the Bering Sea and Gulf of Alaska during the previous thousand years meant that tools, weapons, boats, and clothing were already fairly similar in the two regions. This would explain why such an important linguistic and cultural transition is difficult to detect in the archaeological record.

It should be noted that this apparent influx of Yup'ik people and culture a millennium ago does not imply that the Alutiit are "Eskimos" ("Pacific Eskimo" in some anthropological literature). This label is strongly rejected by many Alutiit as culturally inappropriate and there is little doubt that Alutiiq culture is distinctive and unique in many ways. For the most part, it seems to have been a product of its own independent development in the Gulf of Alaska.

Classical Alutiiq Society

AT THE TIME OF WESTERN CONTACT, AT LEAST EIGHT thousand Alutiit lived in scores of independent villages along the southern Alaska coast. At that time they called themselves Sugpiat ("real people") or Suuget ("people"). Gideon, a Russian Orthodox priest on Kodiak Island in 1804–1807, left one of the most detailed and sympathetic accounts of this complex Native society.[27] His observations were made twenty years after the Russian conquest of Kodiak in 1784. Other writers who described Kodiak during this first generation after the conquest include Archimandrite Ioasaf, Carl Heinrich Merck, Martin Sauer, Gavriil Davydov, and Iurii Lisianskii.[28] For Prince William Sound there are reports by the Cook expedition (1778), Potap Zaikov (1783), Portlock (1789), and numerous other Russian, Spanish, and English voyages.[29] Some of the same sources apply to the Alaska Peninsula, Cook Inlet, and the outer coast of the Kenai Peninsula, although these areas were less frequently visited and described.

An important consideration in the interpretation of history, and in particular the colonial history of the Alutiiq region, are biases that shaped what literate observers recorded about Native society. The content of historical texts and records were shaped by the world view, social position, and commercial, political, scientific, or ideological agendas of the writers. Often, observations and opinions were based on very brief contacts. In some cases, Alutiiq narratives provide an alternative view to what oral historian Julie Cruikshank has called the "intellectual colonialism" of the textual record of contact. In the sections that follow, we attempt to describe Alutiiq society of the late eighteenth century on the basis of historical materials, recognizing at the same time that any such attempt is destined to be partial and imperfect at best.

Cultural Geography of the Alutiiq World

The environment of the Alutiiq region influenced its cultural and economic life. The area occupied by Alutiiq people in historic times spans some 650 miles from Stepovik Bay on the Alaska Peninsula to eastern Prince William Sound, including well over 6000 miles of actual shoreline. Villages were traditionally situated on narrow fringes of land at the foot of rugged coastal mountains and glaciers. The ocean was quite naturally the source for most food, skins, and other necessities, as well as the main highway for travel. Areas of abundant maritime resources, such as Kodiak Island, supported larger villages and greater concentrations of people. Prized raw materials and manufactures such as amber, antler, mountain goat and sheep horn, walrus ivory, and caribou skin clothing were produced only in certain areas, but traded over long distances.

There were variations in language and culture across this broad region. For example, historic observers noted slight differences in speech between the eastern and western villages of the Kodiak archipelago.[30] Variations in the language persist to the present day. The most important linguistic distinction is between speakers of the Koniag dialect in the west (Alaska Peninsula and the Kodiak Island group) and the Chugach dialect in the east (Cook Inlet to Prince William Sound).[31]

Cultural differences paralleled linguistic ones. The Chugach lived in close contact with the Dena'ina, Tlingit, Eyak, and Ahtna, and influences from these Indian groups can be seen in the design of Chugach wooden houses, horn spoons, spruce root hats, iron daggers, and other implements. Koniag culture shared more with adjacent Yup'ik and Unangan peoples, including earthen-walled houses, pottery, and ivory carving.

The Kodiak archipelago The Kodiak archipelago includes Kodiak (*Qikertaq*), Afognak (*Aggwaneq*), and many smaller islands (fig. 20). The northern hills of the mountainous island group are covered with spruce trees, but

The Alutiiq Language

Jeff Leer
Professor, Alaska Native Language Center
University of Alaska Fairbanks

THE ALUTIIQ (OR SUGPIAQ) LANGUAGE IS SPOKEN BY THE people of the Alaska Peninsula (south of Egegik and north of Mount Stepovak), Kodiak Island, the tip of the Kenai Peninsula, and Prince William Sound. There are two major dialects: Koniag, which includes the Alaska Peninsula and Kodiak Island, and Chugach, which includes the Kenai Peninsula and Prince William Sound. However, the Kenai Peninsula subdialect spoken in Nanwalek, Port Graham, and Seldovia, has been significantly influenced by contact with the Kodiak subdialect in the historical period, so that it could be considered to have evolved into a separate dialect transitional between the Chugach of Prince William Sound and Koniag.

When the Russians first came to Alaska, they used the word "Aleut" as a general label for both the Aleut-speaking people of the Aleutian Chain and the Alutiiqs and other people of the mainland who speak Eskimo languages. The name Alutiiq (properly spelled Alu'utíq) is in fact adapted from the Russian word Aleuty "Aleuts." Even now, some of the Yup'ik Eskimos of the Dillingham area and even some Athabaskans from the Iliamna region may refer to themselves as Aleuts. This has understandably resulted in a good deal of confusion about the meaning of the term. For this reason, "Aleut" is now falling into disuse, and linguistically more precise names have come to be used for these different groups: Unangan (or Unangas) for the people of the Aleutian Chain, Alutiiq (or Sugpiaq) and Yup'ik for the Eskimo-speaking people of the southern mainland, and Dena'ina for the Athabaskan of the Cook Inlet area. The language of the Unangan or Chain Aleuts is distantly related to the Eskimo languages. Although the structural similarities between Unangan Aleut and the Eskimo languages are still quite evident, these two branches of the Eskimo-Aleut language family have diverged to the point where they are completely mutually unintelligible (apart from vocabulary borrowed from the Russians).

Before Russian contact, the Koniag and Chugach referred to themselves as Sugpiat, the "real people"—for one person the name is Sugpiaq, a "real person," and the language is referred to as Sugtestun, literally "(speaking) like a person." At the present time, both names, Alutiiq and Sugpiaq, are used. In the 1980s, when I asked people from all the villages whether they preferred to refer to themselves as Alutiiq or as Sugpiaq, most people agreed that Sugpiaq was all right, but that Alutiiq was preferred. Now, however, there is less agreement. For example, the people of Nanwalek prefer the name Sugpiaq, but some of the people of the neighboring village of Port Graham prefer Alutiiq. The preference of one name over the other seems to be based on whether the people identify themselves more with the original or "real" people (Sugpiat), or whether they identify themselves more with the unique blend of heritage and culture that came about due to Russian contact symbolized by the name Alutiiq.

The Alutiiq language has changed since contact with the Russians. Like Unangan, Alutiiq has incorporated hundreds of Russian words into its vocabulary. In a few cases we can observe structural changes in the Alutiiq language that are most likely due to Russian influence, but such structural changes are relatively minor. Russian influence is most noticeable in the northern Kodiak archipelago, especially in the Afognak subdialect.

Alutiiq is currently an endangered language. In most areas there are very few speakers left, and these are for the most part in their sixties or older. The Kenai Peninsula is a notable exception. In the villages of Nanwalek and Port Graham, the youngest fluent speakers are in their thirties, and over a hundred people still regularly speak the language. Nevertheless, even here the language is endangered, since the great majority of the children are being raised to speak English and not Alutiiq.

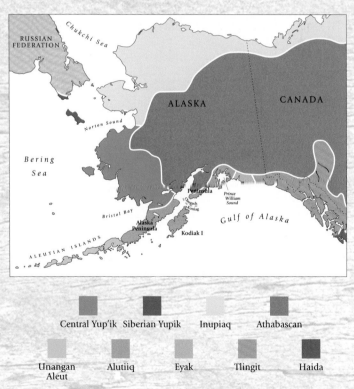

19 The distribution of indigenous languages in Alaska.

Adapted from Alaska Native Language Map, 1982. Courtesy of the Alaska Native Language Center, University of Alaska Fairbanks.

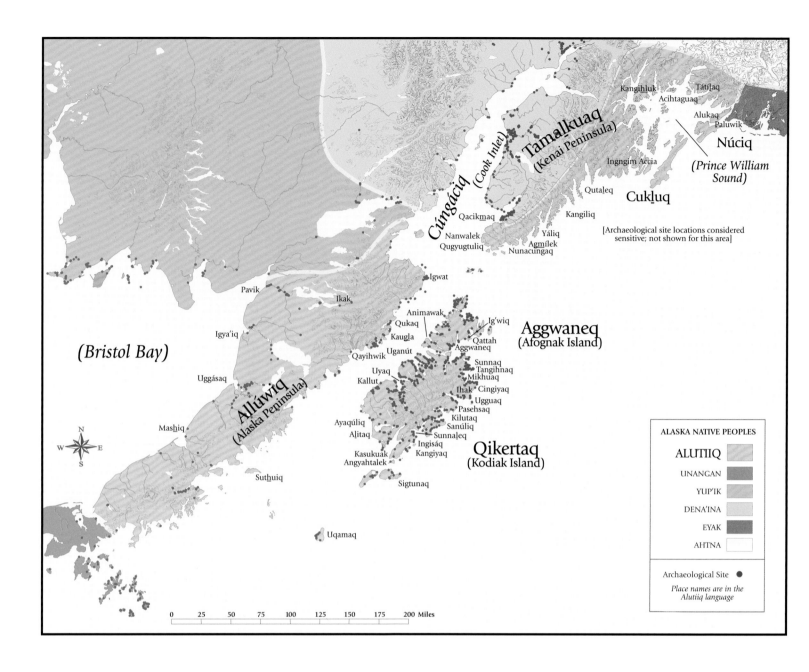

[Archaeological site locations considered sensitive; not shown for this area]

ALASKA NATIVE PEOPLES

ALUTIIQ

UNANGAN

YUP'IK

DENA'INA

EYAK

AHTNA

Archaeological Site ●

Place names are in the Alutiiq language

0 25 50 75 100 125 150 175 200 Miles

the forest thins and vanishes to the west, replaced by treeless tundra.

Kodiak and surrounding islands comprised the most heavily populated Alutiiq area, home to 6500 people or more at the time of Russian contact.[32] Residents of Kodiak called themselves *Qikertarmiut* ("people of the island").[33] Lisianskii recorded about thirty winter villages in the archipelago in 1805 and this is probably close to the original number.[34] Even as late as 1837, when fifty years of epidemics had reduced the population by over fifty percent, there were still about sixty-five active settlements according to the historian Tikhmenev, a

number that included seasonal fishing and hunting camps as well as main settlements.[35] Archaeological sites are also more densely concentrated in the Kodiak archipelago than anywhere else in the Alutiiq region.

The sizeable population of the Kodiak group can be attributed to its rich resource base. Its waters, especially off the northern, eastern, and southern coasts, teem with whales, seals, sea otters, and birds. The Karluk (*Kallut*) and Ayakulik (*Ayaqúliq*) rivers on the southwest side of Kodiak support salmon runs that once included millions of fish. Land animals are few, but people hunted grizzly bears, foxes, and river otters. *Qikertarmiut* families spent the summer at salmon fishing sites and at camps for hunting and gathering plant foods, returning in October to their main villages.

The Alaska Peninsula   Snow-capped volcanic peaks of the Aleutian Range form a chain along the length of the Alaska Peninsula *(Allúwiq)*. Minor eruptions and earthquakes occur frequently, punctuated by major events that cause widespread destruction. On the north side of the mountains lie the lakes and rivers of the lowlands bordering Bristol Bay; to the south is the rugged Gulf of Alaska coast. Residents of Katmai *(Qayihwik)* and Kukak *(Qukaq)* hunted and fished in the coastal waters near their villages, and went inland across the mountain passes for caribou hunting and salmon fishing.

Speakers of Alutiiq or a closely related Yup'ik dialect once resided in villages along the lower Naknek River. This situation changed in about A.D. 1800, when Yup'ik-speaking Aglurmiut migrated into eastern Bristol Bay and forced residents of the lower Naknek to move upriver to the settlement of *Ikak* and west along the coast to Ugashik *(Uggásaq)*.[36] Figure 20 approximates cultural boundaries prior to these changes. Archaeological research demonstrates that the Aglurmiut migration from the north was only the latest population movement in an area that has long been a shifting border zone between Bering Sea and Gulf of Alaska cultures.[37]

Russian estimates of the Alaska Peninsula Alutiiq population between 1792 and 1825 were inconsistent, varying from about 200 to about 900 people depending on which settlements were included.[38] These figures indicate that far fewer people lived here than in the Kodiak archipelago, and the relatively small number of archaeological sites suggests that this may have always been so. Sites are concentrated along the Naknek and Ugashik River drainages where salmon are plentiful, and in Kukak, Amalik, and several other resource-rich bays on the Gulf coast. The western part of the Alaska Peninsula was a border area, shared with the Unangan as a seasonal hunting and fishing ground.

The Kenai Peninsula   In the eighteenth century, Chugach people called the *Unegkuhmiut* lived in several settlements along the glacial fjords of the outer Kenai Peninsula *(Tamaḻkuaq)*.[39] By 1880, only thirty-two people remained at Yalik *(Yáliq)*, the last surviving village. Hundreds of years earlier, people of the ancestral Kachemak culture had occupied Kachemak Bay *(Qacikmaq)* and used fishing camps along the Russian and Kenai Rivers. These areas of Cook Inlet were abandoned for unknown reasons in about A.D. 500, later to became part of Dena'ina territory.[40] In historic times, Chugach of both the Kenai Peninsula and Prince William Sound interacted extensively with the Dena'ina, often traversing mountain passes to Cook Inlet for trade or to do battle.

Prince William Sound   Prince William Sound is encircled by glaciers and peaks of the Chugach Mountains and screened from the open ocean by Montague Island *(Cukḻuq)* and Hinchinbrook Island *(Núciq)*. The sound receives heavy rains and snowfall and its shores and islands are thickly forested with hemlock and spruce. Seals, sea otters, whales, salmon, and birds were traditionally the most important food sources, although some Chugach villages relied heavily on mountain goats for food and skins.

The original Chugach population of Prince William Sound is difficult to estimate. Russian counts are inconsistent and ranged from 423 in 1792 to 1563 in 1825.[41] This relatively low number of people, which does not seem to reflect any scarcity of natural resources, is consistent with archaeological indications.[42]

In addition to Prince William Sound, Chugach territory at the time of European contact included the outer islands of Controller Bay. One of these, Kayak Island, was the site of Bering's landing in 1741.

The Chugach also occupied the Copper River delta but were displaced after contact by Eyak and Tlingit groups who moved in under Russian protection. Chugach Elders in the 1930s remembered that the population of the

Chugach Teachers

Frederica de Laguna
Professor Emerita, Bryn Mawr College

I HAD THE PLEASURE OF WORKING WITH THE CHUGACH people of Prince William Sound in the summers of 1930 and 1933. I was very much impressed by their open welcome when I introduced myself as an anthropologist-archaeologist who wanted to learn about their past. The first summer, 1930, my younger brother Wallace and I were at the village of Chenega in the western sound (a village that was destroyed by a tidal wave in 1964 with tragic loss of life). We were permitted to take pictures freely, and one of the men took me out in his *baidarka* (kayak) and even let me paddle.

In 1933, Kaj Birket-Smith of the Danish National Museum and I collaborated on joint ethnological and archaeological investigations. Norman Reynolds, a graduate student from the University of Washington, was our assistant for the whole season, while my brother and mother (a guest) joined us later. The Chugach of the eastern part of Prince William Sound were equally ready to help us. They not only told about old sites where we might dig, and the sites of rock paintings which they believed had been made by evil spirits, but they also told us myths and stories, and talked freely about their beliefs and customs. They were our patient teachers. More than this, a number became our friends. These were Makari Chimovitski, and his daughter Matrona Tiedemann, a younger brother, Paul Eliah Chimovitski, and also Stepan Britskalov of Chenega. Fred Chimovitski, Makari's younger brother, had befriended my brother and myself in 1930.

Makari and Matrona camped with us for a month, while we were excavating the site of Palugvik, on Hawkins Island, near Cordova. This was the first time I had really lived with Native Americans and it was a delightful experience. I knew at once that Matrona was to be my special friend. She treated me almost like a daughter, so I asked if I might call her "Ma." "Everybody does," she said. She mothered us all, helping us to wash our clothes, cutting Norman Reynold's hair, teaching me to make a delicious chowder (clam or fish) without either milk or tomato, supplying us with an occasional salmon feast (through her white husband, August Tiedemann), and doing many other acts of kindness that were certainly not included in her job as interpreter for her father. She made a sweatbath on the beach which she and I shared before we retired to let the men use it. It was my first sauna; and she laughed

21　Matrona Tiedemann, daughter of Makari Chimovitski, 1933.

Photograph by Kaj Birket-Smith. Courtesy of Cordova Historical Society (83-4-3).

when I had to poke my nose out for fresh air because the steam was so hot. She told me a great deal about her own life and her family—intimate women's talk.

Although I was chiefly responsible for the archaeological excavations at the site, while Birket-Smith concentrated on the ethnographic work with Makari, we often traded places, and we shared our notes. The old man described ancient customs, identified the artifacts we dug up, made little models of tools and weapons to show what his people had used. These included carving a doll for me, an old-time chief with wooden hat and staff, for which Matrona made a frock of rabbit fur.

After a month our Chugach friends had to return to Cordova. My own mother and brother then joined our camp, and in the middle of summer we were all taken by the Forest Service launch, *Chugach*, to Chenega, where Stepan Britskalov became the special friend of Birket-Smith, confiding to him his own religious experiences, something he had never told anyone before.

After all the rest of the party had left at the end of the season, I took a week's trip with the Tiedemanns in "Pa's"

22 Makari Chimovitski (Alingun Nupatlkertlugoq Angakhuna), Prince William Sound Elder, 1933.

Photograph by Kaj Birket-Smith. Courtesty of Cordova Historical Society (83-4-1).

gas boat, during which we dined on all five species of Alaska salmon, in addition to clam chowder, some ducks, and a bear cub, with a barrel of pickled herring just aft of the pilot house for snacks. We stopped at the Tiedemann's sons' place in Sheep Bay. Here, several bear carcasses on the beach aroused Ma's ire and she berated her daughters-in law: "Don't waste all that meat! You get barrels and salt, and put them up! I'll take this one [the cub we ate on the boat], and those ducks." And she sent her sons and their wives scurrying. Later, in Port Gravina, Paul Eliah Chimovitski exhibited his skills as a story-teller.

Because the Chugach shared their knowledge so generously, I feel it not only my duty but my privilege to give back to these wonderful people, or rather to their descendants, as much as possible of what I learned about their ancient culture. I began my many years of Alaska fieldwork among the Chugach, and that experience served to convince me that to understand a people, one should combine a study of their past through archaeology and history with a study of their living culture through ethnography and linguistic efforts.

Returning now to the field notes of 1930 and 1933 in order to edit a volume of "Tales of the Chugach," I have come to realize how much more I owe to my Native teachers of so many years ago. It is that one should endeavor to see their world as they see it, to attempt if only in imagination to adopt their way of life, and to listen to their tales (myth, legend, and personal experience) and to their songs, for these express their joys, sorrows, hopes, fears, their understanding of the world, and their place in it, as well as the fundamental values by which they judge the good and the evil. This then must be translated so that intelligent persons who do not live in that world may understand and respect them.

We were unable to record (on tape) the actual words of the tales we heard, neither those of the Alutiiq speaker, not even the exact English of the narrator or interpreter, although we did our best with pencil and paper. And we had no means for capturing the unfamiliar music of the songs. I realize that it would take a much longer time in the field with the Chugach to be able to approach the kind of understanding I would like to have. Moreover, in 1930 and 1933, we did not even anticipate the questions for which we now want answers.

Yet, because we approached our ethnographic inquiries with a general interest in anything that we might be told, I find that my old field notes may still be mined for overlooked nuggets of knowledge. The more detailed, the more closely written down in the words of the Native teacher, the more valuable such information may become in retrospect, when one is a little wiser.

sound was formerly organized into eight local groups, each with its own chief and a territory that included a main winter village and various seasonal camps.[43] Palugvik *(Paluwik)* and other villages in the outer sound were the wealthiest because of their access to large numbers of sea otters. These rich villages took turns hosting an annual Feast of the Dead, part of the Chugach winter cycle of feasts and hunting ceremonies.[44]

Houses and Domestic Life

The Kodiak Island winter house, or *ciqluaq* (which in the nineteenth century came to be called by the

Kamchadal-derived term, "barabara"), had a driftwood frame, plank walls covered with sod, and a thatched roof. The floor was somewhat below ground. Such houses, according to Lisianskii, accommodated an average of about eighteen residents, consisting of several related families.[45] A large settlement might include ten to fifteen of the houses, with a total population of 200 to 300.[46] The central room of the *ciqluaq*, entered through a doorway at ground level, was connected by low openings to private side chambers that were used for sleeping, storage, and taking steam baths. Houses on the Alaska Peninsula were similar to Kodiak dwellings, but generally lacked these extra rooms.[47]

Floors inside the *ciqluaq* were covered with grass or planks, and there were drains to channel away water. Soft skins and woven mats gave comfort for sitting and sleeping. Each family's area within the main chamber was partitioned off by skins or boards. A stone-lined, wood-burning hearth for cooking and heating occupied the center of the floor, and stone lamps filled with seal or whale oil gave

23 Residents of Old Harbor, Kodiak Island, in front of sod houses *(ciqluat)*, photographed with crew members of the research vessel *Albatross*, 1888–89. The smoke hatch of the house in the foreground is open for ventilation. A kayak frame rests on top of the house in the rear.

Courtesy of the National Archives (22-FA-266).

illumination at night. Smoke rose through a skylight in the roof, which could be closed over with a wooden hatch or a transparent cover made of animal intestine. The top of the house was a storage place for kayaks and other equipment, as well as a sitting area where weather forecasters watched the morning sea and sky.

Chugach dwellings in Prince William Sound were of a style that was more typical of Northwest Coast Indian peoples.[48] The houses were rectangular structures with joined wooden frames, walls of vertically placed boards, grass or bark-covered roofs, and a round doorway at each end. Summer houses were entirely above ground, while those for winter use were partially below ground level. Inside was an open hearth for cooking, with an opening above for the escape of smoke. Each of several families in the typical household had an enclosed sleeping room with a circular doorway and gutskin window. Bedding consisted of mountain goat skins, bear skins, and cormorant blankets. Steam bathing chambers were also built inside, next to the front door. At least one early Prince

25 *Tanqik*—**Lamp**

Cook Inlet, late Kachemak tradition (A.D. 500–1100)
National Museum of the American Indian

"Snow over and they can't hear the wind; they're nice and cozy in there."

—Ephraim Agnot, Kodiak Island Elder, 1986

Stone lamps filled with seal oil and lit with a wick of cotton grass brought light and warmth into the traditional winter house, that also had a hearth for burning wood. Stone lamps of the Late Kachemak period were often carved with human figures, whales, and other designs.

Photograph courtesy of the Anchorage Museum of History and Art.

24 Chugach log house with bark- and grass-covered roof at the village of Nuchek *(Núciq)*, Prince William Sound, 1888. Stretchers for sealskins lean against the front of the house.
Photograph courtesy of the Alaska State Library (PCA 27-60).

26 Mary Peterson (left) and Rena Peterson (right) play *kadaq* at the newly built community barabara in Akhiok, Kodiak Island, 1989. *Kadaq* is a spirited team game that was traditionally played, often for wagers, at winter social events. Pairs or lines of players kneel and face each other, and one of each pair hides a small stick in each hand. The players with the sticks sing humorous songs and move their bodies from side to side, holding one fist to the chest and the other behind the back. When the song is over the others must guess which hand holds the winning stick, which is marked with paint or a groove around the middle; this stick is called the "first chief" in Prince William Sound (Birket-Smith 1953:107–108). Native sea otter hunters are believed to have learned the game from California Indians at the Russian-American Company's Fort Ross during the early nineteenth century (Kari 1983).

Photograph courtesy of the Alutiiq Museum.

27 *Kakangat*—Tossing disks

Woody Island (Tangihnaq), Kodiak Island, 1883
National Museum of Natural History, Smithsonian
    Institution
(NMNH 90436) Diameter of disks 3.5 cm

Kakangaq was a traditional game in which players threw disks of wood or ivory toward a target in the center of a seal skin. Competitors tried to land their disks on the target, or to knock someone else's out of the way. Scores were counted by the positions of the disks and tallied with wooden sticks. Davydov noted in 1802–03 that good hunters were careful not to play in the evenings, because it might bring bad luck to the chase.

William Sound house was decorated inside with paintings of hunting scenes.[49] Chugach people later began using Russian-style log cabins with notched corner joints as winter dwellings (fig. 24).

Throughout the Alutiiq region, provisions harvested in summer were stored inside the winter houses. These might include dried salmon and halibut, whale meat, seal stomachs full of oil and berries, grass baskets filled with plant foods, bark boxes of fish eggs, and bentwood tubs to hold berries preserved in sea mammal fat. Food was roasted by the fire, or boiled in wooden boxes and watertight baskets by adding red-hot stones. Clay cooking pots were also used on parts of Kodiak Island. Food was served on wooden platters and in bowls decorated with beads, crystals, and animal teeth. Simple serving spoons were carved of wood, while decorated spoons for ceremonial use were carved from mountain goat horn.

Inside the house, men and women carried out everyday tasks. When John D'Wolf visited the village of Kukak (Qukaq) in July 1806, he was invited into an Alutiiq home:

> The occupants were principally women, with a few old men; the young men had all gone out hunting the sea otter, in the Russian service. Those at home seemed to be quite happy and contented, and were all employed in making water-proof garments from the entrails of sea-lions, for their husbands and sweethearts. We bought of them a number of articles of their manufacture—curious and very neat work—such as pocket-books, baskets, &c.—and paid them in tobacco and beads.[50]

28   Mountain goat horn spoons

Karluk *(Kallut)*, Kodiak Island, 1879–82 (left)
National Museum of Natural History, Smithsonian Institution (NMNH 72527) Height 15cm

Eagle Harbor *(Ihak)*, Kodiak Island, 1883 (right)
National Museum of Natural History, Smithsonian Institution NMNH 90429) Height 15cm

Alutiiq craftsmen made serving spoons from the horns of mountain goats. They softened the horns with steam, then bent and carved the bowls into shape. Figures on the handles are stylistically unique, but have similarities to Tlingit totemic designs (Holm 1988). These spoons probably reached Kodiak Island through trade with the Chugach region.

29 *Ekgwiutaq*—Woman's sewing bag

Katmai *(Qayihwik)*, Alaska Peninsula, 1879–1882
National Museum of Natural History, Smithsonian Institution
(NMNH 72495) Height 30 cm

"Blow, just like a balloon, that bear gut . . . let sun dry it, like clothes outside. . . . Cut it about so wide. . . . Then they sew it together for a rain jacket."

—Nida Chya, Kodiak Island Elder, 1986

Intestines of bears, seals, sea lions, and whales were used to make waterproof jackets and bags. To prepare intestines for sewing, they were cleaned, inflated, and hung out to dry. This nineteenth century intestine bag is trimmed with sea otter fur and bird down. Colored yarn and hair are tucked into the seams. The bag was made to hold scraps of fur and other sewing materials.

Women wove grass baskets and spruce root hats, and worked with skins, membranes, feathers, fur, and hair to create finely crafted traditional garments. Their tools were bone and ivory needles, awls, gut scrapers, and stone knives. Women's skin sewing skills were also essential for making boat covers. Men built boat frames and made boxes, bowls, spoons, hunting weapons and wooden hats, masks, and many other items. Some households kept eagles as pets, for convenient use of their feathers in fletching arrows and darts.[51] Men's tools were stone and metal adzes, chisels, bone wedges for splitting planks, beaver or porcupine-tooth knives, and knives with curved metal blades. Iron and copper tools were used even before European explorers and Russian fur traders arrived in the region.[52] Copper came from sources in Prince William Sound and along the Copper River, while iron was obtained in trade or found embedded in planks from shipwrecks that washed up on the beach.[53]

Society and Family

One of the notable aspects of classical Alutiiq society was the intricacy of its social arrangements. Although many details of social life in the eighteenth century are unclear from the historical record, it appears that wealth

30   Porcupine or marmot tooth carving tool

Karluk 1 site, Kodiak Island, A.D. 1400–1750
Alutiiq Museum, Koniag, Inc. Collection
(AM193.87:9356) Length 12 cm

The front teeth of marmots, porcupines, and beavers were set in handles to make tools for carving wood. The outer edges of the teeth were used as whetstones to sharpen knives.

31   *Lúgun—*Carving knife

Ugashik *(Uggásaq)*, Alaska Peninsula, 1884
National Museum of Natural History, Smithsonian Institution
(NMNH 90458) Length 21 cm

Knives with curved steel blades are used for carving. The handle of this nineteenth century knife is a caribou rib, and the lashing is made from spruce tree root.

32 "Nangkuq, a Chief from Kodiak Island," painting by
Mikhail Tikhanov, 1818.

Courtesy of the Scientific Research Museum of the Russian Academy of Arts.

and political leadership were concentrated among certain high-ranking lineages.[54] Each village was ruled by a headman or chief (on Kodiak, an *angayuqaq*) who inherited this position as a member of one of the elite families, and some chiefs were recognized as leaders of more than one village.

On Kodiak Island in the early nineteenth century, succession to the chieftainship is reported to have normally passed not from father to son but from a man to his nephew, suggesting that membership in the elite lineages may possibly have been traced through women.[55] In Prince William Sound of the 1930s, a son was first in the order of succession, but the chieftainship could also pass to a brother or nephew on either side of the family.[56] Although men held most positions of political leadership, women became shamans and healers and enjoyed a significant measure of power and influence in their communities.[57] In Prince William Sound they owned winter houses and large skin boats.[58]

Chiefs directed hunting and led expeditions for trade and war, and the wealth acquired through these endeavors was one of the main measures of a leader's success. Gideon recorded a list of clothing, food, equipment, and luxury items that might be owned by a rich man on Kodiak Island. These included many parkas of different furs, a twenty-oar *angyaq*, three kayaks, sea lion skins, whale meat, sea lion stomachs filled with whale oil, bentwood boxes and baskets containing various foods, pieces of amber, dentalium shell ornaments, abalone shell plates, and many glass beads.[59] Several observers noted that chiefs had little actual authority over anyone but their immediate relatives.[60] Instead, they led by strength, intelligence, and by skillfully using their wealth to build support and prestige. Chiefs owned ceremonial houses (*qasgiq*), and hosted feasts and hunting ceremonies that included the distribution of gifts to villagers and guests.[61]

Chiefly and wealthy families represented the upper ranks of traditional society, while ordinary families made up the class of free, common people. At the low end of the social scale were slaves—orphans, chattels acquired through trade, or women and children who were taken during raids against enemy villages. In 1790, Merck reported that a slave could be purchased for twenty glass beads.[62]

Alutiiq society also supported specialists of various kinds. Whalers pursued their difficult and hereditary art with the aid of complex and secret rituals that were passed down to selected apprentices (see chapter 5). Shamans divined the future and the spiritual causes of disease, and *kassat* ("wise men") composed religious songs, dances, and poetry (see chapter 6). Weather forecasters provided advice to sea travelers, and healers and midwives used expert knowledge of herbal cures and other healing techniques. The traditions of midwifery were carried on into recent generations, as discussed by Joanne Mulcahy (p. 44).

It has been pointed out that this kind of society, with its levels of rank and specialized roles, is unusual among the nonagricultural peoples of the world, although the Unangan, Dena'ina, Eyak, Tlingit, and other indigenous coastal societies of the northeastern North Pacific shared similar traits. The rich resource base of the Gulf of Alaska coast, growth of relatively large and settled populations, and need for chiefly leadership to manage economic and political affairs may be involved in the explanation.[63]

33   Woman's food bowl

Chenega (*Caniqaq*), Prince William Sound, 1887–93
National Museum of Natural History, Smithsonian Institution
(NMNH 168618) Width 15 cm

Men's and women's eating bowls were distinguished by shape. This boat-shaped woman's bowl is decorated with glass beads, and may have been used to serve guests at feasts and hunting festivals.

Alutiiq Midwives

Joanne B. Mulcahy
Northwest Writing Institute,
Lewis and Clark College

"OH, THE MIDWIVES BEFORE, THEY WERE SO GOOD! WE never had problems. They took such good care of you. . . . We were really spoiled! . . . I don't know how they knew what to do, but they just knew."

In a 1980 interview, Katherine Chichenoff, respected Elder and mother of ten, alerted me to the symbolic and practical importance of the Alutiiq midwife. For the next fifteen years, I pursued stories about the "knowing midwives" and women's healing roles in Kodiak history. Village midwives Annie Boskofsky, Marina Waselie, Clyda Christiansen, Julia Wolkoff, Sasha Christiansen, and Freida Reft shared their knowledge of herbs and plants, of massage and prenatal care in the banya. They described the steamed alder branches called *wainít* they used to reposition the fetus, how they held the mother during delivery, and offered a week or more of postpartum care. I learned about Oleanna Ashouwak, a renowned healer who cured many of pneumonia and tuberculosis by holding them in the banya to rebalance the pulse and restore health. These stories led to the modern manifestation of the traditional midwife–the Community Health Aide (CHA). The work of CHAs such as Betty Nelson and Stella Stanley, who cared for "every little thing" in village life, as Betty phrased it, underscores a critical historical connection between women's traditional and contemporary healing roles (Mulcahy 1988, 1993, 2001).

Perhaps no one was as pivotal to my exploration of Alutiiq culture as Akhiok Elder Mary Peterson, a midwife and CHA. Mary's stories helped me understand the overlapping sphere of oral histories—individual recollections of experience—and oral tradition, tales handed down intergenerationally. Shaped in social interaction, often told in artistic performance, oral traditions carry on shared cultural values. When Mary Peterson described her first birth experience, she spoke for many women whose ability to heal rested on faith as well as apprenticeship or appointment.

First time by myself, I just knew, just knew what to do, like there was somebody with me, using my hands and my mind. . . . I always think that God was there, using my hands to help this lady.

Stories of faith and the meaning of healing told in banyas and homes, while picking berries and drying fish, were woven into the fabric of daily life. As part of an oral tradition, they transmitted Alutiiq values while resisting attempts to suppress Native identity. Alutiiq women's stories heroically asserted: "This is what we value—family, reciprocity, the healing of individuals and communities."

Many other Elders, including Eunice Neseth, Enola Mullan, and Ephraim Agnot, taught me much about the nature of reciprocity, generosity, and humor in the face of hardship. Their stories are their greatest legacy. Gifts, exist not only in the actual offering, argues poet Lewis Hyde, but in the increase, the meaning that accrues to the gift as it is given again. Alutiiq stories grow with each telling to the next generation, with every person who shares the wonder I remember from my first encounter with tales of women who "just knew" how to heal.

34 Child's necklace

Nuchek *(Núciq)*, Prince William Sound, 1887–93
National Museum of Natural History, Smithsonian
   Institution
(NMNH 168634) Length 19 cm

The four pockets of this child's necklace are sewn shut, and their contents (if any) are unknown. The necklace may be a protective amulet. Elder Lucille Antowak Davis remembers that Kodiak midwives saved and dried the amniotic sac of a newborn, and placed it in a cloth pouch that a child wore around her neck. The amulet provided reassurance and protection.

Children grew up learning the many skills they would need as adults. Girls played with dolls and toy versions of stone knives and other women's tools, and began learning to weave baskets, process skins and sinew, and sew when very young. By age six "they polish thread, plait cords, and do so with sufficient skill," observed Gideon in 1804.[64] Boys played with toy boats, paddles, and spears. They began training to handle kayaks at age fourteen, and by sixteen were hunting at sea with their fathers and kinsmen. Some Alutiiq boys were raised as girls, learned female skills, and wore feminine clothing and tattoos. Such *ahnaucit* (transvestites) often became shamans.[65]

Life's passages were marked by ritual, often involving symbolic separation of the individual from society followed by ritual cleansing and reintegration into community life (see chapter 6). A girl lived for several weeks or months in a separate room or hut after her first menstruation, followed by bathing and a celebration to mark her reappearance in the village as a young woman.[66] Mothers and their newborn infants were segregated for a time after birth, followed by a ritual steam bath for both.[67] A boy's first successful hunt marked his transition to manhood. All of the meat was given away while he was required to fast, and in Prince William Sound there was a community feast and reenactment of the hunt.[68]

35 Doll

Karluk 1 site, Kodiak Island, A.D. 1400–1750
Alutiiq Museum, Koniag, Inc. Collection
(UA85.193.3980) Height 10.5 cm

"There was a time to play with your toys; there was a time to put them away. . . . If you see the geese come from the south, you pray—you make the sign of the cross and say, thank you Lord. The other ones were the swallows. The swallows were when you took your dolls out. That's the sign."
— Lucille Antowak Davis, Kodiak Island Elder, 1997

It was believed in the past that each type of child's play was appropriate to a certain time of the year. Some pastimes were thought to influence seasonal changes, such as tops, which were spun in winter to hasten the return of the sun. Mrs. Davis remembers dolls and many other homemade toys from her childhood in Karluk.

36 Toy bow

Karluk 1 site, Kodiak Island, A.D. 1400–1750
Alutiiq Museum, Koniag, Inc. Collection
(AM193.87) Length 41cm

"Some old people got the best of us. You know they trained us, they trained us to use the bow and arrow. But they played, old men against the young people—they never let us win."
— Ignatius Kosbruk, Alaska Peninsula Elder, 1997

This archaeological artifact brought back memories of Elders' childhoods. When the wild geese migrated in spring, men and boys brought out bows and arrows for shooting competitions on the beach. The target was a reed, a piece of wood, or the bulb of a kelp plant. Elder Mary Peterson remembers the women cheering their favorites. "They were just rooting for their sides, like a ball game. And it was just exciting!"

37   Toy ulu knife *(ulukaq)*, scoop, war club, shield

Karluk 1 site, Kodiak Island, A.D. 1400–1750
Alutiiq Museum, Koniag, Inc., Collection
(ulu and handle, AM15.193:223/ AM193.95:195) Length 5 cm
(scoop, UA85.193.6382) Length 7.5 cm
(war club, AM193.95:1644) Length 16 cm
(shield, AM193.95:749) Length 6 cm

Miniature implements from archaeological sites reveal the grown-up play of children hundreds of years ago.

Marriage partners chose each other, but parents had to approve. Marriage was followed by a period when the couple lived with the bride's family and the groom served her father. Gideon left a description of an early nineteenth century Kodiak marriage ritual:

> If the desired answer is obtained from the latter [the bride's father], the young man the following night goes to the girl's house, and lies down next to her, fully clothed; in the morning, haven risen, he gathers firewood, heats rocks in the front room for a sweatbath, which he then takes together with his bride. As they emerge from the sweatbath, the [groom's] kinsmen bring his gifts, which formerly consisted of sea otter, ground squirrel, marmot, and cormorant parkas, slaves, amber, and dentalium. These gifts were given to the bride's father and the latter's kin.[69]

Death was commemorated according to the wealth and status of the deceased.[70] An ordinary person was dressed in his or her best clothing, beads, and ornaments, and wrapped in seal skins. The final resting place could be a rock or plank-lined grave, rocky cleft, or the collapsed side room of a house. Personal tools, weapons, and sometimes the deceased person's kayak were added to the grave or placed on top of it, and painted memorial poles or other markers were put in place. Grief-stricken mourners cut their hair and blackened their faces. When a chief or other noble person died, the cloth-ing and grave offerings were very rich, and the body was often taken to a hidden place or cave. The bodies of whalers and notable people were preserved in dry caves by mummification.[71] Slaves were sometimes killed and buried with their wealthy owners. The dead were honored with memorial feasts and during the winter hunting ceremonies.

Clothing, Jewelry, and Tattoos

Traditional clothing was a multidimensional expression of Alutiiq culture and values.[72] In functional terms, garments such as fur and birdskin parkas, seal boots, bearskin mittens, and waterproof rain jackets made from animal intestines were practical working clothes for a harsh environment. At the same time, clothing conveyed larger spiritual and social meanings. Beautiful craftsmanship by Alutiiq seamstresses expressed respect for animals, whose skins enveloped the clothed person and whose spirits in the wild were ever alert to human attitudes, actions, and appearance. Mindful of this relationship, hunters wore new, clean garments, and men and women donned their best parkas, beaded headdresses, ermine hats, and other special garments for the winter hunting ceremonies.[73] Clothing, jewelry, and tattoos were equally important as a means of social communication. Variations in style and materials signaled a person's rank, gender, age, and place of origin.

38 Women and children dressed in ground squirrel parkas, Portage Bay, Alaska Peninsula, 1909.

Photograph courtesy of the Alaska State Library (PCA 24-109).

39 *Qanganaq*—Man's ground squirrel parka

Made by Susan Malutin and Grace Harrod, Kodiak Island, 1999
Based on a parka from Ugashik *(Uggásaq)*, Alaska
    Peninsula, 1883

Photograph by Amy Steffian. Courtesy of the Alutiiq Museum (AM 405:1).

Contemporary skin sewers Susan Malutin and Grace Harrod created this parka after studying an 1883 example in the Fisher collection at the National Museum of Natural History (NMNH 90469). It is made from ground squirrel pelts and accented with strips of white ermine along the seams. Mink and white caribou fur are used on the chest and sleeves. The tassels are of dyed skin, sea otter fur, and red cloth with ermine puffs.

The design of this parka (and of the original garment from Ugashik) reflects shared cultural traditions of the Alaska Peninsula. Alutiiq style is seen in the tassels, use of sea otter fur, and the visual accent on horizontal seams. Yup'ik elements include the design and materials of the yoke, sleeves, and collar, as well as the embroidered cloth tabs that hang from the back (Hunt 2000). The finest parkas were worn during the winter ceremonies, and presented by the host as gifts to honored guests.

40   Bobbin for sinew thread

Ugashik *(Uggásaq)*, Alaska Peninsula, 1887–93
National Museum of Natural History, Smithsonian Institution
(NMNH 168633) Height 7.5 cm

After sinews were dried, the tough fibers were separated with
a fingernail or comb. The strands were then moistened and
rolled between the hands to prepare them for use. This bob-
bin held finished strands, ready for use.

42   Sewing tools: needle and gut scraper

Karluk 1 site, Kodiak Island, A.D. 1400–1750
Alutiiq Museum, Koniag, Inc., Collection
(needle, AM193.94:1791) Length 6 cm
(gut scraper, UA84-193/1966) Length 11 cm

Before metal tools were available, an Alutiiq seamstress
punched holes in leather with a bird bone awl and sewed her
seams with fine bone and ivory needles. Spoon-shaped scrapers were used for cleaning fat and tissue from intestines to
prepare them as materials for making clothing.

42   Woman wearing a waterproof seal intestine parka
(kanagluk) at Kodiak (St. Paul) in 1919.

Photo courtesy of University of Alaska Anchorage, Archives and Manuscripts Depart-
ment (National Geographic Society Katmai Expedition Collection, Box 6, 5210).

Unlike parkas from more arctic regions, Alutiiq ones
were loose-fitting and did not have hoods. Men's and
women's designs were quite similar. Parkas often had
armholes below the shoulder so that the wearer did
not have to use the sleeves. In fact, the sleeves were often too short and narrow to be anything but decorative.[74] Many types of furs (sea otter, river otter, fox,
caribou, marmot, marten, bear, arctic ground squirrel,
seal) and bird skins (murres, puffins, geese, eagles,
cormorants) were used. Parkas sewn from the warm,
dense pelts of sea otters, foxes, and bears were symbols
of elite or chiefly status, although Native use of these
commercially valuable furs was forbidden by the
Russians after 1792.[75] As a result, many people on
Kodiak had to dress in puffin parkas, formerly worn
only by slaves.[76] The Kodiak Alutiit were also deprived
of direct access to ground squirrels and instead had to
harvest the animals and sew parkas for Russian-American Company use and redistribution. Ground squirrel
parkas were highly valued, and were often ornamented
with tassels and insets of contrasting furs and trade cloth.

43 Spools

Ugashik (*Uggásaq*), Alaska Peninsula, 1887–93 (above)
National Museum of Natural History, Smithsonian Institution
(NMNH 168632) Length 10.5 cm

Karluk 1 site, Kodiak Island, A.D. 1400–1750 (right)
Alutiiq Museum, Koniag, Inc., Collection
(AM 193.94.16) Length 11.5 cm

The seal-shaped spool was "used by Ugashik women in making fancy work," according to William J. Fisher. Embroidered strips or sinew thread may have been wrapped on the spool for storage. The similar object from Karluk has a ptarmigan carved on one end. Faint grooves and cuts on both spools may be from winding and trimming of materials.

The hooded *kanagluk* rain jacket, also called by the Russian term *kamleika*, was an essential item of apparel (fig. 42). It was stitched from seal, whale, sea lion, or bear intestines or the throats (esophagus) of these animals.[77] Properly sewn and cared for, these garments were waterproof. A kayak hunter would tie the bottom of his *kanagluk* around the hatch opening to seal the vessel against waves.

Bentwood hunting hats and painted basketry hats woven from spruce root fibers held special significance for hunting (chapter 5). Some spruce root hats were topped with a stack of woven cylinders, apparently an indication of high status.[78] Other headgear included embroidered caps of skin and fur for hunting and ceremonies, tall peaked hats worn in ceremonies and by shamans, and beaded headdresses (see chapter 6). Boots were made of sea lion, seal, caribou, marmot, bear, and other skins, although people often chose to go barefoot even in cold weather.

Like clothing, jewelry and tattoos were outward signs of a person's place in society. As George Dixon,

an English fur trader in Prince William Sound, observed in 1786, "Their noses and ears are ornamented with beads, or teeth . . . this I could observe was always in proportion to the person's wealth." There were many styles of labrets (lip plugs) that may have indicated both social status and affiliation with a particular family or village.[79] Women often wore several labrets through perforations beneath the lower lip, from which strings of beads were hung. Men most often wore a single wide labret through a horizontal slit, made of bone, ivory, shell, stone, or wood. Other items of personal adornment included nose pins, necklaces, and earrings.

Tattoos were sewn into the skin with a bone needle and soot-blackened thread. The occasion of a girl's first menstruation was marked by vertical lines that were applied to her chin, and tattoos on a mother's breast helped bring milk.[80] Other tattoos of the face and body signified nobility and wealth. Men and women painted designs on their faces with bright pigments at times of celebration, and with black to signify grief.

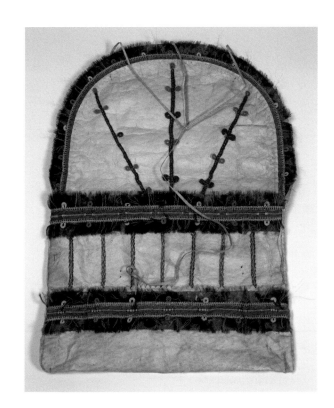

44   *Kakiwit*—Embroidered bags

Katmai *(Qayihwik)*, Alaska Peninsula, 1879–82 (above left)
National Museum of Natural History, Smithsonian Institution
(NMNH 72496) Height 39.5cm

Katmai *(Qayihwik)*, Alaska Peninsula, 1879–82 (above right)
National Museum of Natural History, Smithsonian Institution
(NMNH 72497) Height 39 cm

"All the old people used to have kakiwit. *They would take them along wherever they go, just like a handbag."*
            —Clyda Christiansen, Kodiak Island Elder, 1997

Smithsonian collector William Fisher recorded that these two bags from Katmai village were men's hunting pouches. Women used *kakiwit* to store small sewing items, such as needles and twists of sinew thread. In more recent years, these were made of cloth. Men also carried *kakiwit* at sea for emergency kayak repairs.

45   *Uyamilquat*—Woman's necklace

Ugashik *(Uggásaq)*, Alaska Peninsula, 1879–82
National Museum of Natural History, Smithsonian
    Institution
(NMNH 72467) Diameter 23 cm

Glass beads first reached the Alutiiq region through Native trade connections to the Aleutian Islands, well before Russian fur traders arrived in person. Rare at first, glass beads became common during the early decades of Russian rule. American trading companies imported beads like the ones on this necklace during the late 1800s. Most were manufactured at European glassworks near Venice and Prague.

46   *Agaruak*—Earrings

Ugashik (*Uggásaq*), Alaska Peninsula, 1879–82
National Museum of Natural History, Smithsonian Institution
(NMNII 72465) Length 12.5 cm

"The spectators consisted of native inhabitants, dressed in their fin-
ery. The women were wearing their best dresses . . . while on their
arms and legs, their necks, and in their ears were as many beads as
they could fit in, or all they had."

—G. Davydov, Russian naval officer,
at a winter dance ceremony on Kodiak Island, 1803

Earrings were tied through perforations in the ear lobe or all
around its rim, sometimes six or eight strands on each ear.

47   "Tamaima, an Inhabitant of Kodiak Island" (detail),
painting by Mikhail Tikhanov, 1818.
Courtesy of the Scientific Research Museum of the Russian Academy of Arts.

51

War and Trade

War and trade were two faces of Alutiiq politics, both governed by chiefly alliances between villages.[81] It appears that military allies were at the same time trading partners, and that such relationships were reinforced by reciprocal feasting and marriages. Both alliances and hostile relations existed among Alutiiq villages and also frequently involved Unangan, Dena'ina, Eyak, and Tlingit communities. For example, 1000 Dena'ina ("Kenaitsy") men reportedly traveled in kayaks from the Kenai Peninsula in 1786 to fight alongside the Alutiiq chief of Shuyak Island in his failed resistance to Russian invasion.[82]

Raiding parties set out in *angyat* after a solemn council of war in the ceremonial house, during which the fighters received gifts and food from the chief and war leader. Fighters wore protective helmets and armor made of wooden slats sewn together with sinew. They carried shields and armed themselves with spears, arrows, and war clubs. In Prince William Sound, men also carried long iron knives. Raiders tried to take their enemies by surprise, often at night. They would kill all or most of the men in a settlement, seize valuables, and take young women and adolescents home as slaves. The best defensive strategy was to retreat to the top of a steep-sided islet (refuge rock). Besieged or defeated villages sometimes called on one of their own allies to arrange peace, which was sealed by the provision of high-ranking hostages to the attackers. Retaliation could also follow, as in the Prince William Sound story, "War Between the Chugach and the Koniag" (below).

People of western Kodiak Island traveled to allied villages on the Alaska Peninsula to trade amber and dentalium shells for walrus ivory from Bristol Bay, caribou parkas, caribou antler, and long chest hairs of the animal that were used for embroidery. Eastern Kodiak Islanders traded with Cook Inlet and Prince William

War Between the Chugach and the Koniag: How the Men of Qilangalik Avenged Their Wives

Narrated by Makari Chimovitski in 1933
Translated by Matrona Tiedemann
From *Tales of the Chugach*,
edited by Frederica de Laguna

The Koniag Carry Off the Chugach Women

One summer the men from Qilangalik left their wives on the refuge rock at Johnstone Pont, Hinchinbrook Island, when they went hunting for fur seals. While the women were alone a war party came from Angyahtalek on Kodiak Island. The women did not want the enemy to see that there were no men with them, so they made themselves moustaches of bear fur and brandished spears, but one woman leaned over, and her moustache fell off.

Then the Kodiak Eskimo realized that there were no men there. They made a ladder out of spears and climbed up onto the rock. Some of the women were killed, others they carried away to be slaves or to be their wives.

The Chugach War Party Hears the Kodiak Prophesy Their Own Defeat

In the middle of the winter the men from Qilangalik went to Angyahtalek to avenge their wives.

They arrived while the people were eating supper. They sat down under the window, looking in, and let the snow cover them. The people inside were eating land otter meat. After they ate, they wanted to play dice with a land-otter humerus.

A man threw it. "Tell us the truth about what's going to happen."

Every night the Kodiak people played this game to find out if the Chugach were coming. Before this, the bone had always fallen at "one." This time the bone stuck straight up on the elbow end, at "ten."

"Is that the truth, that the Chugach are going to close in on us?"

Sound people, exchanging ground squirrel parkas for Dena'ina marmot parkas, dentalium shells from the Northwest Coast, and Chugach goat horn spoons.[83] The Chugach traded to the east with the Eyak, Ahtna, and Tlingit for woven mountain goat fur blankets, copper, dentalium shells, and other products.[84]

48   Copper sea otter points

Nuchek (*Núciq*), Prince William Sound, 1887–93
National Museum of Natural History, Smithsonian Institution (NMNH 168631)

Chugach Alutiiq residents of Prince William Sound obtained copper from local sources and through trade with the Ahtna Indians of the Copper River region. William J. Fisher purchased these arrow points when he was a trader at Nuchek for the Alaska Commercial Company.

The man threw it again, and the bone stuck the same way.

"Is that the truth, that they are going to kill us?"

An old man said: "Don't mention the Chugach. They are like the ducks, they may come any minute."

They were outside listening to everything that was said. The bone fell between them.

The Koniag Don't Believe the Chugach Have Come
A young fellow inside the house got up and closed the window. He said:

"I am going outside to see if they are there."

The women were also sitting around the fire. The young man went out (and came back inside). He fell down in front of the fire, but nobody paid any attention, because that's what he was always doing to make people believe that the Chugach had come. They were all afraid of them. They heard him bubbling. The men outside had speared him, and his blood was running out.

The women cried: "See, his blood is running out. The Chugach have speared him already." So they all started to run into the sleeping rooms, and most of them ran

into the bathhouse and closed the door. They heard the men outside, saying:

"Don't kill the old man who was sticking up for us."

They killed all the men but they didn't bother the old man and the women. They found the old man stooping and hiding by the bath house rocks.

The Chugach chief said: "Don't bother him, he was sticking up for us. Take care of him."

Poor fellow, he was all shivering like anything.

The Chugach Return
They recognized their own wives but (some of them) did not take them back. They took young girls, and some took their wives back. They took a lot of young women as slaves. They also took the old man and treated him well. He was always served first when they were eating. They came back home before spring and lived just as they did before. When the old man got (very) old they took care of him, and when he died, they buried him with all kinds of expensive furs. After that, they never left their women alone, but they always left a couple of young fellows to take care of them when they went out after fur seals.

Russian Conquest and Colonial Rule

THE ARRIVAL OF RUSSIAN FUR TRADERS IN THE LATTER HALF of the eighteenth century brought tragedy and almost overwhelming social change. Defeated by Russian force, Alutiiq men and women were forced to work for Grigorii Shelikhov's fur company. Along with systematic exploitation came the loss of political sovereignty, hunger, epidemics of new diseases, and drastic population decline.

Over time, some of the harshest aspects of colonial rule were eased and a bicultural colonial society evolved. Children were born to unions between Russian men and Alutiiq women, and Russian language, customs, and religion gained acceptance in Native communities. Russians in Alaska adopted Native ways as well, and from the beginning they depended on indigenous foods, clothing, boats, and dwellings.[85] Many people began to call themselves "Aleut," a name introduced by the Russians; Alutiiq is a form of this word in the indigenous language.[86]

One of the first Russian voyages to Kodiak Island was by Stepan Glotov in 1763–64.[87] Alutiiq warriors attacked and tried to burn Glotov's vessel, although an exchange of beads for sea otter and fox furs was eventually arranged.[88] Potap Zaikov's voyage to Prince William Sound in 1783 met a similarly hostile reception.[89] It was not until Grigorii Shelikhov's heavily armed expedition in 1784 that the Alutiit of Kodiak Island were defeated and a permanent base of Russian operations was established at Three Saints Harbor.

Shortly after they arrived, Shelikhov's men used cannons and muskets to attack hundreds of men, women, and children who had gathered on a refuge rock near Sitkalidak Island on the east side of Kodiak. Alutiiq Elder Arsenti Aminak recounted the massacre in 1851:

> The Russians went to the settlement and carried out a terrible blood bath. Only a few [people] were able to flee to Angyahtalek in baidarkas [kayaks]; 300 Koniags were shot by the Russians. This happened in April. When our people revisited the place in the summer the stench of the corpses lying on the shore polluted the air so badly that none could stay there, and since then the island has been uninhabited. After this every chief had to surrender his children as hostages; I was saved only by my father's begging and many sea otter pelts.[90]

Izmailov and Bocharov recorded the location of the attack on their 1784 map of Kodiak Island.[91] It was given the Russian name "Razbitoi Kekur" from the Russian word for an off-shore rock (kekur) and the verb razbivat, "to break, crush, defeat." The Alutiiq place name is "Awa'uq" meaning "to become numb."[92] Today most people refer to the site as Refuge Rock.

Hostages and prisoners from the attack were held at Three Saints Harbor, and buildings were constructed there to serve as company headquarters. Over the next several years, Shelikhov's men expanded operations throughout the Kodiak Island group and into Cook Inlet, the Alaska Peninsula, and Prince William Sound. The Shelikhov company and its rival, the Lebedev-Lastochkin company, established reduty (forts), arteli (work stations), and odinochki (small outposts) across the Alutiiq region for control of fur and food production (fig. 51). Competition gave way in 1799 to a single monopoly firm, the Russian-American Company (RAC), which was headquartered first at Pavlovskaia Gavan' (Paul's Harbor, now the city of Kodiak) and after 1805 at Novo-Arkhangelsk (Sitka) in southeastern Alaska.

Under the colonial labor system, Alutiiq men were forced to join sea otter hunting parties commanded by

49 "*Toion* from Igak Bay, Kadiak Island." Painting by Mikhail Tikhanov, 1818. The Russians made Alutiiq chiefs, whom they called *toions,* responsible for fur and food production.
Courtesy of the Scientific Research Museum of the Russian Academy of Arts.

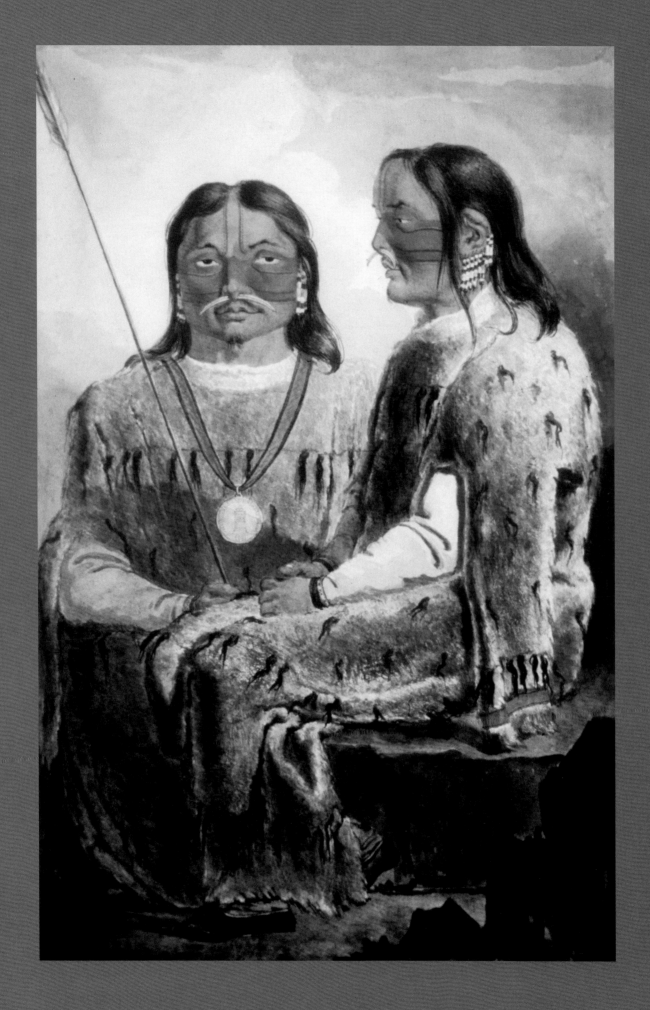

50 The Russian outpost at Three Saints Harbor, 1790. Hundreds of Alutiiq hostages were held at the settlement to guarantee peace with local villages. This romanticized engraving of a drawing by Luka Voronin depicts Alutiiq men and women greeting the arrival of a Russian ship. In later years, Three Saints Harbor was a food production station for the Russian-American Company (Trekh Suiatitel'skaia artel', fig. 51) Excavations at the site revealed details of daily life for Russian and Alutiiq residents (Crowell 1997).

Courtesy of the Elmer E. Rasmuson Library, Alaska and Polar Regions Department, University of Alaska Fairbanks.

Russian foremen. Men from villages around Kodiak Island met at Pavlouskaia gauan' in the spring and traveled east in their kayaks to hunt near Sitka, picking up additional hunters from villages along the way. They would hunt all summer and return in the fall. In the first decade of the 1800s this fleet was as large as 500 boats.[93] Smaller parties went to the south end of the Kodiak archipelago, Ukamok (Chirikof) Island, the mouth of Cook Inlet, and the coast of the Alaska Peninsula. Some men were transported by ship to hunting operations in the Kurile Islands between Russia and Japan and at Fort Ross in northern California. Hundreds drowned at sea or were lost to accidents and in hostilities with the Tlingit. At home, hunters harvested whale meat, halibut, and other

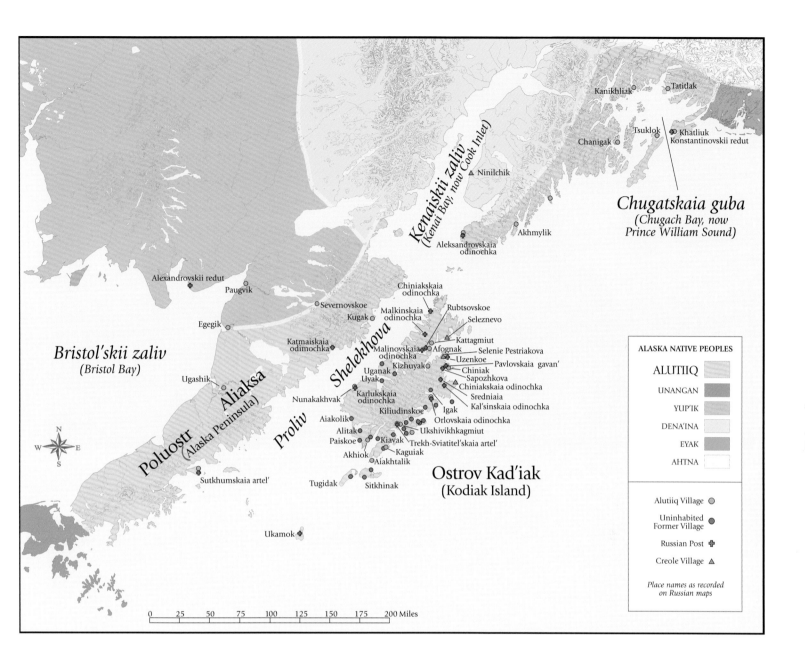

Kanikhliak   Tatitlak

Tsuklok   Khatliuk
Chanigak   Konstantinovskii redut

Kenaiskii zaliv
(Kenai Bay, now Cook Inlet)

△ Ninilchik

Chugatskaia guba
(Chugach Bay, now
Prince William Sound)

Akhmylik

Aleksandrovskaia
odinochka

Alexandrovskii redut

Paugvik

Bristol'skii zaliv
(Bristol Bay)

Egegik

Severnovskoe
Kugak

Chiniakskaia
odinochka

Malkinskaia   Rubtsovskoe
odinochka   Seleznevo

Ugashik

Katmaiskaia
odimochka

Kattagmiut

Shelekhova

Malinovskaia   Afognak
odinochka   Selenie Pestriakova
Uganak   Uzenkoe   Pavlovskaia gavan'
Uyak   Kizhuyako   Chiniak
Karlukskaia   Sapozhkova
odinochka   △ Chiniakskaia odinochka
Sredniaia
Kal'sinskaia odinochka

Nunakakhvak

Aliaksa
(Alaska Peninsula)

Proliv

Aiakolik

Kiliudinskoe   Igak
Orlovskaia odinochka

Ukshivikhkagmiut

Alitak   Trekh-Sviatitel'skaia artel'
Paiskoe   Kiavak
Akhiok   Kaguiak
Aiakhtalik

Poluostr

N
W ✦ E
S

Sutkhumskaia artel'

Tugidak   Sitkhinak

Ostrov Kad'iak
(Kodiak Island)

Ukamok

ALASKA NATIVE PEOPLES

ALUTIIQ

UNANGAN

YUP'IK

DENA'INA

EYAK

AHTNA

Alutiiq Village ◯

Uninhabited ●
Former Village

Russian Post ✚

Creole Village △

*Place names as recorded
on Russian maps*

0 25 50 75 100 125 150 175 200 Miles

food supplies for the RAC, and elderly, young, and disabled people were commanded to trap birds, foxes, and ground squirrels. Women collected plants, dried fish, wove nets, and sewed clothing to meet company quotas.[94]

Compensation for company work was minimal, often consisting of no more than boat skins and parkas sewn for the RAC by Alutiiq women. Small payments of glass beads, tobacco, needles, cloth, or currency were also distributed. The 1821 RAC charter limited the number of Kodiak Islanders who could be drafted to half of the male population between the ages of eighteen and fifty, although repeated protests by local chiefs show that this rule was not always observed. New regulations in the 1820s and 1830s required higher payments for sea

51   Selected Alutiiq, Russian, and Creole settlements in about 1850. Place names are in Russian transliteration, as recorded on nineteenth century maps and documents. Alutiiq villages shown in blue were no longer occupied by 1850, an indication of progressive depopulation as well as resettlement after the smallpox epidemic of 1837–38.

Research by Sonja Lührmann. Map by Mark Matson. Digital map data courtesy of the National Park Service, Anchorage.

52   "Port Dick, near Cook's Inlet," engraved from a 1794 watercolor by Henry Humphreys, showing an Alutiiq sea otter fleet off the coast of the Kenai Peninsula near Akhmylik.

Courtesy of the Anchorage Museum of History and Art.

otter pelts, and that the hunters should no longer be charged for the outfits they needed.[95]

The long absence of so many hunters and the burden of other company tasks meant that not enough subsistence food could be harvested and stored in the villages for winter. Deaths from starvation were reported. Gideon wrote that, "Due to the onerous tasks imposed by the company.... Aleuts in all settlements in wintertime suffer great hunger; when shellfish and kelp become unavailable as the tide flats are covered with ice, they consume even seal bladders ... processed seal skins, thongs, and other things made of sinew."[96]

While the Russian presence was not as strong on the mainland as in the Kodiak archipelago, some Chugach hunted for the RAC out of Konstantinovskii redut (Nuchek) and Aleksandrovskaia odinochka (Nanwalek). On the thinly inhabited Alaska Peninsula, Katmai (Katmaiskaia odinochka) was a trading center and also sent out its own hunting parties. From 1819 on, people on the Bristol Bay side traded with the Russians at Novo-Aleksandrovskii redut at the mouth of the Nushagak River.[97]

Few Russian women came to Alaska, so many Russian hunters married into Native communities. The Creole class included descendants of these marriages as well as others who were assimilated into Russian culture without a direct family relationship. Some Creoles were trained at company expense in Paul's Harbor, Sitka or Russia to serve as clerks, managers, and navigators. Educated Creoles were instrumental in church efforts to foster Alutiiq literacy (see essay by Lydia Black, p. 60). By the 1830s, Creole families had started to settle near St. Paul Harbor and on Afognak and Spruce Islands. In the 1840s, the company settled some Russian and Creole retirees at Ninilchik on Cook Inlet.[98]

A smallpox epidemic in the late 1830s dealt a heavy blow to Alutiiq communities.[99] It was brought to Kodiak

53 Musket lock

Karluk 1 site, Kodiak Island, late 1700s
Alutiiq Museum, Koniag, Inc., Collection
(UA84.195) Length 16 cm

Russian frontiersmen *(promyshlenniki)* did little hunting for sea otters themselves. Their flintlock muskets frightened away the animals, unlike the silent arrows and darts used by Native hunters. Rain, sea salt, and corrosive black powder ruined most guns after a few years of use.

54 Trade items

Three Saints Harbor site (1784–1820s), Kodiak
    Island (bottle glass pendant)
(KOD 083:1033) U.S. Department of Fish and Wildlife

Nunakakhvak Village site (1840s) (ceramic plate fragments)
Alutiiq Museum, Koniag, Inc., Collection
(UA85.195:2986, 3131, 3132)

Nunakakhvak Village site (1840s) (glass beads)
Alutiiq Museum, Koniag, Inc., Collection
(UA84.195:01922-01931)

Nunakakhvak Village site (1840s) (cross)
Alutiiq Museum, Koniag, Inc., Collection
(UA84.195:02743)

Glass beads from Europe and China were among the few types of trade goods that were plentiful under Russian rule. Bottle glass was another new material, used for ornaments and tools. The Alutiit adopted tea drinking from the Russians, along with "China" that was actually made in England. Holes were drilled in pieces of this broken plate so it could be stitched back together, an indication of its value in Alutiiq eyes. The cross was a personal item, worn by Christian converts. Nunakakhvak was a resettlement village for survivors of the 1837–38 smallpox epidemic (Knecht and Jordan 1985).

Forgotten Literacy

Lydia Black
Professor Emerita,
University of Alaska Fairbanks

LITERACY IN THE ALUTIIQ LANGUAGE WAS INTRODUCED to the Natives of Kodiak archipelago, Alaska Peninsula, and Prince William Sound in the first half of the nineteenth century. It took root, had a remarkable vitality, and persisted against all odds until the early twentieth century. But today, the younger generations are not even aware that such literacy ever existed. The development of Alutiiq literacy was closely tied to the establishment of schools, both parish and secular ones, in Russian America (1741–1867). The first school was established at Three Saints Bay, Kodiak soon after the Russian conquest. A number of young Alutiit were also taken to Okhotsk and Irkutsk where they attended school. Thus the idea of literacy, albeit in a foreign language (Russian) began to spread.

By 1804–1807 the Kodiak school was operated by the monks of the First Mission. Three former students, Paramon Chumovitskii, Khristofor Prianishnikov, and Aleksei Kotel'nikov, of Native origin, fully bilingual, served on the staff. Chumovitskii was in charge of linguistic work, compiling Alutiiq vocabulary and developing Alutiiq grammar. Prokopii Lavrov, a senior student and—later—the first Alaskan to become a priest, may also have participated in this work. None of these materials have survived except for the Alutiiq text of the Lord's Prayer (published in 1816). Systematic introduction of literacy, however, dates to 1841, when Il'iia Tyzhnov was sent as a reader to the Kodiak church by the then-Bishop Innocent (Veniaminov) with instructions to prepare materials in the Alutiiq language for use in the church and in parish schools. In 1847 a catechism in Alutiiq was printed, and in 1848 an Alutiiq primer and a Gospel of St. Matthew in parallel Alutiiq and Slavonic texts appeared.

The spread of Alutiiq literacy and its persistence is attested by a number of manuscript fragments collected from various villages. These are compositions of moral character by village Elders intended for the instruction of children, translations of divine services, hymns, songs, and a few secular compositions. The parish schools were bilingual under the Russian regime, and trilingual soon after 1867, when Alaska was transferred to the United States. However, under the policies first articulated by Protestant missionaries such as S. Hall Young and Sheldon Jackson, the first U.S. commisioner for education in Alaska, Native language use was suppressed and the parish schools came under pressure; many eventually ceased to exist.

Nevertheless, many Elders continued their attempts to preserve Alutiiq language and literacy. We know of the efforts of Tikhon Sherotin of Afognak, Emil Kosbruk of Perryville, and Nicholas Moonin of English Bay. Father Michael Oleska provides a few more names of local Elders who continued to act as bilingual teachers: Innokenti Shugak, Larry Ellanak, Vladamir Milovedoff. We have on hand a volume of translation into Alutiiq of services and prayers, as well as short vocabularies, made in 1906–07

from Sitka in the summer of 1837 and spread to Prince William Sound and the Alaska Peninsula in 1838. Although efforts were made to vaccinate the population, 738 people died on Kodiak alone, bringing the combined Alutiiq and Creole population of the island down to under 2000. Starting in 1840, survivors of the epidemic were relocated to seven places, mainly near Russian posts: Woody Island (Chiniak), Orlovskoe (Eagle Harbor), Three Saints Bay (Trekh-Sviatitel'skaia), Aiakhtalik, Akhiok, Karluk (Nunakakhvak), and Afognak. In addition, there was the permanent artel' at Ukamok (Chirikoff) Island.[100] Many formerly thriving Kodiak villages now stood empty.

A Russian Orthodox mission had existed on Kodiak since 1794, with limited success in the first decades. More people began to convert after the 1837–38 smallpox epidemic, and the church assumed a central role in Alutiiq life.[101] Nonetheless, masked hunting ceremonies were still held in some villages in the 1870s and 1880s and perhaps later.[102]

Even before the relocation, each village had a *toion* (headman) whose election had to be confirmed by the company administration. In 1841, his duties were defined in more detail. He was responsible for assigning men to hunting parties and planning the hunt in by Maria Tutoumov and Arsenii Bol'shakov of Tatitlek. The authorship of Alutiiq manuscripts in Akhiok is not known. How many nameless Elders were there who gallantly fought to preserve Alutiiq literacy for over a century? How many grieved when they realized that they were losing the battle? How many shed tears when young people turned their backs on this heritage? We shall never know. But let us honor these Elders now and in the future; may their memory be eternal!

55   Gospel of St. Matthew

St. Petersburg, Russia, Synod Press, 1848
Diocese of Alaska Archive, St. Herman's Theological
    Seminary, Kodiak
Alutiiq Museum
(AM414:1); Height 23 cm

The Gospel of Saint Matthew, translated by Creole church reader Il'iia Tyzhnov, is printed in parallel columns of Alutiiq (left) and Slavonic (right).

consultation with company employees, as well as for keeping people from leaving the new large settlements without permission. *Toiony* also mediated disputes in the village and took care of orphans and poor people. In this way, the Russians tried to integrate traditional leadership roles into their own administration in order to gain better control over the population. At the same time, the *toion* was in a strong position to represent Alutiiq interests because he was indispensable to the company.[103]

Because there were fewer able-bodied Alutiiq hunters after the 1837–38 epidemic, the burden on the survivors of all ages and sexes increased. In 1839, the RAC's chief manager in Sitka ordered the Kodiak office to send as many men on the sea otter hunt as possible, leaving tasks of food production to the women and children. At the same time, fur parkas were increasingly imported from Siberia because Alutiit lacked time to gather enough material.[104] Food supplies for the seven large settlements became a problem, and the naval officer Golovin reported in 1862 that some villages had asked permission to split up. Kaguyak in southeastern Kodiak, abandoned after the epidemic, reappears on midcentury maps.[105]

United States Rule After 1867

Russia sold its Alaska interests to the United States in 1867, but the change had little immediate impact on the daily lives of the Alutiit. The U.S. Army established a large but briefly occupied post on Kodiak in 1868, and the Alaska Commercial Company and several other commercial firms opened stores in many villages and continued to outfit hunting parties, much like the Russian-American Company had done. None of the American companies had a monopoly, however, so they could only hope to bind hunters to their stores by selling them kayak covers and manufactured goods on credit. On Kodiak Island, Kiliuda and Uganik were reestablished, and new villages were founded on the Pacific side of the Alaska Peninsula by people coming from Katmai, Bristol Bay, and Kodiak for subsistence and sea otter hunting. By the turn of the century, however, the sea otter was almost extinct. Many stores closed down even before the hunt was officially ended in 1911. Sea otter hunting villages like Aiaktalik, Nuchek and Douglas shrank as people looked for other ways to obtain goods such as tea, flour, sugar and clothing.[106]

Smithsonian collector William J. Fisher, who purchased many of the objects presented in *Looking Both Ways*, arrived in St. Paul (Kodiak) in 1879, during the early years of American rule. The settlement was still an important center of the sea otter trade, where Alutiiq men assembled in their kayaks for the annual hunt. The town had 500 residents, most of mixed Russian and Alutiiq descent. There were about 125 Russian-style log houses, several Alutiiq barabaras, and stores and warehouses of the Alaska Commercial Company and Western Fur and Trading Company. Fisher observed that tuberculosis ("consumption") was the most common health problem among the residents, and that their dietary staples were fresh and dried fish. All were members of the Russian Orthodox church, and Alutiiq and Russian were the common languages. Very few people spoke any English.[107]

56 Men and women on the beach at Old Harbor, Kodiak Island, 1888–89. The hunters standing next to the double-hatch kayak are wearing hooded, waterproof *kanagluk* coats (*kamleika* in Russian) made from sea mammal or bear intestines. One of the women is dressed in a ground squirrel parka.
Courtesy of the National Archives (22-FA-268).

57   Docks and warehouses at St. Paul (formerly Pavlovskaia Gavan', later Kodiak), 1892.
Courtesy of the National Archives (22 FFA-463).

58   Alutiiq family in front of their barabara at Pillar Creek, Monashka Bay, Kodiak Island, ca. 1908–1919.
Courtesy of the Kodiak Historical Society (P386-85N).

59   Salmon seining crews and canneries at the mouth of the Karluk River, 1889. Nets were deployed by rowboat, then pulled into the beach by hand.
Courtesy of the National Archives (22-FFA-1145).

The salmon canning industry came to southern Alaska in the 1880s. Canneries at Karluk, Alitak, Chignik, Nushagak, Kasilof, and many other places were making enormous profits at a time when the Alutiiq population faced economic hardship. Most canneries employed few Natives at first, preferring to bring in Scandinavians and Italians as fishermen and Chinese and other Asian contract laborers as cannery workers. Alutiiq fishermen were able to sell some of their catch to the canneries, and in the early twentieth century more Alutiit were hired. The commercial fishing industry came to be the main source of employment, cash and credit in most Alutiiq villages. In chapter 7, Elder Lucille Antowak Davis shares her memories of the men at Karluk fishing for the Larsen Bay cannery in the 1930s. People from Old Harbor also worked in the commercial whaling operation at Port Hobron on Kodiak Island (1926–37). Other Alutiit worked at the coal mine on Kachemak Bay or as guides and porters for gold prospectors heading from Valdez into the interior. Tatitlek grew into the biggest Native village on Prince William Sound because of its

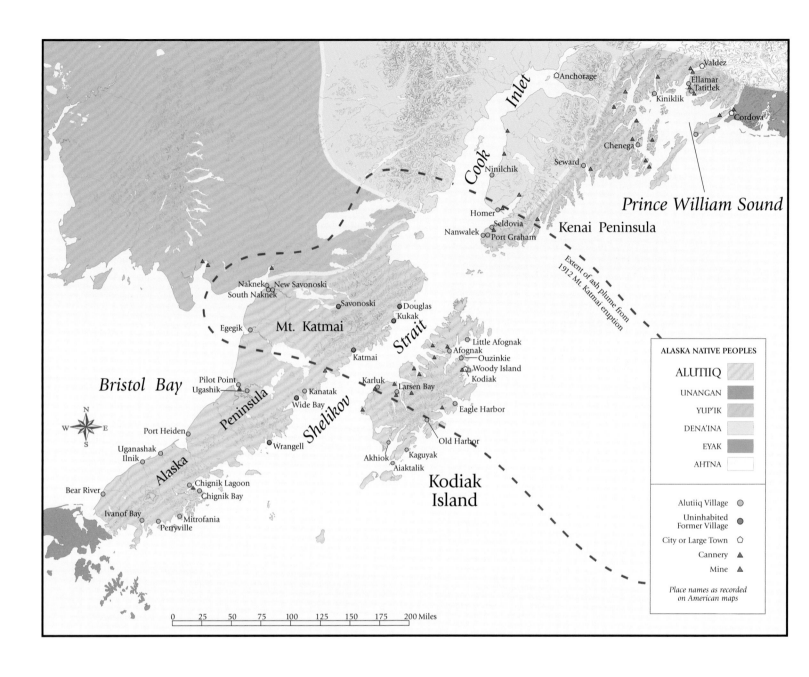

60 Settlements, canneries, and mines in the Alutiiq region, 1920. The area covered by volcanic ash during the Katmai/Novarupta eruption of 1912 is indicated. Villages closest to the eruption (Katmai, Douglas, and Savonoski) received up to one meter (three feet) of ash fall and were no longer habitable. No one was living at Kukak at the time of the eruption.

Map research by Sonja Lührmann; illustration by Mark Matson. Digital map data courtesy of the National Park Service, Anchorage.

61 Refugees evacuated from Kodiak following the Katmai/ Novarupta volcanic eruption, on board the U.S. Customs Service cutter *Manning*, June 1912.
Courtesy of the Kodiak Historical Society (P600-6.7 N).

62 Children making "ash pies" out of volcanic ash. Kodiak, 1912.
Courtesy of the Kodiak Historical Society (P. 90 N).

proximity to Valdez and the mining town of Ellamar.[108] Many immigrants from Scandinavia and the U.S. who came for the fishery married Alutiiq women, and some Japanese cannery workers also married into Native villages and stayed as storekeepers or cooks.[109]

In 1912, the violent eruption of the Novarupta volcano near Katmai destroyed several villages on the Alaska Peninsula and covered the ground with ash as far away as the city of Kodiak. The skies darkened and many Alutiit believed that the biblical Judgment Day had arrived. Some fled out to sea in kayaks, as described by Ignatius Kosbruk in chapter 7; others were rescued by government ships. The inhabitants of ash-covered Katmai village moved west to found Perryville, while the people of Savonoski (Severnovskoe) in the interior of the Alaska Peninsula founded New Savonoski at the mouth of the Naknek River.[110]

Many villages did not have a U.S. government school until well into the twentieth century. In an effort to acculturate Alutiit to American ways, the government ordered a strict English-only policy. Children who spoke Alutiiq in school were physically punished, a practice

63 The mission and school in Tatitlek, Prince William Sound, 1902.
Courtesy of the Alaska State Library (PCA 277-7-25).

64   Woody Island Baptist Mission calendar (1899)

Alutiiq Museum
(AM291:1) Width 14 cm

Woody Island, opposite the city of Kodiak, was home to the Kodiak Baptist Mission from 1893 until the late 1930s. Baptist missionaries opposed the Russian Orthodox church, and took some Alutiiq children from their families for a non-Orthodox upbringing. Other children at the Mission's orphanage had lost their parents to epidemics.

65   In the kitchen of the Kodiak Baptist Mission, Woody Island, about 1918. The girl on the left is Elizabeth Agizza.
Courtesy of the Kodiak Historical Society (P386-27).

that is remembered with anguish by many Elders (see chapter 7). The school system and new American churches also sought to diminish Russian cultural influences. The Baptist mission on Woody Island, founded in 1893, was criticized for taking children from their parents and refusing to let them attend Orthodox services.[111] Many of the children who resided at the mission's orphanage had lost their parents in the 1918 influenza epidemic, a tragedy that brought the total Alutiiq population to its historical low point of about 2300 at the 1920 census.[112]

Two late-twentieth-century disasters tested the resilience of Alutiiq communities. On March 27, 1964 (Good Friday), the earth quaked and rolled so strongly that cracks opened in the ground, and large tidal waves pulsed across the Gulf of Alaska. Twenty-seven Alutiiq villagers drowned, and damage to coastal villages was extensive. People at Afognak, Chenega, and Kaguyak had to relocate their homes, although these lost villages live on in memory. Earthquake survivors built the new settlements of Chenega Bay and Port Lions.[113] In March 1989, the tanker *Exxon Valdez* ran aground in Prince William Sound, spilling almost eleven million gallons of Alaska crude oil. It was the largest tanker spill in United States history. Oil fouled 1500 miles of pristine coastline including hunting and fishing areas used by fifteen

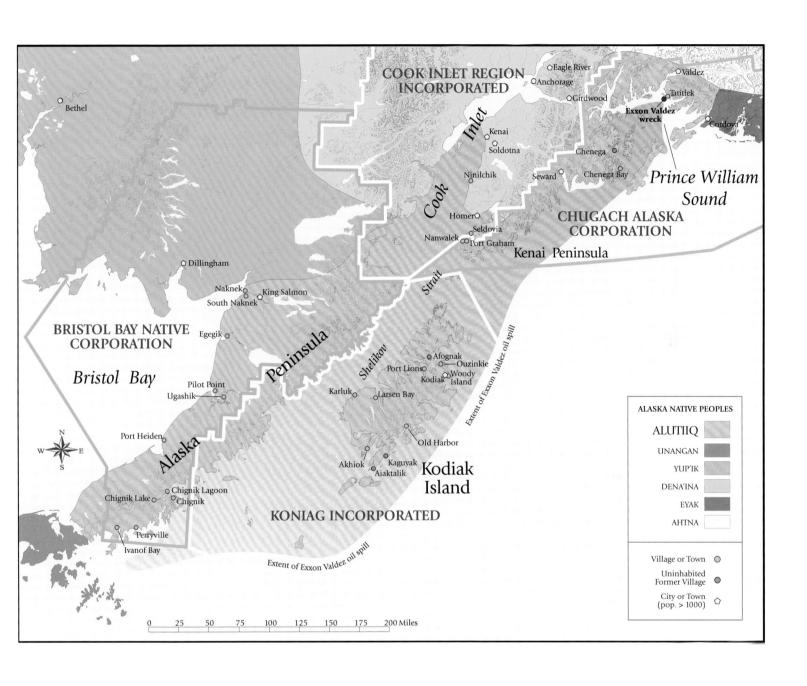

66 The Alutiiq region in 2000. The Alutiiq homeland includes all or part of four different regional Native corporations: Koniag, Inc., Chugach Alaska Corporation, Bristol Bay Native Corporation, and Cook Inlet Region, Inc. The map shows the extent of the 1989 *Exxon Valdez* oil spill (ochre shading), which spread westward from Prince William Sound.

Map research and illustration by Mark Matson. Digital map data courtesy of the National Park Service, Anchorage.

67

Alutiiq villages (fig. 66). More than a decade later, seals, herring, clams, and crabs are still scarce along some parts of the coast.

Today, Alutiiq people live in twenty-five villages and in larger towns and cities including Anchorage, Kodiak, Homer, King Salmon, and Cordova. Employment is in commercial fishing, logging, retail businesses, politics, education, and many other fields. Russian, American, and Scandinavian surnames reflect generations of intermarriage with non-Native traders, trappers, and fishermen. English is the language of everyday communication, and in most communities there are few fluent speakers of Alutiiq who are younger than sixty years old. The Russian Orthodox church, joined by other Christian faiths, supplanted the traditional religion and its ceremonies more than a century ago (chapter 6). Coexisting with tribal governments are regional Native corporations established under the Alaska Native Claims

Alutiiq Identity

Patricia H. Partnow
Vice President of Education,
Alaska Native Heritage Center

"THIS STORY WAS TOLD TO ME BY THE OLD MAN—WASCO." So my mentor, the late Perryville Elder Ignatius Kosbruk, began many a narrative. He allowed me to record his knowledge, live with his family, and learn by example from 1990 until his death in 1998. Ignatius was one of many wise and generous teachers who led me toward an understanding of what it means to be Alutiiq. I was also privileged to work with Ignatius's wife Frieda; Emil and Mary Phillips, Ralph Phillips, Polly Shangin and Polly Yagie, also of Perryville; Mike and Olga Sam of Chignik Lagoon; Olga Kalmakoff of Ivanoff Bay; Walter Stepanoff of Chignik Bay; Christina Martin, Emil Artemie and Doris and Bill Lind, all of Chignik Lake, as well as many others who offered me hospitality, advice, and information. Sadly, seven of my instructors have passed away since I began my research.

As an anthropology student, I had chosen the Alaska Peninsula as my study area, and Alutiiq oral tradition, particularly as it showed the effects of 200 years of Russian influence, as my dissertation topic (Partnow 2001). The work began in 1988 when I was in Anchorage teaching a class of Alaska Native high school students—a third of whom were Alutiiq—and was struggling to find relevant material on their cultures and histories. One narrative that I did find especially intrigued me. It was an Alutiicized version of an old Russian folktale, told a decade and a half earlier by Dick Kamluck, Sr., of Port Graham. I decided to look for other Alutiiq-Russian stories. I believed they would provide insights into the meaning of contemporary Alutiiq culture, through the merging of Russian and Native cultures.

Soon after I entered the field, my Russian-folklore focus faded and a new set of questions, more relevant to the lives of the Alaska Peninsula Alutiiqs, took its place. I began to investigate what, in an era of rapid cultural and technological change, it means to be Alutiiq. I watched for ways that Alutiiq identity is enacted in everyday and ceremonial life. My earlier quest for the Russian past was relegated to the background.

The more I asked, talked, listened, and wondered about Alutiiq identity, the more I questioned my insistence on marking cultural boundaries. Unlike me, my Alutiiq hosts were not concerned with unraveling the disparate threads of their cultural inheritance. They identified themselves as Alutiiqs, usually unhyphenated. In anthropological jargon, they were privileging one part of their genetic and cultural background and underplaying their Athabascan, Russian, Scandinavian, Irish, and Yup'ik parts. Why, I wondered, is Alutiiqness so central to their beings?

Answers often come from unexpected quarters. Mine came from stories Ignatius Kosbruk told me—both the old *unigkuat* that explain how the world came to be the

Settlement Act of 1971—Bristol Bay Native Corporation, Koniag Incorporated, Chugach Alaska Corporation, and Cook Inlet Region, Inc. The regional and village corporations hold land and manage resources for their shareholders.

Identity is a complex issue in this contemporary context, negotiated with the contradictions of history. Shared traditions, practices, and beliefs provide a foundation for ethnicity, as Patricia Partnow observes in her essay. Yet each individual confronts this legacy in a different way and makes different choices. In the next chapter, Gordon Pullar and contributors Roy Madsen, Sven Haakanson, Jr., Mary Jane Nielsen, Marlane Shanagin, Ruth Dawson, John F. C. Johnson, and McKibben Jackinsky examine the modern dilemmas of Alutiiq identity and the cultural priorities of Alutiiq communities.

way it is, and the more recent *quliyanguat* that tell how heroes and others dealt with the challenges of life on the peninsula. The tales suggested that a simple answer to the question, "Who is an Alutiiq?" might be: "A person who grew up with these stories." A more complex answer consists of the following five points of Alutiiq ethnic identification, all illustrated in the *unigkuat* and *quliyanguat*:

♦ Ties to the land
♦ A shared history and continuity with the past
♦ The Alutiiq or Sugcestun language
♦ Subsistence
♦ Kinship

In the old stories, every character shares all five points of ethnic identity with every other character. But in today's life, people are more diverse. They may follow different religions, or move away from the village, or take a wage-earning job. With such variation in lifestyle, it has become impossible for all Alutiiqs to exemplify all five points equally. Instead, people accentuate different parts of their Alutiiqness at different times and in different places.

If a contrast between the stories and contemporary life highlights changes in Alutiiq identity paralleling the history of cultural contact, it also demonstrates that ethnic identity is still a very vital issue. Those Alutiiq students I knew in 1988 were searching—not for relevant school curriculum as I was, but for themselves. It is, fittingly, their Elders who are helping them and their younger brothers and sisters in this quest.

67   Chief Alexie and sons at Chignik on the Alaska Peninsula, 1930–38.
Courtesy of the Alaska State Library (PCA 105-3).

Chapter 2 notes

1 Black 1988.

2 Oswalt 1979; Collins 1984.

3 Steller 1988:66–75.

4 Steller 1988:102–105; Okladnikova 1987; Davydov 1977:97; Khlebnikov 1994:4–5.

5 Beaglehole 1967:1108. The latter idea was correct. Russian fur traders had already pushed as far eastward as Kodiak Island.

6 López de Haro 1788; Arteaga 1779; Fidalgo 1790.

7 Damas (1984:6). According to Damas, the word "Eskimo" may be derived from the Montagnais ayassime.w related to "snow-shoe netter." The common belief that "Eskimo" is a derogatory term meaning "raw meat eaters" appears to be erroneous.

8 As a self-designation, Inuit ("real people") is used primarily in Canada and western Greenland. It is also preferred to "Eskimo" as an inclusive name for related cultures of northeastern Siberia, Alaska, Canada, and Greenland. Its use in this way was officially adopted by the Inuit Circumpolar Conference in 1977 (see Damas 1984:7). "Eskimo" is used and accepted by indigenous people in some areas but rejected in others, including the Alutiiq region.

9 Krauss 1988; Woodbury 1984. Inuit or Eskimo languages include Siberian Yupik, Sirenikski, and Naukanski in northeastern Siberia; Siberian Yupik on St. Lawrence Island; Central Alaska Yup'ik in southwest Alaska; Alutiiq (also called Sugcestun, Sugpiaq, or Pacific Yup'ik) in southern Alaska; and Inuit-Inupiaq in northern Alaska, Canada, and Greenland.

10 Dumond 1987a.

11 Several key implements associated with northern Inuit life appeared at relatively early dates in the Gulf of Alaska region. Pecked stone oil lamps and compound bone fish hooks were used at the Rice Ridge site more than 6000 years ago (Hausler-Knecht 1993). Slate projectile points for sea mammal hunting were common by 4500 years ago in the Ocean Bay II phase of Kodiak Island (Clark 1979). Small slate ulu knives and several types of stone weights for fish nets were in use by 3400 years ago in the early Kachemak phase (Clark 1997). Labrets appeared by about 4600 years ago at Hidden Falls (Davis 1989) and other Northwest Coast sites (Matson and Coupland 1995) and were adopted in the Alutiiq region during the later Kachemak period (see chapter 4).

12 Donald Clark (1994:145–146) suggests that "much of what is Neoeskimo [Bering Strait cultures after about A.D. 100] actually could be Pacific in origin" and believes that both southern Alaska and the Northwest Coast of Canada contributed to the development of Eskimo-Inuit culture.

13 West 1996.

14 Yesner 1998.

15 Dixon 1993; Fladmark 1978; Laughlin 1975.

16 Arutiunov and Fitzhugh 1988; D. Clark 1982a, 1982b, 1984a; Crowell 2000; de Laguna 1975; Dumond 1987b:101–127; Heizer 1956a; Workman 1980.

17 Arutiunov and Fitzhugh 1988; Collins 1937; Mason 1998.

18 Moss and Erlandson 1992.

19 Dumond 1988:386; see also Dumond 1987a, 1994a.

20 D. Clark 1984a, 1988, 1992, 1994.

21 Jordan and Knecht 1988; Knecht 1995.

22 Gideon 1989:59; Pinart 1873; Wrangell 1980:59.

23 Leer 1991; Woodbury 1984.

24 Birket-Smith 1953; de Laguna 1956; Lantis 1938, 1947; Black 1991, 1994.

25 Dumond 1987a; Scott 1991, 1992, 1994; Turner 1988.

26 Scott 1994.

27 Gideon 1989.

28 Black 1977; Davydov 1977; Lisianskii 1968; Merck 1980; Sauer 1802.

29 Arteaga 1779; Beaglehole 1967; Birket-Smith 1953; De Laguna 1956; Dixon 1968; Fidalgo 1790; López de Haro 1788; Merck 1980:110–124; Portlock 1789; Vancouver 1801; Zaikov 1979.

30 Davydov 1977:147.

31 *Koniag* is an Americanized pronunciation of an Aleutian Islands term for people of the Kodiak archipelago and the Alaska Peninsula (D. Clark 1984b: 195). It was introduced by the Russians and may have become a self-designation during the early years of contact (Davydov 1977:148). Variations of the name *Chugach* were reported for the people of Prince William Sound from earliest Russian contact (Merck 1980:111; Zaikov 1979:1), possibly from the self-designation *Suaciq* (Birket-Smith 1953:19) or from the Alutiiq place name for Cook Inlet, *Cúngáciq* (Leer in D. Clark 1984b:195).

32 The earliest Russian census figures for the Kodiak Island group are 5696 people in 1792 (Khlebnikov 1994:7); 6206 people in 1795–96 (Tikhmenev 1978:47; Khlebnikov 1994:7); and 5464 people in 1800 (Khlebnikov 1994:7). According to a Russian-American Company list published in Langsdorff (1993:Vol. 2, pps. 30–31) the population of the Kodiak group declined from 6362 in the year 1795 to 4705 in 1804 (excluding counts for Kukak on the Alaska Peninsula). The magnitude of population decline before these various estimates were made is unknown. Lisianskii (1968:193) suggested that the original population of the Kodiak archipelago was about 8000. Oswalt (1967) made a more conservative estimate of 6500. Sporadic Russian landings on Kodiak Island started in the 1760s and intensive contact began with Shelikhov's subjugation of the island in 1784 (Black 1992).

33 Pullar 1994:23.

34 D. Clark 1987; Lisianskii 1968:172–186. Langsdorff (1993:Vol. 2, pps. 30–31) gives the names of thirty-two Kodiak archipelago villages and three small islands inhabited in 1795 and 1804, close to Lisianskii's estimate. Place names on figure 19 were provided to Jeff Leer by contemporary Alutiiq Elders on Kodiak.

35 Tikhmenev 1978:200. Russian census data from 1825 show a surviving Kodiak population of only 2917 (Khlebnikov 1994:8).

36 Dumond and Van Stone 1995; Harritt 1997; Wrangell 1980:64.

37 Dumond 1981.

38 Khlebnikov 1994:7–8; Petroff 1884:33-34.

39 Crowell and Mann 1998; De Laguna 1956:34–36.

40 Workman and Workman 1988.

41 Birket-Smith 1953:22; Khlebnikov 1994:7-8; Petroff 1884:33–34.

42 de Laguna 1956.

43 Birket-Smith 1953:20–21.

44 Birket-Smith 1953:112.

45 Lisianskii 1968:193.

46 Holmberg 1985:43.

47 Late eighteenth- and early nineteenth-century Kodiak Island houses were described by Billings (1980:204); Davydov (1977:154); Gideon (1989: 39–40): Lisianskii (1968:212–213); Merck (1980:100); and Shelikhov (1981:55-56). Langsdorff

(1968:235) and D'Wolf (1968:66–67) described houses at Kukak on the Alaska Peninsula in 1806. Kodiak Island-style houses with multiple side chambers have been described from archaeological data at Paugvik at the mouth of the Naknek River, Alaska Peninsula (Dumond 1994b).

48 Birket-Smith 1953:53–55; Portlock 1789:253; Walker 1982: 140–141; Zaikov 1979:4.

49 Walker 1982:141.

50 D'Wolf 1968:66–67.

51 Lisianskii 1968:184.

52 Davydov 1977:186; Shelikhov 1981:43.

53 Merck 1980:107.

54 Birket-Smith 1953:92. One English edition of Davydov's account (1977:190) suggests that all chiefs are "descended from one tribe," but this is a mistranslation. What Davydov (1812:113) actually says is that those villages that have a common chief are descended from one tribe, i.e., have split up from one original village (see Lührmann 2000:78–79).

55 "In earlier times the status of the chiefs was hereditary–but the choice of a successor rarely fell upon the sons but more likely upon one of the nephews" (Davydov 1977:190). Matrilineal descent, if it existed on Kodiak, would have been consistent with inheritance by the sister's son. Gideon (1989:41), on the other hand, indicated that the successor could be a son, brother, uncle, nephew, or son-in-law.

56 Birket-Smith 1953:92.

57 Davydov 1977:165.

58 Birket-Smith 1953:96.

59 Gideon 1989:41–42.

60 Davydov 1977:190; Merck 1980:109.

61 Jordan 1994.

62 Merck 1980:109.

63 Townsend 1980.

64 Gideon 1989:49.

65 Davydov 1977:166; Lisianskii 1968:199; Merck 1980:104-105; Sauer 1802:176.

66 Birket-Smith 1953:87-88; Fisher 1882; Holmberg 1985:53.

67 Gideon 1989:49.

68 Birket-Smith 1953:87.

69 Gideon 1989:50.

70 Birket-Smith 1953:88-90; Gideon 1989:53; Holmberg 1985:53; Lisianskii 1968:199-200; Merck 1980:107–108; Sauer 1802:177; Shelikhov 1981:54; Walker 1982:142-143.

71 Birket-Smith 1953:90; Dall 1878: de Laguna 1956:55, 92-93; Pinart 1873.

72 Birket-Smith 1941; Hunt 2000; Varjola 1990.

73 Hunt (2000) summarizes ethnohistoric information on Alutiiq ceremonial use of beaded headdresses, hats, and other garments. Alphonse Pinart (1872:23) and Smithsonian collector William J. Fisher (Smithsonian Institution Archives, Record Unit 305, Accessions 12209, 14024, 15687) reported that beaded headdresses were worn at Kodiak Island dances and winter ceremonies in the late nineteenth century, usually by women and girls (Hunt 2000:107–111).

74 Davydov 1977:151; Hunt 2000:91–94.

75 Gideon 1989:66.

76 Gideon 1989:48.

77 Davydov 1977:152.

78 Black 1991:23; Davydov 1977:153; Merck 1980:102.

79 Holmberg 1985:38; Steffian 1992a.

80 Birket-Smith 1953:69; Davydov 1977:149; Gideon 1989:58; Lisianskii 1968:195; Merck 1980:103; Shelikhov 1981:53.

81 Davydov 1977:159, 187–88; Gideon 1989:42–44; Izmailov and Becharov in Shelikhov 1981:89; Zaikov 1979:4.

82 Shelkihov 1981:48.

83 Davydov 1977:152; Gideon 1989:57; Holmberg 1985:45.

84 Birket-Smith 1953:100-101; Zaikov 1979:5.

85 Crowell 1997; Fedorova 1973; Gibson 1987.

86 See sidebar "The Alutiiq Language" by Jeff Leer, p. 31. Native use of the name Alutiiq (recorded as "Aljutik") was reported in 1851 on Kodiak Island (Holmberg 1985:35).

87 Black 1992.

88 Coxe 1780:106–123.

89 Shelikhov 1981:41: Zaikov 1979:1–6.

90 Translation modified from Holmberg 1985:59. Although Aminak's description of the attack is confirmed by Russian accounts, Russian-American Company and Orthodox church records do not support the statement that the island (Sitkalidak) was deserted in the aftermath. A number of villages were actually occupied there until the 1830s, in most case until the 1837–38 smallpox epidemic and 1840 resettlement. These included Anikinskoe, Ezopkino, Begletsovo, Prokliatovskoe, Sanulik, Mysovskoe, Razbitovskoe, and probably Kolpakovskoe (Lührmann 2000:35-45). Lisianskii's visits to some of these locations in 1805 are discussed by D. Clark (1987).

91 Efimov 1964:Map 178.

92 Pullar and Knecht 1995.

93 Davydov 1977:194.

94 Gideon 1989:64–65.

95 Khlebnikov 1994; Sarafian 1970:157–169; Russian-American Company communications sent, vol. 42: 152 ad passim.

96 Gideon 1989:70.

97 Sarafian 1970:228; Morseth 1998:12,37.

98 Black 1990; Arndt 1996; Golovin 1979:18–19; Gibson 1976:100; Russian-American Company, communications sent vol. 29: 246–247.

99 Fortuine 1989:230–235; Lührmann 2000.

100 Lührmann 2000:49; Tikhmenev 1978:200; Russian Orthodox Church records, reel 175 (1844 confessional register, Kodiak parish).

101 Oleksa 1992; Pierce 1978.

102 Crowell 1992; Desson 1995.

103 Russian-American Company, communications sent, vol. 15: 248–253, vol. 20: 73–81, 170–173.

104 Russian-American Company, communications sent vol. 17: 50–52.

105 Golovin 1979:24; Russian-American Company, "Merkatorskaia karta kad'iakskago arkhipelaga, sostavlena Rossiiskoiu-Amerikanskoiu Kompanieiu po noveishim svideniiam" (Mercator map of the Kodiak archipelago, compiled by the Russian American company from the newest reports.)1849. On display at the Baranov Museum, Kodiak.

106 Russian Orthodox Church Records; Morseth 1998:54–58; Cook and Norris 1998:65–70; Lethcoe and Lethcoe 1994:40–43 .

107 Crowell 1992; Fisher 1880.

108 N. Davis 1984; Morseth 1998:87–94; Moser 1898; Roppel 1987; Russian Orthodox Church Records, reel 204 (report by Andrei Kashevarov, Nuchek, April 8, 1898).

109 Morseth 1998:99–104; Lethcoe and Lethcoe 1994:98–100; Matfay 1988:26; U.S. census records, 1910, 1920.

110 Griggs 1922; Hussey 1971: 248–256; Partnow 1993.

111 Antonii 1900a:114–119; Antonii 1900b:143–146; Russian Orthodox Church Records, reel 172 (report by Fr. Tikhon Shalamov, Kodiak, June 9, 1894).

112 Including persons listed as "mixed," but who appear to be of Alutiiq ancestry by language or other indications.

113 N. Davis 1984

3

CONTEMPORARY ALUTIIQ IDENTITY

Gordon L. Pullar

Identity encompasses a contrast between being identical and being unique. In short, as symbolizing beings, people are by definition identity-seeking creatures.

—Selma van Londen[1]

Are you Alutiiq or are you Sugpiaq? Our identity is mixed up. Who are we?

—Lydia Robart (Port Graham, Kenai Peninsula), 1997[2]

Today's Alutiiq identity configuration is characterized by ties to the land, a belief in a shared history with other Alutiiqs, acknowledgement of Alutiiq as the ancestral language, adherence to some level of subsistence lifestyle, and kinship link to Alutiiqs of the past.

—Patricia H. Partnow, 1993[3]

WHEN I RETURNED TO KODIAK ISLAND IN 1983 AND assumed the presidency of the Kodiak Area Native Association, I had little idea of what it meant to be Alutiiq. My mother, Olga Rossing[4] died in 1967 and had told me almost nothing on this topic. She was born in the Alutiiq village of Woody Island (Tangihnaq) in 1916 and was predominately Alutiiq, at least biologically. Yet, when asked, she would identify herself as Russian. I was puzzled by why she would choose Russian when her nearest Russian ancestors, members of Alexander Baranov's Russian-American Company crew, were eight generations in her past. I did not challenge her self-designation but could not bring myself to identify as Russian.[5] Instead, I tended to avoid the topic altogether.

During the enrollment period under the Alaska Native Claims Settlement Act (ANCSA), Alutiiq individuals who had previously identified as Russian (or another nationality) were put to the test. Most clearly qualified to become shareholders in Alaska Native corporations under ANCSA but could not receive this benefit without enrolling. This was a difficult choice for some. At the time, an Alutiiq friend from Prince William Sound told me of her father's reluctance to enroll despite being encouraged by his children. "I am an American!" he told them, feeling that to enroll would somehow damage the

68   Afognak. Gordon Pullar, Kodiak Island, director, Department of Alaska Native and Rural Development, University of Alaska Fairbanks.

Afognak photograph by Patrick Saltonstall. Portrait by Carl C. Hansen, Smithsonian Institution

strong reputation he had built over his lifetime as a "hardworking American." He later relented. At the height of the enrollment process in 1972, my grandmother, born Afanasiia Rysev in Woody Island village in 1896, displayed her ambivalence about enrollment to me at an ANCSA informational meeting. "Are they trying to make an Aleut out of you?" she asked. Once again, I found puzzlement in how Kodiak Native identity was perceived but was becoming increasingly interested in learning for myself.

69 Olga Rossing, the first high school graduate from Longwool School on Woody Island, 1934.
Courtesy of Gordon Pullar.

70   Man's cap

Woody Island (Tangihnaq), Kodiak Island, 1879–82
National Museum of Natural History, Smithsonian Institution (NMNH 72477) Diameter 22 cm

Circular skin caps were everyday headgear for Alutiiq men in the 19th century. Like many other objects and cultural practices, they reflect the blending of traditions. The shape was Russian, but the decorations were Alutiiq: strips and cutouts made from dyed sea lion esophagus and decorative stitching in caribou hair, sinew, and yarn. The leaf and petal designs may have been inspired by European embroidery.

Tides and Ties of Our Culture

Roy Madsen
Kodiak, Alaska

CLOSE YOUR EYES AND VISUALIZE STANDING ON A SHORE where a stream meets the sea. The tide has just begun to fall, and as it releases its hold on the river water, you gaze into the clear waters of the stream at the multicolored stones in its bed, and at the bits of seaweed and twigs that are being carried off to unknown destinations. Those bits and pieces are our Alutiiq culture as it has been pushed, shoved, jostled and propelled from the time of our earliest ancestors to the present day.

The first man to brave contact with the Russians, whom our ancestors thought were devils, was named Ishnik. Kashkak was the name of the man Shelikhov put in charge of 400 prisoners who were furnished provisions and needed appliances for trapping and hunting for the Russians. This was the era of the Sugaks, Ashowaks, Adongas, Azuyaks, Kahutaks, Karluks, Yakanaks, Takaks, Ignatins, Ingas, Agnots, Zeeders, Amuknuks, Waselies, Tunohuns, Kewans, Knagins, Lukins, Noyas, Maliknaks, Matfays, Tudawhans, and others.

How was the island population affected during the Russian time? In addition to being decimated by the ravages of diseases such as smallpox, influenza, venereal disease and alcoholism, there were the losses due to enforced sea otter hunting and in the Russians' war against the Tlingits.

Then the Koniag blood was diluted through intermarriage. This was the period of the Pavloffs, Larionoffs, Chichenoffs, Katelnikoffs, Kvasnikoffs, Wolkoffs, Shuravloffs, Panamarioffs, Chernofs, Simeonoffs, Pestrikoffs, Kalmakoffs, Squartsoffs, Fadaoffs; the Metrokins, Petrovs, Patarochins, Petellins, Sharatines, etc. I think of this as a maternal generation, because these are the families of the mothers of many of us.

The next period I will refer to is the Scandinavians' Era, and arbitrarily set it from about 1900 until 1939. During this time there was an influx of seafaring men involved in the whaling, cod, salmon and herring fishing industries. This I will refer to as a paternal generation because these are the names of the fathers of many of us. The Johnsons, Jensons, Swansons, Swensons, Larsons, Nelsons, Nortons, Ericksons, Olsons, Andersons, Carlsons, Christiansons, Hansens, Petersons, Madsens, Magnusens, Sholls, Johansons, Haakansons, Gundersons, Mahles, Opheims, Linds, Von Scheeles, Pajomans, and others are included. They came from countries with similar climates and where opportunities were limited to fishing and farming. They left their homes, sailed halfway around the world, and ended up on our shores where they met, mingled with, and married our people and further diluted the blood of our ancestors.

During this period the population was further reduced by the Great Influenza Epidemic of 1918, by tuberculosis, which took a heavy toll, and, of course, alcoholism. Craig Mishler and Rachel Mason coauthored a study entitled "Alutiiq Vikings; Kinship and Fishing in Old Harbor, Alaska," which was printed in a journal called *Human Organization* in 1996. The article brought to mind the term "Smoked Norwegians" or "Smoked Scandinavians," a sobriquet which I attribute to Sven Haakanson, Sr., since he was the first person I recall using it.

I certainly don't want to downplay or minimize the influence of other cultures and nationalities that blended with the Koniag, Russian and Scandinavian during this same period. They were the English, Irish, Celts and Germans: the Sargents, Frosts, Kings, Heitmans, Hubleys, Mullans, Coyles, Cohens, and McCormicks. They flavored the mix, like herbs applied to a dish after the salt and pepper.

So as we talk about the tides and currents, we're talking about the flow of events that influenced and acted upon our ancestors' culture to modify, alter, change and transform it. We celebrated American Christmas and Russian Christmas, Russian New Year and Russian Easter. English was the most common language at home, our mother only spoke Russian outside the home when visiting relatives, and our father never spoke anything but English, although he could speak Danish, German and seven Eskimo dialects. There was only one church in town, the Russian Orthodox, and the services were all in Slavonic. Dances were a common social event and during the Russian New Year's celebration they were held every night of the week. Although this was a celebration of a Russian holiday, the music was mostly Scandinavian—polkas, schottisches, Rhinelanders, and of course waltzes and fox trots, and so it has continued on to today.

So the homogeneous culture of our ancestors has been transformed into the heterogeneous culture that we experience today, mixed, mingled, blended and combined with those many other cultures, retaining some of each but still with some recognizable and acknowledged aspects of the culture of our Alutiiq ancestors.

The Impact of Traumatic Events on Alutiiq Identity

THE SHARED HISTORY OF THE ALUTIIT INCLUDES A number of traumatic events that have influenced both culture and identity.[6] While we cannot know what took place before Russian contact marked the beginning of written history, we can be certain that the massacre at Refuge Rock by Grigorii Shelikhov and his men in 1784 had a tremendous impact. The slaughter of people by cannons, which they had never seen before, was followed by executions and the taking of children as hostages. The apparent absence of this story in contemporary oral history gives credence to the belief that the memory was collectively suppressed by generations of Alutiiq people. Sven Haakanson, Jr., an Alutiiq from Old Harbor and a Harvard-educated anthropologist, said, "People had made themselves forget about it."[7]

Russian atrocities abounded during the first three decades of Russian rule after 1784.[8] It is probably safe to say that a collective depression engulfed the Alutiit during this era. This depression was witnessed by the young Russian naval officer, Gavriil Davydov. His descriptions of Alutiiq ceremonies[9] are often quoted in modern texts but his observations of peoples' emotional condition are less noticed. While it is most likely that he was witnessing Alutiiq villages in a state of despair, he interpreted the behavior and actions he saw as signs of weakness and laziness.

> On the other hand it is hard to believe some of their bad traits. For instance, the irreconcilable attitude towards their traditional enemies with a constant desire for revenge. Their ingratitude; their lack of affection for family or friends; their indifference to the suffering of those who should be dear to them; their cunning and their habit of dissimulating their real feelings and intentions. One never sees a Koniag show excitement; he controls his feelings. He calmly figures his revenge for real or fancied wrongs.[10]

Davydov goes on to say:

> Like all savage people, they are not given to worry. They are lazy and only urged to activity by their necessities. In a village where I once lived, I noticed that they lay in bed all day long, never speaking. Once in a while one would get up and pound a drum and begin to sing in a lazy way, then several would join him in the same listless fashion.[11]

Much attention has been given to the epidemic of self-destructive behavior that has been sweeping across Alaska and its Native villages in recent years.[12] Alutiiq villages have not escaped this epidemic. Psychologists and other social scientists have concluded that this behavior stems from a sense of hopelessness brought on by decades of dependency on outsiders.[13] Davydov's observations show that Native reaction to Russian rule included the desire for death as a release from oppression:

> They commit suicide over trifles. If one announces his intention of drowning himself, no one tries to dissuade him, nor does any one interfere if he is seen carrying out his threat. They desire freedom above all things and cannot endure the thought of living under restraints of any kind.
>
> Once we went to a new village to get acquainted and sent several Russians to ask them to come to our boats. They got the idea that they were to be made prisoners and immediately began the slaughter of their wives and children, and finally themselves.
>
> I asked a man 'How is your family?' He said his wife had recently given birth to a son and he had wished to kill him, but the wife said she wanted him. Asked why he should do such a thing, he replied that he thought it better to kill him now rather than let him live to possibly become a slave later on.[14]

The conditions described by Davydov would have other names if witnessed today. Psychologists Jane Middleton-Moz and Eleanor Fedrid compare Native American survivors of traumatic events to Holocaust survivors. The result, they say, is "multigenerational grief,"

and "survival guilt" which in turn creates difficulties with identity.[15] This state, Middleton-Moz says, leads to feelings of helplessness and hopelessness within a culture.[16]

Social worker Margaret Knowles, an Alutiiq descended from the people of Afognak and of Prince William Sound, concludes that a similar state has existed in Alutiiq communities after the traumatic events of history, from the Refuge Rock massacre to devastating epidemics to the loss of life and communities during the great earthquake and tidal wave of 1964:

> And what happens to a people who . . . when they experience or see something so devastating . . . (and they have) nothing to receive that information, they go into kind of a—a shock mode. We refer to it as post-traumatic stress disorder . . . . They called that shell shock after World War II when they observed, you know, some of the soldiers who had come home with these symptoms. Well it's the same thing. . . . When there's nothing inside that will help you process this information, an actual physiological thing happens in the brain.[17]

72 "Man of Kadiak Island," 1790. A Russian artist drew this portrait at Three Saints Harbor, the first Russian headquarters on Kodiak Island. This Alutiiq hunter wears a birdskin parka, spruce root hunting hat, nose pin, and labret (Sarychev 1826: Plate 29).
Courtesy of The Bancroft Library, University of California.

73 *Awa'uq* (Refuge Rock), a small islet in the Kodiak archipelago, was the site of a Russian massacre of Alutiiq men, women, and children in 1784. People from many villages had gathered on top of the rock for safety from attack. A Russian force commanded by Grigorii Shelikhov fired on the settlement with cannons. The attack was a turning point in the Russian conquest of Kodiak Island.
Photograph by Richard Knecht, 1991.

Anthropologists and Alutiit

IN CHAPTER 2, ARON CROWELL AND SONJA LÜHRMANN present some of the anthropological views on Alutiiq culture and identity. The results of academic research are, of course, important in describing how Alutiiq people have come to view themselves today. But, at the same time, the reader must decide how the various views of Alutiiq culture and identity fit together. Listening to Alutiiq people about how they see themselves and how they view their own history is equally important. There are times when the indigenous viewpoint is diametrically opposed to that of Western scholarship. The age-old question "What is truth?" may be appropriate in this circumstance. The proposition that there can be more than one truth is often overlooked.

Archaeologists often define periods of the past, and thus the identities of the people living during that period, by the name of a geographic location where archaeological remains representing that time were discovered. In the Alutiiq region, archaeologists use a number of such labels. Thus, we have "Kachemak people," so called because of archaeological discoveries at Kachemak Bay on the Kenai Peninsula, and "Ocean Bay people," the result of archaeological discoveries at Ocean Bay on Sitkalidak Island in the Kodiak archipelago. These labels, however, mean absolutely nothing to Alutiiq people in describing their own culture and history.

Despite aspects of archaeology that may run contrary to Alutiiq beliefs, archaeologists have played an important role in efforts by Alutiiq people to reconstruct their own cultural history. Archaeology, when not viewed as the supreme truth, offers a valuable (and at times, the only) way to know about the distant past. However, as British archaeologist Stephan Shennan says, "As far as reconstructing the past is concerned, traditional origin myths are as good as archaeology, which is, in fact, simply a way of producing origin myths which are congenial to the way of thinking of a particular kind of society. It is all a matter of upbringing."[18]

By the 1960s, the presence of anthropologists in Alutiiq communities was common. They came as individual researchers and as representatives of government agencies. It was often difficult for village residents to understand why the anthropologists had arrived and what they wanted. Despite this lack of understanding, anthropologists usually found Alutiiq people to be cooperative. There was generally a high degree of cooperation and sharing of information with these inquisitive scientists. The 1930s had seen such noted anthropologists as Frederica de Laguna spend extended periods in the Alutiiq culture area. In the following decades new names from faraway universities and government agencies appeared.

By the 1980s anthropologists were beginning to wear out their welcome. From the perspective of many Alutiiq residents they were becoming more intrusive. There was still little understanding of why they were there, and the only evident results were technical reports written in a style that few people other than specialists could interpret. Sometimes these reports were not sent to the villages at all, in the belief that local residents would not be interested or able to understand them. In some cases, anthropologists—or people who represented themselves as such—would spend just a day or two in an Alutiiq village and then write about their findings as if they were experts on Alutiiq culture. Activism among indigenous peoples throughout the world caused the Alutiit to become more guarded about how cooperative they would be. Resentments had built over the anthropologists' definition of who Alutiiq people were, as if their version of Western science was the only truth.

With new caution and even distrust against anthropologists, new concepts emerged throughout the world that would change the ways that scientific research was carried out in indigenous communities. Codes of ethics originating from indigenous groups began to appear. The theme was consistent. Scientists would be required to secure permission to conduct research and they would

Can There Be Such a Thing as a Native Anthropologist?

Sven Haakanson, Jr.
Director, Alutiiq Museum
and Archaeological Repository

74 Sven Haakanson, Jr., at the Settlement Point site, Afognak Island.

Photograph by Richard Knecht.

THE LETTER ASKED ME TO WRITE ABOUT ALUTIIQ IDENTITY, a seemingly simple request. However, after studying anthropology at Harvard University and working with other Native peoples in Siberia I find it ironic that only Natives are asked to write in an "emic" (culturally "inside") voice about contemporary Native issues. Non-Natives, on the other hand, are asked to write from a scientific ("etic") point of view about Natives and their culture. Why are Natives always pigeon-holed into being spokespeople for their specific groups, even when they may have never experienced growing up in a rural community? Why is it that Alutiiq researchers were not requested to write from a scientific point of view, as were outsiders? I ask this question not to criticize this work but to bring up larger issues about the nature of collaborative work between Natives and anthropologists, and to note that research by Native anthropologists is often not accepted in the academic community because of a prevailing belief that it is biased.

If one examines most supposedly collaborative work, it appears that Native contributors are the ones who are interviewed and documented, while few Natives end up working together with anthropologists in true collaborative fashion. One would think that we were beyond this exclusionary approach, which is a clear example of how Natives are not in control of their history and what is said about them.

Furthermore, why is it that when Natives do research they have to clarify their approach, stating that they are coming from either an etic or emic perspective, while with others it is simply assumed they are writing as scientific observers? Is not the whole purpose of research to learn, including the exploration of different approaches to knowing (hermeneutics)? If Natives cannot write from *both* Native and scientific perspectives then what is the purpose of doing anthropology? More to the point, if this is the case can there ever be a such a thing as a Native anthropologist? I argue that Natives can do valid scientific research from an emic perspective and that this work should be respected as part of the genre.

There are several indigenous authors that I know of who utilize an emic approach and do it well. Knut Rasmussen, who was Greenlandic Inuit and Danish, worked with Inuit peoples across the North American arctic in the 1920s and 30s. His emic view provides the reader with a deeper understanding of Inuit peoples' lives prior to the changes that occurred under assimilation policies enacted by outside entities. His respect for and understanding of Inuit peoples' lives is deeper than any other author of his time. Alfonzo Ortiz achieves something similar in his book about the San Juan Pueblo Tewa in New Mexico, *The Tewa World: Space, Time, Being, and Becoming in a Pueblo Society*. Ortiz, a Tewa himself, uses an emic perspective to discuss the intricacies of Pueblo social organization. AlaskanYup'ik researcher Oscar Kawagley examines how outside educational systems are changing Native world view. By utilizing an emic perspective to critique the system, he is able to point to another way of knowing and learning, through a traditional world view. These individuals demonstrate that an emic approach can be effectively applied. It could be argued that more work of this type has not been done because Native anthropologists have been discouraged from attempting it.

I am not suggesting that a Native emic perspective is any better than an etic scientific approach for the study of Native peoples. What I am pointing out is that anthropology needs to embrace a new and more inclusive definition of collaboration, in which Native approaches to the field are just as valid as any others.

have to keep the local group informed. The results of all studies were to be shared openly with the people involved. Above all, indigenous peoples were to be full partners in all research involving their communities and would have direct input into developing research agendas.

From the partnership model of cooperative research between indigenous peoples and Western scientists the next step could be anticipated—Natives as researchers. The concept that an Alutiiq (or any indigenous person) could gain an education that would provide him or her with credentials to conduct scientific inquiry posed new challenges. Could these Native scientists be accepted by the Western scientific community? The Alutiiq culture area seems an ideal place to challenge old ways of doing things. There has been and continues to be considerable anthropological research conducted among the Alutiit such that a whole generation has grown up witnessing it. As a result, several Alutiit have gone on to institutions of higher education to pursue degrees and achieve the required credentials. Old Harbor's Sven Haakanson, Jr., received a Ph.D. in anthropology at Harvard University in the spring of 2000 and in doing so became the first village-raised Alutiiq to earn a doctoral degree. Haakanson poses the penetrating question in his attached essay, "Can there be such a thing as a Native anthropologist?" His points are worth considering. He doubts that anthropologists who also happen to be Alutiiq can be taken seriously when they speak about their communities from an anthropological perspective. "If Natives cannot write from *both* a Native and scientific perspective then what is the purpose of doing anthropology?"

Language and Identity

When we speak our language we hear our ancestors' voices. . . . It is our desire that each new Alutiiq generation will learn to speak Sugcestun so they will always know who they are.

—Rhoda Moonin, 1999[19]

We were told not to speak our language in Aleut in school ground and we got spanked. And I said, I'm not gonna' have no teachers spank me! I quit going to school. No school teacher spank me. But by reading, I—I read a lot, and that's how I learned, you know, how to speak more in—in English. And dad never taught us how to talk in Russian. My mom—our mom did a little; what she knew. So that's all I have to say.

—Julia Knagin Pestrikoff (Afognak/Port Lions)[20] 1997[21]

There was not a school in Kaguyak.[22] And then the people in Kaguyak they say, 'I'll send you to Old Harbor to go to school.' So I did. I went over. . . . I didn't speak English. When I went to school in—in the classroom and the teacher came to me and speak to me in English. I said, 'I wondering what he's saying?' I talked back to him in Aleut. He said he didn't understand me either. I didn't understand him in English. So I kept on and then later that year and they sent five of us to Wrangell Institute on the S.S. Denali.

—Senafont Zeedar (Kaguyak) 1997[23]

LANGUAGE IS A MAJOR MARKER OF INDIGENOUS identity throughout the world. Indigenous people who speak a Native tongue are considered to be more legitimate than those who cannot, regardless of the reasons behind the loss of language. Sadly, the majority of Alutiiq adults today do not speak their language, called Sugtestun. This name for the language, which means "to speak like a true human being" derives from the self-designation Sugpiaq, "genuine human being." The language suffered a serious, if not fatal, blow when the imported American education system prohibited Native students from speaking it in the classroom. Many Alutiiq children born in the nineteenth century and the early twentieth century were trilingual, speaking Sugtestun in the home, Russian in church, and English in school. Russian was also spoken as a first language in many Alutiiq homes, especially in the villages of northern Kodiak Island. There is a small and decreasing number of Elders alive today who continue to be fluent in all three languages.

Like other social scientists, linguists applied their own labels to the language of the Alutiiq people. The terms "Pacific Eskimo" and "Pacific Yup'ik" have been used in the published literature, but these terms are considered offensive by many Alutiit who identify themselves more closely with the Aleuts (Unangan) of the Aleutian Islands than with Yup'ik people of the Alaska mainland. Linguists have relented under pressure and no longer use the objectionable labels. The name most commonly used today, by both linguists and the Alutiit, is "Alutiiq." Use of the term Sugtestun is no longer widespread. Alutiit of the Prince William Sound area and the lower Kenai Peninsula communities are the main holdouts for maintaining this original name for the language.

The existence of historically imposed external names for the language and culture have contributed to identity confusion, as described by Margaret Knowles at the 1997 Alutiiq Elders' Conference in Kodiak:

> I realized that we are *not* the true Natives and the fact remained that we really didn't even know who we were. And that really bothered me. It angered me because I . . . well, who are we? . . . I was embarrassed when I'd be around other groups, Yup'iks, who absolutely knew who they were and where they were from, . . . and I didn't. I didn't know. And they said, 'Well, it depends on what anthropologist you talk to.' I always believed I was Aleut and then somebody said, 'No, you're really Koniag.' And, 'No, you're really Pacific Eskimo.' 'No, you're Sugpiaq.' 'No, you're really more related to the Yup'ik'.[24]

75 School children at Perryville, 1939–41.
Courtesy of the Alaska State Library. (PCA 222-370).

Alutiiq Land, Land Claims, and Identity

A SPECIAL, EVEN SPIRITUAL, ATTACHMENT TO THE LAND is a central theme among all indigenous people. Often, this concept comes into direct opposition to attitudes of the dominant Western culture. A strong connection to the land continues to help define Alutiiq identity just as it does for other Native peoples of the world.

If indigenous people belong *to the land*, it becomes difficult for them to accept the notion that land can belong *to them*. In the Alutiiq world, this connection to the land continued to be strong long after the American takeover of Alaska from Russia. This situation became problematic in the western world of development and legal titles. The federal government claimed it owned the land in Alaska and in turn gave or sold it to outsiders,

including individual homesteaders and companies such as fish canneries and oil businesses. Land traditionally used by (but never thought of as being owned by) the Alutiit was designated as U.S. national forests and wildlife refuges.

These new land statuses left Alutiiq people without the right to live where they and their ancestors had been for millennia. In some cases, it was not until the 1950s and 1960s that Alutiiq people even had a mechanism to acquire legal title to the very land where their homes

76   Man at the village of Uganik on Kodiak Island.
Courtesy of the University of Washington Libraries (UW 7559).

were situated. For example, the Secretary of the Interior announced on January 20, 1954, that residents of the Alutiiq village of Afognak would be allowed to purchase the lots on which their homes were sitting.[25] The $2.50 per acre price might seem reasonable enough until it is considered that this was the home ground of countless generations of ancestors, none of whom could have conceived of *owning* it.

Another practice that could not be comprehended by outsiders was the Alutiiq propensity to relocate their villages. Some Western scientists assume that the empty settlements they find on the landscape have been left behind forever. Thus, such terms as "abandoned village" or "abandoned area" are commonly used.

Yet, from the archaeological evidence itself comes the realization that Alutiiq people commonly moved their settlements from time to time. Granted, these occasions may have been centuries apart, but moves took place nonetheless. Resettlement may have come about for a variety of reasons, including a change in the food supply, threats from enemies, or even simply because a more comfortable location was found. In historic times, Alutiiq communities moved or dispersed because of epidemics, volcanic eruptions and earthquakes, or, more commonly, for economic reasons. Evidence from oral histories strongly suggests that although people occasionally move they seldom think of actually abandoning a village site. They continue to feel a spiritual connection to the former location and may intend to return, even at some point in the distant future. These village connections are a persistent aspect of identity, often passed down from generation to generation. Thus, younger Alutiit may feel connections to villages they have never even seen. Marlane Shanigan's article about the Alaska Peninsula village of Kanatak, where she spent her childhood, shows that the now-empty village still defines identity and tribal affiliation.

In 1971, an event took place that had perhaps the most profound effect on Alutiiq identity of any in the twentieth century. The Alaska Native Claims Settlement Act (ANCSA), passed by Congress in December of that year, settled the legal issue of aboriginal land claims in Alaska. Under the act, Alaska Native people were to receive legal title to forty million acres of land as well as a cash settlement of nearly a billion dollars for land given up.[26] Under ANCSA, Alaska was divided into twelve geographical regions that largely coincided with culture areas. The approach worked fairly well in most parts of the state

but the Alutiiq culture area found itself divided. Alutiiq communities are located in four different ANCSA regions, each represented by a separate regional corporation (see fig. 66).[27]

Eligible Alutiiq people became shareholders in the Native corporations and thus a new identity quickly emerged.[28] Being a "Native shareholder" became the dominant way of validating identity, for Alutiit as well as other Native groups in Alaska.[29] One of ANCSA's most confusing provisions was that Natives could enroll in the corporation representing the geographical area where they resided when the act was passed, regardless of their ethnic or cultural affiliations. As a result, some enrollees in what would have been exclusively Alutiiq corporations were not Alutiiq at all, but members of other Alaska Native groups. Corporations representing the two regions with exclusively Alutiiq communities—Chugach Alaska Corporation and Koniag, Inc.—have had corporate leaders who were Athabascan, Inupiaq, Tlingit, and Tsimshian. Bristol Bay Native Corporation and Cook Inlet Region, Inc., represent geographical areas that include Alutiiq villages but also other culture groups.[30]

The enrollment process was made even more complex by the fact that each eligible Native could also enroll to a village. The village was required to be within the enrollee's region but there was considerable flexibility (and some confusion) in the process. One could choose the village where he or she resided when ANCSA was passed, the village of birth, or where parents, grandparents, or other ancestors were born.

Alutiiq Elder Roy Madsen, born in Kanatak and raised in Kodiak with stops at various other locations in the area, described the dilemma faced by many in choosing where to enroll:

> [I]t made me think back to the time when we were enrolling people in Koniag [Inc.] and then we had to enroll in a village corporation. And when we started looking around, of course, the natural thought was, 'Well, I live in Kodiak so I should be enrolled here.' But then I started looking at the other connections and I could've enrolled in Karluk, in Larsen Bay, in Uyak, in Uganik, Afognak, or Ouzinkie, and I ended up enrolling in Leisnoi.[31]

Emotions flared during the enrollment process and beyond. The eligibility question became particularly controversial within the Alutiiq culture area. Rather than affirming Alutiiqness, the process promoted a pan-Native identity based on corporate affiliation. Because

The Spirits Are Still There: Memories of Katmai Country

Mary Jane Nielsen
General Manager, South Naknek
Alaska Peninsula Corporation

77 Mary Jane Nielsen.
Courtesy of Mary Jane Nielsen.

NOVARUPTA AND KATMAI BLEW UP IN 1912, WHEN MY father, Trefon Angasan, was two years old, forcing an evacuation of all the villagers of Katmai Country. The villagers from Grosvenor and Savonoski crossed Naknek Lake and went down the Naknek River, taking refuge in a new place that was aptly named New Savonoski. Those villagers eventually moved to South Naknek and beyond. Our relatives on the Shelikof Strait side of Katmai from the villages of Katmai and Douglas moved to safer places. Most went to Perryville, named after the captain of the ship that transported them there. Descendents of Katmai eventually migrated to various parts of the Alaska Peninsula or Kodiak and are now all over the world.

The first three of the ten children born to my parents, Vera Kie from Ugashik, and Trefon Angasan of Old Savonoski were born in this new place of refuge. Nothing stands in the village now except for parts of

of the events of history, the Alutiit were much more biologically diverse that many Natives in other parts of Alaska. Virtually all had some degree of Russian ancestry while some had Scandinavian blood or other mixtures brought about by more than a century of U.S. rule.

Over the decades leading up to the passage of ANCSA, Alaska Natives, including the Alutiit, had been treated as second-class citizens. In fact, those identified as Natives were not even conferred American citizenship until 1924. Natives who could pass as non-Natives could achieve citizenship and all the benefits that go with being a member of the dominant part of American society. An option exercised by many of those who could get away with it in the eyes of the dominant society was to take advantage of their Russian blood (even if it was minimal) and declare that they were Russian rather than Native. This was easier for those who were fluent in the Russian language. Nearly all Alutiit were members of the

Russian Orthodox Church, which also aided in validating a Russian identity.

Those Alutiit who had chosen to try to conceal their Native blood but then chose to enroll under ANCSA were ridiculed by those who had not followed this course. The phrase "He/she was never a Native until 1971" became common. Many believed that those who had not identified as Alutiiq before ANCSA and to varying degrees had escaped the hardships associated with being Native in Alaska now wanted to cash in through the benefits of ANCSA.[32]

ANCSA was a controversial piece of federal legislation from the outset. There were concerns about its equity because some regions were rich in natural resources and others were not. Regional corporations that extracted natural resources were required to share seventy percent of their profits with the other regions. This caused considerable divisiveness throughout Alaska because many shareholders in the well-endowed regions were reluctant

Agafia and Andrew Wassillie's windbreak and remnants of Mike McCarlo's house. On the hill overlooking the village, the Russian Orthodox Church still stands as if in testimony of the enduring spirit of our ancestors.

My parents and grandparents brought us up the Naknek River and across Naknek Lake to visit their ancestral homelands. My sister "Kata" (Katharine Groat) says that she still starts feeling the spirits when we get to the rapids on the Naknek River. Grandma Palakia would ready her tea and dried fish to feed the "eating rock." The driver of the skiff or boat would pass as closely as possible so that Gram could throw her offerings to the rock and say her words in Sugcestun, which meant, "Eat. Our nets... Let the fish come back to them." We still do this, both going up and coming back down the river. Only now, it is fed potato chips, bread, marshmallows, or whatever modern-day campers carry with them. When my brother-in-law Charley Savo first married my sister Viola, he didn't feed the rock. He had to be towed back when his outboard engine shaft was broken, or whatever other misfortune befell him. He started feeding the rock.

When we got to the dad's cabin at the mouth of Naknek Lake, we would be anxious and excited about how close we were getting to Kittiwick. Upon arrival, Grandma would joyfully go ashore, cross herself and venerate the ground by kneeling and pressing her forehead to the earth. We tease my brother Ralph to this day. He thought that Gram was kissing the ground so that is what he would do.

A small contingent of Council of Katmai Descendants went to Kittiwick. Jeff Anderson, Margie Macauly-Waite, and Edna Smith were there for the first time. It was moving to see how the land affected them and how happy they were to be in Katmai country.

to distribute so much of their income. For the predominately Alutiiq regional corporations, however, this sharing proved to be an important difference between corporate survival and failure.

Among some Alutiit, ANCSA produced anger and resentment. Alan Panamaroff, a leader of Kaguyak Village on Kodiak Island, said in 1981, "Corporations were forced on my people–they didn't understand it when it passed. They still don't understand it. They don't understand people telling them they have certain boundaries. My people didn't need the money. They didn't need the value of being important. All they needed was a duck or two, or to get a deer, so two or three families could share. The most valuable thing they knew was seal liver. My people were the richest people in the world."[33]

For Alutiiq people, the positive impact of ANCSA, however, may best be measured in ways other than financial. The struggle for a just land settlement brought people together, in some cases reuniting families that had been separated for years. During the land claims process leading up to ANCSA, a new unity was forged. Roy Madsen gives a glimpse of the spirit of that era, saying, "I think back to the times when we were working on the Alaska Native Claims Settlement Act in the 1960s.... I have never seen such enthusiasm and unity among the people on Kodiak Island as existed then."[34] On November 9, 1984, I testified before the Alaska Native Review Commission headed by Justice Thomas Berger during one of the hearings held on Kodiak Island. The words I said then still ring true today, with one exception. "While there may seem to be many flaws in ANCSA, that Act is not without its positive effect. For many people the Act restored a sense of Native identity."[35] If I could change those words of the past I would insert "Alutiiq identity" for "Native identity."

Kanatak Tribal Council

Marlane Shanigan
Kanatak Tribal Council

ALL APPEARS QUIET AND CONTENT AS THE WIND BLOWS its strong breath of ownership through the ruins of a once-popular Alutiiq village and its oil fields. Surely, the wind does own this now-quiet town nestled between the grand Pacific Ocean and the magnificent mountains of the Alaska Range.

Kanatak, located across from Kodiak Island on the mainland, was once a major town. It sprang to life in the 1920s with the beginning of oil exploration and died almost as quickly in the late 1940s after all efforts to profitably recover oil had failed. Needless to say, when the oil companies left so did the stores, the bakery, the hotels, and the merchants. This was followed by the closing of the post office and later the Bureau of Indian Affairs (BIA) school. Residents eventually chose to spend a majority of their time in Kodiak, Egegik, and Chignik, communities that offered jobs and a place for the children to go to school. My family was the last to move in 1955.

From the late 1950s to the 1970s, the Native village of Kanatak had sporadic visits from strangers, mostly commercial fishermen and hunters with light planes. These visitors became aware of a treasure chest of personal property. It didn't take long to empty out the homes of rifles, photos, and other items of value. Although some of the former residents also periodically returned to the village by trekking over the mountains or by boat or small aircraft, these visits eventually declined. Because of this, many writers have referred to Kanatak as "abandoned." However, I disagree. Abandonment means that one leaves without the intention of returning.

In 1938, the Natives of Kanatak organized and formed a tribal governing body with the assistance of the BIA school teachers. On March 1, 1941, tribal leaders drafted a constitution and bylaws under the authority of the Indian Reorganization Act (IRA). As a result, the Native Village of Kanatak went on record as a federally recognized tribe, complete with IRA standing.

One might ask what relationship the Kanatak Tribal Council has to the land and the people. Today there are several so-called landless tribes in Alaska, and Kanatak is one of them. Although public records indicate that the village of Kanatak was surveyed, there are no records to indicate that a townsite was ever approved. There were no Native allotment filings, nor did anyone apply for group status under the terms of the Alaska Native Claims Settlement Act.

In the fall of 1993, while working at the Bristol Bay Native Association (BBNA), I learned that the BBNA Tribal Operations department was seeking information on members from Kanatak. BBNA's intention was to provide documentation to the Department of the Interior that would substantiate the existence of all tribes in the Bristol Bay area. This effort was timely because for many years I had compiled notes about all of the former residents of the village from my grandfather and my father. I had researched my family's ties to Kanatak and gathered stories about its history.

My interest in this research was personal. The first five years of my life when I lived in Kanatak with my family include some of my happiest memories. Kanatak was my father's birthplace, and I felt very strongly that my family and other families that owned homes there had a right to return and to reestablish residency.

Since the Kanatak Tribal Council had preexisting tribal authority and was already a federally recognized tribe, the main tasks were to complete the enrollment process and to establish programs for tribal members such as vocational training, higher education, and social services. I realized that this process would enable us to acquire other federal and state funding and might even allow for historic preservation programs and tourism. It would enable us to rebuild our homes and to establish a direct connection to our land.

While our tribal entity has experienced difficulties in getting reorganized, it is my hope that the newly elected council will make choices that will allow a cooperative agreement to be signed by organizations with ownership interests both in and around the boundaries of Kanatak–Koniag, Inc., the Becharof Wildlife Refuge, and the tribe itself. This will allow a dream to come true: having a direct tie to our land and thus to our Alutiiq culture.

78 Family at Kanatak, 1920s.
Courtesy of the Anchorage Museum of History and Art (B64.1.354).

Alutiiq Cultural Reawakening

ACCORDING TO ANTHROPOLOGIST MARGARET LANTIS, A cultural revitalization movement began for Alaska Natives during the land claims movement of the 1960s.[36] This may have been the case, but it was not very noticeable in the Alutiiq culture area. There were some starts and stops in an effort to have an Alutiiq museum and cultural center built in Kodiak during the 1970s. This effort was revived in the early and mid-1980s when I was president of the Kodiak Area Native Association. After many meetings and discussions, the board and management of KANA decided that each program within the organization should have a cultural base and a cultural component, no matter how small. New cultural activities were initiated, including language classes, mask carving, bentwood visor making, basket making, and ar-

79 Instructor Lydia Robart leads students in a traditional dance at Núciq Spirit Camp, 1998. At the camp, students learn traditional arts and skills and participate in professional archaeological research.

Courtesy of John F. C. Johnson and the Chugach Heritage Foundation.

chaeological excavations with Alutiiq students participating. In a short time, similar activities were taking place
throughout the Alutiiq culture area from Prince William
Sound to the Alaska Peninsula.

In 1995, the Alutiiq Museum, built with funds from
the legal settlement of the *Exxon Valdez* disaster, was
opened in Kodiak. The museum is a state-of-the-art
facility operated by a board made up of representatives
from all the Kodiak area Native corporations. The museum is a source of pride for all Alutiiq people. Its spectacular collections erase any doubt that the Alutiit do
have a history and that the culture they lived for thousands of years was one to behold and admire.

In recent years, collaborative efforts among the
Smithsonian's Arctic Studies Center, the Alutiiq Museum,
and corporations representing Alutiit throughout the

80 The Alutiiq Museum in Kodiak.
Photograph by Patrick Saltonstall.

region have bought Elders and youth together to share
their culture. The Afognak Native Corporation began the
Dig Afognak project that joins the efforts of archaeologists, Alutiiq Elders, and youth in order to delve into the
past. Ruth Olsen Dawson eloquently describes the positive impact of archaeology on the revitalization of Alutiiq
culture in her included essay.

Bridging Traditions and Science

Ruth Alice Olsen Dawson
Chair, Alutiiq Heritage Foundation

CAMAI. MY NAME IS RUTH ALICE OLSEN DAWSON. I am the daughter of Nina Knagin Olsen, Koniag Alutiiq of old Afognak village, and Pete Olsen, Chugach Alutiiq from Cordova in Prince William Sound. I have served on the board of Afognak Native Corporation for over thirteen years, five of those as president. I want to share with you part of my journey of discovery of being Koniag Alutiiq, and how scientific research has helped me find my Native heart.

My people, the people of Afognak village, have only in my lifetime been recognized as Native. Prior to the Alaska Native Claims Settlement Act, my people were not recognized or distinguished in any way from all the newcomers to Kodiak and Afognak Island. Through the intense lobbying of the Alaska Federation of Natives, the Alaska Native Claims Settlement Act was signed into law in 1971, only thirty years ago. We in Alaska were told to organize into corporations to receive the settlement of land and money and we began the job of governing our people through a corporate structure.

Kodiak has one of the hardest and cruelest histories of cultural impact. We lost much during the Russian period. An estimated Native population of 10,000 or greater was reduced to a handful of villages in less than a hundred years. We lost Elders, stories, songs, ceremonies, and our identity. This downward spiral continued until recently. But a number of events have contributed to the rekindling of Alutiiq heritage on Kodiak, and the light of our ancestors' oil lamps is now burning bright. And it is modern science that has enhanced this process.

A number of events have fed this light. The first battle was ANCSA itself. There were a number of powerful people who believed that we here in Kodiak were not Native enough to be included. We were Creole, Russian, Scandinavian, anything but Native. There were those among our own people who did not want to admit to Native blood, and so hindered our efforts to join in the act and be recognized. It was through the efforts of archaeologists and anthropologists who submitted evidence to Congress that our federal lawmakers were convinced that we were indeed Native. Archaeological data clearly established that Kodiak had been occupied by indigenous people for thousands of years, and the remains of our ancestors' bodies showed that we were indeed descended from these prehistoric ancestors. Without this evidence, it is doubtful I would be sharing this story today.

The second major event that contributed to our identity as a people was *glasnost'*. How could there possibly be a connection between the opening of Russia and my Native people? Though the Russians were the destroyers of my people's ancient way of life, they were also later its salvation. Many trained scientists traveled with the Russian-American Company, and they kept notes and journals and collected ethnographic materials in large quantities from Kodiak. In the 1990s the now famous Smithsonian exhibition, *Crossroads of Continents: Cultures of Siberia and Alaska*, traveled to Anchorage, Alaska. That exhibition included numerous items from museums in Russia, many of them returning to Alaska for the first time. That exhibit was a mind-blower. For the first time we saw "snow-falling" parkas made out of bird skins and decorated with puffins' beaks. We saw ceremonial masks, regalia, baskets, rattles, pictures, and drawings. The impact for me was overwhelming. The exhibit sparked the start of the first Native dance group in Kodiak in years. And instead of wearing European calicos, we wore snowfalling parkas, shook puffin beak rattles, and wore beaded headdresses. It was a revelation. Again, the science of anthropology allowed us to regain a little of what had been taken from us.

At the same time, archaeological research was underway on Kodiak Island. A very large and well-preserved site had been discovered at the village of Karluk. However, we on Kodiak had no museum to store what was being found. It might have been the same old story. Researchers come in from the outside and take what they have found to their universities. The Native people being researched never get to see, feel, or learn from the scientists' discoveries. However, Kodiak has managed to reverse this trend. Through the efforts of Gordon Pullar, a young archaeologist named Rick Knecht was hired to start our own museum. The dream was realized when funds from the *Exxon Valdez* oil spill settlement were provided to build the museum. Today, the board of directors of the museum is made up of representatives from the various Native organizations in the Kodiak Archipelago. Policy is made by the Native board, and the museum is there to serve as a facilitator for ongoing research on our Native lands. This has not been an easy journey for us, but we are already seeing the rewards. Children from the Kodiak schools now come to the museum to touch our past and learn about our people. The museum has helped turn

around local prejudices about being Native. And the researchers now must come to Kodiak to study the collections, instead of us begging for them.

But most exciting to me has been my corporation's commitment to continued learning about our culture. While I was president, the board was presented a proposal from our staff for a program called "Light the Past, Spark the Future, Dig Afognak." Dig Afognak was a new model, where archaeologists would work for the Native corporation, and paying participants would provide much of the labor.

The research efforts of Dig Afognak have had a major impact on our corporation and its shareholders. First, every summer we have a touchstone, a place we can go to be on our island and live simply. It is a place where we can touch the old clay storage pits, find oil lamps, help build a model barabara, our traditional house, and simply visit and share stories.

Second, Dig Afognak is helping our youth find their identity. We sponsor a youth intern program and every summer some of our teenagers work at the camp, learning both the science and how to run a professional tourism program.

Third, we are able to share the information we learn from the sites with our people. The archaeological staff are required to devote a large part of their time to educational efforts, including articles for our newsletters, slide shows for our informational meetings, and visits with our people. This helps the scientists to understand and become more sensitive to issues, particularly involving burial sites, and allows us to understand how we can best manage our cultural resources.

Fourth, through cooperation with all the other village corporations in Kodiak, we now have an Alutiiq controlled and funded museum to store our treasures and history.

Afognak is now one of the leaders in research. And I understand that this can be controversial. I understand that many object to archaeological research as they feel it would be better left alone. For some this may be appropriate. But for me, archaeology has opened a new world. The key is that the Native people must control the research effort. Research cannot happen on Native land without the Native people themselves directing the effort. Otherwise, its just another rip-off, with scientists coming in and taking instead of sharing.

What our Dig Afognak project site at the old village of Katenai has taught me is that through working together with mutual respect for each other's views, Native people and scientists can learn from each other. And by adding our youth and paying participants, we complete the circle and share knowledge with others.

My mother, an Alutiiq Elder and one of the few who still carried our language, was a source of inspiration and encouragement for all of us through our growing days of finding our roots. She felt strongly that archaeological research has its place if properly done. One time when we were visiting we talked about our Dig Afognak program, and she was concerned that I would be hurt when some people disapproved of what the corporation was doing. She said, "Ruth Alice, we must never stop learning." And I offer that to you, that we can never know too much about our people, our ancestors, and who we are. We must never stop learning.

Quyaná
Thank You.

Repatriation

BEGINNING IN THE LATE NINETEENTH CENTURY, scientists began collecting human remains from the Alutiiq culture area. Famed Smithsonian naturalist William H. Dall described stealing the much-revered remains of whalers on Kodiak Island during the 1870s.[37] This was merely the beginning of the expropriation of human remains from Kodiak Island and other parts of the region.

In 1931, Aleš Hrdlička, curator of physical anthropology at the National Museum of Natural History, Smithsonian Institution, began the first of the several summers on Kodiak Island where he gathered human remains from burials.[38] Most of these were taken from the village of Larsen Bay but Hrdlička also traveled around the island seeking "specimens." His usual procedure, practiced on expeditions throughout Alaska, was to visit Native villages and ask where the "very old" burials were. He apparently believed that there would be no objection if he collected bones of ancestors who were not specifically remembered. His writings about visits to interior Alaska villages reveal that he also dug up graves that were quite recent.[39] Even on Kodiak Island some of the human remains he removed were from victims of the 1918 influenza epidemic.[40]

Alutiiq Elders Lucille Antowak Davis of Karluk and Mary Peterson of Akhiok remember when Hrdlička and his crew visited their villages. Unable to comprehend why anyone would want to dig up graves to collect skeletal remains, they assumed he must have been searching for jewelry buried with the bodies.

> I was about eight or nine years old when these people came from the Lower 48. At that time I guessed they were archeologists, maybe. But they were not Natives. They were digging back of the church there. Nikita was in charge of the cemetery at that time, Sophie's father. And so they came and they were digging back there. Okay. And they—he just said that they were white people digging the graves. And . . . and what they were doing was digging them old ones that had been buried; taking . . . taking things from them empty coffins and taking their—I guess they took. . . . At that

82 Aleš Hrdlička at the Uyak site excavation, Kodiak Island, 1930s.

Courtesy of the National Anthropological Archives (93-12628).

Repatriation and the Chugach Alaska People

John F. C. Johnson
Chairman, Chugach Heritage Foundation

THE INDIGENOUS PEOPLE OF OUR REGION HAVE BEEN called by many names over the years, such as *Aleuts, Alutiiqs,* and *Chugach*. We also call ourselves *Sugpiaq,* which means "Real People." Another name is *Suaciq,* which refers to warriors of the eastern portion of Prince William Sound.

My ancestors were from the settlement of Nuchek, which was the largest Native historic village in Prince William Sound and the location of a Russian trading post, built in the 1790s called "Fort Saint Constantine and Helen."

I hold my head high when I say that my grandmother's uncle, Peter Chimovitski, was the last traditional chief of this village until his death in 1928. Recently I had the honor of respecting his son's last wish by burying him next to his family's grave site at Nuchek. Our roots go deep into the ground where the ancient ones have been put to rest. Respect for the dead is just as important as having respect for the living. The boundary between life and death is a very fine line. Death is not the end, but rather the beginning of a new cycle in life.

Nowadays, I wear many hats. I am currently the chairman of the Chugach Heritage Foundation, director of the board for the Chugach Alaska Corporation, and president of the Keepers of the Treasures for the State of Alaska. This statewide organization is dedicated to assisting Alaska Native people in the preservation of our culture and implementing the recent federal repatriation law called the Native American Graves Protection and Repatriation Act (NAGPRA).

For the past twenty years I have been active in documenting archaeological sites and oral history of the Chugach, Tlingit, and Eyak Native people. My interest in repatriation became keen when I traveled to old pillow-lava burial caves and rock shelters and found them looted, vandalized, and empty.

These caves once held the mummified remains of our Chugach warriors, chieftains and shamans. At the time of their deaths, some had armor plates on their chests and wooden dance masks by their sides. Others had kayaks and weapons nearby to protect them in the afterlife. On the cave walls above these prehistoric burials were red pictographs made of blood, seal oil, and red ocher.

Over the years these caves were looted in the name of science, greed, and just plain stupidity. Curio hunters would rob these graves of mummies so they could make a profit and be placed on display at various world fairs across the country. Scientists would remove these remains so they could try to understand the origin of mankind. Others would rob these graves just to get a souvenir.

As a result of the *Exxon Valdez* oil spill, the Chugach people had to pull together again and fight once more for our cultural survival. Souvenir collecting of artifacts and human remains happened during the *Exxon Valdez* oil spill cleanup. The desecration of these burial sites brought outrage to the Native people. Many wondered why the treatment and respect for the dead were not the same for all cultures. Why were we any different?

The Chugach have been very active and successful in obtaining Chugach human remains that were stolen during the oil spill and those that were removed earlier to various museums and universities in the United States and Europe. Once our ancestors were returned, we placed them back into their place of origin with dignity, with honor, and with respect.

Our children are the next generation of leaders that will be responsible to keep our culture alive and not let this cycle be broken. The fight for indigenous rights is our destiny and duty. The voices from the past must be heard. We cannot turn back the hands of time, but we can learn from the mistakes and make corrections for the future.

Repatriation is not the end to the thirst for knowledge, but is a new starting point in building trust and cooperation. As one of my friends from the Smithsonian said recently, "The best studies that have been completed on human remains recently are on the ones that have been returned." Cooperation and a partnership with science and the Native community is important if we want to understand the full picture of human history. The sharing of knowledge and respect for cultural beliefs is important if we are truly to advance into the next level of civilization.

An example of this sharing is from the oral history that I have collected from Alaska Native Elders. One legend tells of a Chugach migration from western Alaska some 10,000 years ago, when Prince William Sound was covered by a solid sheet of ice during the Pleistocene period.

A cultural renaissance is now sweeping across Alaska like a winter storm. Native cultural centers and spirit camps for the Native youth are being built across this great land and in record numbers. The Chugach assisted in the creation of the Alaska Native Heritage Center in Anchorage, Alaska, which opened in May of 1999. For the past five years, the Chugach have maintained the Nuchek Spirit Camp, at an old remote village in Prince William Sound. This camp is designed to teach the younger generations the importance of our culture, language, and subsistence way of life.

Sometimes during our lives we have a window of opportunity to correct past injustices and mistakes. We now have this opening before us and we need to accept the challenge to make a difference in this world. A concentrated effort must be made to return all human remains to their places of origin. This may be a hard pill to swallow, but the positive outcome will outweigh the pain. When I travel to various museums across the land, I feel a sense of joy and spiritual uplifting in being able to bring my relatives back home. It has been a long journey, but it is worth every single step.

83   Mask

Prince William Sound, 1875
National Museum of Natural History, Smithsonian Institution
(NMNH 20269) Height 38 cm

"The graves were situated rather far from the village. Those of poor people were not hidden, but rich persons were put in inaccessible places."
—K. Birket-Smith, *The Chugach Eskimo*, 1953

This mask may have been worn by a member of a secret men's society in Prince William Sound, the *aqlat*, or "winds." An opening through the forehead allowed the dancer to see, and attachments (now missing) were inserted in holes around the edge of the mask. The mask was one of seven that were taken from a cave in Prince William Sound by the Alaska Commercial Company in 1875, and sent to the U.S. National Museum (Smithsonian Institution). Because the masks were found with human remains, federal repatriation laws required that they be returned to the people of Prince William Sound. This mask was repatriated in 2000, and is shown with permission from Chugach Alaska Corporation.

time they buried the chiefs and everything with their garments and what not and that's what they were after when they found the skulls with . . . some of 'em had gold teeth and that's what they were taking. Taking their jewelry and everything like that. That's what I've been told. So we never went back there.

—Lucille Antowak Davis (Karluk) 1997[41]

I . . . I remember they did that in Akhiok, too. And there were people—I don't know what they were. . . . And they were digging. . . . When I see him, I remember. And they were going up and . . . we thought somebody died. You know. And then we didn't know. We followed him. We went and we were late for school. We followed. They were digging. . . . Why are they digging? Who are they digging? Who are they going to bury? . . . They were digging the graves looking for jewelry from the dead people. Looking to see if they had

jewelry; rings and old jewelry. . . . What they had on their ears and their nose and stuff like that. They were asking, which—what part of the graveyard is long time ago.

—Mary Peterson (Akhiok) 1997[42]

In the early 1980s, Indian tribes in the Lower 48 began seeking the return of human remains so that they could be reburied. Virtually all major museums in the United States housed Native American remains. The Smithsonian Institution had an astounding 18,500 with about 4,000 from Alaska. Of these, well over a quarter were from Kodiak Island. The Larsen Bay collection, estimated at 1,000, was the largest from a single location held by the Smithsonian. Attempts at repatriation touched off a national and international debate pitting indigenous peoples against museums and western scientists, primarily archaeologists and physical anthropologists.[43]

Who is an Alutiiq?

THERE ARE A NUMBER OF DIFFERENT, AND SOMETIMES conflicting, methods of identifying an Alutiiq, or any other indigenous person, for that matter. For some, biology and physical appearance provide the clearest means of identification. Biology has its limitations, however. The "blood quantum" method became particularly prevalent during the land claims enrollment when a person had to prove one-quarter Native blood to be eligible. The problem, however, was that very few people could say with absolute certainty what their Native blood quantum was. There had been eight to ten generations of outside genes entering the Alutiiq population by the time of ANCSA. Few records of blood quantum had been maintained, and those that existed were unreliable.[44]

A related method is the "appearance test." Some people may say, "I can't define an Alutiiq but I know one when I see one." Yet, because of the high percentage of non-Native ancestry now carried in the Alutiiq gene pool, it is often unpredictable what any new off-

spring will look like. Within some families, siblings are very different in appearance.

During the twentieth century many Alutiiq people moved to the lower forty-eight states. Adoptions, job opportunities, and marriages to outsiders were the most common reasons.[45] The children, grandchildren and great-grandchildren of those who left often have little sense of Alutiiq identity even if they appear to be Native and are able to prove one-quarter blood quantum. In many instances they have never even visited Alaska and know little about it.

To many Alutiiq people, the most important way to define another Alutiiq is to witness how much that person actually lives the culture. Making one's home in a village, speaking the Alutiiq language, practicing subsistence, and belonging to the Russian Orthodox Church all add credibility to a person's Alutiiqness, regardless of appearance or blood quantum. These people are accepted by other Alutiit regardless of whether they were able to enroll under ANCSA.

The repatriation effort came at a time when the search for identity and cultural pride was underway on Kodiak Island. It became a symbol for tribal self-determination as tribes challenged the government's right to own the remains of Native ancestors. The October 1991 reburial of repatriated remains at Larsen Bay was an important step toward enhancing cultural pride on Kodiak Island and reaffirming the strength and resolve of the people against seemingly long odds.

84 Orthodox priests bless the reburial of human remains at Larsen Bay, 1991.

Courtesy of the Anchorage Daily News/Erik Hill.

As no one can feel what is going on in another person's head and heart it is difficult to define precisely who is an Alutiiq. Some people may feel themselves to be Alutiiq based on ancestry and an intangible connection to the culture even if many others don't accept them as Alutiiq.

In the end, however, Alutiiqness is usually based on kinship. It is not uncommon for the descendents of Alutiit who left Alaska to return seeking their Alutiiq roots. Usually knowing no one and armed with only the names of ancestors, they want to establish a connection. Their legitimacy usually comes down to how they answer one question—"Whom are you related to?" Once they have established that they are indeed descended from Alutiiq families they are accepted. Alutiit *know* who another Alutiiq is and decide regardless of blood quantum or any other criteria. A similar system seems to be in place in Greenland; as Greenlandic scholar Robert Petersen said, "it is generally known at a personal level who is a Greenlander and who is not. But it is difficult to explain exactly how this is determined."[46]

Conclusion—The Mosaic of Identity

The incredible complexity of contemporary Alutiiq identity presents problems in western society, where science demands that definitions be crisp and clear. Instead, identity is defined by a mosaic of historical events and overlapping criteria. Alutiiq identity has been profoundly molded by eight millennia of cultural development and 220 years of massive change brought on by contact with the outside world. Numerous attempts have been made by outsiders to define Alutiiq identity as they believe it should be defined. These definitions and labels have sometimes caused anger, resentment, and confusion as Alutiiq people have tried to fit themselves to these varying and contradictory definitions.

Through generations of gradual cultural change and rapid transitions brought on by colonization and traumatic events, the Alutiiq people have remained adaptive and resilient while maintaining a strong connection with their distant past. They maintain the ability to decide who they are despite outsiders' attempts to decide for them. The right to decide who they are and what they will be called is clearly the exercise of self-determination.[47]

Kinship

McKibben Jackinsky
Ninilchik Native Descendants

MAGGIE RUCKER'S VOICE flooded ME WITH CHILDHOOD memories, its strength in sharp contrast to her fragile seventy-year-old frame. Rich with the accent of Ninilchik's ancestors, it rolled across me like Cook Inlet surf on Ninilchik's gravel shores, bringing the scent of a coal fire, baking bread, salmon in the smokehouse. Like an eagle sailing on salty breezes, it lifted in the room.

On that afternoon, a roomful of Elders were discussing who could best represent Ninilchik at the second Alutiiq Elders and youth gathering in Kodiak. Maggie was volunteering to go. The theme of the conference was Alutiiq kinship ties. With sixteen brothers and sisters, she provided numerous links to other villages. Tiffany Stonecipher (age fifteen) and I would travel with her.

The uncovering of ties to other villages began on the flights to Kodiak as Maggie became reacquainted with people from her past. Memories ignited by names overheard, words spoken and songs sung. Arriving in Kodiak, Tiffany and I were quickly absorbed in the excitement as invisible lines connecting villages came into focus. Family names and points of origin were exchanged, frequently followed by surprised gasps of recognition. A family tapestry was being woven, the warp and weft drawing us together.

The opening ceremonies created an atmosphere in which strangers became family. With a flurry of dancing feet and blessings offered, the gathering began. Honor was given and bread broken. As the days passed, we made new friends, found family relations we'd never met, and got to know each other better. We logged miles on our rental car, eager to see country our ancestors called home. Hearing Alutiiq spoken, Maggie excitedly recognized words from her childhood. Tiffany constructed her family tree, the expanding information making it necessary to tape more and more pages together. We told Ninilchik's

history, and found our experience much like others, binding us even closer to those around us

On Sunday morning, we retraced our steps of a few days earlier. Only now Tiffany and I lugged suitcases filled with memories, addresses, and rolls of film. We quietly sipped coffee and smiled as now-familiar faces joined us waiting for flights home. Silently, we wondered how to take what we'd experienced back to Ninilchik. I thought of the way Maggie's voice affects me. Full of scents and sounds. Full of strength and power. Like a salmon coming home, I recognized its source. It comes from a riverbed of experiences over which flows the powerful current of generation upon generation. Birth . . . death . . . and all the shared experiences filling the years between. A strong, proud current.

Within a few short days we had acquired a better understanding of who we are. We are three women with Alutiiq ancestors, representing three different generations. We speak with one voice. And our voice is strong.

85 Maggie Rucker.
Courtesy of McKibben Jackinsky.

Chapter 3 notes

1   van Londen 1996.

2   Alutiiq Elders' Planning Conference for *Looking Both Ways*, 1997.

3   Partnow 1993.

4   Olga Vasili Rossing (my mother) received her name from her father, Vasili Shmakov, who adopted the name of his stepfather, Anton Rossing, a Norwegian ship captain.

5   I grew up during the 1950s while the Cold War was in full swing. National animosities against the Soviet Union did not make "Russian" a popular identity to claim.

6   Pullar 1992.

7   National Geographic Society (video) *Giant Bears of Kodiak Island*, 1994.

8   Black 1992.

9   Davydov 1977:107–111.

10 Davydov 1932–33:5.

11 Davydov 1932–33:6.

12 Alaska Federation of Natives 1989; Alaska Natives Commission 1994.

13 Alaska Natives Commission 1994 Vol. 1:3–81.

14 Davydov 1932–33:7.

15 Middleton-Moz and Fedrid 1987.

16 Middleton-Moz 1990.

17 Alutiiq Elders' Planning Conference for *Looking Both Ways*, 1997.

18 Shennan 1989:2.

19 Chugachmiut (video), *Sugpiat Lucit: The Ways of the Sugpiaq*, 1999.

20 Afognak was an Alutiiq village on Afognak Island that was destroyed by the 1964 tsunami. The residents moved to a new location on Kodiak Island and named it Port Lions.

21 Alutiiq Elders' Planning Conference for *Looking Both Ways*, 1997

22 Kaguyak was an Alutiiq village on the south end of Kodiak Island that was destroyed in the 1964 tsunami. The residents relocated to Akhiok, Old Harbor, and Kodiak.

23 Alutiiq Elders' Planning Conference for *Looking Both Ways*, 1997.

24 Alutiiq Elders' Planning Conference for *Looking Both Ways*, 1997.

25 *Kodiak Mirror*. January 22, 1954, page 1.

26 The ANCSA cash settlement amounted to about three dollars an acre for lands relinquished.

27 The Alaska Native regional corporations representing Alutiiq villages are Chugach Alaska Corporation (Prince William Sound and lower Kenai Peninsula), Cook Inlet Region, Inc. (central Kenai Peninsula/Cook Inlet), Bristol Bay Native Corporation (Alaska Peninsula), and Koniag, Inc. (Kodiak Island).

28 To be eligible for enrollment under ANCSA, a person must have been living on December 19, 1971, and be able to prove one quarter degree Native blood. People born after that date could only be enrolled through acquisition of corporation shares, usually through wills on the death of an original shareholder.

29 Two particularly contentious components of ANCSA were those that would make all Native-owned land taxable and all stock saleable on the open market twenty years after its passage. Amendments to the Act in 1988 corrected these shortcomings but in the meantime it was common for many Alaska Natives to say there would be "no more Natives after 1991," somehow believing that if the land was lost for unpaid taxes and Natives sold their shares of stock in the Native corporations because of needed income then Native status would be eliminated.

30 The Bristol Bay Native Corporation represents mostly Yup'ik villages and Cook Inlet Region, Inc., represents the Dena'ina Athabascan communities of Cook Inlet as well as the multicultural city of Anchorage.

31 Leisnoi, Inc., is the ANCSA village corporation formed for the village of Woody Island near Kodiak. Quoted from the Alutiiq Elders' Planning Conference for *Looking Both Ways*, 1997.

32 Pullar 1996.

33 Parfit 1981.

34 Alutiiq Elders' Planning Conference for *Looking Both Ways*, 1997.

35 Alaska Native Review Commission 1984.

36 Lantis 1973:116.

37 Dall 1878.

38 Bray and Killion 1994.

39 Hrdlička 1930:76.

40 Pullar 1994:20.

41 Alutiiq Elders' Planning Conference for *Looking Both Ways*, 1997.

42 Alutiiq Elders' Planning Conference for *Looking Both Ways*, 1997.

43 The story of the Larsen Bay repatriation is told from multiple perspectives in *Reckoning with the Dead: The Larsen Bay Repatriation and the Smithsonian Institution* (Bray and Killion 1994).

44 U.S. Bureau of Indian Affairs annual "censuses" of Alutiiq villages in the 1930s and 1940s commonly listed blood quantums differently from year to year for the same people.

45 The U.S. government policy of relocation during the 1950s and 60s also took many Alaska Natives away from Alaska to urban centers in the Lower 48 for job training and attempted assimilation.

46 Peterson 1985:295.

47 Dybbroe 1996:40.

4
CUMMILLALLRET—ANCESTORS

Amy F. Steffian

THROUGHOUT THIS CATALOG, AUTHORS BLEND information from a diversity of sources to tell the story of the Alutiiq people. From contemporary voices to historic narratives, and from archaeological data to museum collections, each source provides a distinctive view of Alutiiq culture and heritage. This chapter explores how both Alutiiq people and those who have studied their heritage perceive events that are beyond the reach of living memory and recorded history. It elaborates on the theme of Alutiiq origins introduced in chapter 2 and examines ancient cultural connections through the legacy of traditional myths and stories. It summarizes archaeological interpretations of Alutiiq history and illustrates how new perspectives on the past are emerging through research partnerships.

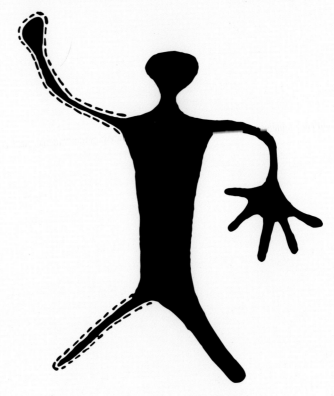

86 Archaeological excavations at the Malina Creek village site on Afognak Island in the Kodiak archipelago. Layers of seashells and animal bones—the remains of meals consumed by the inhabitants—are visible. The lowest levels at Malina Creek are 5000 years old.

Photograph by Richard Knecht, 1993.

87 Rock painting of human figure, Bear Island, Kachemak Bay. The date is unknown.

From de Laguna 1975, Plate 65.

Time and Tradition

EVERY SOCIETY HAS A CONCEPT OF TIME, A WAY OF thinking about the past that orders the universe and ties people together. Westerners tend to think of time as linear—tracking the evolution of species, charting the progress of industry, and following family histories from one generation to the next. Gordon Pullar suggests that time is circular and more fluid for the Alutiit.[1] From this perspective, the past is part of the present and events from distant times continue to inform daily life and shape the future. Ancestors remain a central part of contemporary society through their connections to families and through the stories, legends, songs, dances, artwork, and artifacts they have bestowed to the circle of time.

Alutiiq stories and legends (*quliyanguat*) are links to ancestors and past events—a hunter's trip to a distant shore, a fierce storm, or a battle waged for revenge. As this catalog illustrates, oral narrative remains an important way of sharing history, values and cultural meanings. Through stories, Elders provide younger generations with a sense of heritage and connection to previous generations.

Myths *(unigkuat)* are pathways to the beginning of time, explaining the universe and its mystical events. Alutiiq legends tell of the origin of people, the formation of the heavens, the propagation of animals, and the settlement of the Alutiiq homeland.

> A raven, he said, brought the light from heaven, while a bladder descended at the same time, in which a man and a woman were enclosed. At first this pair of human beings enlarged their dungeon by blowing, and afterward by stretching their hands and feet; and it was thus mountains were constructed. The man, by scattering the hair of his head on the mountains, created trees and forests, in which wild beasts sprang up and increased; while the woman, by making water, produced seas, and by spitting into ditches and holes formed rivers and lakes. The woman, pulling out one of her teeth, gave it to the man, who made a knife of it; and, cutting trees with the knife, threw the chips into the river, which were changed into fish of different kinds.

> —Recorded by Iu. Lisianskii, May 1805, Kodiak Island[2]

88 Telling stories at the 1997 Alutiiq Elders Planning Conference for *Looking Both Ways*. Left to right: Ignatius Kosbruk, Ed Gregorieff, George Inga, Sr., and Sven Haakanson, Sr.
Photograph by Maria Williams, Arctic Studies Center.

89 Portrait carving

Uyak site, Kodiak Island, A.D. 1–1100
National Museum of Natural History, Smithsonian Institution
(NMNH 363739) Height 21 cm

This Alutiiq creation myth shares many elements with Yup'ik and Inupiaq origin tales. The formation of waterways by urination and the creation of fish from wood chips are common themes, but the act of pushing up the mountains with hands and feet is uniquely Alutiiq.[3]

Another story recorded by Lisianskii tells how Alutiiq people descended from a union between a Native woman and a dog. "Dog husband" legends occur in Alaska, Canada, and Greenland, although the place names vary to fit each homeland.[4] These mythological similarities suggest that coastal peoples across the North American arctic preserve elements of a shared ancestral culture. The Lisianskii story also indicates that Alutiiq forebears migrated to the Gulf of Alaska from the Alaska mainland to the north:

> To the northward of the peninsula of Alaska [the Alaska Peninsula] lived a *toyon* [chief], whose daughter cohabited with a male of the canine species, by whom she had five children, three males and two females. The *toyon* being displeased with this degenerate conduct of his daughter, took an opportunity, in the absence of her lover, of banishing her to an island in the neighborhood. The lover, coming home, and finding none of his family, grieved for a long time: at last, discovering the place of their exile, he swam towards it, and was drowned on the way. The whelps in the meantime were grown up, and the mother had acquainted them with the cause of their banishment; which exasperated them so much against their grandfather, that when he came to see them they tore him to pieces. The mother, on the melancholy event, resolved in return [to go back to] her native place, and gave free leave to her offspring to go wherever they chose. In consequence of this permission, some went northward; while others, passing the peninsula of Alaska, took a southerly course, and arrived at the island of Cadiak [Kodiak], where they increased and multiplied, and were the founders of the present population.
>
> —Recorded by Iu. Lisianskii, May 1805, Kodiak Island[5]

Russian-American Company administrator Ferdinand von Wrangell reported a similar origin tale among the Chugach of Prince William Sound in 1839: "According to tradition they came from the north and their fellow countrymen may still be met along the coastline which stretches from Bristol Bay to Bering Strait."[6]

Alutiiq myths also look to the south and east, revealing ties to the Indian peoples of southeastern Alaska. Information gathered by French linguist and collector

Alphonse Pinart provides an Alutiiq perspective on cultural connections with the Tlingit. [7]

When the Koniagmiut [Kodiak Alutiit] came to establish themselves on the archipelago, they at first lived only on the part of Kodiak lying along Shelikof Strait (which according to their tradition was no longer than a long stream); they lived in this area for a long time without suspecting that the northern part of the island was occupied by Koloch [Tlingit] tribe. Little by little, as they became more numerous and wished to expand their familiarity with the other parts of the island, they encountered the Koloch. From that moment wars ensued; the Koniagmiut were vanquished and the Koloch proposed peace, on the condition that the chief or leaders of the village would be chosen among them, thus forming in the end a kind of hereditary nobility, the chief passing on his power to his son or to other members of his family. It is reasonable to suppose that under such conditions the blood of the two races came to be mixed; but that which would have had the strongest influence is that of the Eskimo, because we see that by the end of a certain period of time they had grown to outnumber their conquerors and succeeded in driving them from the archipelago altogether. Despite the fact that they had driven away the Koloch, the retained the system established among them of hereditary chiefs."

Recorded by Alphonse Pinart, 1873,
Kodiak Island[8]

These accounts of Alutiiq interaction with neighboring peoples of the Gulf of Alaska and Bering Sea, passed down by many generations, are supported by archaeological evidence. Cross-cultural similarities in technology, subsistence, social organization, art, and ceremony demonstrate long-term connections with the Unangan, Inuit (Eskimo), and Tlingit culture areas.

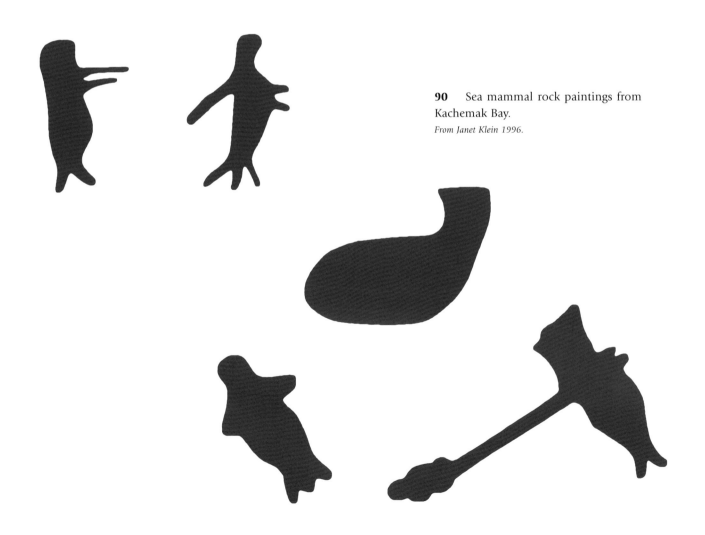

90 Sea mammal rock paintings from Kachemak Bay.
From Janet Klein 1996.

Deep History: An Archaeological Perspective

ARCHAEOLOGISTS HAVE LOCATED MORE THAN 3,000 SITES in the Alutiiq homeland.[9] These include villages that dot the coast, streamside camps, burial caves in secluded mountain settings, stone weirs built to trap fish, images pecked and painted on cliff faces, ridgetop cairns, stone quarries, and even ancient trails. Accumulations of cultural material at many of these sites have resisted decay in the region's persistently cool, wet environment. In addition to the stone tools commonly found in ancient settlements, many of Alaska's coastal sites contain shell, bone, antler, and ivory objects. A rare few hold spectacular assemblages of wood and fiber artifacts. Coastal settlements are also rich with architectural features, including houses, tent rings, hearths, clay-lined storage pits and slate boxes. This well-preserved archaeological record documents thousands of years of continual settlement and chronicles the adaptation of Native societies to the region's productive marine environment.

Archaeologists assign cultural materials from the Gulf of Alaska to a sequence of traditions, each reflecting a different way of life. Although there are many similarities in archaeological materials across the region, there is no single cultural sequence used to describe all areas. This reflects differences in local economy as well as interaction with different neighbors. For example, the Chugach Alutiit of Prince William Sound live in a forested environment, traditionally hunted mountain goats, and traded with their Athabaskan and Tlingit neighbors. In contrast, Alaska Peninsula Alutiit inhabit a tundra-dominated landscape, hunt caribou, and interact with their Yup'ik neighbors. Differences in economy and trade relationships resulted in the use of different tools and raw materials, and thus geographic variation in the objects found by archaeologists.

The variety of archaeological culture names also reflects the history of research. Surveys and excavations have been conducted unevenly across the Alutiiq region and each area has been studied by a different group of archaeologists. Kachemak Bay and the Kodiak Archipelago have been extensively investigated, but the Pacific coast of the Alaska Peninsula, the outer Kenai Peninsula, and Prince William Sound have received less intensive study. This situation has sometimes made interregional comparisons difficult and focused attention on local developments rather than wider trends.

First Arrivals—The Paleoarctic Period (8000–5500 B.C.)

Settlement of Alaska's gulf coast began at least 10,000 years ago, as glaciers of the last ice age (the Pleistocene) melted, sea level rose, and plant and animal communities flourished in warming coastal environments. Based on the proximity of the North American and Eurasian continents at Bering Strait and on shared technological traits, archaeologists believe that these first coastal Alaskans traced their ancestry to Upper Paleolithic hunters of eastern Siberia and Japan. Ancient Asian craftsmen chipped tiny stone blades, known as microblades, from nodules of chert. These thin, parallel-sided flakes of stone were set into the edges of slender bone points to form sharp-sided lances and arrowpoints.

Sites with blade-based technologies in coastal settings are rare, but they have been found from the Aleutian Islands to southeastern Alaska. The oldest known settlement on the gulf coast is Ground Hog Bay 2 in southeast Alaska's Icy Strait, near Glacier Bay. This site was inhabited roughly 10,000 years ago.[10] At On-Your-Knees Cave, a site on Prince of Wales Island, archaeologists uncovered a barbed harpoon for sea mammal hunting and the skeletal remains of a man who lived more than 9200 years ago. Chemical studies of the man's remains, conducted with permission of the local Tlingit tribal council, revealed that his diet was composed almost entirely of marine foods.[11]

Archaeologists assign these very early materials to the "Paleoarctic" era, with dates from about 10,000 to 7500

Radiocarbon Years B.P.	Glacial Advances			Alaska Pen. North Coast/ Interior	Alaska Pen. Pacific Coast	Kodiak Archipelago	Lower Cook Inlet (Kachemak Bay)	Outer Kenai Coast	Prince Wm. Sound
	Alaska[1] Pen.	Kenai[2] Coast	Prince[3] Wm. Sound						
0	Minor undated advances	LIA	LIA	B. R. Bluffs		Koniag	Dena'ina	Chugach (provisional)	Chugach
				B. R. Camp	Mound				
1000				B. R. Falls	Beach	Three Saints	Yukon I. Bluff Site	SEL-188 Site	Palugvik
				B. R. Weir	Cottonwood		Kachemak III		
2000				Smelt Creek			Kachemak Sub-III		
						Old Kiavik	Kachemak II		
3000				Brooks River Gravels	Takli Birch		Kachemak I		Uqciuvit
4000				Brooks River Strand		Ocean Bay II	Ocean Bay II	No known sites	
5000		HYPSITHERMAL			Takli Alder				
6000						Ocean Bay I			
7000									
8000				Koggiung	PALEOARCTIC (presumed across entire region)				
9000				Ugashik Narrows Site					
10,000			Remnant ice						
11,000									

1. Detterman 1986; Pinney and Beget 1991
2. Wiles and Calkin 1990
3. Heusser 1983

91 Archaeological cultures of the Alutiiq region. "LIA" is the abbreviation for Little Ice Age. Earlier periods of colder climate when glaciers grew are indicated. During the Hypsithermal period temperatures were warmer than at present.

From Crowell and Mann 1998.

years ago (8000–5500 B.C.). Although a few site locations provide evidence of early coastal life, the Paleoarctic tradition is best known from interior regions, including upland areas of the Alaska Peninsula.[12] The oldest evidence of occupation on the peninsula comes from the upper Ugashik River drainage, where archaeologists have found stone implements up to 9000 years old.[13] These are presumed to be the tools of ancient caribou hunters. Across interior Alaska, people of the Paleoarctic pursued caribou, bison, and other land mammals, and fished in fresh water lakes and streams.

Did these interior residents colonize the coast? Data from some early coastal sites of southern Alaska suggest intermittent use of shoreline environments by people with a land-based subsistence economy, although other evidence points to colonization by fully developed maritime societies.[14] Archaeologists have considered the possibility that Northeast Asian settlers worked their way into Alaska by following the southern shoreline of the Bering Land Bridge.[15] It must be kept in mind that Alaska's coastal geography is quite different today than at the end of the Pleistocene, when large sections of the continental shelf were exposed by lowered sea levels and the two continents were connected by dry land. The sea began to rise as the climate warmed and glaciers melted, increasing quite rapidly until 8000 years ago and at a

92   Columbia Glacier, Prince William Sound

"'Let's go see what that black thing is sticking out of the ice.' So the hunters paddled closer and closer to see what it was. Within a short distance, they could see mountain tops emerging from the retreating ice. Thus these ocean travelers settled along the ice-free shores of Prince William Sound."

—Legend told to John F. C. Johnson
by Prince William Sound Elder John Kalashnikoff

The Gulf of Alaska coast was first settled about 8000 B.C., by descendants of Native Siberians who had crossed to Alaska almost 2000 years earlier. The climate was warmer than present, as Ice Age glaciers withdrew.
Photograph Courtesy USDA Forest Service, Chugach National Forest.

slower pace ever since.[16] Given the changing relationship between land and sea, many of the earliest coastal settlements are probably under water and therefore inaccessible for study.

Early Coastal Life (5500–1500 B.C.)

Coastal archaeological sites dating to between 7500 and 3500 years ago are relatively numerous. Settlements from the earlier part of this time range are assigned to the Ocean Bay I phase on Kodiak Island and to a closely related variant on the Pacific coast of the Alaska Penin-

sula known as Takli Birch.[17] Both are named for the geographic areas where early discoveries were made—Ocean Bay on Sitkalidak Island in the Kodiak archipelago, and Takli Island in Amalik Bay on the Alaska Peninsula. Later phases on Kodiak and the Alaska Peninsula are called Ocean Bay II and Takli Alder, respectively, distinguished from earlier sites by changes in housing and subsistence technologies.

The oldest known settlements in Prince William Sound and on the Kenai Peninsula are about 4500 years old, and are included in the Ocean Bay II and Uqciuvit phases respectively. The absence of earlier sites in both

Ocean Bay— The Luck of Science

Donald W. Clark

IN 1961 THE ALEUT-KONYAG PROJECT AT THE UNIVERSITY of Wisconsin began a series of excavations in the Kodiak islands. Thirty years earlier Aleš Hrdlička of the Smithsonian Institution had initiated what was then the largest dig in Alaska, at Larsen Bay on Kodiak.[18] Only now have we discovered the magnitude of Hrdlička's "big new story." These are my personal recollections of how the span of ancient history on Kodiak, as adumbrated by Hrdlička, was doubled through discovery of the Ocean Bay culture in 1963.

Hrdlička's remark "learned definitely of a whaling site on the south shore [of Sitkalidak Island]...in Ocean Bay"[19] was on my mind before I had ever seen Sitkalidak. Then, in 1961, from the peaks behind Rolling Bay I saw Ocean Bay and the surf line sweeping for miles into the distance. I had to go there. The opportunity came two years later. When I reached the McCord Ranch at Port Hobron during a site survey, I learned that the ranchers had cut a dirt road across the island to Ocean Bay. After supper, my assistant and I put on our packs and headed across. Just before the road reached the Pacific side it cut through a thick soil deposit. There, in the evening light, we saw charcoal streaks and found a flaked spear point deep in the orange and brown soil. Then we found more

artifacts, some flaked, some fragments of ground slate spears. Part of the slate was unfinished and showed traces of fashioning by sawing and scraping. These artifacts were unlike ones found previously on Kodiak, and had to be older. Later we learned how old: 4000 years for late Ocean Bay slate work and up to 7000 years for flaked chert artifacts.

Discovering the site was only the beginning. The crew, then digging at Kiavak, was willing to stay extra days at the end of the season while stoically enduring the torrential rains that started falling as we filled in the trenches at Kiavak and broke camp. We set off in the *Kiska* for Old Harbor on August 22. We had exhausted our supplies and were stopping there for foodstuffs. I had determined that the Old Harbor store was open, but neglected to ask if they sold food. They didn't. That nearly ended our expedition. Seeing our plight, the boat operator took us to Mrs. Christiansen and the project was rescued with supplies from her winter shipment from Shearwater. But the torrential rains did not forget us. Without the help of the ranch staff and Ned Roberts, who got us in and out of the site through seas of mud with a chained-up six-wheel-drive truck, operations would have been onerous. The first Ocean Bay excavations were on a small scale, but the artifacts and technology were so distinctive that we were able to recognize two phases of a new cultural tradition.

Ocean Bay remained poorly known although similar material was soon found on the Alaska Peninsula. So in 1971 I went to Ocean Bay culture sites that we had discovered at the mouth of the Afognak River in 1964. This was a joint project by the Alaska Methodist University, places may reflect the loss of cultural deposits due to local geological processes including sinking shorelines and the readvance of glaciers rather than a true absence of settlement.[20] Archaeologists believe that Kachemak Bay at the tip of the Kenai Peninsula was available for settlement as early as 10,000 years ago,[21] and Prince William Sound by about 9000 years ago.[22]

Unlike Paleoarctic times, when the coast may have been visited only sporadically by inland hunting and gathering peoples, Ocean Bay and Takli sites give ample evidence of a true adaptation to hunting and fishing on the ocean, including possession of skin boats. Occupants

of Tanginak Spring, Zaimka Mound, and other early sites in the Kodiak archipelago–all more than 7000 years old—could only have arrived by boat.[23] Colonization of much of the rest of the Alutiiq homeland would have also required crossing substantial bodies of water in well-designed watercraft.

The early Holocene climate was warmer and drier than at present and lightweight, portable skin tents appear to have been the shelter of choice. At old camp sites, archaeologists find rock rings that held down the edges of the tent covers, small post holes left by tent frames, and thin layers of occupation debris. Such camps seem to

under William Workman, and the Canadian Museum of Man. The crew left Kodiak on a sunny May 5 on a conservatively powered seiner, thus dubbed "silver slug." But the happy face of the sun soon frowned, remembering that our lot was to be drenched. The rain arrived in the evening, followed by a full blizzard. That was not the first time it snowed on us at Afognak that spring, and the storm tides rose to drive us off the shore, still much depressed after 1964, into the snow banks in the woods. We recovered a lot of stone artifacts, though.

93 Ocean Bay, Sitkalidak Island, 1963. The surf-pounded beaches and spectacular landscape of Ocean Bay provided the setting for the discovery of Kodiak's earliest cultural tradition. The lowlands behind the beach were once a protected inner bay that teamed with resources. Hunting and fishing parties camped on the surrounding hillsides, leaving evidence of their activities many thousands of years ago.

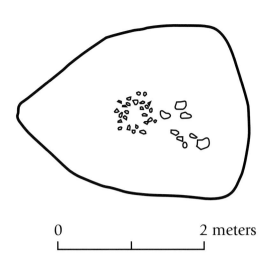

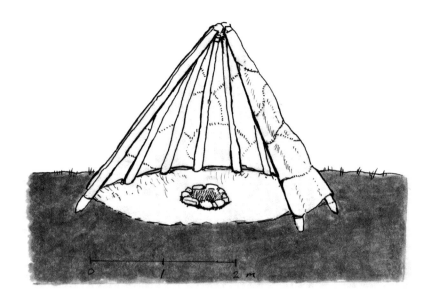

0   2 meters

94   Early period tent floor and reconstruction

Tent floor at Brooks River on the Alaska Peninsula (B. R. Strand phase, about 2500–1900 B.C.) and suggested reconstruction.

Archaeologists believe that early inhabitants of the Alaska Peninsula and Kodiak archipelago lived in skin tents. These structures are inferred from oval, circular, or tear-drop-shaped occupation floors with charcoal and red ocher stains, food bone, and artifacts. At the Blisky Site on Near Island in the Kodiak area, tent floors with simple hearths were surrounded by hunting tools (Steffian et al. 1997). Ground slate lances and chert projectile points suggest that the site was an Ocean Bay era hunting camp. Sea mammal hunters shaped and sharpened their tools between trips to nearby rookeries.

Drawing by Mark Matson, adapted from Dumond (1981:117).

95   Oil lamp

Zaimka Mound, Kodiak Island, ca. 5500 B.C.
Alutiiq Museum, Leisoni, Inc., Collection
(AM411:7700) Length 24 cm

Stone oil lamps shaped from sandstone and other rocks are one of the most ancient and enduring pieces of technology in the Alutiiq world. This lamp, among the earliest ever discovered, was found just 3 centimeters above glacial deposits at the bottom of Zaimka Mound.

have been occupied seasonally, although repeated visits were made. The dwellings were relatively small, between four and eight meters in diameter,[24] suggesting that households consisted of nuclear family groups. Parents and children of the household would have slept around the central stone hearth, and used oil lamps carved from sandstone for additional light and heat. Many sites contain layers of red ochre, a pigment ground from a naturally occurring iron oxide, as well as large stone mortars and grinding stones for ochre processing. Although the function of ochre is unknown, it often covers structure floors[25] and may have been used to tan hides for bedding or tent coverings.

Site locations, animal remains, and tools indicate that people of this era were skilled mariners who harvested the full range of marine resources. Camps occur in locales appropriate for both marine hunting and riverine

fishing,[26] and animal remains from early settlements include those of sea otters, small whales, seals, sea lions, and porpoises, in addition to auklets, murres, ducks, salmon, cod, halibut, a variety of shellfish, and even bears.[27]

Hunting on the open ocean required specialized tools and equipment. The earliest tool kits contain stone microblades similar to those made during Paleoarctic times. The tiny, parallel-sided flakes were set into the edges of slender bone points to make hunting spears or lances.[28] These tools were used along with a variety of bilaterally barbed bone harpoons and chipped stone points for sea mammal hunting, special points for bird hunting, and bone hooks for fishing. Significantly, evidence of marine hunting and fishing is coupled with evidence of fine sewing. Delicate bone needles from the Rice Ridge site suggest that residents fabricated waterproof gut

96   Microblade core, slotted point, and microblades

Rice Ridge site, Kodiak Island, about 4000 B.C.
Alutiiq Museum, Rice Collection
(core, 363-89-7-144-250) Height 3 cm
(slotted point, 363-89-3-77-236)

The earliest settlers in the Gulf of Alaska made extensive use of narrow, sharp-edged flakes of stone (microblades) that were struck from nodules of chert (microblade cores). Microblades were placed in rows along the edges of slotted bone spear heads or knives to make long, sharp edges. This technique was used widely throughout ancient Alaska and illustrates ancestral ties to the Upper Paleolithic hunters of eastern Asia, including Siberia and Japan.

97   Early prehistoric technologies

Needle, barbed harpoons, and leaf-shaped lance points
Rice Ridge site, Kodiak Island, 4000–2000 B.C.
Alutiiq Museum, Rice Collection and Afognak Native
    Corporation Collection
(needle, 363-89-3-39-211) Length 4 cm
(barbed harpoons: left, 363-90-106-16-102; right, 363-89-5-
    124-256) Longest 11 cm
(lance points: left, AM221:14; right, 363-89-7-90-219)
    Longest 11 cm

By Ocean Bay times, Gulf of Alaska residents were adept at harvesting resources from the sea. They used throwing boards to cast bone-tipped harpoons at sea mammals and killed wounded animals with chipped-stone lances. Delicate sewing needles suggests that waterproof gutskin clothing was available for protection against wind, rain, and sea spray.

98　Fish hooks

Rice Ridge site, Kodiak Island, 4000–2000 B.C.
Alutiiq Museum, Rice Collection
(large hook: 363-88-4-30-116 and 363-88-7-17-111)
　　Length 11.5 cm
(small hook: 363-88-4-66-148 and uncataloged) Length 4 cm

Early settlers in the Kodiak archipelago fished for cod, halibut, and other bottom fish with deepwater rigs. The hooks (shown here) were made by attaching a sharp bone barb to a curved shank. A hook was suspended from each end of a wooden bar, and a grooved stone weight was tied below the bar so that the hooks would float just above the sea floor. Deepsea fishing gear from the earliest sites is nearly identical to the gear in use at the time of Russian colonization.

clothing to protect boaters from rain and sea spray.[29] Similar clothing, an essential piece of a hunter's tool kit, has long been manufactured by Unangan and Inuit peoples across the Arctic.

In later centuries modern weather patterns began to dominate the annual meteorological cycle.[30] The weather became colder and wetter and people developed a new form of housing. They dug shallow pits and erected wooden frames inside, then covered the frames with sod blocks to create warm, weather-resistant homes. Although the size and configuration of these houses changed over time, semisubterranean structures became the primary form of dwelling and were used well into the historic period.

In addition to these more permanent houses, people continued to use temporary shelters and to move between harvesting areas. At the Blisky site on Near Island in the Kodiak group, a pair of stone tent rings is associated with hunting tools and the remains of sea mammals and fish.[31] At Pedro Bay on the shore of the Alaska Peninsula's Illiamna Lake, a collection of hunting tools and mammal bones suggests a seasonal caribou hunting camp occupied temporarily by coastal peoples.[32]

Artifacts of this era also occur in an estuary setting at the Beluga Point site in Upper Cook Inlet.[33]

Another important technological change was the proliferation of ground slate tools. Although a small number ground slate items are present in earlier assemblages,[34] it was not until about 2500 B.C. that slate grinding became widespread.[35] From thin leaves of slate, people formed long slender killing lances and broad-bladed butchering tools known as flensing knives. In the Kodiak archipelago and on the Alaska Peninsula, they employed a distinctive "saw and snap" technique to create these tools. Using a sharp-edge boulder flake, artisans carved parallel grooves into a piece of raw slate and then snapped along the grooves to produce a long, linear preform. They abraded this preform with a harder rock to form a lance and sharpen its edges. These ground slate lances replaced the large chipped stone projectiles that were formerly used, although people continued to chip a variety of smaller points, many of which may have been inset into the tips of bone harpoons.

Slate grinding spread rapidly among the societies of the Gulf of Alaska coast, appearing in cultural deposits from southeast Alaska to the Aleutian Islands by about

99 Ground slate lances

Ride Ridge Site
Alutiiq Museum, Rice Collection

Slate grinding technology may have its origins in the Alutiiq region, where the first slate hunting tools are more than 6000 years old. By about 4500 years ago, techniques for crafting long, sharp-edge bayonets and double-edged butchering knives had been perfected. Similar tools begin appearing in adjacent regions about 4000 years ago. At Hidden Falls, a site on Baranof Island in southeast Alaska (S. Davis 1989), ground slate points 4600 to 3200 years old are similar to those found on the Alaska Peninsula and Kodiak, suggesting that the technology spread from the west.

Photograph by Patrick Saltonstall.

2500 B.C. However, this technology was not carried north at this time to the western Alaska Peninsula or the Bering Sea coast, where a very distinctive culture known as the Arctic Small Tool tradition (ASTt, ca. 2500–1000 B.C.) was flourishing.[36] This suggests that Gulf of Alaska coast societies were developing fairly independently of their northern neighbors, although some ASTt tool forms do appear in assemblages from the Pacific Coast of the Alaska Peninsula,[37] Kachemak Bay,[38] and the Kodiak archipelago.[39]

Coastal Villages of the Middle Era (1500 B.C.–A.D. 1100)

Sites dating to the 1300 year period between 1800 and 500 B.C. are scarce, and some archaeologists believe that the region was only sparsely populated during these centuries.[40] Part of the reason may have been the onset of the Neoglacial (ca. 3200 years ago), a period of colder, wetter weather.[41] In Prince William Sound, a gap in the occupation of the Uqciuvit site corresponds closely with the first major glacial advance related to this climatic period, and researchers suggest that ice drove residents to outer regions of the sound.[42] Others believe that sites have been lost to changes in sea levels or have been poorly sampled.[43] Recent studies of settlements in the Chiniak Bay region of Kodiak Island demonstrate that sites of this period may simply be harder to recognize.[44] Known deposits display very poor organic preservation, are well buried with few surface features, and are located away from the modern shoreline on more ancient coastal features.

Sites from the middle era of Alutiiq cultural history span the period between about 1500 B.C. and A.D. 1100, and are named for Kachemak Bay where they were first found.[45] Kachemak era sites are also well known from the Kodiak archipelago, and culturally related materials are assigned to the Palugvik phase in Prince William Sound and the Takli Cottonwood and Kukak Beach phases on the Alaska Peninsula.[46] These archaeological cultures are not strictly like Kachemak, although they include many tools in common. Also present, however, are unique objects that reflect both distinct adaptations and connections with adjacent culture areas. For example, Cottonwood and Beach phase sites include pottery and chipped stone implements suggesting ties with culturally distinct groups in the peninsula's interior.[47]

Were Kachemak and related people descended directly from earlier inhabitants of the region? The lack of archaeological samples from the early centuries of the middle period has made this question difficult to answer. However, data from the Kodiak archipelago point to an ancestral connection, and archaeologists note continuities in both technology and lifestyle across the transition.[48] In Kodiak's Chiniak Bay, for example, sites with deposits from both periods show similarities in activities and the use of raw materials. People were making and employing many of the same tools, using the landscape in similar ways, and even trading in a similar manner. On the other hand, some major social and economic changes were underway.

For one thing, the middle period is characterized by the development of larger coastal villages, composed of many single-roomed sod houses. The houses were square or rectangular with a central stone-lined hearth. Around these hearths people built clay-lined pits for food preparation—oil rendering, butchering, stone boiling, and fermentation of fish and meat.[49] Many houses also had raised sitting and sleeping platforms and entrance tunnels to trap cold air. Like dwellings of Ocean Bay times, these houses were small (twenty-five to thirty-six square meters) and probably designed for nuclear families.[50] However, the number of structures at some sites is quite large. Villages with more than thirty houses are not uncommon, although it is not clear how many structures would have been occupied at one time.[51]

Increases in site size are accompanied with increases in the number of sites, a trend that seems to reflect substantial growth in the Native population. For the first

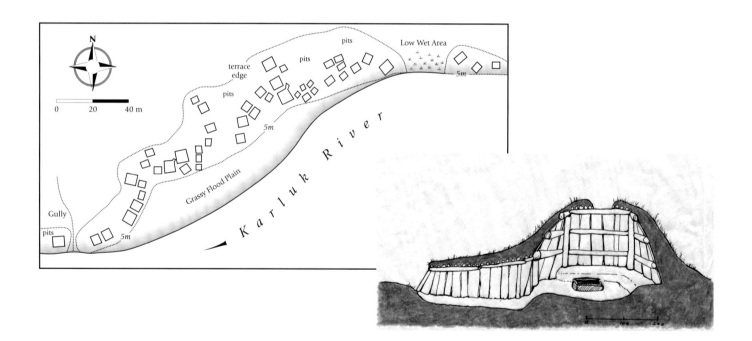

100 Kachemak Era Village on the Karluk River

Clusters of rectangular depressions, 4 to 5 meters across, are the remains of houses at a middle prehistoric village. Each house was probably home to a single family.

Illustration by Amy Steffian.

101 Late Kachemak house floor and reconstruction

Uyak site (A.D. 600–1100), Kodiak Island.

Kachemak dwellings had walls made of sod that were supported by wooden posts and planks. There were earthen benches for sitting and sleeping. A stone-lined fireplace provided heat, surrounded by clay pits for holding and cooking food. Some late Kachemak houses like this one had entrance tunnels, dug below the level of the house floor which kept out cold air.

Illustration by Mark Matson, adapted from Steffian 1992b.

Back To Uyak

Amy F. Steffian
Curator and Deputy Director, Alutiiq Museum

SMITHSONIAN PHYSICAL ANTHROPOLOGIST Aleš Hrdlička died in 1943, nineteen years before I was born. Yet his work has dramatically shaped contemporary Alutiiq archaeology and my own career. Hrdlička's interest in the origins of Native Americans led him to Alaska in the 1930s, where he sought to understand biological relationships across the Bering Strait.[52] His primary intent was to collect Native skeletal remains though he recognized that archaeological data would help to corroborate his findings. Surveys and excavations produced many large collections, the most extensive from Kodiak's Uyak site. From 1931 to 1936 he removed an estimated 8501 cubic meters of this coastal shell midden,[53] collecting the skeletal remains of hundreds of individuals and recovering several thousand artifacts. The rich archaeological data from Uyak led to many controversies. Hrdlička's theories on population migrations set the stage for decades of debate over the origins of Alutiiq people, and his unorthodox excavation and collection methods created a legal battle that ultimately changed the practice of American archaeology.

As a graduate student at the University of Michigan, I signed on as a field assistant with the massive KANA—Bryn Mawr College Archaeological Project (1983–87) to investigate the deep history of Alutiiq societies (Knecht, this chapter). Three years of intensive field work led to a dissertation project restudying the Uyak site. Conveniently located in the village of Larsen Bay, the deposit offered the opportunity to explore Kachemak social and economic organization, involve local students in research, and live with modern amenities—a post office and hot showers. At the time, I was naively unaware that the village

was engaged in a heated debate with the Smithsonian Institution over the return of the human remains collected by Hrdlička from this very site, a battle they would ultimately win.[54] Many archaeologists would have argued that I was headed for the wrong place at a bad time.

But in 1987, the city of Larsen Bay gave permission for the project and I began a two-year study.[55] The Uyak site produced tremendous archaeological data. The well-preserved shell midden yielded a Kachemak village with numerous complete houses. We documented cooking features, entrance tunnels, and storage structures never seen before and recovered a wealth of artifacts highlighting the intensive trade, craft production, and artistic symbolism of the era. These data have significantly enriched the picture of Kodiak's Kachemak tradition, helping to illustrate the strong temporal continuities in Alutiiq culture and to dispel Hrdlička's migration theory.

But the archaeological discoveries at Uyak are only half the story. Our ability to do this work is of equal historic importance. To many, the Larsen Bay repatriation case is emblematic of the competing views of Native people and scientists. The tiny community's ability to prevail over the Smithsonian and bring Hrdlička's collection of Alutiiq ancestral remains home is now legendary. What few people realize is that this was neither a fight against archaeologists, nor a condemnation of museums. It was an issue of respect.[56] Alutiiq people were not opposed to archaeology, only to research imposed from outside, to disrespect for the past entrusted to their care. This is clearly evident in their support of my work. The funding, food, transportation, and warm hospitality extended to my crew during this frustrating time reflect a true commitment to collaborative heritage preservation. I was in precisely the right place at the right time.

This point was driven home again in 1995. Just days before the Native-governed Alutiiq Museum opened its doors, we received a call from Larsen Bay Mayor Frank Carlson. Would the museum care for the artifacts from Hrdlička's excavations returned by the Smithsonian? They had not been reburied, or even unpacked, but carefully stored to share with future generations. In an ironic and wonderful twist of fate, objects from Hrdlička's controversial collection became the first formal accession to the Alutiiq Museum.

102 Whale-tail spoon or gut scraper
Uyak site, Kodiak Island, A.D. 1–1100
National Museum of Natural History, Smithsonian Institution
(NMNH 377796) Length 15 cm

103 Walrus ivory portrait carving

Uyak site, Kodiak Island, A.D. 600–1000
National Museum of Natural History, Smithsonian Institution
(NMNH 365582) Height 8.5 cm

104 Middle prehistoric technologies

Left to right: barbed harpoon, toggling harpoon,
    slate point, net sinker
Uyak site, Kodiak Island, A.D. 600–1000
Old Karluk site, Kodiak Island, A.D. 600–1000
Alutiiq Museum–Larsen Bay Collection and
    Koniag, Inc., Collection

(harpoon, far left: UA88-78-2414) Length 10cm
(harpoon, middle left: UA88-78-1376) Length 6.5 cm
(point: UA88-78-2405) Length 7 cm
(net weight:UA85-209/5298) Length 4 cm

New technologies were developed in the middle period for
harvesting larger quantities of food. Nets made with wooden
floats and stone sinkers permitted the mass capture of salmon
and a new form of harpoon—the toggling harpoon—improved
a hunter's ability to capture sea mammals. This type of harpoon head turned sideways in its prey, decreasing the animal's
chance of escape.

time, the landscape seems to have been filled with settlements and people may not have been able to move their
communities in response to changes in the availability
of resources. People of the middle-period responded to
this reduced mobility in three important ways.

First, they began harvesting a broader range of resources from a broader range of environments.[57] Shellfish, used modestly during earlier times, occur in
enormous quantities in middle period sites. Clams,
mussels, urchins, cockles, chitons, whelks, and limpets
are ubiquitous finds in garbage deposits. Similarly, village sites of this era occur more frequently along the
courses of major rivers, on inland lakes, and in outer
coastal settings. In interior regions of the Kenai Peninsula, people of the middle prehistoric era even established year-round settlements along major rivers, relying
on terrestrial resources for the bulk of their subsistence
needs.[58] In contrast, coastal areas show a true dichotomy
between summer and winter settlements. Large winter
villages were centrally located in outer bays to provide
access to sea mammals, marine fish, and birds, while
smaller summer salmon camps, perhaps used by extended families, occur at the mouths and along the mar-
gins of large fresh water streams, particularly those
draining bay heads or lakes.

Second, people of this era developed technologies for
extracting greater quantities of food and raw materials
from existing sources. They made nets to harvest salmon
in bulk and produced slate ulus and storage structures

105 Whale-tale pin

Uyak site, Kodiak Island, A.D. 600–1000
Alutiiq Museum, Larsen Bay Collection
(UA88-78-3525) Length 12.5 cm

Decorative ivory carvings are a hallmark of the Kachemak tradition, an era when large quantities of walrus ivory and other trade goods flowed across the Alutiiq region. This ivory pin depicts a whale's tale, a common motif in Late Kachemak art.

to process and care for these larger catches. They adopted a more efficient type of small harpoon—the toggling harpoon—possibly to increase the efficiency of seal hunting. The success of these endeavors is preserved in massive accumulations of middens (trash piles) that are rich in fish, bird, and mammal remains.

People also began to trade extensively with their neighbors—both locally and in adjacent regions. In the Kodiak archipelago, sites of this period contain large quantities of basalt, caribou antler, walrus ivory, bituminous coal, pumice, exotic chert, and limestone obtained through trade with the Alaska mainland.[59] Trade was in both finished items and raw materials, and the volume of exchange was enormous. Nonlocal materials such as antler were used to produce even the most basic tools, illustrating the ease with which people obtained goods from distant sources. Such trade networks moved resources to people rather than people to resources, creating ties to different ecological settings that could be called on in times of need. In a sense, these nonlocal materials were a form of currency. They were small, portable, valuables that could be readily exchanged as needed.

Changes in economic life correspond with changes in the social and spiritual realms of middle-period societies. Kachemak sites are well known for their jewelry and small pieces of decorative art. The labret, a decorative plug worn below the lower lip, appears for the first time, as do beads, nose pins, pendants, and intricate ivory

106 Spirit face carving

Uyak site, Kodiak Island, A.D. 1–1100
National Museum of Natural History, Smithsonian Institution
(NMNH 395188) Length 7.5 cm

Carvings from the middle era depict animals, people, and supernatural beings. This small ivory piece shows one, possibly two, spirit-like faces.

115

107 Caribou hoof carving

Uyak site, Kodiak Island, A.D. 1–1100
National Museum of Natural History, Smithsonian Institution
(NMNH 377893) Length 6 cm

This carving represents a caribou's split hoof and dew claws. Caribou are not indigenous to the Kodiak archipelago, where the carving was found, though caribou antler was a common trade item during the middle prehistoric period. Antler was prized for its density and resilience. It was used to make many common objects, from harpoon points to wedges for splitting wood and bone.

108 Coal labret (lip ornament) and nose ring

Uyak and Old Karluk sites, Kodiak Island, A.D. 1–1100
Alutiiq Museum, Larsen Bay Collection and Koniag, Inc.,
    Collection
(labret, left: UA88-78-2658) Length 3 cm
(nose ring, right: UA85-209/5348) Width 1.3 cm

Pieces of bituminous coal were fashioned into jewelry and small carvings. The raw material was chipped to a rough shape, ground, then polished to a lustrous finish. Although coal occurs in many regions of the Alutiiq homeland, only certain varieties were suitable for working. Studies of coal from Kodiak sites suggest that artisans obtained their material from the Alaska Peninsula.

109 Beads

Uyak and Old Karluk sites, Kodiak Island, A.D. 1–1100
Alutiiq Museum, Koniag, Inc., Collection and Larsen Bay
    Collection
(left to right: UA85.193:4507, length 3.5cm;
    AM193.87:8854; AM14.193:6; UA88-78-3289)

Before the introduction of glass beads, the Alutiit decorated clothing and created jewelry with beads carved from coal, shell, amber, slate, bone, and ivory.

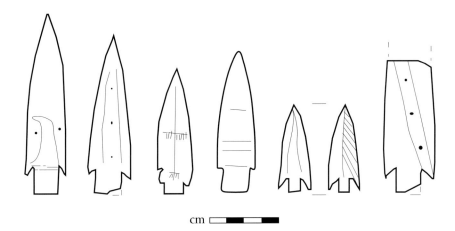

cm

110 Incised slate lances

Designs incised on slate lances may be the marks of individual hunters. They occur in a wide variety of types: people, animals, geometric patterns, and designs that mimic motifs from masks.

Adapted from Clark 1970a.

carvings. The use of jewelry may reflect a growing interest in social status. Although archaeological data do not indicate the presence of the distinct social classes recorded in the historic era, they do suggest a growing concern with social identity, particularly family affiliation.

Evidence of increasing family loyalty may be preserved in labret styles.[60] Sites of this era typically contain sets of discrete labret styles, each of which may have been worn by a different social group, perhaps an extended family or clan (see chapter 2 of this volume for a description of ethnographically recorded practices). Interestingly, regional differences in labret styles correspond with trading patterns preserved in the distribution of nonlocal materials. People of the Kenai Peninsula and the northern Kodiak archipelago appear to have worn similar-style labrets and traded regularly, whereas people of the Pacific Coast of the Alaska Peninsula and of southern Kodiak were socially and economically linked. This suggests the presence of two broad social and economic spheres of interaction.

Family affiliation and territorial control were also symbolized through treatment of the dead. Middle-period societies are known for their elaborate burials. The dead were placed in pits around the village; some lined with wood or slate slabs. These graves were occasionally reopened to add additional people or to remove bones, possibly for ritual purposes.[61] Grave goods and elaborate treatment of individual skeletons are also recorded. At a site in Kachemak Bay, de Laguna found human crania with inset ivory eyes and one with an elaborate clay mask.[62] The use of crypts, presumably for related individuals, and the great reverence for the dead expressed in the treatment of human remains suggest the development of corporate groups—extended families that traced

their ancestry through a common line. These groups may have emerged to exert control over fishing and hunting spots in a more densely settled landscape. People of the middle period may have signaled their claims to hunting and fishing areas by burying their dead in traditionally used lands and by reminding others of those ties by incorporating ancestral remains into rituals.[63]

This increasing control of resources may also be indicated by the development of makers' marks. Hunters began to incise simple geometric designs on slate hunting lances. These appear to be ownership marks, easily recognized designs that tied specific hunters to their weaponry and their kills (fig. 110).

In addition to formal burials, sites of this period often contain human remains that have not been carefully buried or that show signs of trauma. These remains may belong to victims of violence, as they are treated quite differently from those found in purposeful burials.[64] Given the apparent increases in population size and long-distance trading, it seems likely that fighting increased as well. Strong family affiliations and increasing control of subsistence territories probably created both social and economic competition between communities. This idea is supported by the use of refuge sites at very

Alutiit on the Alaska Peninsula

Don Dumond
Professor Emeritus, University of Oregon

WHEN THE FIRST SUSTAINED ARCHAEOLOGICAL RESEARCH on the northern Alaska Peninsula was begun by the University of Oregon in the 1960s, we were surprised to find that the ancient culture of the Naknek River basin bore little relationship to that of Kodiak Island, but was essentially identical to cultures as far north as Bering Strait and beyond—and had been so for at least 4000 years.[69] And yet the closest relationship of the language of the Native Alutiiq people of the northern Gulf of Alaska was to that of the Yup'ik people of the southern Bering Sea, suggesting some connection between Kodiak and the Bering Sea.

Questions regarding this seeming conflict led us into a program of research on both sides of the Alaska Peninsula. The result was the realization that the Native people on the two sides of the peninsula had relatively little contact with each other before 2000 years ago, when clear signs of contact appeared and finally peaked after A.D. 1000, as the cultures on the two sides of the Aleutian Range became indistinguishable from one another. We interpreted this as probable evidence of a movement of people southeastward across the peninsula about 900 years ago, a movement that can explain why the Alutiiq language is more closely related to Yup'ik than to any other form of speech, including the Unangan language spoken in the Aleutian chain.[70]

But when Russian administrators and fur hunters arrived on the Gulf of Alaska, they named the inhabitants of Kodiak Island and the mainland coast of Shelikof Strait with the same term they had applied to people of the Aleutian Islands, *Aleuty* or Aleuts—even though they were aware of linguistic and cultural differences between them. As the Russians expanded onto the coast of the Bering Sea and met people speaking a form of the Central Yup'ik language, they did use other names. The people they found around the head of Bristol Bay they called Aglegmiut (which linguists now say should be Aglurmiut).

In the American period, these terms brought confusion—not, of course, to Native people, but to the outsiders. There was never doubt of the Alutiiq affiliation of inhabitants of the Shelikof Strait coast of the Alaska Peninsula, but outside commentators argued about the boundary between Alutiiq and Aglurmiut. Most agreed that the mouths of the Egegik and Naknek rivers held settlements that were predominantly Algurmiut, but they differed regarding the Ugashik River region. Some said it was Aglurmiut territory,[71] while at least one of them said it was inhabited by partly "Aleut" (i.e., Alutiiq) people whose relatives controlled the Naknek, Egegik, and Ugashik rivers from mouths to headwaters. Russian officials believed that the people at Ugashik and the interior settlement known as Severnovsk (Savonoski to the Americans) had been driven there from eastern Bristol Bay by invading Aglurmiut in about the year 1800.[72]

Only after the mid-twentieth century did it become possible to unscramble the erroneous impressions of earlier American officials and scholars, when the Library of Congress made available the long-stored papers of the Russian Orthodox Church in Alaska. Then it was clear that on the peninsula the Central-Yup'ik-speaking Aglurmiut held only settlements at the mouths of the Naknek and Egegik rivers, while all the other villages as far southwest as Port Heiden and Chignik were home to Alutiiq people. This included the interior settlements in the upper Naknek region that the Russians called Severnovsk as well as the village of Ugashik on the river of the same name. From Ugashik in particular have come important objects collected by William J. Fisher in the 1880s that are included in this exhibition.

Like nineteenth- and early twentieth-century ethnologists, archaeologists working on the northern peninsula were also misled. The first fairly comprehensive report on the Oregon excavations in the Naknek region[73] attributed the entire four-thousand-year cultural sequence to the Aglurmiut and their ancestors. When the impression was corrected the extensive area of occupation of prehistoric Alutiiq people was recognized,[74] although as was the case in the Kodiak Island group the Alaska Peninsula probably included some differing dialects of Alutiiq.[75] Still more recently it has become evident that many prehistoric cultural characteristics mark an especially close relationship between the peninsula and the Kodiak Islands in the period after about A.D. 1500.[76] This was the period of the final development of the Alutiiq people whose way of life is featured in *Looking Both Ways*.

111   Fieldwork on the Alaska Peninsula, 1960s

The Brooks River, with Naknek Lake on the left and Brooks Lake on the right.

Photograph by Don Dumond.

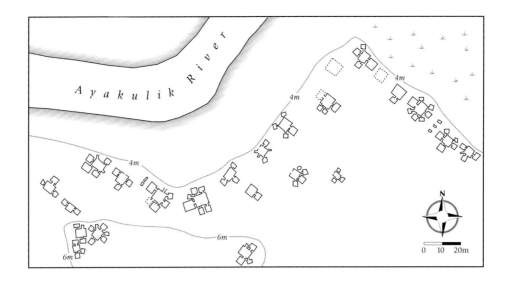

112 Map of a Koniag phase village

Depressions from prehistoric sod houses reveal the layout of a 500-year-old Alutiiq community on the Ayakulik River, southern Kodiak Island. This settlement is one of five that lie well inland along the banks of the river. Variation in the size and configuration of structures illustrates the complexity of late prehistoric communities. The number of side rooms suggests differences in household size, as each chamber provided sleeping quarters for a nuclear family.

Adapted from Knecht (1995).

113 The Karluk River is Kodiak's most productive salmon stream. All five species of Pacific salmon spawn in the shallow river from Karluk Lagoon to Karluk Lake, 33 km upstream. This food-rich locale attracted Native settlement for more than 5000 years. Archaeologists have documented forty-six sites along the river, with the greatest density around the lagoon. Karluk 1, a remarkably well preserved late prehistoric village, once lay at the lagoon entrance, but the meandering river has recently reclaimed this unique piece of Alutiiq history.

Photograph by Richard Knecht.

114 Disk for playing *kagangaq*

Karluk 1 site, Kodiak Island, A.D. 1400–1750
Alutiiq Museum, Koniag, Inc., Collection
(AM251.193:1) Height 9 cm

end of the period. [65] These remote rocky islet functioned as community retreats—places where families could flee for protection from raiding parties.

Alutiiq Societies: The Late Precontact Era (A.D. 1100–ca. 1760)

Roughly 900 years ago, societies of the middle era began transforming into the complexly organized Alutiiq communities recorded at historic contact. Like their Tlingit and Unangan neighbors, the Alutiit encountered by Russian traders were socially stratified with a hereditary ruling class, slavery and warfare, and specialized community occupations—chiefs, priests, whalers, shamans, and midwives. [66] This social system was built on the accumulation of wealth and the perpetuation of social standing through elaborate ritual (see discussion in chapter 2).

There has been extensive debate over the causes of this transformation. How did more simply organized societies develop institutions that favored social inequality and the accumulation of wealth? Some interpretations of Alutiiq history suggest that Inuit people from western Alaska colonized the Gulf coast in the late precontact period, displacing and acculturating existing societies. [67] In short, a new way of living was introduced by outsiders. This idea is supported by a suite of archaeological and linguistic data (see chapter 2) that suggests population movement across the Alaska Peninsula. However, the results of recent studies, particularly

excavations at the remarkably preserved Koniag village of Karluk 1 on Kodiak Island, suggest that late precontact Alutiiq culture developed primarily in place. [68] Most likely, the observed changes resulted from a combination of changing cultural relationships, population growth, and adaptation to significant climatic and environmental changes.

This cultural transition is well evidenced in most areas of the Alutiiq homeland. In the Kodiak archipelago, the Koniag phase follows Late Kachemak and in Prince William Sound the Chugach phase follows Palugvik. [77] The transition is more complicated on the Alaska Peninsula, where archaeological data show interaction across the Alaska Range. Sites of the Kukak Mound phase appear about A.D. 1100 on the Pacific coast and contain tools nearly identical to those found along the Brooks River, a productive interior fishing stream. Up to this time, Pacific coast and interior sites produced largely independent artifact assemblages, reflecting culturally distinct groups of people (Dumond, this chapter). However, archaeologists believe that both regions were occupied by Alutiiq people after about A.D. 1100. Perhaps families traveled from coastal winter settlements to interior summer camps on productive salmons streams. [78]

An exception to this pattern of change occurs at Kachemak Bay, on the north side of the lower Kenai Peninsula. By about A.D. 1000, the middle period societies of the lower Kenai Peninsula began to disappear. [79] Sites postdating this era hold artifacts of the Dena'ina, who spread south from upper Cook Inlet. It is not yet clear why people of the Kachemak culture left the area, although archaeologists do not believe that they were actually forced out by the Dena'ina.

One possible answer is climate change. The beginning of the late precontact era coincides with the onset of the Little Ice Age, a period of cooler, damper weather that began about A.D. 1100 and continued until A.D. 1850. In the Gulf of Alaska, cooler air temperatures and greater precipitation led to substantial glacial advances between A.D. 1440 and 1710. Perhaps environmental changes associated with the Little Ice Age made Kachemak Bay a less desirable place to live. Overexploitation of resources and warfare may also have contributed to the decline of the region's relatively small population.[80]

The abandonment of Kachemak Bay was coupled with increases in the size and number of settlements in the Kodiak archipelago. Residents of Kachemak Bay may have moved in with their Kodiak relatives.[81] Whatever the case, faunal remains at sites and the distribution of late precontact villages on Kodiak suggests an economy that was more intensely focused on salmon harvesting. Regionally, the size and number of villages found along salmon streams increases dramatically. Some of these settlements contain up to 200 house depressions and occur several miles from the coast (fig. 112).[82]

Some of the richest data on life during the late precontact era comes from Karluk 1, an exceptionally well-preserved village at the mouth of Kodiak Island's Karluk River. At about A.D. 1200, people began to build sod houses on the beach at the mouth of this prolific salmon stream.[83] Over the succeeding 700 years, repeated house construction, occupation, and abandonment created an enormous mound of cultural material with layer upon layer of household debris. Over time, water from nearby streams seeped through the deposit, creating cool wet conditions that slowed decay. Wood, bark, bone, antler, ivory, baleen, spruce root, grass, fur, human hair, and feathers all survived, providing an unparalleled look

at Koniag-era culture. Many of the items in the *Looking Both Ways* exhibit are from this remarkable site.

Technological changes in Karluk 1 artifacts illustrate changing subsistence practices. There is a notable difference in the proportions of fishing and hunting technologies in different layers of the site. At the base of the deposit, sea mammal hunting gear occurs in proportions equivalent to or exceeding fishing gear. In upper levels, however, fishing gear far exceeds hunting gear, and animal bones show a corresponding increase in fish remains relative to sea mammal remains. This increased reliance on fish corresponds with the development of a new fishing technology. People of the middle period harvested salmon with nets. Their descendants wielded fishing harpoons, small, composite projectiles used to dispatch salmon trapped behind stone or log weirs.[84]

Greater dependence on fish is also associated with increases in storage. As people harvested more salmon they needed additional space for processing and holding their catches. At Karluk 1, the size of bentwood vessels increases with time, there is a proliferation of basketry, and people begin to build large, plank-lined storage boxes. In at least one case, an entire room was used to store fish. Split fish were carefully laid on a bed of alder branches covering a complete side chamber of a house. A similar pattern was preserved at Settlement Point, a Koniag village on southern Afognak Island. Here house floors were covered with clay-lined pits and slate slab boxes.[85] Although these features are similar to those from Kachemak-era houses, they are strikingly larger. Residents dug depressions up to two meters across, lining and encircling them with clay. A number had carefully fashioned covers, contained salmon bones, and were associated with slate *ulukat*—the semilunar knives traditionally used to process fish. Many of these features probably functioned as fish storage, fermenting, and cooking facilities.

Economic changes in the late prehistoric era also prompted social reorganization. A regrouping of family units is evident in new house styles. Dwellings of this

115 Koniag subsistence technologies

Left to right: slate lance point and wooden case, barbed
  harpoon for sealing, harpoon head for salmon fishing
Settlement Point site, Afognak Island, A.D. 1400–1600
Karluk 1 site, Kodiak Island, A.D. 1400–1750
Alutiiq Museum, Afognak Native Corporation Collection
  and Koniag, Inc., Collection
(lance point AM33-94-138) Length 14.5 cm
(lance case: AM14.193:38 & 39) Length 16 cm
(barbed harpoon UA85-193:5628) Length 11.5 cm
(salmon harpoon AM193-87-7924) Length 6.5 cm

During the Koniag period on Kodiak Island, people began to
harvest even greater quantities of salmon. Sea mammals remained important and continued to be hunted with barbed
harpoons and slate lances, but fish became the focal resource.
In addition to nets, salmon were captured with small, two piece
harpoons. Carved from bone, these points were designed to
pass through a swimming salmon completely—to enter one
side and exit the other. Fishermen dammed a stream then stood
in the water to harpoon the fish as they passed.

116 Bentwood box

Karluk 1 site, Kodiak Island, A.D. 1400–1750
Alutiiq Museum, Koniag, Inc., Collection
(UA193-95-1068) Width 13 cm

Bentwood boxes were used for food storage, stone boiling, and
other common household tasks. A thin plank of steam or wa-
ter-softened wood was bent at the corners to make the sides
of the box; the overlapped seam was then lashed together with
spruce root or baleen. The final steps were to peg the sides
onto a wooden base and to make a cover.

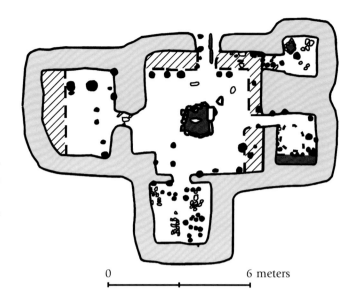

117 Koniag style house—*ciqluaq*

Koniag houses were much larger than in Kachemak times, to accommodate groups of fifteen or more related people. The floor was excavated below ground level, and large posts held up a heavy timber roof frame that was covered with grass and earth. Side chambers served as sleeping quarters for individual families or were used for steam bathing and storage. Smoke from a large fireplace in the central room escaped through an opening in the ceiling.

Drawing by Mark Matson. Adapted from Knecht and Jordan 1995.

0   6 meters

era are substantially larger than those of the preceding Kachemak tradition and include side rooms for sleeping, storage, and sweat bathing. It is as if the single-roomed houses of the Kachemak era were grouped together around a large central space to form a communal living area. This change suggests a switch from nuclear to extended family households, perhaps the better to manage the labor necessary for harvesting, processing, and storing very large quantities of food. Coordination of labor is also evident in the construction of enormous stone fishing weirs, large inland villages far from coastal driftwood resources, and refuge sites above precipitous cliffs.[86]

Massive food storage, larger communities, and increasing control of labor, are all accompanied by increasing evidence of social inequality. Site maps illustrate a reorganization of villages from clusters of equally sized houses to linear arrangements of structures with an internal hierarchy in house size. Groups of larger houses tend to cluster near the center of late prehistoric villages, and were presumably occupied by wealthy, powerful people. The use of labrets also changes. This highly visible facial jewelry increases in size and is more elaborately decorated. These trends seem to reflect a heightened concern with social status and display.[87]

Other concurrent developments include a greater frequency of nonlocal raw materials reflecting long distance trade and a greater number of artifacts and refuge sites indicative of warfare. Clubs, war arrows, and slats from vests of armor all suggest a new emphasis on raiding as does the increased number of refuge sites—settlements on inaccessible cliffs and islets where communities retreated to protect themselves from invaders. Ethnographically, both trade and warfare were used by affluent members of society to obtain riches and maintain economic power. An increase in these activities supports the idea of emerging social classes.

The use of petroglyphs and pictographs—carvings and painting applied to cliff faces, boulders, and cave walls—along the coast[88] may also be related to increasing interaction and competition. These images depict people, land and sea mammals, birds, fish, boats, harpoons, lamps, and geometric designs. Perhaps people were marking their territories with highly visible artwork to signify ownership in a period of more intense competition. Kodiak petroglyphs tend to occur at the mouths of bays, facing the open water (fig. 120).

This period is also characterized by larger household hearths and more evidence of sweat bathing and woodworking. Sweat bathing tools, fire-cracked rock dumps, and wedges become progressively more common and a new form of grooved splitting adze is adopted.[89] These changes may reflect adaptation to colder conditions, the construction of larger houses, and an increased use of

118 Labrets (lip ornaments)

Karluk 1 site, Kodiak Island, A.D. 1400–1750
Uyak site, Kodiak Island, A.D. 600–1100
Alutiiq Museum, Koniag, Inc., Collection and
    Larsen Bay Collection
(top left to right: UA85.193.6881, ivory, width 2
    cm; UA85.193.2868, limestone, width 2.5
    cm; AM193.87:9320, wood, height 3.5 cm)
(bottom: UA88-78-1144, coal, width 5cm)

Labrets were facial ornaments that visually communicated the social status and perhaps family
affiliation of the wearer. During the late prehistoric era, labrets became larger and more varied
in decoration, perhaps an indication of greater
social inequality.

119 Barbed arrowhead and wooden armor slats

Karluk 1 site, Kodiak Island, A.D. 1400–1750
Alutiiq Museum, Koniag, Inc., Collection
(arrowhead: UA87-193-9254) Length 25.5 cm
(slats: UA85.193:6367, 6380, 6381) Length 9 cm

Shields, clubs, armor, and war arrows occur in the
late prehistoric archaeological record and coincide
with the development of refuge sites—isolated
settlements where communities retreated to avoid
raids. Here, families prepared shelters and stock-
piled supplies. Archaeologists believe that as the
Alutiiq population grew and strong political leaders emerged, warfare became more common.

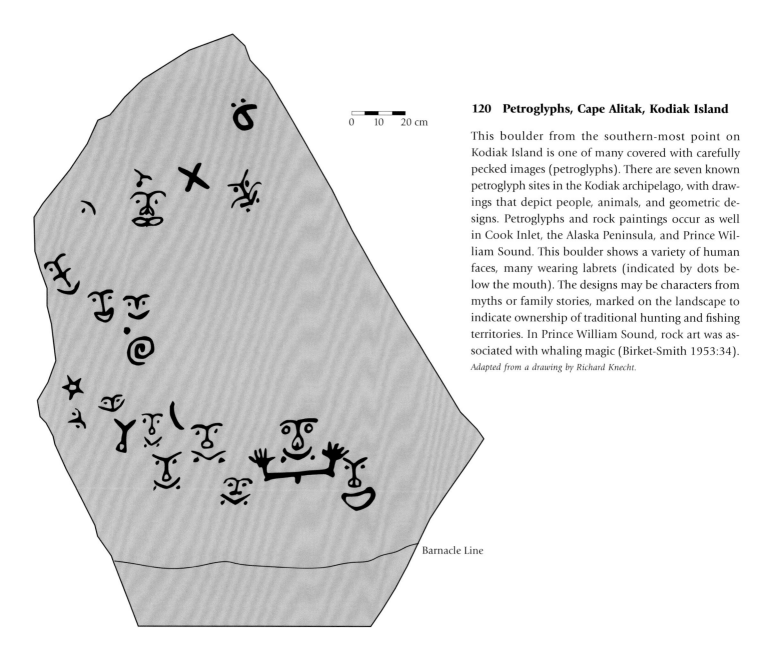

0   10   20 cm

120 Petroglyphs, Cape Alitak, Kodiak Island

This boulder from the southern-most point on Kodiak Island is one of many covered with carefully pecked images (petroglyphs). There are seven known petroglyph sites in the Kodiak archipelago, with drawings that depict people, animals, and geometric designs. Petroglyphs and rock paintings occur as well in Cook Inlet, the Alaska Peninsula, and Prince William Sound. This boulder shows a variety of human faces, many wearing labrets (indicated by dots below the mouth). The designs may be characters from myths or family stories, marked on the landscape to indicate ownership of traditional hunting and fishing territories. In Prince William Sound, rock art was associated with whaling magic (Birket-Smith 1953:34).

Adapted from a drawing by Richard Knecht.

Barnacle Line

sweat bathing for ritual purposes. The remains of huge meat-roasting pits at the Settlement Point site on Afognak Island also hint at more community feasting.[90]

This growing emphasis on public ritual is evident in the construction of *qasqit*—ceremonial buildings. Enormous single-roomed structures in late precontact villages match ethnographic descriptions of community buildings maintained specifically for social, political, and ceremonial gatherings. At Karluk 1, emphasis on public ceremony is preserved in an array of artwork, ceremonial gear, and gaming pieces. Based on ethnographic data, these public events reinforced the social position of the Alutiiq elite while integrating potentially competitive social groups.

In sum, many changes in the archaeological record point toward both economic and social reorganization in the late precontact era. Some archaeologists hypothesize that colder environmental conditions of the Little Ice Age led to a greater reliance on anadromous fish, causing widespread social reorganization[91] Population growth or redistribution, as well as increasing contacts with neighboring peoples, were also probably important factors in the transformation. There is no simple answer. Whatever the causes, the prehistoric sites on the Gulf of Alaska will continue to enhance and enrich the Alutiiq story. There are thousands of ancient tales left to be told.

121   Incised pebble

Settlement Point site, Kodiak Island, ca. A.D. 1300
Alutiiq Museum, Afognak Native Corporation Collection

Incised pebbles—small pieces of slate etched with drawings of people in ceremonial clothing—appear in Alutiiq village sites at around A.D. 1300. Bird-skin parkas, gut-skin jackets, headdresses, rattles, and jewelry are all depicted, providing the rare opportunity to study clothing from the distant past. The purpose of the drawings is unknown.

Photograph by Patrick Saltonstall.

122   Miniature mask

Karluk 1 site, Kodiak Island, A.D. 1400–1750
Alutiiq Museum, Koniag, Inc., Collection
(UA85-193-6311) Height 4.5 cm

Miniature wooden masks were found in the upper levels of the Karluk 1 site. Although their function is unknown, the masks may have been carried as amulets, used to teach stories to children, or served as masks for dolls. A proliferation of masks and other ceremonial gear during the Koniag era seems to indicate an increasing emphasis on public ritual.

Partnerships in Archaeology

ON THE SURFACE, ARCHAEOLOGY IN THE CONTEMPORARY Alutiiq homeland looks much like archaeology anywhere. Muddy excavators wielding trowels carefully peel back layers of earth to expose ancient houses and layers of garbage. Artifacts are mapped where they lie and then delicately placed in plastic bags labeled with laundry markers. But a closer look shows a difference. Throughout the central Gulf of Alaska, archaeologists are working in partnership with Alutiiq people to combine traditional knowledge with scientific practice. Archaeology is no longer performed only by scholars who design their research in distant libraries, but by teams of Alutiiq people and researchers who are exploring questions of mutual interest and benefit.[92]

At Mink Island, a tiny grass-covered islet at the entrance to Geographic Harbor in the Katmai National Park and Preserve, Park Service archaeologists collaborate with

123 Shauna Lukin helps to excavate a 500-year-old house floor and storage box at the Settlement Point site on Afognak Island. The excavation was sponsored and managed by the Afognak Native Corporation as part of *Light the Past, Spark the Future, Dig Afognak!*

Photograph by Patrick Saltonstall.

124 A prehistoric oil lamp, lit for the first time in hundreds of years to mark the opening of Spirit Camp at Afognak Island in 1996. This annual camp, organized by the Kodiak Area Native Association, provides children from ages ten to eighteen the chance to explore traditional culture with peers from communities throughout the Kodiak archipelago. The first two seasons of camp were hosted by the Afognak Native Corporation at *Dig Afognak*, allowing campers to participate in the excavation of Alutiiq archaeological sites.

Photograph by Amy Steffian.

volunteers from the Council of Katmai Descendants to save ancient tools threatened by vandalism and insure the most reverent treatment of ancestral remains. At Dig Afognak, a heritage project run by the Afognak Native Corporation, graduate students in archaeology excavate sites on Native lands, train Native youth, and provide tourists with the opportunity to explore Alutiiq heritage while gathering information for dissertation research (see Woodhouse-Beyer, this chapter).[93] In Old Harbor, archaeologists lead Alutiiq high school students in a community excavation as part of their school curriculum (see Fitzhugh, this chapter).[94] On the Kenai Peninsula, the Port Graham Corporation recently provided permits, crew salaries, travel expenses, and widespread community support for a collaborative excavation with the University of Alaska Anchorage.[95] And in Prince William Sound, participants in Núciq spirit camp, a heritage program run annually by the Chugach Alaska Corporations, work with Alutiiq archaeologist Lora Johnson to study ancient settlements.

These partnerships have taken years to form. Although archaeologists have been studying Alutiiq heritage for nearly seven decades, it has only been only in the past twenty years that Alutiiq people have been asked permission to conduct archaeology, invited to participate in field research, and consulted on the disposition of cultural materials. Like many indigenous peoples, the Alutiit have had their share of unfortunate experiences with archaeologists. It was the remote Alutiiq village of Larsen Bay, population 180, that challenged the Smithsonian Institution to return hundreds of ancestral remains collected without permission in the 1930s (Pullar, this volume).[97] The success of their efforts set a precedent that directly influenced passage of the Native American Graves Protection and Repatriation Act (NAGPRA). This landmark federal legislation now requires museums to repatriate ancestral remains and sacred objects, and archaeologists to consult tribal councils when they encounter human

Historical Archaeology at the Afognak Artel

Katharine Woodhouse-Beyer
Ph.D. Candidate, Brown University

I FIRST VISITED THE KODIAK ARCHIPELAGO IN THE summer of 1987, when Professor Richard Jordan of Bryn Mawr College invited me to participate in collaborative archaeological excavations at Karluk under the auspices of the Kodiak Area Native Association as well as the college. When I began archaeological research with the Afognak Native Corporation in 1993, I realized that the Karluk project was at the vanguard of a new, and positive, set of relationships among Native Americans, local peoples and anthropologists. The Karluk model guided my professional behavior as both observer and participant, in learning such values as listening, valuing oral traditions, and fostering mutual respect. I have come to realize that anthropological consultation is a process, not an end product. Native Americans and archaeologists can be strong partners with mutual objectives in preservation as well as promote global respect for cultural and traditional heritage.

The archaeology of more recent periods can be used as a tool to explore the dynamic social processes of history, cultural transformation and ethnic understanding. From 1994–98, I was the director of excavations at the Afognak artel (ca. 1790s–1840), an early nineteenth-century Russian-American Company provisioning post at the mouth of the Afognak River. Here Russian and Alutiiq hunting crews set out to hunt sea otters while at camp Native women gathered food and processed pelts for clothing, kayaks and the China fur trade. Our archaeological team recovered the artel manager's house, storage houses, and workers' barracks. The collection comprises nearly 50,000 artifacts of both Alutiiq and Euro-Russian manufacture. During our collective journey we learned that, contrary to the history books, Alutiiq culture did not die with Russian implantation, but displayed a tenacious resiliency. While the artel manager's house possessed Russian-style hewn spruce planking and frame construction, Alutiiq workers at the Afognak artel were still building traditional barabara structures and using ground slate ulus, bone harpoons, and greenstone adzes. My particular interest at the Afognak artel has been to explore the changes in the Alutiiq community that occurred and which were catalyzed by Russian contact. While other studies have focused on genocide, loss of land, relocation and warfare, I am particularly keen to provide new insights into Russian contact from research focusing on gender relations and the emergence of Creoles.

From the excavation of the Afognak artel over the past five field seasons, we have gained a unique understanding of the Russian-American period on Kodiak and its many effects on the daily life and material culture of the Alutiiq people. The archaeological excavations have been enhanced by many interdisciplinary scholars, guests and shareholders who have visited the site and have contributed their skills, muscles and emotional support over the years. My role has been but one part of the teamwork remains. Why, then, would Alutiiq people embrace archaeology as a means of studying their past?

This seeming paradox is itself an artifact of history. The Alutiit are the least known of Alaska's Native people. The rapid conquest of the Alutiiq homeland by Russian fur traders and the introduction of devastating diseases disrupted Native life. When the first anthropologists arrived in the central Gulf of Alaska, the Alutiit had been participating in the Western economic system for nearly 150 years and many traditional practices had disappeared. With the exception of Kaj Birket-Smith's monograph on the Chugach,[98] there is little traditional Alutiiq ethnography. As such, archaeology offered a chance to access unrecorded traditions and reclaim a vanishing history. In a very real sense, archaeological sites are the Alutiiq library and the information they contain provides an irreplaceable addition to oral traditions, historical accounts, and museum collections. A partnership with archaeologists could help to unlock this history, a situation Alutiiq leaders recognized in the early 1980s.[97]

Second, and perhaps more important, archaeology can instill cultural pride. Well-preserved sites throughout the Alutiiq homeland hold treasures from the past that reawaken the memories of Elders, inspire youth, and excite artists. By funding, governing, and participating in archaeology, the Alutiiq community could rightfully make decisions over the treatment of its heritage and

towards the larger goal of preserving Alutiiq traditions. I am grateful to the Afognak Native Corporation, Alutiiq Museum, and Kodiak community, who have supported and encouraged my research over the years and look forward to a lifetime of friendship, dialogue and cooperative ventures.

125 Mary Fearne assists with midden excavations at the Afognak artel.
Photograph by Amy Steffian.

endow its members with a powerful sense of identity. Martha Demientieff expressed this idea at the 1997 Alutiiq Elders conference: "I touched these [artifacts] and it made me realize that schools don't have to and cannot teach me self-esteem. It's knowing how smart our ancestor were that makes me know where I come from and I should have high self-esteem . . . it was a religious experience for me."

Archaeology, however, is not a traditional way of looking at the past and it has taken time to get used to. While the younger generation is thrilled to search for tiny glass trade beads in a muddy hole or to handle harpoons in a museum collection, Elders still approach ancestral objects with caution. They maintain a reverence for the past that they wish to pass along, but they learned as children that artifacts can be dangerous. Artifacts are associated with ancestors, which aligns them with the powerful spirit world, and some are believed to be tainted with shamans' poisons. Clyda Christiansen said, "My husband believed in that, too. He didn't believe much, but . . . even now he tells me he wouldn't touch artifacts. He never touches mine at home. He just looks at 'em and he says 'I remember when I found an artifact and I went and I showed it to my mom and she just got mad at me and she said, go and put that thing back where you found it from and come home and wash your hands.' After that he never did touch any kind of artifacts. He got just so scared."[100]

Community Archaeology, Old Harbor Style

Ben Fitzhugh
University of Washington

ALMOST EVERY YEAR SINCE 1993, I HAVE BEEN TRAVELING to Old Harbor on southeast Kodiak Island to explore the region's archaeological heritage, and with each visit, I am overcome with the warmth, hospitality, and support I receive. The Old Harbor community has supported my research, welcomed me into their homes, and shared their knowledge generously. What could I do to repay this kindness? The following is a personal account of a partnership in Old Harbor community archaeology from 1993 to 1997.

I began as many archaeologists do in this age of increased responsiveness to local interests by presenting the results of my field work to the community in an evening of "show and tell." At the end of each field season, I discussed the archaeological history of Kodiak, explained the purpose of my research—to find archaeological sites of all ages and use them to understand the development of Native economies, social patterns, and politics over the past 7000 years—and displayed a sample of artifacts recovered that season. The audiences were large, full of adults and children eager to know more about my activities and finds. This was all well and good, but it fell far short of satisfying the local desire to know more about Kodiak cultural history. People wanted to be involved. Many had artifact collections from beach fronts and road cuts, mementos of a misty past cloaked in the obscurity of rapid culture change and imposed Americanization. They wanted to know more; they wanted to do more.

In the spring of 1995, the Old Harbor School and I found a way to promote this interest. With the backing of the Old Harbor Native Corporation and Tribal Council, high school and junior high students started digging at a 135-year-old Russian-Alutiiq site located in Old Harbor itself. The school was interested in the project's hands-on application of cultural, historical, scientific, and mathematical knowledge and skills; the students saw it as a chance to get out of the classroom and do something new and different; and I saw it as an opportunity to further illustrate how archaeology could help to recapture misplaced Alutiiq heritage.[96]

For a few weeks during the springs of 1995 and 1996, we excavated portions of two historic-period Alutiiq houses, dating to the Russian era just before the sale of Alaska to the United States. Students learned to read the layers of earth defining floors, walls, and other parts of past houses. They mapped the artifacts they found in place, showing how objects were used in and around living areas, and they screened the dirt for unseen items. Below the Russian-Alutiiq houses, the students found a thick layer of artifacts and other debris roughly 5000 years old. The historic Alutiiq village was resting on top of this much older settlement. In the end, the students studied the finds and presented the results to the community in a formal conference-style presentation. They had become the experts, with the right to boast that they knew at least as much as anyone alive about the ways of the inhabitants of these two moments in Old Harbor's history.

In 1997, with the help of Elders' accounts, we turned our archaeological experience into the construction of a replica *ciqluaq* (sod house or barabara) that remains an educational resource in Old Harbor. The dedication of the house was an auspicious occasion, joined—quite by chance—by a national delegation of Native Americans who spoke eloquently of continuity between past and present, the preservation of culture and tradition. Throughout this work, it was tremendously gratifying to see Old Harbor students go from novice enthusiasts to experts in studying their own heritage. I look forward to the day when some of these young people assume active roles as promoters and protectors of their archaeological heritage, as teachers, tour guides, and professional archaeologists. This day might indeed be close at hand.

126 This traditional style sod house in Old Harbor was built by school students, community volunteers, and archaeologist Ben Fitzhugh.
Photograph by Amy Steffian.

127 Lena Amason with her "Salmon Mask." The mask is both an aesthetic work and a symbol of connection to Alutiiq ancestry. Lena is a student at the University of Alaska Anchorage.

Photograph by Amy Steffian.

Although many Alutiiq people feel that artifacts should be left in peace, others see them as a gift—something left by the past to inspire the future (Dawson, this volume, pp. 89–90). In 1984, the Kodiak Area Native Association took a bold step, giving $10,000 to the Karluk Archaeological Project, spearheaded by Richard Jordan of Bryn Mawr College.[101] The plan was to involve Alutiiq youth in the excavation of sites in their community. The project was enormously successful, both in reawakening a sense of Native identity and in recovering world-class collections. The Karluk project continued for a number of years and gave rise to numerous other collaborative heritage programs. In recent years, it has been Alutiiq organizations, and not just archaeologists, that have initiated research.

Of course, archaeology generates collections that need care and storage. Across the Alutiiq homeland, the process of preserving and studying heritage is continuing at museums—another Western field that is being reshaped to serve Alutiiq people better. Kodiak's Alutiiq Museum was built in 1995 to bring collections home, provide an outlet for public education, and create facilities for the research fueling the heritage movement. The operations of this archaeological repository are funded and governed by eight Alutiiq corporations who

infuse exhibits, educational programs, and collections care with traditional values. In Prince William Sound the Chugach Alutiiq have received a similar grant to build a Native-governed museum and a series of connecting cultural centers in outlying communities. And in Port Graham, artifacts from a collaborative excavation with the University of Alaska Anchorage are being worked into displays for the school and community hall, and a CD-ROM of the entire collection is under production.[102] For Alutiiq people, these efforts mean that the archaeological materials recovered from area sites can receive culturally sensitive care in their community, and exhibits, lectures, and publications based on the collections are readily accessible to the people whose heritage they most closely reflect.

The success of these endeavors is hard to measure. The volume of artifacts recovered from sites, numbers of museum visitors, and growing public recognition of Alutiiq culture are surface indications of a deeper movement toward cultural knowledge and self-respect. One outward sign is that Alutiiq students are translating their personal explorations of heritage into degrees in anthropology, education, and the arts. Although archaeological field methods have changed little over the past twenty years, the spirit of research and it's meaning to the Alutiiq community have been altered dramatically.

The Karluk Archaeological Project and the Changing Cultural Landscape of Kodiak Island

Richard A. Knecht
Director, Museum of the Aleutians

128 Daryl Squartsoff at the Nunakakhvak village site, 1984. Excavations of a sod house at Nunakakhvak—an historic Alutiiq settlement near Karluk village—were conducted by archaeologist Richard Knecht in 1984 with help from local students. The project was funded in part by the Kodiak Area Native Association to help youth explore their Native heritage.

Photograph by Richard Knecht.

THE KARLUK ARCHAEOLOGICAL PROJECT BEGAN ordinarily enough in 1983 when armed with grant from the National Endowment for the Humanities, Dick Jordan of Bryn Mawr College began surveying and testing sites in the Karluk area. Less than two decades ago, the cultural landscape of the Kodiak Archipelago had been eroded by time and collective neglect in a way that is difficult to imagine today. Alutiiq artwork was nowhere to be seen, and there was an uncertain sense of how "Russian" or "Aleut" cultural identities were defined within the Native community.

We started with the standard professional etiquette of asking for permission from Koniag, Inc., and the Karluk Village Council, and it was simply good manners to invite our village neighbors in to see the day's finds. But local interests far exceeded our expectations. Young people, teachers, and Elders first watched, then joined in the excavations—and with good reason, for the finds at the Karluk One site were truly spectacular. Kneeling together in the mud, we thrilled at the exquisite workmanship and enigmatic stare of a wooden doll, the weave of a spruce root basket, the still green folds of rye grass on a 500-year-old house floor. At the season's end we displayed the treasures in the Karluk school gym, and the village gave a potlatch dinner to invite guests from around the island. In Kodiak crowds filled the Senior Center for a similar display. The call went out for a local museum facility capable of curating these splendid collections. The enthusiasm and commitment was real. Quite by accident we had tapped into an enormous and long pent-up reservoir of curiosity about Kodiak's past and what it meant to be Native.

Gordon Pullar, then president of the Kodiak Area Native Association, formed a Culture Committee charged with planning a museum. In 1987 I began to work with KANA full time on the project. It was also the last year of the Karluk Archaeological Project. Dick Jordan moved on to the University of Alaska Fairbanks, and continued to work closely with KANA until his untimely death in 1991. KANA, along with Native Corporations like Koniag, Inc., the Afognak Native Corporation and the Old Harbor Native Corporation continued to support archaeological field work. The Alutiiq Culture Center was opened in 1990, evolving into the Alutiiq Museum and Archaeological Repository by 1995.

Nearly all of the archaeologists working in the Kodiak Island region first arrived as crew members on the Karluk Archaeological Project, including Aron Crowell, Chris Donta, Ben Fitzhugh, Philomena Hausler, Amy Steffian, Patrick Saltonstall, Katharine Woodhouse-Beyer, and me. Senior scholars such as Don Clark returned to Kodiak to resume field work after a fourteen-year hiatus. Others have entered the profession through the numerous projects of the past seventeen consecutive field seasons, including Native Alutiiq anthropologists Sven Haakanson, Jr., and Mark Rusk. Through the Alutiiq Museum, the Native community has assumed full stewardship of its own heritage.

The Alutiiq cultural landscape has been forever changed by the cultural renaissance that was nourished by the Karluk finds. In the long evolution of a culture there is no convenient cut off point between past and present, for culture exists as a continuum. As archaeologists we had come to Kodiak to study Alutiiq culture but while doing so unwittingly became an inextricable part of the very culture history we had sought to understand.

Chapter 4 notes

1 Pullar 1994:19.
2 Lisianskii 1968:197.
3 Lantis 1938:131.
4 Lantis 1938:132–133.
5 Lisianskii 1968:196. Davydov (1977:185) and Merck (1980: 167–168) heard versions of this origin tale on both Kodiak Island and in the eastern Aleutian Islands.
6 Wrangell 1980:59. See also Pierce 1978:11 for another version of the migration to Kodiak Island from the north coast of the Alaska Peninsula.
7 The Russian spelling was Koloshi.
8 Pinart 1873.
9 Erlandson et al., 1992.
10 Ackerman 1992.
11 Dixon et al., 1997.
12 Dumond 1998:190; Henn 1978.
13 Henn 1978:87.
14 Ackerman 1992:23; Moss 1998.
15 Laughlin 1975.
16 Crowell and Mann 1998:18.
17 D. Clark 1979, G. Clark 1977.
18 Hrdlička 1944.
19 Hrdlička 1944:21.
20 Crowell and Mann 1996, 1998.
21 Workman 1998:152.
22 Yarborough and Yarborough 1998.
23 Saltonstall and Steffian 1999; Fitzhugh 1996; Hausler-Knecht 1993.
24 Dumond 1998:193, Steffian, Pontti, and Saltonstall 1998:52.
25 Jordan and Knecht 1988:240.
26 Fitzhugh 1996:329; Jordan and Knecht 1988:320; Reger 1998:168–169.
27 Dumond 1998:193; Hausler 1993; Partlow 1999.
28 Clark 1979; Hausler 1993.
29 Hausler 1993.
30 Heusser et al. 1985.
31 Steffian, Pontti and Saltonstall 1998:85.
32 Dumond 1998:193.
33 Reger 1998:168–169.
34 Hausler 1993:12.
35 Clark 1982a.
36 Dumond 1998:194.
37 Dumond 1998:194.
38 Workman 1998:151.
39 Hausler 1993:16; Steffian, Pontti, and Saltonstall 1998:59.
40 Fitzhugh 1997:368.
41 Heusser et al. 1985:486.
42 Yarborough and Yarborough 1998:138.
43 Dumond 1998:194.
44 Steffian, Pontti, and Saltonstall 1998.
45 de Laguna 1975.
46 Yarborough and Yarborough 1998:140.
47 Dumond 1998:196.
48 Clark 1997:85; Steffian, Pontti, and Saltonstall 1998:92-93; Saltonstall and Steffian 1999.
49 Steffian 1992b.
50 Steffian 1992b.
51 Jordan and Knecht 1988:232.
52 Street 1994; Hrdlička 1944.
53 Steffian 1992b.
54 Bray and Killion 1994.
55 Steffian 1992b.
56 Pullar 1994:19-21; Pullar this volume.
57 Erlandson et al. 1992:53; Lobdell 1980; Yesner 1992.
58 Reger 1998:164.
59 Steffian 1992a.
60 Steffian and Saltonstall 1995.
61 Simon and Steffian 1994.
62 de Laguna 1975:43-44.
63 Simon and Steffian 1994.
64 Simon and Steffian 1994.
65 Fitzhugh 1996:332.
66 Townsend 1980.
67 Dumond 1987a.
68 Jordan and Knecht 1988; Knecht 1995.
69 Dumond 1981.
70 Dumond 1987a.
71 e.g., Dall 1877; Petroff 1884.
72 e.g., Wrangell 1980.
73 Dumond 1962.
74 Dumond 1981.
75 Harrit 1997.
76 Dumond and Van Stone 1995.
77 Yarborough and Yarborough 1998:138; Knecht 1995.
78 Dumond 1998:198.
79 Klein 1996:65.
80 Workman 1998:152–153.
81 Workman 1998:153.
82 Jordan and Knecht 1988; Knecht 1995.
83 Donta 1993; Jordan and Knecht 1988; Knecht 1995; Steffian and Knecht 1998.
84 Knecht 1995.
85 Saltonstall 1997:24–25.
86 Knecht 1995.
87 Steffian and Saltonstall 1996.
88 Alaska Packers Association 1917; Clark 1970b; Heizer 1956b; Klein 1996:23–27; de Laguna 1956:102–109.
89 Knecht 1995.
90 Saltonstall 1997:26.
91 Knecht 1995.
92 Knecht 1994.
93 Saltonstall 1996; Woodhouse-Beyer 1998.
94 Fitzhugh 1996.
95 Workman, Workman, and Yesner 1997:16.
96 Pullar 1992:1.
97 See Bray and Killion 1994.
98 Birket-Smith 1953.
99 Pullar 1992.
100 Alutiiq Elders' Planning Conference for *Looking Both Ways*, 1997.
101 Pullar 1992; Jordan and Knecht 1988.
102 Workman, Workman, and Yesner 1997:16.

5

SÚGUCIHPET—
"OUR WAY OF LIVING"

Aron L. Crowell and April Laktonen

My grandmother always says, "You always cook your food when it's still moving!" and I say, "Well, that's when it's the best, you know, when it's still fresh." Salmon is excellent that way, it has to be totally fresh. After it's frozen for a while it loses its quality and it's not as good . . . (laughing) I usually take all of my stuff out of the freezer and send it to my children in Anchorage.

— Virginia Aleck
(Chignik, Alaska Peninsula), 1997[1]

IN RURAL ALUTIIQ COMMUNITIES, FISHING, HUNTING, and collecting of plants, eggs, and shellfish occupy people of all ages during many parts of the year. Each harvesting activity builds connections among people and with the land. Traditional knowledge about plants, animals, geography, and weather is shared and passed on. Out with the adults, young people learn local place names that map the cultural landscape: *Lugsuhwik* ("place to eat wild chives"), *Amikum Yámai* ("octopus rocks"), and *Caqalqahsuhwik* ("Place to get seaweed").[2]

The importance of fresh and preserved wild foods is shown by surveys of fifteen Alutiiq communities conducted during the 1980s by the Alaska Department of Fish and Game.[3] There was much variation between villages and regions, but nearly every household used locally gathered foods. The average amount per person varied from 220 lbs to more than 600 lbs, and typical families used between ten and twenty-five different types of resources over the course of the year, depending on where they lived. Because few Alutiiq communities are served by roads and store-bought foods are very expensive, the subsistence harvest is not only culturally important—it is economically indispensable.

The *Exxon Valdez* oil spill in 1989 caused great destruction in Prince William Sound, and the oil spread

129 Artemie Kalmakoff, Sr., of Ivanof Bay with dried fillets of silver (coho) salmon, 1990.
Photograph by Lisa Hutchinson-Scarbrough.

137

130 Sophie Katelnikoff and grandson picking highbush cranberries at Larsen Bay, Kodiak Island, 1990.

Photograph by Priscilla Russell.

westward on ocean currents to affect almost every Alutiiq village on the Gulf of Alaska coast. People feared that beach foods, birds, fish, and sea mammals had been contaminated, and subsistence harvests went down dramatically. In the less damaged areas of Kodiak, the Alaska Peninsula, and Cook Inlet, most Alutiiq communities have now fully resumed their prespill consumption of these foods.[4] In Prince William Sound, where residual oil lurks beneath the surface of the beaches, residents still feel the impact of the disaster. Seals and herring remain scarce, and there is worry over the loss.

> I miss the lifestyle. I mean my subsistence living . . . I miss it. Because that's a lot of what isn't there anymore, or it isn't like it used to be. You got to go a long ways for it if you get anything. And after the oil spill especially they say it didn't affect it but you could notice year after year this stuff is still disappearing slowly and it ain't going to be long before we ain't going to be able to have any of that stuff anymore. And that makes me feel bad. I like that Native lifestyle, I mean that subsistence lifestyle.
>
> —Ed Gregorioff, Prince William Sound Elder, 1997[5]

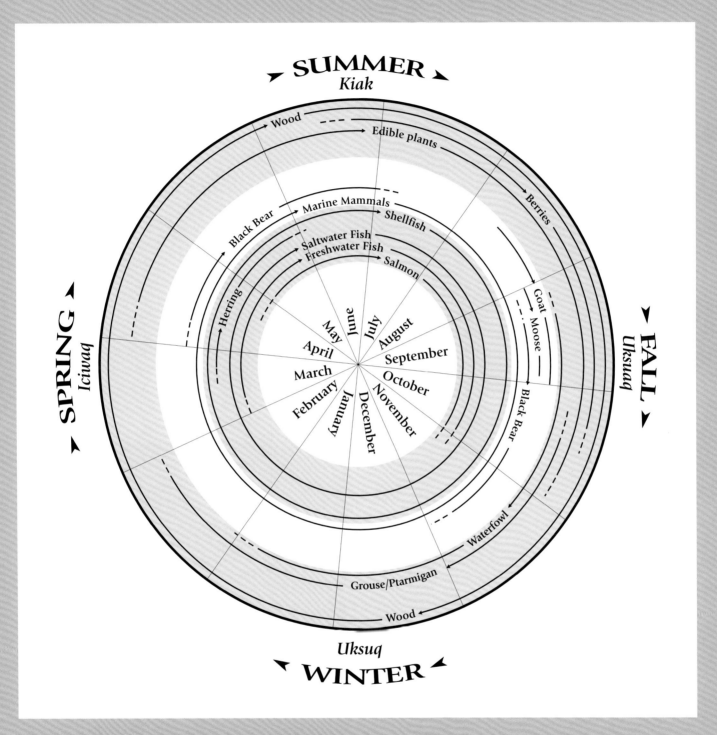

SUMMER
Kiak

Wood

Edible plants

Black Bear

Marine Mammals

Berries

Shellfish

Saltwater Fish
Freshwater Fish

Salmon

Herring

Goat

May June July August
April September
March October
February November
January December

Moose

Black Bear

SPRING
Iciwaq

FALL
Uksuaq

Waterfowl

Grouse/Ptarmigan

Wood

Uksuq
WINTER

131 This chart represents the annual subsistence cycle in the village of Nanwalek. The harvest of wild foods shifts its focus from season to season, but the process continues all year.

Drawing by Ron Stanek. Courtesy of the Alaska Department of Fish and Game.

Súgucihpet— Our Way of Living

McKibben Jackinsky
Ninilchik Native Descendants

A Piece of the Whole

Alutiiq people reclaim their identity through hunting and gathering. The sustaining of life encompasses the physical, the mental and the spiritual. A reverent awareness and respect for all things provides an ancestral warp over which are woven threads of modern beliefs and economics. Involvement in the part is involvement in the whole.

Passed To the Future

The white-haired man knelt on uneven gray beach rocks, his eighty-year-old body bending slowly. Whispering waves of cold inlet water rolled up behind him, lapping at his toes. In the distance, mountains formed a snow-covered horizon along the bottom edge of a cloudless blue Alaska sky. Overhead, noisy seagulls spiraled and dipped in a salt-laden breeze, loudly voicing their hunger.

The freshly caught salmon flooded the Elder with a graceful agility. His daughter's attempts to steady him went unheeded. Others placed buckets of water at his side, leaving him the decision of how much to use. Around him stood the people of his village. Excited youngsters pressed close to see how he cut and cleaned the salmon's head, readying it for preserving. Their wide eyes recorded his movements, their ears strained to hear his voice. They bent their heads of black, brown and blonde hair toward him, the colors a testimony of cultural blending.

The salmon in the man's hands and the movements he made carried a changeless history. The eagerness of his village crowding around him and the silence as they listened were a strong sinew-thread running through the present, connecting past to future, the anchor in a historically tumultuous sea. With a sharp knife the Elder opened the salmon head, swept it clean of blood and removed the feathery gills. His smiling eyes sparkled with satisfaction. His actions, sure and graceful, came automatically. Ancestral memories guided him.

Drawn together by the activity, the people celebrated the survival of another winter. Smells of ocean salt and smoke from fires heating nearby homes filled the air. The salmon had returned. It was spring. The season of new life. The wisdom of generations was passing through an Elder to the youth of his village.

132 Woven spruce root fiber basket

Prince William Sound, early 1900s
American Museum of Natural History
(AMNH 16.1/1602) Height 49 cm

Woven grass and spruce root fiber baskets are a woman's art. Some old baskets were tight enough to hold water, which could be brought to a boil by adding hot rocks. Others were for storing plant foods, fish, clothing, and household goods. Dyes for coloring baskets were made from berries, barks, and minerals.
Photograph by C. Chesek. Courtesy of the American Museum of Natural History.

Touching Hands

The women, many having traveled considerable distances to attend this Saturday morning class, crowded into the small conference room. Some had their young children with them, some were with friends, some came alone. Finding chairs around a large table, they sat down, took off their coats, stared around the room. On tables lining the walls were examples of Alutiiq style baskets, reference books, and colorful photographs. As the women settled into place, quiet filled the room like that in a library or a church, an expectant sort of reverence.

The instructor introduced herself and said what village she was from. She talked about where she learned to weave baskets and how long she'd been weaving. She invited the women to introduce themselves. Going around the table, they gave their names, many of them strangers to each other.

That done, the instructor began passing around the baskets, describing steps taken to gather the grass, time involved in the weaving, different techniques. She pointed out patterns and the perfect fit of lid to basket.

The women asked questions and made observations. Rising voices and warm laughter replaced the room's quiet.

Photos showed detail too minute to be seen without enlargement. There was color to discuss and delicate shapes to consider. Books provided a history of weaving and a list of weavers' names.

Someone in the room gasped, her face breaking into a smile. On the page before her she discovered a relative's name from generations passed. Her interest in weaving stretched back in time, the hands that held the book connected with hands that wove grass. The other women in the room smiled in response, drawn by her discovery.

When all the samples had been examined and the photos and books looked at, the women put their coats back on and went to the nearby beach. They learned the kind of grass used for weaving, when it should be picked and how it should be stored. Their fingers slid over the grass's surface, felt its smoothness, practiced stripping it into usable pieces. It was the knowledge of a people thousands of years old, made new in their hands.

Celebration

In the corner of the boathouse the two women sat like queens, celebrating their eightieth birthdays. Purple feather boas (gifts from a granddaughter) were wrapped around their shoulders and sparkling silver crowns rested atop their gray hair. Around them, five generations of family and friends brought flowers and offered good wishes.

Balloons filled with helium floated up to the ceiling. A table spread with food kept people munching. The two guests of honor told the stories of their births and childhood in the village. Sitting beside them was a skiff, its layers of paint peeling, that the women played in years ago. The older guests remembered; the younger guests listened. Music played, toes tapped, and laughter rose with the eagles circling overhead. Behind them the river curved, drawing them in its embrace, holding memories of a younger time.

Another guest arrived. He was younger than the two women were. In his arms he carried the gift that meant more than any other placed around them. From the end of the plastic wrapping protruded the tail of a spring king salmon, one of the season's first. Recognizing its importance, the partiers broke into a chorus of "Happy Birthday."

The birthday queens gladly accepted his gift. Greedily removing the wrapping, they found a beautifully cleaned salmon. Suddenly, looks of disappointment flooded their expressions. "Where's the head?" Everyone laughed, understanding the importance of what was missing.

Saying Goodbye

She had lived in the village longer than some could remember. Before there was electricity. Before there was running water. Everyone had a story about her they could tell. They knew her husband and his family. They knew her children, had seen them grow and have children of their own.

That afternoon her family sat together, holding hands, wiping away tears of grief. Others came to share their loss. They offered their stories for comfort. They brought pictures telling of her life, bouquets of flowers meant to cheer. They hugged one another for support. Tried to smile.

The songs that were sung were her favorites. Words her voice would never sing again.

When the service ended, when the last prayer was said, food was set out on tables. Tablecloths in her favorite colors. Vegetables fixed the way she'd liked them. Her favorite desserts.

In the center of the table was a pirok, a salmon pie, its crust a golden brown. Across the top was written her name: a gift of love, prepared in her memory.

Our Way Of Living

These moments are a brilliant flame in the eyes of Alutiiq people, overcoming shadows of the past, bringing light and hope to the future. Activities that say, "We are alive." Actions that say, "This is our way of living."

Subsistence and the Spiritual Universe

When I've been with the hunters, what I've seen them do is cut off the tip of the heart and set it in four directions on the ground. It's giving back to the animal spirits.

> —Margie Macauly-Waite
> (Chignik Lake, Alaska Peninsula), 1998[6]

My Dad always told me that before you go out on any kind of hunt, you have to cleanse yourself. And this was like a ritual. And you kept yourself quiet. In order to catch what you're going to get, you have to get your whole body, mind, and soul ready.

> —Virginia Aleck
> (Chignik Lake, Alaska Peninsula), 1997[7]

THE RITUALS OBSERVED BY ALUTIIQ HUNTERS TODAY, and the respectful, personal attitude that Alutiit hold toward animals and the land, express a world view that has absorbed Christian teachings but flows from a much older tradition. In 1933, Makari Chimovitski and other Elders in Prince William Sound told about this system of beliefs.[8] Imam Sua was the spirit owner of the sea, and she ruled over all of its creatures. When hunters set out in their kayaks, they invoked her name to call for game to appear. Similarly, all land animals were controlled by the female diety Nunam Sua. In traditional belief, every animate and inanimate thing, including animals, plants, tides, winds, stars, and ice, possesses a *suk*, or human-like possessor that gives it personhood and awareness. These concepts, discussed more fully in chapter 6, are widely shared with Inuit peoples of Alaska and Canada.[9]

In Alutiiq tradition, personal rituals, hunting ceremonies, and rules of behavior maintained harmony with the supernatural beings upon whom human life depended. In the nineteenth and early twentieth centuries, hunters used decorated clothing and weapons to show respect to the *suk* spirits, who chose to let themselves be captured if they were pleased or to avoid hunters if offended. In Prince William Sound, the hunting of land and sea creatures on the same trip was prohibited to avoid angering their *suk*,[10] nor was their meat to be cooked together or their skins used in the same garment.[11] Although some women have always hunted and trapped, men had to minimize contact with any woman who was menstruating, nor could she touch hunting weapons or clothing. As a girl, Lucille Antowak Davis helped her father to trap foxes at Karluk, but, he told her, "Pretty soon when you hit your teens you're not going to go with me no more because you're going to dirty the ground where I trap."[12] Menstruating women could not cross the bridge over the Karluk River, for fear that the salmon would cease swimming upstream.

Elders today teach that animals should not be killed unless needed, that no parts of them should be wasted, that their remains should be thoughtfully treated, and that their increase should never be threatened.

> We couldn't hunt ducks when they have eggs in 'em. We couldn't hunt bear, seal, and stuff when they have pups in 'em. And that was their way of life, because they know they're gonna' reproduce. And they get awful mad if people now, they shoot seals with pups.... Back in the old days you would've been punished for that.
>
> —Sven Haakanson, Sr., Kodiak Island
> Elder, 1997[13]

133 *Agayu̱lqútaq*—Mask

Sitkinak Island *(Sigtunaq)*, Kodiak archipelago, 1883
National Museum of Natural History, Smithsonian Institution
(NMNH 90466) Height 31 cm

Masks revealed themselves in dreams. Each represented a spirit
that was summoned by dances and songs at the winter hunting ceremonies. This mask has a bird's beak and the pointed
head of an *íyaq*, a dangerous being who was the reincarnation
of a man or woman who had led an evil life. An *íyaq* could be
adopted by a shaman as one of his helping spirits. This mask
is charred on one side and may have been purposely burned
after it was used; masks were often destroyed or placed in caves
after the end of a ceremony.

134 Hunter with fox pelts, Woody Island (Tangihnaq),
1909–29.
Courtesy of the Kodiak Historical Society (P 386.97N).

The Heritage of Skin Boats

ALUTIIQ LIVES ARE LIVED BY THE SEA, AND ON BOATS. Skills for reading the weather, navigating, and surviving on the tempestuous waters of the Gulf of Alaska, Bristol Bay, Cook Inlet, and Prince William Sound in today's fishing vessels are the practical heritage of earlier times. Many Elders remember when fishermen and families traveled in heavy wooden dories pulled by oars. Some grew up around a much older tradition of hunting, fishing, and traveling in graceful kayaks *(qayaq)* made from sinew, wood, and skins. A larger type of skin boat, the *angyaq*, once traveled the waters of the Alutiiq region on expeditions of trade and war.

As a young child, in about 1915, the late Kodiak Island Elder Larry Matfay and his sister rode inside a kayak, looking out through the translucent cover of the boat, freshly waterproofed with seal oil. "It was just like glass—you can see the water line," he remembered.[14] Bobby Stamp, who grew up in the village of Chenega in Prince William Sound, recalls joyful women making new sealskin covers for the boats in spring: "I remember the ladies sitting in the houses, laughing and . . . sewing. You know, everybody helped everybody."[15]

135 Alutiiq hunters in Bear Cove, Kachemak Bay, 1905.
Photograph by Adam Widenius, courtesy of the National Museum of Finland.

In recent years, Larry Matfay, Bobby Stamp, and other Elders have taught kayak building to a new generation of artisans and students. This knowledge almost vanished during the first decades of the twentieth century as the use of kayaks for sea otter hunting came to an end and work in the salmon canneries reduced time available for travel and subsistence hunting. By the 1930s, relatively few of the boats were in use.[16]

Today, kayaks are new symbols of cultural pride and indigenous craftsmanship. In the Cook Inlet village of Nanwalek, students and community members have been constructing kayaks since 1996, and paddling the boats to *Tamamta Katuhluta,* an annual cultural festival in Homer. Boats built by students through the Kodiak Area Native Association's Alutiiq Arts Program, under the direction of Joe Kelley, are on display at the Alutiiq Museum and at other museums in the U.S. and Japan.

136 Kayakers from Nanwalek at the *Tamamta Katuhluta* heritage festival, Homer, Alaska, 1997.

Photograph by Lena Anderson.

Kayak Design and Construction

It is likely that skin-covered watercraft were used by the very earliest people to travel the coasts and interisland passages of the Alutiiq region between 7500 and 10,000 years ago. Parts of kayak frames have been found at the Karluk 1 archaeological site, some as old as A.D. 1600.[17] Designs were perfected over many generations, producing boats that are fast, light, and extremely seaworthy. The wooden frames are lashed together with cord, rawhide, spruce root, or sinew. This gives great strength and flexibility, letting a kayak bend in heavy seas that might otherwise break its thin wooden skeleton. Metal nails or screws are avoided because they would make the frame too rigid, and might also cut through the skin covering and cause a leak. Another aspect of rough water design is the split and sharply upturned bow of the Alutiiq kayak, a feature shared by Aleutian Island boats. The complex curves of the bow skim the water and safely lift the front of the boat over incoming waves.[18]

Alutiiq kayaks, also known by the Russian name *baidarka,* were traditionally made with spaces for one, two, or three paddlers. Single-hatch boats *(qayanguaq)*

137 Kayak prow

Carved by Ki-cuk, Akhiok, Kodiak Island, late 1800s
Alutiiq Museum
(53:1) Width 59 cm

The solid wooden prows of Alutiiq kayaks are divided into two parts; a knife-like lower portion and an upturned horn. This split construction allows the bow to be slightly hollow along the sides, increasing its buoyancy and efficiency. Strong sinew cords, which passed through holes along the bottom of the prow, were used to bind the frame. Kayaks need to bend with the waves, so nails are never used. The late Elder Larry Matfay learned the art of kayak building from his father, Sava, who learned from his own father Ki-cuk. Ki-cuk carved this heirloom prow in the late 1800s. Mr. Matfay rescued it from his old home in Old Harbor after a tidal wave washed away much of the village in 1964. An unknown person had cut a section from the bottom.

were used for fishing, travel, and the pursuit of fast animals like dolphins. The more common double-holed boats (*qayahpak*) allowed the person forward to fire a gun, arrow, or dart while a hunting partner used a paddle to steady the boat. The three-hatch type (*paitálek*) came into use during Russian colonial times. Such boats were used by ordinary sea otter hunters, but on other occasions served to convey Russians or *toions* (village chiefs).[19]

Building the boats was a cooperative effort, and men and women each brought special skills to the task. The men carved the frame pieces with crooked knives and adzes, softened the ribs in water and bent them into shape, then lashed the parts together. Hemlock, alder, or spruce wood was used, and materials were carefully selected for strength. Fresh green wood was best for ribs and stringers, especially from trees made tough and flexible by exposure to the wind. Bow pieces had to be very strong to take the stresses of heavy waves, and were carved from natural crooks with curving grain.

Kayak frames were built to human measurements, like tailored suits of clothes. Stephan Britskalov from Ellamar in Prince William Sound knew all of the frame-maker's rules of thumb. The width of a baidarka was one arm length, including the hand, and the length of the cleft in the prow was two thumbs plus two hand widths with outstretched thumbs.[20] Larry Matfay's grandfather, even though blind, could tell if a frame was true:

> And he goes round, feeling right long here, and feeling with his hands back and forth, and he said, "Sava, this is not good.... This is out a little bit. That's how.... He knows what's right."[21]

Alutiiq women carefully prepared the seal or sea lion skins and seamed them into a waterproof sheath that would stretch over the frame like a tight glove. Selection of the skins was an important first step. Skins of female sea lions were the best because they were not scarred by fighting like the males' hides.[22] Six to twelve seal skins were needed to cover a kayak, depending on its size. A cover needed to be freshly oiled each spring, and replaced every three to four years.

From his memories of seeing the process in Prince William Sound, Bobby Stamp explained how skins were cured and the cover prepared. First, fresh pelts were washed and rolled up with moss, a process that loosened the hair and allowed it be removed with a dull-edged *ulukaq*, or women's knife of slate or iron. The skins

138   *Paitálek*—Three-hatch kayak

Kodiak Island, 1874
National Museum of Natural History, Smithsonian Institution (NMNH 16275) Length 51 cm

Hunters usually traveled in one-man or two-man kayaks. Three-place boats were invented during Russian times, originally to carry fur traders or other passengers. Weapons lie on the deck of this model, ready for use. The middle paddler wears a hunting helmet that is carved to resemble a seal's head. The others wear conical hunting hats.

139   Toy kayak *(qayaq)* and boatman

Karluk 1 site, Kodiak Island, 1400–1750
Alutiiq Museum, Koniag, Inc., Collection
(kayak AM193.87.8835) Length 21.5 cm
(figure AM38:11) Height 5 cm

Boys still play with toy boats in spring, pulling them along the shoreline on strings. This miniature kayak from long ago is carved from the bark of a driftwood log. The boatman wears a bentwood hunting visor.

were often dried and stored away until needed, then softened in sea water, stretched out on wooden frames, and given a final scraping. With an older, experienced woman in charge, the skins were then tied to the frame, marked by eye, carefully cut to fit, and stitched together with sinew thread:

> This older woman would, the one that was in charge of the sewing, she would give each one of the ladies a piece to sew together. And the older women would be making the thread as they're going along. It was porpoise sinew. I remember, they would take it and they would roll it in their hands and they would even take it in their mouth to moisten it, then keep rolling it. They made an endless thread out of that sinew.[23]

According to Joe Tanape of Nanwalek, women used large and small sewing needles made from bird bones.[24] The finished cover was pulled over the frame using seaweed to lubricate the wood, drawn tight with rawhide lacings, and sewn into place. The skin cover was then treated with seal or shark oil as a final waterproofing and preservative.

Learning these intricate tasks was once part of growing up in an Alutiiq village. On Kodiak Island in 1804, the Russian priest Gideon noted that girls began their training as seamstresses by age six, when they started making sinew thread and learning to plait cord. Boys at age seven were already making toy *qayat* and paddles, and practicing with spears on the beach to prepare for their adult roles as sea-going hunters.[25] They learned to paddle full-sized boats in the surf, their fathers pulling them in with safety ropes if the boat overturned.[26]

A feast and dance was hosted by the owner of a newly completed kayak. Kayaks were given as marriage gifts, and passed on to children or placed on the owner's grave if there were no heirs. Women could own kayaks, especially through inheritance, and went out in the boats with their husbands or brothers.

140 Gunnel board

Eagle Harbor *(Ihak)*, Kodiak Island, 1883
National Museum of Natural History, Smithsonian Institution
(NMNH 90420) Length 101 cm

"The hunters would ask the whales to bring them some seals or sea lions."

—Herman Moonin, Cook Inlet Elder, 1980

Gunnel boards were lashed to the bow of a kayak with skin cords. They helped to hold a hunter's weapons securely on deck. The painted images depict sea otters, which the hunters hoped to catch, and killer whales, which could help in the hunt. The carved head of a cormorant, a seabird that dives for fish, summons another companion hunting spirit.

141 Wrist clip

Karluk 1 site, Kodiak Island, A.D. 1400–1750
Alutiiq Museum, Koniag, Inc., Collection
(UA85.193.3540) Width 6.5 cm

A hunter in a kayak on the cold ocean had to keep dry or risk dying of exposure. He wore wooden wrist clips to keep water out of the sleeves of his *kanagluk,* a waterproof hooded jacket made from the intestines of bears or sea mammals.

Kayaks at Sea

Alutiiq paddlers customarily knelt on boards or pads of skin, clothing, or grass, using their knees to help steer the boat in rolling waves. Larry Matfay laughed at the idea of sitting in a kayak, saying "you might as well be in a rocking chair in front of the television."[27] Single-bladed paddles with spear-shaped blades and T-shaped handles were generally used, and were switched from side to side with every few strokes. The job of steering with a special draw stroke fell to the man in the rear. Double-bladed paddles were used rarely on Kodiak but more commonly in Cook Inlet and Prince William Sound.[28] Paddlers wore hooded, waterproof intestine shirts called *kanagluk* and tied the bottom of the garment around the cockpit to keep water from coming into the boat. Alternatively, an intestine spray skirt *(akkuilitaq)* would be used.[29] Water that leaked inside was sucked out with a hollow wooden siphon, or with a kelp stem.

142   *Punehpak*—**Braided sinew line**

Katmai *(Qayihwik)*, Alaska Peninsula, 1879–82
National Museum of Natural History, Smithsonian Institution
(NMNH 72492) Length of bundle 13 cm

Alutiiq women twisted sinew fibers from whales, porpoises, and bears into strong lines for hunting equipment and kayaks. Learning to make braided cords was one of a young girl's first lessons. This cord is decorated with colored thread and strands of caribou hair.

143   **Basketry quiver**

Kodiak Island, late 1800s
Phoebe Hearst Museum of Anthropology
(PHMA 2-6594a,b) Length 101.5 cm

"I said 'Why don't you shoot 'em? You get more.' 'Well, if you shoot 'em they won't be coming back after this . . . you scare 'em. . . . With arrows, they keep coming back.' "
—Larry Matfay, Kodiak Island Elder, 1997,
about hunting eider ducks with his father

A quiver was carried on the deck of a kayak to hold arrows for sea otters and ducks. This quiver is woven from spruce root fiber and embroidered with grass and colored wool yarn. The wide top accommodated the feathered ends of the arrows. Similar quivers were used in southeast Alaska and on the Northwest Coast of Canada.

Photograph courtesy of the Phoebe Hearst Museum of Anthropology.

If the hatches were properly closed off, a tipped boat could be rolled upright with an underwater stroke by the paddler. A kayak could be ballasted with rocks, to avoid flipping on a rough passage, and two or three boats at sea might be lashed together to ride out a storm. The men would seal the hatches and crawl completely inside, leaving a small air gap to avoid suffocation.[30]

Landing on a wave-pounded shore and leaping from the boat without swamping required great skill, and launching into the surf was equally challenging. Bobby Stamp recalled:

> You'd count the breakers. One, two, three, four, or whatever the rhythm was. Like the fourth would be the big one. And then you tried to get in after the big one. . . . And then, in the meantime you had to jump in and get that *kamleika* on you. . . . Jump in and snap that in around you. It was already tied to your wrists and around your face. . . . Yea, it was a lot of teamwork.[31]

Kodiak Alutiiq Weather Lore

Craig Mishler
Alaska Department of Fish and Game (retired)

THE PROPER ASSESSMENT OF WIND AND WEATHER conditions is critical to survival in many parts of rural Alaska, and the way people read the weather and talk about it is of great interest to folklorists and cultural anthropologists because it is orally transmitted, based on a complex system of traditional ecological knowledge, and remains at the focus of everyday conversation.

I have gathered notes on Alutiiq weather lore from the Kodiak archipelago because my research on subsistence uses of wild foods led me there about once a month between 1989 and 1994 and about once every two or three months from 1995 through 1998. During that time I gathered weather lore from the Alutiiq communities of Ouzinkie, Larsen Bay, Old Harbor, and Akhiok. On nearly every visit I have been struck by the special sensitivity local people have to wind direction and wind speed, things largely ignored or misunderstood by outsiders and mainlanders.

For subsistence purposes, especially the gathering of shellfish, one must know about the complex interaction between winds and tides. Around Ouzinkie, for example, when the winds blow easterly, you can hardly find any clams, *bidarkies* (chitons), or urchins, even on a strong minus tide, but when there are westerlies, the winds can turn a small minus tide into a big one, allowing you to find clams, bidarkies, and urchins everywhere.

In Larsen Bay northeasterlies can be problematic because there are two kinds. A northeasterly accompanied by a falling tide builds up the swell, but a northeasterly accompanied by a rising tide is smooth and good. The adversarial northeasterly with the falling tide is humorously known in Alutiiq as *qallí'iq*—the noisy woman's wind.

Ouzinkie residents are very sensitive to winds according to season. In the summer, easterly, southeasterly, and northeasterly winds are warm and rainy, contributing to conditions when the salmon are eager to run up into the spawning streams. However, southerly, southwesterly, westerly, and even northwesterly winds bring fair and clear weather, which are very good for salmon fishing. Residents say they need three good days of westerly winds to make dry fish or *tammúq*. Hot weather without any wind at all is no good—the fish will turn sour and spoil before they are dry.

In the winter months, by contrast, Ouzinkie's northwest winds are generally cold and stormy, bringing lots of snow. Northwest winds are also very strong and may be bad for flying. A northerly brings dry snow while a northeasterly brings wet snow. The worst winter winds for Ouzinkie are the easterlies, which bring warm air and a driving rain that melt off the snow and create lots of ice. These easterlies produce about a six-foot chop and create very dangerous conditions for small boats. But wind lore is very localized and wind directions can signify radically different things in different communities. In contrast to Ouzinkie, an easterly coming through Akhiok produces very moderate weather.

When I first started flying to small Kodiak Alutiiq communities in 1989 following the *Exxon Valdez* oil spill, I found myself spending hours or days in the Kodiak City

Many different items of equipment were carried on and in the boat, so that hunters would be prepared for any hunting opportunity or emergency. Harpoons, darts, lances, throwing board, spare paddle, axe, bow, quiver full of arrows, shotgun, and seal club were among the items arrayed on deck in front of each man, secured beneath deck straps.[32] On some boats, the deck straps ran through carved and painted gunwale boards. Inside, hunters carried water in covered wooden boxes, food, blankets, bladders for emergency flotation, bags of spare lance tips, arrowheads, and other necessities, and a sewing kit *(kakiwik)* for repairing rips in the boat cover. Nick Ignatin of Old Harbor recalled that such a repair could even be done at sea, by bringing two boats together and overturning the damaged one.[33]

Because weather is such a critical factor in sea travel and subsistence, forecasting has always been a highly developed Alutiiq skill (see Craig Mishler, below). As

144 Afognak Island sky.
Photograph by Patrick Saltonstall.

airport terminal, waiting for the weather to improve, and sometimes I returned home to Anchorage without ever reaching my destination. Except in extremely foggy conditions I could almost always fly from Anchorage to Kodiak City, where IFR (instrument flight rating) landings are possible by twin-prop or jet, but then I would end up stuck there because bush flights in small single-engine planes operate only under VFR (visual flight rating) conditions. Now, armed with indigenous local knowledge of what a northeast or a southeast wind forecast means, I save myself a lot of time and trouble by simply rescheduling for another day or another week.

Gideon noted, "A diligent hunter often goes outside during the night to observe the clouds, assesses the weather, and in accordance with his observations, leaves very early."[34] Sven Haakanson, Sr., says, "Shamans and weather forecasters were up all night while the rest were sleeping, watching the moon and stars, and would tell the hunters the next morning whether to go or not, and which way to go so they could come home with the wind at their backs."[35]

145 *Angyaq*—boat model

Kodiak Island, 1860s–1870s
National Museum of Natural History, Smithsonian Institution
(NMNH 1130) Length 39cm

The men in this model of a small *angyaq* wear three kinds of headgear: seal hunting helmets, spruce root hats with tall tops that indicated wealth, and bentwood hunting hats in the form of open-topped cones with slanting brims, a style from the Alaska Peninsula. Sprays of colored yarn depict water thrown back from the surging bow of the boat.

The *Angyaq*

The *angyaq* (plural, *angyat*) also called by the Russian term *baidara*, was a large, open boat used for long-distance trading expeditions, warfare, and intervillage travel. *Angyat* varied in length from about twenty-five to forty feet and could carry up to twenty paddlers as well as many additional passengers and hundreds of pounds of cargo. The boats were ideal for hauling home supplies of dried salmon from fishing camps, for towing whales, and other heavy tasks. Their range and speed were impressive as well. With good weather, war parties of thirty boats with twenty men each were reported to cross from Shuyak Island at the northern end of the Kodiak archipelago to Cook Inlet in two days, a distance of about fifty miles.[36] When carried up on the beach and overturned, *angyat* became travel shelters for their crews.

Angyat are depicted in early Cook Inlet rock paintings, and pieces of boats built hundreds of years ago have been found at the Karluk 1 archaeological site. Explorers' accounts from the late eighteenth century describe trading for furs with *angyaq*-borne parties of men, women, and children in Prince William Sound and Cook Inlet.[37] The Chugach always began these encounters with shouted greetings and signals of peace—a bunch of green plants

held high, uplifted arms, and raised flags made of white skins.

Before the arrival of the Russians, every Alutiiq village had *angyat*. They represented prosperity and ties to loyal kinsmen who built and crewed the boats. *Angyat* were used to bring home riches and slaves from trading expeditions and raids on distant enemies. Gideon wrote that ownership of a large *angyaq* was a hallmark of wealth on Kodiak Island.[38] In Prince William Sound, the wives of prominent hunters and political leaders owned the boats, and thus enjoyed this distinction.[39]

The strategic importance of these watercraft was recognized by the Russian fur companies, and by 1790 most *angyat* on Kodiak Island were owned by the Shelikhov-Golikov Company.[40] The boats served Russian needs to move men, furs, wood, and food, but the larger effect of Russian ownership would have been to decrease the autonomy and mobility of the indigenous population. In 1804, Gideon recorded the words of a song by Aleksei Ikuik of Aiaktalik that mourns this change and speaks of longing for the ancestral way of life. It begins:

My grandfather had riches; I am looking diligently for him

(*Apaka qasqangqehtelhia, iwahpagaqa*);

My grandfather had *baidary*, Aminaq, I am looking diligently for him,

(*Apaka angyangqehtelhia Aminak, iwahpagaqa*).[41]

146 Rock painting of an *angyaq*, Cook Inlet. The age of the painting is unknown.
de Laguna 1975:Plate 64.

147 Overturned *angyat* being used as shelters at a Chugach camp in Prince William Sound, 1790.
Courtesy of the Alaska Polar Regions Department, Elmer E. Rasmuson Library, University of Alaska Fairbanks.

Angyaq Design and Construction

Construction of the boats required a large investment of time and resources, and was a joint effort of men, who built the frame, and women, who seamed the waterproof cover from seal and sea lion skins. Baleen was used for the lashings.[42] Although an Alutiiq *angyaq* was similar to a northern Alaska *umiaq*, it also incorporated unique design features needed in the stormy, open waters of the Gulf of Alaska. The rounded, two-part bow, which James Cook thought "bears some resemblance to the head of a Whale," gave buoyancy to the front of the boat that allowed it to be launched into heavy surf and to survive in stormy seas. Because their bottoms were relatively flat, *angyat* could be landed on wave-pounded beaches where keeled boats would have been swamped.[43] The stern was deeper than the bow to hold extra cargo or ballast, increasing the stability of the craft.[44]

Under Russian rule, a hybrid style of *angyaq (baidara)* was developed. A rudder, mast, and sails of leather or grass matting were added, and some *baidary* even carried cannon. These boats were propelled with oars instead of paddles. A remarkable account of traveling in an Aleutian Islands Russian-style *baidara* was left by Archibald Campbell, an English sailor. Cambell was en route to the town of Kodiak ("Alexandria") in 1808 after surviving a shipwreck in the Aleutian Islands. Leaving Uganik Bay on the west side of Kodiak Island, he noted:

> The wind being fair we hoisted a square sail, and ran before it, at a great rate. There is a group of small islands a-breast of the south point of North Island, at which place the tides meet, causing a heavy breaking sea; and as the *Baidarai* was deeply loaded, it had a frightful appearance. The frame of the vessel was so extremely slight, that between the waves, she was bent into a deep curve, and whilst on the top of the wave the two ends were as much depressed, I was in constant apprehension that the frame would give way. She, however, went through the sea drier than a stiffer vessel would have done, and we reached the harbor of Alexandria [Kodiak] upon the ninth without incident.[45]

According to Holmberg, both *angyat* and Russian-style *baidary* were still in use on Kodiak Island in 1851,[46] but it is not known when the such last boats were built. Models of these watercraft may have been used in ritual reenactments of journeys and war at the winter ceremonies, preserving knowledge of their construction. Although no full-sized Alutiiq *angyat* now exist, Russian-era drawings and descriptions, models, and archaeological finds tell the story of these imposing skin boats.

148 *Angyaq*—Boat

Karluk *(Kallut)*, Kodiak Island, 1883
National Museum of Natural History, Smithsonian Institution
(NMNH 90464) Length 75 cm

The *angyaq* had a light, strong wooden frame made up of many individual pieces that were lashed together with whale baleen. This gave great flexibility and let the boat bend in rough water. As many as twenty large seal skins went into making the covering. The rounded bow, carved from a naturally curved piece of driftwood, lifted the boat over oncoming waves. This nineteenth-century model shows the frame in accurate detail; identical full-sized parts have been recovered at the Karluk 1 archaeological site (Knecht 1995:312-317).

Hunting Hats

FROM THE EARLIEST WESTERN CONTACTS, BEGINNING WITH Russian fur trader Stepan Glotov's arrival on Kodiak island in 1763, outsiders took special note of the hats worn by Alutiiq hunters.[47] There were wooden helmets in the shape of seal heads, round basketry hats woven from strips of spruce root, and curved visors and peaked hats shaped from thinly shaved planks of wood. To the painted imagery of the hats were added dentalium shells (delicate, cone-shaped mollusk shells traded in from the Vancouver Island region in British Columbia), glass trade beads, and sprays of sea lion whiskers. The "closed-crown" style of bentwood hat—to use terminology developed by Lydia Black—was worn in the Kodiak Island region and eastern Aleutians, while a "truncated cone" shape was typical of the Alaska Peninsula. Spruce root hats were worn throughout the Alutiiq region and down the Northwest Coast, where this style probably originated.

The heritage of hunting hats had largely faded by the end of the nineteenth century, although the late Martha Matfay and Nida Chya both recalled that some older women still made the painted basketry hats on Kodiak Island into the 1920s. Artist Jacob Simeonoff creates

149 Bentwood whaling hat entitled "Kiluda" made by Jacob Simeonoff, 1980s

Alutiiq Museum, Kodiak Area Native Association Collection (AM56:6) Length 81.5 cm

This hat is rich with symbols of animal spirits and ancestors. The ivory side panels and painted spirals (representing eyes) refer to mythical birds that could swoop down to pluck whales from the ocean. Sea lion whiskers (artificial) bristle from the back. The sharp teeth of killer whales are painted along the bottom rim. Other painted figures include leaves (symbols of life), a loon, a woman's *ulukaq* knife, and abstract hunting masks.

The seated ivory man is "a place for my father or grandfather to sit and watch and be joyful," says artist Jacob Simeonoff. Ancestors had to be spiritually present on the hunt to ensure success. The small grass pouch on the back of the hat is there to carry a hair or fragment from an ancestor's body.

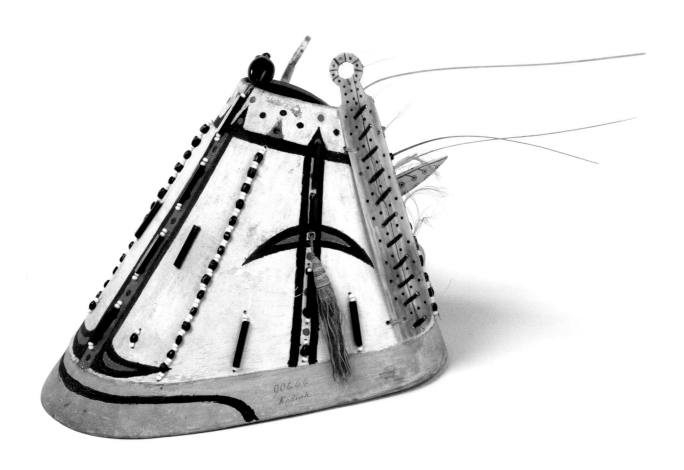

150 *Caguyaq—Bentwood hunting hat*

Katmai *(Qayihwik)*, Alaska Peninsula, 1883
National Museum of Natural History, Smithsonian Institution
(NMNH 90444) Length 52 cm; height 20 cm

"These hats are highly prized and natives do not like to part with them. These hats are supposed to have the power of attracting sea otters, and by parting with the hat they also part with all luck in getting the animals."
      —William J. Fisher, notes on Katmai hunting hat 90444
(Smithsonian Institution Archives 1882–94)

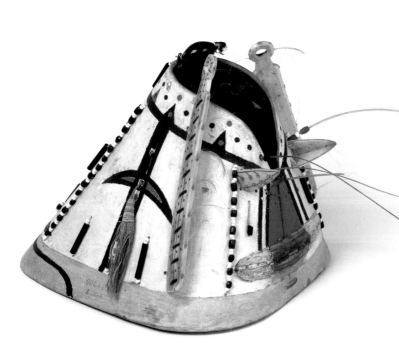

This complex hat is an abstract representation of an animal's head. Painted designs include a down-turned mouth line on the front of the brim; a long snout and nostrils (accented by white beads and black tubular beads); and crescent-shaped eyes. On the back of the hat are pointed ears carved from walrus ivory. Ivory side panels are decorated with human or animal hair. Cone-shaped ornaments with finely woven tassels of colored yarn and thread dangle from each eye, and sea lion whiskers are inserted into ivory plates at the back. The hat has a chin strip (not shown) made of braided sinew. The basic shape of the hat, an open-topped cone, was typical of the Alaska Peninsula.

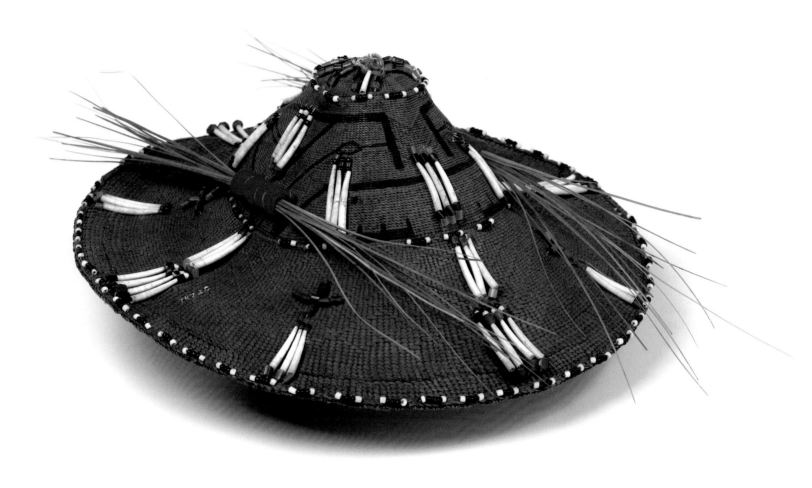

151 *Awihnaq*—Spruce root hunting hat

Karluk *(Kallut)*, Kodiak Island, 1884
National Museum of Natural History, Smithsonian Institution
(NMNH 74720) Diameter 38 cm

A creature with oval eyes, erect ears, and a toothy mouth is painted on the crown of this spruce root hat from Kodiak Island. The hat is ornamented with glass trade beads, dentalium shells, sea lion whiskers, and red cloth. There is a cloth chin strap (not visible). The style of painting and decoration is distinctively Alutiiq, while at the same time there are strong resemblances to hats worn by the Tlingit and other Northwest Coast peoples (Holm 1988). In a collection note pertaining to this item, Fisher wrote that Alutiiq kayak hunters wore spruce root hats to attract sea otters and believed strongly in their power. The painted image may represent a helping spirit similar to those seen on bentwood hunting hats. Fisher also recorded that hunting hats were valuable heirlooms that were passed down through generations. Some beads on this hat are surprisingly old, including green-centered "cornaline d'Aleppo" beads and a clear-over-white variety that were most common in Alaska during the late eighteenth and early nineteenth centuries (Crowell 1997).

152 Rock painting from Sadie Cove in Kachemak Bay, Cook Inlet (de Laguna 1985:Plate 68). The painting may represent wolves transforming into killer whales. Black (1991) suggests that the iconography of bentwood hunting hats depicts the "killer whale-wolf" known from Yup'ik mythology, a creature that changed its form to be able to hunt on both land and water (Nelson 1899:444). This rock painting may indicate that the same theme was part of Alutiiq oral tradition. Herman Moonin, an Elder from the village of Nanwalek, said that long ago in Cook Inlet people believed human beings changed into killer whales when they died (Moonin 1980:75–76).

vivid contemporary interpretations of bentwood visors and hats.

Even though the last generations of traditional makers have passed away, insights into the meanings of the hats may be drawn from historical materials, study of museum collections, and traditional Alutiiq stories. Both bentwood and spruce root styles of hunting hats were believed to aid the hunter in his quest for animals at sea, an idea that Smithsonian collector William Fisher interpreted in terms of a simple concept of luck. Writing about a bentwood hat purchased in Katmai in 1883 (fig. 150), he noted, "These hats are highly prized and natives do not like to part with them. The hats are supposed to have the power of attracting sea otters, and by parting with the hat they also part with all luck in getting these animals."[48]

Close examination of this hat reveals a deeper level of meaning. As the painted lines are visually traced, the face of a wolf-like creature emerges—a downturned mouth along the brim, a long snout with curving nostrils, and crescent-shaped eyes. The eyes are set in motion by dangling tassels of finely woven hair and grass. On the back of the hat is a pair of pointed ears made of walrus ivory. Attached to the side of the hat are ivory panels that, angle out like bird wings, each topped with a ring or eye.

Similar imagery was used on bentwood hats and visors made by Yup'ik, Unangan, and Iñupiaq artists. Russian scholar Sergei Ivanov made the original suggestion that such hats were "masks of a religious and magic character" that represented and attracted the animals sought

by sea hunters.[49] Anthropologist Lydia Black argues that the hats are symbolically complex "images of power" that depict the killer-whale wolf, a mythical predator that hunted on both sea and land.[50] She further suggests that the ivory side-panels represent bird wings, heads, beaks, and eyes, symbols that imparted to the hunter the power of the thunderbird or eagle which could sweep down from the skies to catch whales.

An Alutiiq story from Kodiak Island, recorded in the early years of this century under the title "The Un-Natural Uncle," illustrates this idea. It tells of a boy who drifts in a box to the land of the Eagle people. When he puts on one of their skins, he becomes an eagle himself and is able to pluck whales from the sea and bring them back to his home village.[51] Raven, another powerful figure in Alutiiq mythology, captures a whale in the Kodiak tale, "The Raven and His Grandmother."[52]

While bentwood headgear links the Alutiiq region to Inuit and Unangan traditions, spruce root hats *(awirnaq)* reflect the strong Northwest Coast strand of Alutiiq heritage (fig. 151). Such hats were woven like baskets and heavily embellished with beads, prized dentalium shells, and sea lion whiskers, especially in the late nineteenth century. Styles of weaving and decoration are similar to hats worn by northern Tlingit people.[53] As among the Tlingit, stacks of basketry cylinders were added to the top to mark "men of the first consequence."[54] Animal faces—like the toothy creature with large ears who graces the front of the Karluk hat—suggest that these hats were also a type of hunting mask.

Sea Mammals

SEA MAMMALS ARE AMONG THE MOST PRIZED subsistence foods in Alutiiq villages, now as in the past. The right of Alaska Natives to hunt these animals is protected under the federal Marine Mammal Protection Act of 1976. When a harbor seal, sea lion, or beluga whale is taken, it is shared through extended family networks and with Elders and others in the community who might be in need. Other kinds of sea mammals—whales, dolphins, sea otters, fur seals, and porpoises, whose bones litter archaeological sites—were important in former times for food and many other uses. Seal and sea lion skins were fashioned into boat covers, and intestines were material for waterproof garments and bags. Sinews were made into thread and cord, and whale baleen into lashings. Seal stomachs became containers for fresh water, food storage containers, and hunting floats. Oil was used to preserve dried fish, seaweed, and berries, to waterproof clothing and skin boats, and to fuel stone lamps for heat and light.

153 Mike Totemoff of Tatitlek fleshes a harbor seal skin for tanning, 1998.
Photograph by William Simeone.

Harbor Seal and Sea Lion

Harbor seals and sea lions are hunted with rifles in bays near the villages and at places where they haul out on rocks. Hitting one of the animals in the water from a bobbing boat demands excellent marksmanship.

Traditional methods for hunting these animals were varied and ingenious. One way to kill a sea lion or seal from a kayak was to surprise it while it slept in the water. Hunters used heavy toggle harpoons, which remained important even after the introduction of rifles (fig. 156). According to Innokenty Inga of Old Harbor on Kodiak Island, "A fat seal would always float, but we had to use the harpoon for seals which had only been wounded by the bullet. The harpoon was attached to a line that was in turn connected to an air bladder. The bladder was always carried on the kayak. It would help us to get the seal if it tried to swim away or if it had been only slightly wounded by our shot."[55]

Working from his kayak, a hunter might spread a sinew net, suspended by wooden floats and stone sinkers, across the mouth of a cove while the animals slept on the shore or on rocks. Then he would yell, frightening the animals into the net.[56] Another technique was to place inflated sealskins on the shore as decoys. Wearing a painted wooden seal helmet, the hunter would partially conceal himself behind rocks and imitate seal calls and movements until a curious animal came within harpooning distance. Sven Haakanson, Sr., relates his memory of a woman who practiced a variation of this method:

> She'd come to our house and borrow one .22 shell.... I'd give her a shell. She'd walk behind Ousinkie on the bog. And somebody almost shot her once. She'd put a sealskin over her head, that was cut out with the face. And she'd go crawl down on the rocks with her .22. And cry like a baby seal or a mother seal.... And the seal would come right into it, to where she's

154 Ivory carvings

Naknek, Egegik, and Ugashik villages, Alaska Peninsula, 1885–86
National Museum of Natural History, Smithsonian Institution (NMNH 127799) Longest 6 cm

Miniature animals and mythical creatures were probably fashioned for children. This set—which includes a beluga whale, seal, sea otter, sea lion, and ten-legged insect with a bird's head—was collected from Alutiiq and Yup'ik villages on Bristol Bay.

like ten feet [away], and she'd shoot it and wade out and get it. And she'd come back packing a seal.[57]

Traditionally, seal and sea lion meat was eaten raw, dried, stone-boiled, or roasted. Seal meat today is cooked as a roast, fried, or made into a stew. Intestines, lungs, liver, kidneys, and heart are prepared using traditional recipes, and baked flippers are a delicacy prized by Elders. Seal oil is an essential ingredient for *akutaq* ("ice cream") made out of various combinations of oil, salmon eggs, mashed potatoes, berries, and sugar.

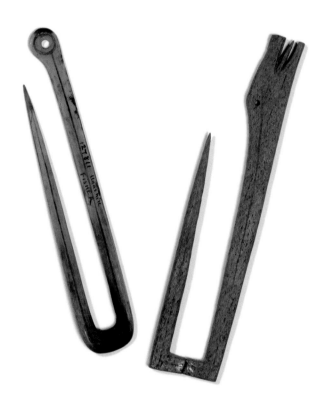

155 Childrens' blubber hooks

Ugashik *(Uggásaq)*, Alaska Peninsula, 1885–86
National Museum of Natural History, Smithsonian Institution
(both NMNH 127811) Length 18 cm (left) and 19 cm (right)

" [W]e're all well schooled in the way of living. . . . If you got some meat or some fish or something like that . . . you shared with the whole village."

—Natalie Simeonoff, Kodiak Island Elder, 1991

In Ugashik in the 1880s, when a hunter brought home a seal or beluga whale, the entire village shared in the feast. Each child received a small piece of blubber, and carried it away on a special bone or ivory hook (Fisher note, Smithsonian Institution Archives 1882–94, Accession 18490).

156 Toggling harpoon

Prince William Sound, 1887–93
National Museum of Natural History, Smithsonian Institution
(NMNH 168625) Length 25 cm

Until the early 1900s, Alutiiq hunters used harpoons mounted to kill seals and sea lions. This heavy bone harpoon with a triangular slate blade is mounted on a wooden foreshaft that would have in turn been attached to a long handle. It has a ring of twisted bark that slipped over the spur of the harpoon head to keep it straight until the harpooner made his strike.

"Big Ed" Gregorieff

William Simeone
Alaska Department of Fish and Game

EDWARD GREGORIEFF HAS LIVED IN PRINCE WILLIAM Sound over seventy years, most of that time in the village of Tatitlek. He is an articulate and cosmopolitan man, fluent in three languages—Alutiiq, Russian, and English. He is also possessed of an encyclopedic knowledge of Alutiiq culture and history. I first met Ed in 1990 when I went to Tatitlek to learn about the effects of the *Exxon Valdez* oil spill on subsistence. Ed invited me to have coffee and for hours I listened to stories about his life and how the oil spill disrupted life in the community. During subsequent visits Ed told me more about subsistence and the history of the village.

Harbor seals are an important source of food and skins for Tatitlek people. Now hunters use rifles with telescopic sights to kill seals but in the past they had only iron sights. To improve their aim, hunters filed down the V of the back sight. When they aimed at the head of a seal the hunter placed the bead of the front sight at the bottom of the V and the head of the seal on top of the bead. The idea was to place your shot just below the water line. This was called *imlayuk* or "giving it a little water."

In spring and fall migrating ducks were hunted using various techniques. One day Ed followed an Elder to the beach but lost sight of him. After looking around Ed saw the man lying on the beach with his shotgun pulled tight against his chest with his eye on a flock of ducks feeding just off shore. Each time the ducks dived below the surface of the water the hunter rolled across the beach toward them and each time they surfaced he stopped. Finally, when he was within twenty yards of the ducks, he waited until they dived and then stood up. When the ducks surfaced the hunter let them have it with his twelve-gauge shotgun.

Ed spent much of his adult life as a commercial fisherman. "It was a fun life," he said "just like a big picnic for us, just the family. What amount of fish we got was all ours. . . . We didn't get as much fish as most of them did, but we made as much money, you know just for the family. My wife enjoyed the outdoors and traveling around different places, anchor up somewhere else every night. Usually close to a steam bath some place and make a steam bath on the beach. Kill a seal and barbecue it over an open fire on the beach. I think we just picnicked about half of the time we were fishing. We had a lot of fun."

In the 1930s Ed worked as a hand logger. He and his partner hand logged with cross cut saws, double bladed axes, and springboards (boards set into notches in the tree, where loggers stood while sawing). At first Ed didn't know what a springboard was. The owner of the logging company provided them with a chain saw but neither Ed nor his partner knew how to start it so they didn't use it. Eventually, a tree fell on it. The pay was $5 dollars a tree, limbed, and cut into forty-foot lengths. At that time there were no jobs at home except for the CCC (Civilian Conservation Corps) and they paid $2 a day or sixty dollars a month. Ed said that when they got going he and his partner could cut down twenty-five trees a day.

157 Seal-shaped food bowl

Chenega *(Caniqaq)*, Prince William Sound, 1887–93
National Museum of Natural History, Smithsonian Institution
(NMNH 168619) Length 37 cm

Men ate from round and animal-shaped bowls. This bowl depicts a seal with its head and tail above water. Ripples from the swimming seal form the rim. The wood is stained with the rich oils of Alutiiq cuisine.

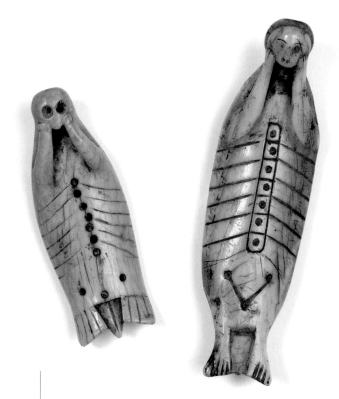

Sea Otter

Although few are hunted today, sea otters were historically of great importance. Images on hunting equipment reflect the spiritual dimensions of the sea otter quest. A traditional Chugach belief held that the sea otter *(ahnaq)* was a man who was surprised by the tide when he was out looking for chitons and then cried: "I wish I might turn into a sea otter."[58] Evidence for this kinship between human and animal was seen in the otter's internal organs, which are "exactly like those of a human being."[59] Respect for the animal's soul was shown by sinking its bones in the sea, or by burying them if it had been killed on shore. Some hunters were lucky enough to learn a secret song from the sea otter, and could then attract the animal by singing. Hunting amulets of many kinds were used. Larry Matfay said, "There was a little sea otter in there. [Dried] Baby sea otter. And the guy told me, 'That's for our good luck. We put that up on kayak and pretty soon we find a sea otter.'"[60]

Sea otter fur made luxurious, warm parkas that early European explorers saw people wearing in Prince William Sound and the Kodiak archipelago.[61] The same qualities created the world market for otter pelts and motivated the Russian fur trade that engulfed the Alutiiq region in the eighteenth century. Huge flotillas of sea otter hunters were sent out by the Shelikhov-Golikof company and Russian-American Company, and the Alutiit were no longer allowed to use the fur themselves.

158 Ivory sea otter amulets

Napartalek, Bristol Bay, 1887–93
National Museum of Natural History, Smithsonian Institution (both NMNH 168626) Length L 7 cm (left) and 10 cm (right)

According to traditional Alutiiq belief, sea otters *(ahnat)* were formerly human beings. These walrus ivory amulets—made to be fastened inside the cockpit of a kayak—may be of Yup'ik manufacture, but similar carvings were made in both the Unangan and Alutiiq regions (Black 1982). An archaeological example was found at Seldovia in Cook Inlet (de Laguna 1975:Plate 52-9). The incised designs depict the animal's ribs and spine. The Chugach of Prince William Sound returned the bones of a killed otter to the sea so that the animals would be reborn.

Gideon wrote, "Since 1792 the company has prohibited all inhabitants engaged in its enterprises to make for themselves parkas out of sea otter and fox pelts, and issued the strictest orders that if anyone were to wear such clothing, it would be torn off the person's back and confiscated for the company without any recompense. This has actually happened. This is why nowadays, all inhabitants generally wear bird skin parkas, formerly used only by the poor and the slaves."[62]

The hunt continued under American rule, but with fierce commercial competition that decimated remaining populations of the animals and drove up prices. The hunting continued until the animal was protected under the Fur Seal Act of 1911. Larry Matfay told about one hunter who built a house during the boom years using expensive red cedar lumber brought to Akhiok by schooner: "How much did that cost? One sea otter!"[63]

On the morning of a hunt, a party of eight to fifteen double-hatched kayaks would set out in a line, spaced widely apart. When a man saw an otter, he would silently raise his paddle as a signal for the boats to form a circle. The otter would dive to escape, but on calm days its underwater movements could be followed by the air bubbles trailing from its fur. When the otter surfaced to breathe, the man who first saw it would throw his harpoon or shoot an arrow.[64] Larry Matfay explained what would ensue. "When the first arrow hits the sea otter, they'll dive. The arrow's got a string attached on the arrowhead to slow the otter down, but it will dive again and again. The arrow goes crossways in the water. Everyone can see which way the arrow is going; and after the first hit, anybody can shoot it."[65]

With each successive dive the otter weakened, and finally surrendered. After killing an otter, the hunters would not drink water until they were once again on land. To quench the thirst the animal must have felt in the salty water of the sea, they poured fresh water over its mouth.[66] The hunter whose arrow was the first to strike the sea otter earned the right to keep the valuable skin.

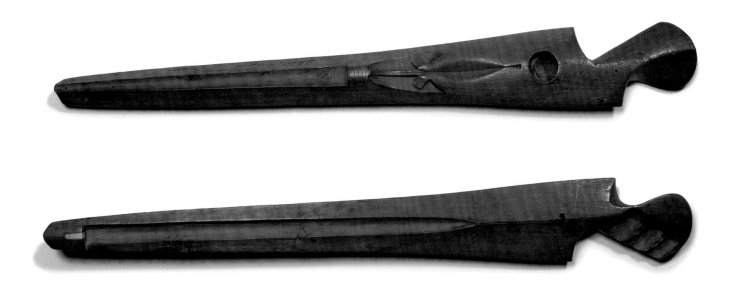

159 *Qehuq*—Sea otter arrow

Copper River, near Prince William Sound, date unknown
National Museum of Natural History, Smithsonian Institution
(NMNH 382243) Length 79 cm

Hunters encircled a sea otter with their kayaks, shooting arrows or darts each time the animal surfaced. When an arrow hit, its barbed point remained in the animal while the shaft came loose and floated away, still attached to the point by a sinew cord. The cord (here seen wrapped around the arrow) was tied so that the shaft would drag sideways through the water, causing the swimming otter to exhaust itself. The animal was finally caught and killed with a club. Arrow points could be made of bone or copper.

160 *Nuqaq*—Throwing board

Kodiak Island or Prince William Sound, 1867
National Museum of Natural History, Smithsonian Institution
(NMNH 2533) Length 48 cm

The design on this board shows the feet and tail of a sea otter, depicted as though it has just slipped through the finger hole. The carving may depict the moment of death, when the animal passed from its own watery world into the care of human hunters.

161 Unangan hunters in the Aleutian Islands use a throwing board to launch a hunting dart. Illustration by Luka Voronin, 1790–92.

Courtesy of the Alaska Polar Regions Department, Elmer E. Rasmuson Library, University of Alaska Fairbanks.

162 Ornament for whaling ritual

Uyak site, Kodiak Island, A.D. 1–1100
National Museum of Natural History, Smithsonian Institution
(NMNH 365592) Length 19 cm

Whalers summoned spiritual power for the hunt through songs and charms. This archaeological carving from Kodiak Island has a grip on the back so it could be held in the mouth, probably by a dancer. Images of whales and a human face with whale-tail mouth are carved on the front. Birds' heads on the ends may represent helping spirits and the small holes around the edges probably once held feathers.

Whales

The whale was so close now he could touch it with his paddle. The whaler stood up and, after motioning to the boy to dip his paddle deep to steady the kayak, struck with all his might, sinking the spear point deep into the whale. Then he pushed the shaft hard to the side and jerked it loose. The whale, feeling the spear in its side, threw its fluke high in the air and went down in a steep dive.

—Ahhuhsulek (The Whaler), told by
Ralph Demidoff, Afognak Island Elder,
1962[67]

Each spring, migratory whales arrive in the Gulf of Alaska from their southern breeding grounds, to spend the summer feeding along the coasts of the Alutiiq region. Young humpback and fin whales were once an important resource for the Alutiit, providing meat, blubber, intestines for gutskin garments, baleen, bone, and sinew. Until the early decades of the twentieth century, whalers set out in kayaks to kill them, armed only with slender, poison-tipped darts or spears. Whalers summoned spiritual power for the hunt through special songs, talismans, and complex, secret rituals.[68]

The Alutiiq method of killing whales was unique, practiced nowhere else but in the eastern Aleutian Islands, where it seems to have spread in late precontact or early historic times.[69] It contrasts with the whaling traditions of Bering Sea peoples to the north and the Makah to the south in Washington state, who harpoon whales and tow them ashore using large, open boats.[70] Alutiiq whalers relied on the effects of the poison and on ritual practices to prevent the whale's escape. Several other types of whaling seem to have been practiced in Prince William Sound. Groups of kayak hunters surrounded the whale (as in sea otter hunting), or pursued it from *angyat* with toggle harpoons like Bering Strait hunters.[71]

The *ahhuhsulet*, "shamans who hunt whales," were ritual specialists. On Kodiak, whaling and its secrets were passed from father to son within certain families, although in Prince William Sound any young man could choose the profession.[72] Whalers were highly respected but also feared because of their knowledge of deadly poisons. During the whaling season they were shunned and considered unclean, and lived away from the village in remote areas.[73] For their part, the *ahhuhsulet* avoided other people, especially women, because whales were very sensitive to the "vapors" that surrounded them.[74]

163 *Ulukahsút*—Whaling dart blades and sheath

Karluk (*Kallut*), Kodiak Island, 1885–86
National Museum of Natural History, Smithsonian
    Institution
(NMNH 127759) Length 19 cm (right) and 25 cm
    (right)

Alutiiq whalers coated the long stone blades of their weapons with a poison made from the root of the monkshood, mixed with human fat and other magical ingredients. The small quantity of aconite poison that could be painted on a dart blade was not strong enough to kill a whale directly but could paralyze its tail or flipper and cause the animal to drown (see Crowell 1994). When a dead whale was found, often two or three days after the strike, markings on the blade identified the hunter who had made the kill. These were abstract designs, like the chevron and dot motif seen here, or sometimes the actual name or initials of the hunter spelled in Cyrillic characters. The blade on the left is encased in a protective sheath, probably a hollow stem of wild celery.

Whale poison was brewed from the root of the monkshood *(Aconitum sp.)*. Sauer learned about this aspect of whaling in 1790 on Kodiak Island. He wrote, "Selecting the roots of such plants as grow alone, these roots are dried and pounded, or grated; water is then poured upon them, and they are kept in a warm place until fermented: when in this state, the men anoint the points of their arrows, or lances, which makes the wound which may be inflicted mortal."[75]

Human fat was mixed into the aconite poison, giving it magical potency. To obtain this ingredient, the corpses of prominent people or other whalers were taken to caves and soaked in water before rendering out the fat over a fire.[76]

The resulting mixture of fat and aconite was believed to be incredibly strong and dangerous. In Prince William Sound, it was said that birds who flew over a kayak where it was stored would fall dead from the sky.[77] On Kodiak Island, where the last traditional whaling took place before about 1920, the late Larry Matfay was taught never to drink water from a stream that trickled down from a whaler's cave for fear that it would be contaminated.[78] Elders grew up with warnings from their parents never to touch old artifacts that they found in the ground, for fear that shamans had rubbed the objects with poison. Sven Haakanson, Sr., said, "But they said the reason why we weren't supposed to touch 'em is some of the shamans used to have some awful strong poisons. They even poisoned the whales or paralyzed the whales with stuff they used. . . . And I've heard many stories where people touched them and they got sick or hands start rottin' 'till they put 'em back."[79]

The poison was applied to long, slender blades of slate that tipped the whaling dart or spear (fig. 163). The fragile blade was designed to break off inside the whale, killing the animal by paralyzing its flipper or tail and causing it to drown or to be unable to dive or feed.[80] Each whaler engraved his own mark in the slate, which enabled his kill to be identified when a dead whale was found:

> One . . . drift up in the Clam Beach. Old Arsenti looked at it, take it out. Go out there and wash it. I was watching him pretty close. He looked back and turned around and he said, "Now this is Ambrose's whale." Then we have to go over there and notify him,

his whale has drifted over here. He said he's been looking for it after he spear it.

—Larry Matfay, Kodiak Island Elder, 1990[81]

During the Russian colonial period, the Russian-American Company kept a register of whalers' marks, and appropriated two thirds of the whale for its own stores.[82]

Ritual, ceremony, and special clothing were connected with all phases of whaling. In accounts collected by Dominique Desson, whalers wore a type of peaked shaman's cap during preparation of the poison and preenacted the hunt with a miniature weapon and a wooden model of a whale.[83] Rock paintings and carvings of whales and whale-people were made to foster success in the hunt.[84] Black suggests that the closed-crown style of hunting hat, discussed above, was worn by whale hunters to invoke the predatory power of killer whales and eagles. Before and after striking the whale, its movements were restricted by trailing a line of human fat through the water which the animal would not cross.[85] Songs called on the winds to make the whale drift to the beach, and the whalers' wives had to stay in their houses, to keep the whale from traveling away. When the whale drifted ashore, the whaler's wife took fresh water to it to drink, a sign of respect shown to sea otters and seals as well.[86]

Finally came the harvest of the whale's incredible bounty, which provided food, oil, and raw materials to the whole community. People went to wherever the whale had drifted ashore and camped there to cut it up. Seagulls and eagles were observed to see what parts of the carcass they avoided, a sure sign that the meat was spoiled or contained poison. A small amount of oil rubbed on the arm or forehead caused numbness if any of the toxin was present. A Chenega Elder told Bobby Stamp about the butchering of probably the last whale to be killed in Prince William Sound, in about 1885, capturing the excitement of the event:

> He could see [his uncle] way up there, on top of the whale, cutting it you know. You could imagine what it was like, they're barefooted them days. They down on the beach and they were slipping around in that whale oil after they cut it open.[87]

164 *Aḷḷugaq*—Skin hat

Sutkum, Alaska Peninsula, 1883
National Museum of Natural History, Smithsonian Institution
(NMNH 90446) Height 26 cm

Tall peaked hats were worn by shamans and whalers on the
Alaska Peninsula and Kodiak Island (see also fig. 197). The
red-painted front panel of this hat is embroidered with caribou hair, yarn, and strips of thin painted skin (probably
esophagus), and further embellished with puffs of ermine and
sea otter fur. The side panels are made of ground squirrel fur.
Long strands of unidentified white hair and red yarn are
worked into the seams. Iridescent cormorant breast feathers
can be seen on top of the hat.

Land Animals

165 Ivory carvings

Naknek, Egegik, and Ugashik villages, Alaska Peninsula,
  1885–86
National Museum of Natural History, Smithsonian
  Institution
(NMNH 127799) Longest 6 cm

These carvings include a caribou, fox with spots, a seal-like
animal with ten legs, and a weasel.

166 *Ekgwiutaq*—Hunting bag

Woody Island (Tangihnaq), Kodiak Island, 1879–82
National Museum of Natural History, Smithsonian
  Institution
(NMNH 72500) Height 21.5 cm

Men carried bags to hold percussion caps, ammunition, tobacco, arrowheads, and other small necessities for hunting. This
skin bag is embellished with colored thread, yarn, and caribou
hair embroidery. Appliquéd designs are made of thin, dyed skin,
probably sea lion esophagus. The mouth of the bag is trimmed
with seal skin and the strap is made of twisted sinew.

167 Gun cap box

Nuchek (*Núciq*), Prince William Sound, 1887–93
National Museum of Natural History, Smithsonian
  Institution
(NMNH 168630) Height 8.5 cm

The Alutiit increasingly used guns after the 1860s. Flintlock
muskets were eventually replaced by muzzle-loaded percussion guns, which used small metal caps to ignite the gunpow-
der charge in the barrel. This horn box held a supply of the
caps, which were valuable trade items.

DEPENDING ON LOCATION, CARIBOU, BLACK BEAR,
grizzly bear, moose, mountain goats, and Dall sheep, as
well as elk and Sitka deer (introduced species), are available to Alutiiq hunters. Many smaller species are hunted
or trapped for furs and food: porcupine, marmot, weasel, marten, mink, land otter, snowshoe hare, and red
squirrel. Land animals are particularly important in the
economies of Alaska Peninsula villages.

Caribou

For communities on the northern Alaska Peninsula,
seasonal migrations of caribou provide a valuable subsistence food that is not available elsewhere in the Alutiiq
region. The northern Alaska Peninsula herd travels south
to its calving grounds in late winter and early spring,
then returns to its winter range in the northern peninsula. Villages along this route stock their freezers with
meat as the herd passes or winters in their area. When
the season comes for hunting, everybody is ready for
fresh caribou meat.[88]

A caribou provides a varied feast: The tongue is con-
sidered a delicacy, and often the entire head is boiled.
Fat is used for sausage, ground meat, or flavoring roasts.
The heart, liver, intestines, kidneys, and arteries are used.
Alutiiq families on the Alaska Peninsula eat caribou
steaks, roasts, soups, and stews, as well as dried caribou.
Hides, which were once saved, are one of the few things
today that are discarded.[89]

In the past, tanned hides were sewn into shirts and
warm coats. Caribou fur and hairs were often used for

decoration on clothing. Alutiit on Kodiak Island traded with those on the Alaska Peninsula for these materials. They desired antlers for arrows and the long caribou chest hairs used for embroidering clothing. Caribou hunters on the Alaska Peninsula also traded with villages in Prince William Sound and on the Kenai Peninsula.[90]

Today caribou are hunted with guns by men in small parties of two or three. Some women join the hunt.[91] Caribou hunters share the meat throughout their communities, with special attention to relatives, elderly people, and the disabled.[92]

Before guns were available, caribou were hunted with bows, arrow, and special hunting tactics.

> One man goes behind the deer [caribou] and frightens them. The animals rush straight at the people who are hiding who shoot them with bows and arrows. Deer [caribou] hunting is very difficult, except at that time when they are crossing. In order to hunt them you have to go high up in the mountains and stalk them with the greatest of care, and out of the wind as well.[93]

Bears

Bears–including brown or grizzly bears (*Ursus arctos*, throughout the Alutiiq region) and black bears (*Ursus americanus*, present on the Kenai Peninsula and around Prince William Sound)—are prominent in Alutiiq legend and surrounded by a rich body of contemporary lore and hunting ritual. Traditional stories illustrate identification and kinship with bears. Clyda Christiansen recalls a Kodiak Island legend, "The Woman Who Turned into a Bear," in which a woman transforms herself and her daughter in order to exact bloody revenge upon her cheating husband.[94] Lydia Robart of Port Graham told a traditional story about a shaman who changed into a bear.[95] Some Alutiit believe that humans are descended from the animals, and many have noted bears' human-like characteristics, including occasional bipedalism and similar diet.[96]

Bear hunters also hold a special status in Alutiiq folklore. The great whaler and hunter Atlutaq, who lived near Montague Island in Prince William Sound, was said to be able to kill bears with only a club.[97] Davydov recorded a nineteenth-century story about two brothers who waged war on the bears of Kodiak Island:

> A bear killed and ate a little girl and her brothers proposed to take vengeance on the bears for this; they would kill them all until in the stomach of one they found the earrings which had been in the girl's ears, or some other sign.[98]

After many bears were killed on Kodiak, the hunters eventually found the girl's belongings in the stomach of a bear on the Alaska Peninsula, far across the water from Kodiak.

Bear products have traditionally had many uses. The meat, fat, skin, and bone were used, and little was thrown away. Today on the Alaska Peninsula, the skins and skulls of brown bears are left in the field by subsistence hunters, but there is little waste. One woman from the Alaska Peninsula noted that the few things they leave behind are the same few parts that are kept by trophy hunters.[99]

Some communities today hunt more bears than others, and not all Alutiiq people have a taste for it. Some

168 Pete Pavloff with a bear skin at Woody Island (Tangihnaq), after 1908.
Courtesy of the Kodiak Historical Society (P386-127).

consider the meat to be too strong in flavor, or too tough. The ribs, front and hind quarters, feet, and fat of brown bears are saved, as well as the tongue for boys (which prevents them from being bitten by bears), and the front paws for women (men who eat the hands may be slapped by bears).[100]

Margie Macauly-Waite remembers how her father used bear meat to ensure her brother's future as a hunter:

> My father went out and . . . got a brown bear and then took the muscles . . . and tied them around Steven's wrists and ankles. . . . And I guess that is something to go ahead and give them strength—make them strong . . . and brave like a bear.

> —Margie Macauly-Waite
> (Chignik Lake, Alaska Peninsula),
> 1997[101]

Anakenti Zeedar and Nida Chya said that the same practice with brown bear veins was common on Kodiak in the village of Old Harbor. Baby boys would have the veins of a bear tied around their wrists to ensure future strength.[102]

In the past, bear skins were used for bedding and clothing. In Prince William Sound, hides were stretched on wooden frames, then washed in a solution of bear's fat and spruce bark, scraped, rubbed, and dried again.[103] Bear skins were also made into garments for bad weather that utilized the skin of the head for a hood, the legs and paws for sleeves and mittens, and the back legs for trousers and boots. Rain parkas (*kamleikas*) were made from horizontally sewn strips of bear intestines.[104] However, the intestines of brown bears can only be used when harvested in the spring, according to the late Larry Matfay of Kodiak Island, because in the fall they are full of holes from the sharp bones of salmon that the bears have been eating.[105]

Bear hunting requires spiritual preparation. The most important thing to remember is respect for the animal. Hunters are never supposed to brag about their hunting abilities, and some refrain from even speaking about the hunt before it happens. A contemporary Chignik Lake hunter explained that is because the animals might be listening.[106] Virginia Aleck's father told her that to be

ready for bear hunting she had to cleanse herself, keep quiet, and prepare her whole body and soul for the hunt.[107]

On Kodiak Island there were many rules that hunters and women at home had to follow. Lucille Antowak Davis remembers, "If there was a woman that was pregnant—If her husband [sic] was pregnant, he was not allowed to go bear hunting. That's how they respected the bears. Otherwise, the bears will attack him."[108] Nida Chya said that if a woman was menstruating, her husband would not be chosen to go out on a bear hunt. Men also had to keep their guns and shells in the shed, where women were not allowed.[109] Women typically are not hunters, but there are some exceptions. Virginia Aleck of Chignik Lake, an active bear hunter, had to earn the respect of the men: "I told Uncle Bill, I said, 'You take the first shot. And you know I'll shoot after you.' He took the first shot and the guys were shooting like everything. I shot, and the bear went down. And after that, you know, he said you can come bear hunting with me anytime."[110]

In the past, first-time bear hunters on the Alaska Peninsula and Kodiak Island were initiated in special ceremonies. Some had to "walk in the maggots someplace on the beach" to toughen their feet so they could track bears barefoot. This bestowed silence and stealth.[111] Hunters took sweat baths before the hunt, slept on clean sheets, and wore clean clothes to prevent the bears from smelling them. This tradition has changed in that today men usually take a steam bath after, not before the hunt.[112] On the Alaska Peninsula, formal initiation into bear hunting continued into the 1960s, and some training still remains. Following the custom of silence, some Chignik Lake boys were not notified in advance of their first hunt, and were quite confused about their steam bath, special dinner, prayers for protection, and early wake-up in the morning.[113] The most frightening of the initiation practices occurred both on the Alaska Peninsula and Kodiak Island. After the kill, novice boys had to stick their arms down the bear's throat. "You know, bears [without] open eyes are not dead," said Anakenti Zeedar, speaking of his first hunt. Like many boys, he and his brother were terrified when they realized their kill had not yet expired.[114] Wilfred Alexanderoff had a

169 *Uhluwaq*—Sinew-backed bow

Probably Alaska Peninsula, 1867
National Museum of Natural History, Smithsonian Institution
(NMNH 2528) Length 128 cm

Wooden bows strengthened with sinew cord were powerful and
accurate weapons. They were used for sea hunting, for taking
bears and other large land animals, and for warfare. Painted
figures on this bow include bears, birds, caribou, and hunters
with rifles.

170 *Íngirsún*—Snow goggles

Ugashik *(Uggásaq)*, Alaska Peninsula, 1879–82
National Museum of Natural History, Smithsonian Institution
(NMNH 72515) Width 13.5 cm

Unless a hunter wears eye protection, gazing at a snowy
landscape in the bright sunlight of spring can lead to snow
blindness.

similar experience: "When I first went, I was only fifteen
or sixteen," he said, "and we got a bear.... After they
kill it, it's nice and warm, you know, just smoking. They
opened that mouth and stick my whole arm in. Something moved, I pulled it [out]!"[115]

Bears are hunted in their dens during the winter as
they hibernate, and occasionally in the spring. According to Mike Tunohun, an Alutiiq Elder from Old Harbor who was interviewed in 1987, bear hunting is best
between the second and third quarters of the moon.
"When it gets below half then it's still moonlight in the
morning by three, four o'clock." Hunters can see by the
light of the moon in these early morning hours, when
the bears start "traveling, looking for food."[116] Traditional
hunting methods included snares, deadfall traps, and
spears or arrows.[117] Davydov described other methods
used in the early nineteenth century:

On Kad'iak sometimes two or three people in a group
creep up on an animal and fire arrows at it, and if it
attacks them they fight it off with spears. The Alaskans, like the Koniagas, always send their best hunter
alone against bears. He takes his bow and just two
stone-tipped arrows, for the stone causes quite serious wounds. The hunter will lie in wait near the bear's
habitual path and shoot at the bear at absolutely
point-blank range, after which he dodges away to the
side, leaving his parka. If the bear is not killed by the
first shot and attacks then he falls upon the coat and
tears it to pieces and this gives the hunter time to
aim his other arrow.[118]

Respect for bears and their spirits is evident in rituals
associated with the hunt. In Prince William Sound, bears
were traditionally addressed before any shots were fired,
so the animal would not be offended. The hunter would
say: "We do this because we need you." The skull of a

dead animal was buried at the place where it was killed, facing inland so that the remains might turn into a new bear.[119] In a contemporary permutation of this latter custom, Virginia Aleck said, "You always point the bear's head to the East . . . because that's the direction that Christ is going to come in."[120]

Other rituals are carried out to protect the hunter and his family. At Chignik Lake, the bear's eyes are removed and put up its nostrils to prevent it from seeing or sniffing out the hunter. Similar measures are taken with its ears, mouth and paws. Some hunters remove the heart, cut off the tip, and split it "like a cross" to ensure the bear will not come back alive.[121] Nick Ignatin of Old Harbor stated that it is important to cut the eyes of a dead bear so that its spirit will not return to the body.[122]

The meat is shared among the hunters' extended families, and especially with Elders. Bear fat is considered very valuable, with a buttery taste and slightly chewy texture, and has been used in the past (melted) as an all-purpose oil. Some hunters age the meat for a few weeks to give it a better flavor.[123]

Bear hunting has changed much in modern times. Bear hunters on the Kenai Peninsula have reported that getting a black bear is becoming more difficult, and attribute this to the increase in hunting by nonlocals.[124] Some villagers are concerned that younger hunters are forgetting the rules taught by the Elders, and that they brag about their bear hunting skills and do not give the animals the respect they deserve. Other concerns have been raised about bears becoming too accustomed to humans and eating garbage, which makes their meat unsafe.

Fish

FISHING SETS THE PACE OF THE SUBSISTENCE YEAR. IN summer, five varieties of salmon gather in the bays or ascend rivers to spawn—king, red, chum, pink, and silver. Ancestral salmon fishermen used harpoons or nets with stone weights and wooden floats. Today, nets are used for both subsistence and commercial fishing. By fall, salmon fill freezers and hang in the smokehouses, a wealth of food preserved for winter. Halibut and cod can be caught the year around, but are most important in winter and spring.

Dried and smoked fish have always been important staples during the long lean winters. Alutiiq people have traditionally been very careful to appease the spirits of the fish they take. In Prince William Sound fish intestines were customarily returned to the water because these parts were the home of the animal's soul. The first fish caught each year was eaten entirely except for the gall and the gills. If anything was wasted, it was believed the fish would not return.[125]

Halibut, a large bottom fish, were caught in early spring with the aid of large V-shaped wooden hooks (fig. 172). The herring fishery began in June, tapered off in July and August when herring feed offshore, and resumed in September. Cod were fished in spring and early summer using large hooks rigged to a weighted kelp line that suspended the bait just off the sea bottom.

In May, king salmon arrive in the streams to spawn; red, dog, pink, and finally silver salmon runs follow. The traditional method of harvesting the fish was to build V-shaped weirs of wood or stone across spawning streams. Fish trapped behind the weir were caught by spear, gaff, dip net, or even bare hands.[126] Pink or chum salmon spawn in the intertidal zone, where they were caught in weirs or with traps made of roots, grass or bark.[127] Christine Lukin, who lived in Afognak as a child during the early twentieth century, remembers using nets for intertidal pinks:

> In the summertime, pink salmon would come very close to Afognak, right in front of the village. I used to fish myself, you know; me and two other girls would make a set near the creek when the tide was right. We would often catch two hundred fish at a time. After catching them, the wheelbarrow would be used to haul them to the creek where they were cleaned and hung in the smokehouse or canned.[128]

Salmon are cleaned, split, and hung on racks to dry, and are also smoked or canned. Salmon roe is sometimes an ingredient in *akutaq*, and also is eaten fresh or fermented as a treat. Lukin said, "Many women knew how to fix salmon eggs to eat, and they were really tasty. I never did manage to pick the correct recipe. Years ago, they would smash them up, set it aside, and let it rot. It was used for flavoring in various dishes. We didn't have flavorings like those you buy on the shelves today."[129]

The introduction of dories and large fishing boats and the arrival of canneries in the late nineteenth century gave Alutiiq fishermen both the means and incentive to catch fish in numbers that exceeded the amount needed for subsistence. While the canneries provided work for the Native people, they also were an important factor in the disruption of the marine ecosystem. Overfishing became a problem that deprived villages of a traditionally reliable and crucial food source.

171 Commercial gillnet fishermen harvesting salmon, Bristol Bay.

Photograph © Tom Souchek/AlaskaStock.com

172 *Iqsak*—Halibut hook

Probably Kodiak Island, 1899
National Museum of Natural History, Smithsonian Institution
(NMNH 200831) Length 25 cm

Halibut are very large fish, sometimes weighing hundreds of pounds. V-shaped halibut hooks floated just above the bottom of the sea, held down by a stone weight. A strong line made of kelp (a type of seaweed) ran to the surface, attached to a seal stomach buoy. The opening of the hook was just wide enough for the fish to put its mouth over the bait. Hooks of this type probably originated on the Northwest Coast.

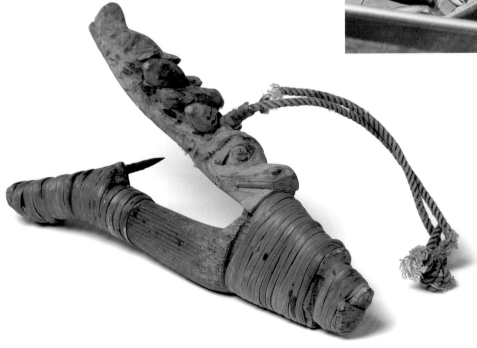

Subsistence Fishing

Shauna Lukin

I REMEMBER IN THE SUMMERTIME MY DAD WOULD wake my sisters and me up early to go fishing. My dad, sisters, cousin, and I would spend several hours prepping the boat: cleaning, putting everything in its spot, checking and double checking the engine and all the equipment. Finally, we'd leave the dock in our beat-up thirty-two-footer headed for the nearest site. I always had to plunge. With that oversized toilet bowl plunger in hand I'd hang over the side of the boat trying to keep all the fish from escaping from the net. It always seemed like the skiff man, my cousin, would take hours to close up the seine. Then we'd pull with all our might to get the fish on deck. My dad would turn around when the sun was still high in the sky and head for the harbor.

But that wasn't the worst of it, then we had to clean 'em. The *cíwat* (flies) were always in our ears and on the fish, they were everywhere pestering us as we worked. My dad would sometimes pull out on open water to escape their relentless torture but a couple of them always found us. When we had finished splitting and salting the fish, the sun was usually low in the sky. We'd pull the dory up the beach in front of our house and pack the fish to the smokehouse. My dad would stand on a ladder as we handed him salmon. After a week or so of constantly watching the fire to make sure it wasn't putting out too many flames or not enough smoke, the fish would be ready. We'd pull them down and pack them into the house. My sisters, cousin, and I would spread vegetable oil over the meat and skin of the smoked fish to keep them from drying out. After the fish were covered in oil, and usually all of us kids, my dad would pull out the vacuum sealer to protect the fish during the long winter months in the freezer.

I haven't gone fishing with my dad for a couple of years now, since I left my village to pursue a college degree. Work is scarce at home so I have remained in Anchorage. Although I complained about the early morning hours, the *cíwat*, and the work of plunging, I have gained an appreciation for the subsistence way of life. I've come to learn that all those mornings when I had to get up early my father was teaching me. He was teaching me to survive the harsh Kodiak climate and how to feed my family and myself. I have come to understand that although my family gathers and preserves our subsistence food differently than my ancestors used to, we are still sustaining a main component of our Alutiiq culture.

173   Ivory fishing lure

Uyak site, Kodiak Island, A.D. 600-1000
Alutiiq Museum, Larsen Bay Collection
(UA88-78-4181) Length 7 cm

Birds

LAND AND SEA BIRDS DO NOT MAKE UP A MAJOR PART of the Alutiiq diet, but they hold great cultural significance. Bird imagery exists on bentwood hunting hats as well as hunting amulets. Traditional Alutiiq parkas were often made from the feathered iridescent black skins of cormorants, and rattles were made from puffin beaks.

Birds and ducks were actively hunted for their feathers and skins, and eggs have always been considered a special treat. Southcentral Alaska is home to many species of resident and migratory birds. Eagles, seagulls, murres, puffins, ducks, and cormorants were most useful to Alutiiq communities of the past, and hunters used various methods to capture them:

When several *baidarkas* sight a flock of these birds [ducks] they paddle up to them, suddenly fire several arrows and shout for all they are worth. At this some of the ducks take fright, but before they can fly out of the water they have to dive. Thus they surely fall into the hands of the Americans, who give them no chance to draw breath, firing a constant barrage of arrows at them. In the end the ducks become so tired that they pass out, and are killed with paddles, or they escape ashore where they are caught by hand.[130]

Another method of catching ducks in the early nineteenth century was to stretch a net above the water across a river mouth or narrow strait to entangle low-flying

174   Bird-shaped feast bowl

Chenega *(Caniqaq)*, Prince William Sound, 1887–93
National Museum of Natural History, Smithsonian Institution
(NMNH 168623) Length 38 cm

Guests at feasts and ceremonies ate fish, meat, lily roots, and berries mixed with seal and whale fat. They were served from bowls shaped like animals and decorated with beads. This large bowl is inset with white beads.

175 *Neqlehtesútet*—**Goose snares**

Ugashik *(Uggásaq)*, Alaska Peninsula, 1885–86
National Museum of Natural History, Smithsonian Institution
(NMNH 127778) Length of bundle 18 cm

Each snare in this bundle consists of a wooden stake with a slippery loop of whale baleen. The snares were set up in a line along the grassy edge of a pond where geese gathered. A bird's foot, head, or wing might become caught in the loop.

waterfowl. Gulls and other birds were taken by means of baited floating noose traps and snares.[131] Larry Matfay remembered using a trap made of sticks and sinew netting to catch diving ducks.[132] Guns were available when he was younger, but he most often hunted with arrows, because he believed the ducks would be permanently frightened away by a shotgun.[133]

Sven Haakanson, Sr., said many people used to collect bird eggs at rocky island rookeries around the Kodiak archipelago. "In the spring everybody [would] get into *biadarkas* and go to the islands and then live off of eggs, it was a big treat! But they'd always leave so many and they'd have all kinds of eggs. They'd have their egg feast and then the fish hit and then they'd switch to fish."[134] Villages would invite other villages to the egg feast, which was an important occasion for young people to meet marriage partners.

Harvesting eggs and bird skins was part of the labor system imposed by the Russians. Young, elderly, and sick men who could not hunt sea otters were sent to rookeries to gather bird skins for parkas, and women gathered eggs which were preserved in fat for the company use.[135]

Intertidal Life

BEACH FOODS ARE USUALLY HARVESTED IN the early spring. In the traditional economy, stored fish and other supplies were usually low by this time. Davydov in 1802–03 noted, "the months are named after various phenomena in nature, and this in its turn produces months of uneven length. For example, *Kepnehciq* [February: "cutting the *yukola* [dried fish] into strips"] is the longest month for it covers the whole period during which the islanders are short of food supplies and eat only shellfish or pieces of the remaining *yukola*. . . ."[136] When bad weather prevented hunting or gathering expeditions, Alutiiq people only had to walk down to the beach to find abundant food sources.

The lowest tides of spring are eagerly awaited, as they reveal much more of the intertidal zone where herring spawn and clams, cockles, urchins, octopus, and other marine invertebrates can be found. Spiny urchins are part of this harvest, and are collected for their roe. *Bidarkies*, also known as chitons, are pried off of rocks. The term *bidarkies* refers to their shape, which resembles an overturned *biadarka* [kayak]. Some Alutiit collect snails and sea cucumbers. Octopus are caught on the beaches where they hide under rocks. Villagers use a funnel and hose to pour Clorox-water into an octopus's lair. The octopus comes out from under the rock to escape the bleach, and is captured.[137] Roy Skonberg quoted a common axiom, "You always hear people say, 'When the tide's out the table is set,' you know, if you're starving you're just a lazy guy."[138]

Herring spawn along the beaches in Prince William Sound, and leave the seaweed in those areas covered in eggs, or spawn. Alutiiq families collect the spawn-seaweed, which they boil for just a moment "until it turns green." Elders like this dish flavored with seal oil, while younger generations prefer butter.

176 Karen Kalmakoff of Ivanof Bay displays her beach harvest of *bidarkies* ("little boats," or chitons), 1990.
Photograph by Lisa Hutchinson-Scarbrough.

Competition with sea otters and overharvesting in the early part of this century led to declines in the number of clams in some areas. At other places, shellfish habitat was disturbed by the 1964 earthquake. Alutiiq residents also perceive long-term declines in herring as a result of the *Exxon Valdez* oil spill, and worry about the safety of other beach foods. Another problem facing communities that depend on shellfish is paralytic shellfish poisoning (PSP), which is also known informally (and inaccurately) as "red tide." PSP is caused by a tiny microorganism that is safely ingested by shellfish, but acts as a neurotoxin on humans who consume contaminated shellfish. Many people on Kodiak Island who regularly went clam digging in the past have been told to avoid consumption due to the high PSP risk.

Plants

177 Clyda Christiansen with beach chickweed, Kodiak Island, 1990.

Photograph by Priscilla Russell.

FOR ALUTIIQ GATHERERS, FOREST, TUNDRA, BEACH, AND mountain environments are stocked with edible plants. Numerous varieties of wild greens, berries, roots, and even seaweed add to the Alutiiq diet. These foods provide vital nutrients and flavorful seasonings for fish and game. Other plants contribute to the economy by providing raw materials–wood for fuel, construction, and carving; spruce root, grasses, and birch bark for basket making; and natural dyes and pigments. Plants are also the sources of many traditional medicines. Healers use herbal remedies to treat everything from scrapes and swellings to more serious illnesses like fever, arthritis, and respiratory problems.[139]

The Alutiit harvest plants throughout the year. In spring, as the landscape begins to green, people gather tender young vegetables from the beach. In the past, this was also the time when fresh, dry grass was cut to provide a clean cover for house floors and sleeping areas. By midsummer, vegetable collecting is supplemented by berry picking, which continues well into the fall. People often wait to pick certain varieties till October or November, when they have been sweetened by a frost. Some berries can even be collected in the winter, when they are dug from beneath the snow. In fall and winter, storms replenish the supply of driftwood that is collected for fuel. And in late winter, the Alutiit gather seaweed, when other sources of fresh food are hard to obtain.

All members of Alutiiq communities participate in plant collecting, although men and women harvest different species. Men are in charge of procuring plants for raw material, particularly the wood used to fuel fires, smoke fish, and build structures. Women collect plants primarily for food and medicine. Berry picking, vegetable harvesting, and herb collecting are activities traditionally conducted by women of all ages, often with the help of their children. Children are taught to respect plants. Overpicking, breaking branches, stepping on plants, or eating too much while you are collecting are considered poor etiquette.[140]

178 *Suqaq*—Seal stomach container

Kodiak Island, early 1900s
Alutiiq Museum
(AM 53.2) Length 62 cm

"They'd hang it up and put anything inside, any kind of berries they used, and put seal oil in there, to keep the berries from getting spoiled."

—Mary Peterson, Kodiak Island Elder, 1997

Until the mid-1900s, people stored food in dried seal stomachs that were hung from the ceilings of their houses. Berries, tubers of the Kamchatka lily, dried fish, fish eggs, or blubber might be put inside with seal oil, which acted as a preservative.

Although plants are collected widely, particular families are considered to own certain collecting spots and visit them each year. A woman may harvest berries from the same patch annually, perhaps one visited by her grandmother. Similarly, men collect driftwood from habitually visited beaches. Piles of driftwood may even be stacked or marked in unique ways to indicate ownership.[141] In classical Alutiiq society, plants were harvested with a simple set of tools. Digging sticks fashioned from sea mammal ribs were used to unearth roots, and large carrying baskets woven from spruce root held berries, vegetables and medicinal herbs picked by hand.

Today, most plant foods are cleaned and eaten raw, although people also boil, bake, fry, roast, and dry plants. In the past, vegetables were cooked in large wooden tubs filled with water. Hot rocks dropped into these containers heated their contents. Dipping plants in oil is also a long-standing tradition. In the past people immersed vegetables in seal oil. Today many use cooking oil.

To extend their availability beyond the growing season, plants were preserved and stored in a variety of ways. Some plants, particularly berries, were once mixed with blubber, oil, and fish eggs, and placed in seal stomach containers (fig. 178). The containers were then tightly sealed and stored for later use. When opened, the resulting cheese-like mixture could be sliced and eaten. Other plants were stored in grass-lined, underground pits, hung from house rafters to dry, or mashed and spread to dry into a fruit leather. Today people make a tempting variety of jams and jellies for winter use and preserve wild fruits and vegetables in their freezers.

In addition to wild plant foods, the Alutiit have come to enjoy fruits and vegetables introduced by Western settlers. The most commonly grown garden crops are rhubarb, potatoes, turnips, carrots, and raspberries, which are fertilized with seaweed and peat from local beaches.

The collection and preparation of medicinal herbs is a specialized and fading art, once widely practiced by women who treated the sick and acted as midwives. Knowledge of plant medicines was passed from one generation of healers to the next through apprenticeship. Young women assisted established healers to learn the art of curing. Healers were careful to offer a small gift to the plants they harvested, to insure the potency of the medicine. A strand of thread, a match, or bit of tobacco might be left as a thank you and sign of respect.

Medicinal herbs are used both fresh and dry. They are employed in washes and poultices, or steeped in hot

179 Phyllis Peterson with berries, Kodiak Island, 1990.
Photograph by Priscilla Russell.

water to create soothing teas. Some herbs are also used in the *banya*—or sweat bath—where steam releases their rejuvenating powers.

Wild Vegetables

One of the most well-known edible plants is beach lovage *(pitrúsekáq)* often referred to by its Russian name *petrushki* or as wild parsley. This flavorful herb is used in soups and to season boiled or baked salmon and fish patties. It is also boiled and tossed in salads. Another coveted salad vegetable is sour dock, known as wild rhubarb, wild spinach, or *átunaq*. This leafy green is also eaten boiled and its rhubarb-like stem added to pies. Sour dock is also used to purge the system and alleviate fever.[142]

Goosetongue *(wegguaq)* is a small grass-like plant that grows along beaches. It has delicious salty leaves that are eaten raw or boiled, and can be added to fish soup. People enjoy eating goosetongue with bacon or oil for added flavor. Oil is also added to bulbs of the chocolate lily *(láqaq)*—a flowering herb with a ricelike root. Mashed bulbs were once used in *akutaq*, but have been replaced with mashed potatoes. Cow parsnip *(ugsútet)*, known also as *puchki* or wild celery, is another commonly eaten green. The plant's stem, which resembles celery, is peeled and eaten. The leaves are not eaten, but can be used to flavor fish. *Puchki* root poultices are considered to be strong medicine for infections, aches and pains.[143]

Berries

Alutiiq people harvest at least fifteen species of berries and berrylike fruits, more than any other type of plant food. In the past, a family might gather fifty pounds of berries in one season. Salmonberries *(alagnat)* are picked in the greatest quantity, although crowberries, cranberries, and blueberries are also important. Salmonberries

are traditionally eaten raw, with fish, or in *akutaq*—a beloved dessert. There are many recipes for *akutaq*. Basic ingredients include wild berries, sugar, shortening, and milk. In the past, mashed potatoes, lily roots, dried fish, and salmon eggs were also potential ingredients. Today, salmonberry tarts, pies, and cobblers are popular.

There are two varieties of blueberry *(atsaq)* in the Alutiiq homeland: the early blueberry, or blue huckleberry, and the alpine blueberry, or bog blueberry. The Alutiit typically gather blueberries in August and September. Blueberries are primarily harvested for food, although their juice can also be used as a dye to color wild grasses for decorating woven baskets.[145] In the Kodiak region, the Alutiit once stored blueberries in seal-stomach containers filled with water or oil. In Prince William Sound, they dried blueberries on special wooden grates over an open fire. The berries were then stored in containers and rehydrated as needed. The Chugach Alutiit also mashed fresh berries into a paste and spread them on skunk cabbage leaves. The paste was allowed to dry and then stored on the leaves for later use.[144] Like salmonberries, blueberries are now enjoyed in sweet preserves and luscious desserts.

The crowberry *(pakik)*, also called the blackberry or mossberry, is the favored berry for *akutaq*. Crowberries grow in mountainous areas, and are often eaten raw by men when out hunting. In Akhiok and Old Harbor, the leafy stems of crowberry shrubs were once burned in homes to prevent and cure illness. Visitors to these communities were asked to jump over burning plants and stand in their smoke. This destroyed diseases and chased away evil spirits.[145]

Alutiiq people harvest two kinds of cranberries: the low-bush cranberry, or lingonberry *(kenegtaq)*, and the high-bush cranberry, or sour berry *(inaqqamciq)*. Both varieties are collected in August and September, and stored in quantity. Although they can be eaten raw, they are usually chosen to flavor meat sauces, especially for seal and sea lion, and for making jams and jellies. Cranberries are also recognized for their medicinal properties. People prepared tea made from the leaves to treat colds. Eating raw cranberries is also recommended for sore throats, canker sores, and kidney problems.[146]

Seaweeds

The Alutiit harvest at least eight different seaweeds, from the tender green leaves of sea lettuce *(kappúsetáhuaq)* which grows in rocky intertidal areas to the hefty stems of the bull kelp *(nasquluk)* that washes onto beaches each winter. Seaweeds are collected year round, but are harvested in greatest quantities in the early spring. They are most tender at this time and easily accessed during the lowest tides of the year. Seaweeds are often eaten raw with other beach foods—chitons, urchin eggs, mussels—and, like many other plant foods, are often dipped in oil. Some are made into pickles and relishes and others are dried and crumbled for seasoning.

Seaweeds are also a source of raw material and medicine. Leaves of ribbon kelp are used to wrap burns. The hollow stem of the bull kelp makes a handy siphon. Pieces about two feet long and one inch in diameter were kept in kayaks and used to empty water from the vessel. In a pinch they can even be used to funnel fuel into an outboard motor. The thinner parts of the stem were traditionally dried and used for line. The line was soaked in salt water to make it supple, and then used to anchor kayaks or as fishing line to jig for halibut, cod, and rockfish.

Chapter 5 notes

1 Alutiiq Elders' Planning Conference for *Looking Both Ways*, 1997.

2 Lower Cook Inlet place names from Leer (1980).

3 Fall 1999.

4 *Exxon Valdez* Oil Spill Trustee Council 1999.

5 Alutiiq Elders' Planning Conference for *Looking Both Ways*, 1997.

6 *Allriluukut "We Are One"* Alutiiq Elders and Youth Conference, 1998.

7 Alutiiq Elders' Planning Conference for *Looking Both Ways*, 1997.

8 Birket-Smith 1953:119–123; see also Desson 1995.

9 Fitzhugh and Kaplan 1984; Fienup-Riordan 1998; Birket-Smith 1953.

10 Bobby Stamp, interview 1987 or 1988, Alutiiq Museum oral history archive.

11 Birket-Smith 1953:117–118.

12 Interview at Arctic Studies Center August 11, 1997.

13 Alutiiq Elders' Planning Conference for *Looking Both Ways*, 1997.

14 Alutiiq Elders' Planning Conference for *Looking Both Ways*, 1997.

15 Interview November 6, 1987, Alutiiq Museum oral history archive.

16 Innokenty Inga, as told to Henry Lundsgaarde 1962 (Alutiiq Museum oral history archive); Birket-Smith 1953:46; Stanek 1985:56-59.

17 Knecht 1995:301-312.

18 Chris Cunningham, personal communication, 1996. Information about traditional Alaska Native kayaks and their construction is presented by Dyson (1986) and Zimmerly (1986). Complete instructions for building an Alutiiq kayak can be found in an article in *Sea Kayaker* by Joe Kelley (1996).

19 Birket-Smith 1953:45; Davydov 1977:202–203; Holmberg 1985:44.

20 Birket-Smith 1953:47-48.

21 Alutiiq Elders' Planning Conference for *Looking Both Ways*, 1997.

22 Bobby Stamp, interview November 6, 1987, Alutiiq Museum oral history archive; Larry Matfay, Alutiiq Elders' Planning Conference for *Looking Both Ways*, 1997.

23 Bobby Stamp, interview November 6, 1987, Alutiiq Museum oral history archive.

24 Stanek 1985:59.

25 Gideon 1989:49.

26 Davydov 1977:164.

27 Alutiiq Elders' Planning Conference for *Looking Both Ways*, 1997.

28 Beaglehole 1967:364; Davydov 1977:203; Dixon 1968:242; Ledyard 1963:80; Birket-Smith (1953:104) says this type was used for racing.

29 Merck 1980:172.

30 Larry Matfay, Alutiiq Elders' Planning Conference for *Looking Both Ways*, 1997; Davydov 1977:203.

31 Interview, November 6, 1987, Alutiiq Museum oral history archive.

32 Birket-Smith 1953:47.

33 Interview, July 24, 1986, Alutiiq Museum oral history archive.

34 Gideon 1989:56.

35 Interview, 1987, Alutiiq Museum oral history archives.

36 Gideon 1989:43–44.

37 Beaglehole 1967:344, 1112, 1115; Dixon 1968:67–69; Portlock 1789:112–113.

38 Gideon 1989:41.

39 Birket-Smith 1953:96.

40 Sauer 1802:171; Lisianskii 1968:211. Langsdorff (1993:19) noted that the RAC was similarly in possession of all the *baidary* at Unalaska in 1805.

41 Gideon 1989:47–48.

42 Davydov 1977:202; Birket-Smith 1953:49.

43 Holmberg 1985:45.

44 Chris Cunningham (*Sea Kayaker* magazine) and Joe Kelley (Kodiak Area Native Association) contributed significantly to this discussion of *angyaq* design features, based on study of boat model 90464 in the William J. Fisher Collection at the National Museum of Natural History (see fig. 197).

45 Campbell 1816:100.

46 Holmberg 1985:45.

47 Black 1991; Coxe 1780:114; Davydov 1977:153; Hunt 2000.

48 Smithsonian Institution Archives Record Unit 305 (United States National Museum, Registrar, 1834–1958). Accession Record 14024, "List of Ethnological Specimens Collected by Wm. J. Fisher," 1884.

49 Ivanov 1930:488–489.

50 Black 1991:30–41, 1994. The killer whale-wolf is not directly attested in known Alutiiq oral traditions, although it is recorded among the Yup'ik (Nelson 1899:444).

51 Golder 1903:90–95.

52 Golder 1903:16–19.

53 Holm 1988:285–293. At least some hats were locally made on Kodiak Island (Davydov 1977:153), although others may have been traded into the Alutiiq region.

54 Holm 1988:287.

55 1961 interview, Alutiiq Museum oral history archive.

56 Gideon 1989:57.

57 Interview, June 29, 1991, Alutiiq Museum oral history archive.

58 Birket-Smith 1953:33.

59 Birket-Smith 1953:33.

60 Larry Matfay, interview August 1986, Alutiiq Museum oral history archive.

61 Beaglehole 1967:346; Merck 1980:102; Portlock 1789:238.

62 Gideon 1989:66.

63 Alutiiq Elders' Planning Conference for *Looking Both Ways*, 1997.

64 Matfay 1987; Vick 1983: 4-5; Gideon 1989:56.

65 Vick 1983: 5.

66 Birket-Smith 1953:32.

67 Demidoff 1962, quoted in Desson 1995:109.

68 Desson's recent dissertation on Alutiiq rituals of the Kodiak archipelago includes a valuable discussion of whaling (1995:75–125) based on research by linguist Alphonse Pinart during 1871–72. Demidoff (1962) provides a detailed oral narrative that is also incorporated into Desson's analysis. With regard to the history of the rituals, the Kodiak Island whaler Tik-nakaak told Pinart that real whaling ceremonies were

discontinued after the devastating smallpox epidemic of 1837–38 (Desson 1995:108). It is clear from the narratives of living Elders, however, that the use of aconite poison and some aspects of whaling ritual continued into the early twentieth century.

69 Black 1987.

70 Crowell 1994.

71 Birket-Smith 1953:34–36.

72 Lisianskii 1968:209; Birket-Smith 1953:34.

73 Lisianskii 1968:174; Pinart 1875:7.

74 Demidoff 1962:9–10; Desson 1995:115–117.

75 Sauer (1802: 177–178).

76 Demidoff 1962; Desson 1995:79-88; Gideon 1989:60; Lisianskii 1968:174.

77 Birket-Smith 1953:34.

78 Larry Matfay, interview July 1986, Alutiiq Museum oral history archive.

79 Alutiiq Elders' Planning Conference for *Looking Both Ways*, 1997.

80 Davydov 1977:223–224; Gideon 1989:68.

81 Interview December 14, 1990, Alutiiq Museum oral history archive.

82 Davydov 1977:224.

83 Desson 1995:83–93.

84 Birket-Smith 1953:34.

85 Hrdlička 1944:126.

86 Birket-Smith 1953:34.

87 Bobby Stamp, interview December 14, 1987, Alutiiq Museum oral history archive.

88 Fall 1993:6–7.

89 Fall 1993:7–8.

90 Gideon 1989:57.

91 Virginia Aleck, Alutiiq Elders' Planning Conference for *Looking Both Ways*, 1997; Fall 1993:5.

92 Fall 1993:4.

93 Davydov 1977:212.

94 Interview, June 3, 1997, Alutiiq Museum oral history archive.

95 Alutiiq Elders' Planning Conference for *Looking Both Ways*, 1997.

96 Fall and Hutchinson-Scarbrough 1996:10; Hallowell 1926.

97 Birket-Smith 1953:4.

98 Davydov 1997:167.

99 Fall and Hutchinson-Scarbrough 1996:5.

100 Fall and Hutchinson-Scarbrough 1996:5.

101 Alutiiq Elders' Planning Conference for *Looking Both Ways*, 1997.

102 Nida Chya and Anakenti Zeedar, interview June 4, 1987, Alutiiq Museum oral history archive.

103 Birket-Smith 1953:75.

104 Birket-Smith 1953:65.

105 Vick 1983:6.

106 Fall and Hutchinson-Scarbrough1996:8.

107 Virginia Aleck, Alutiiq Elders' Planning Conference for *Looking Both Ways*, 1997.

108 Lucille Davis, Alutiiq Elders' Planning Conference for *Looking Both Ways*, 1997.

109 Nida Chya, interview July 25, 1986, Alutiiq Museum oral history archive.

110 Virginia Aleck, Alutiiq Elders' Planning Conference for *Looking Both Ways*, 1997.

111 Nida Chya and Anakenti Zeedar, interview June 4, 1987, Alutiiq Museum oral history archive.

112 Fall and Hutchinson-Scarbrough 1996:8.

113 Fall and Hutchinson-Scarbrough 1996:10.

114 Nida Chya and Anakenti Zeedar, interview August 7, 1987, Alutiiq Museum oral history archive.

115 Wilfed Alexanderoff, interview August 6, 1987, Alutiiq Museum oral history archive.

116 Mike Tunohun, interview August 5, 1987, Alutiiq Museum oral history archive.

117 Birket-Smith, 1953:37.

118 Davydov 1977:209.

119 Birket-Smith 1953:38.

120 Virginia Aleck, Alutiiq Elders' Planning Conference for *Looking Both Ways*, 1997.

121 Fall and Hutchinson-Scarbrough 1996:9-10.

122 Nick Ignatin, interview July 24, 1986, Alutiiq Museum oral history archive.

123 Fall and Hutchinson-Scarbrough 1996:5.

124 Stanek 1985:180.

125 Birket-Smith 1953:42.

126 Birket-Smith 1953:41, 96; Davydov 1977:231; Portlock 1789:118; Stanek 1985:59–69.

127 Birket-Smith 1953:41.

128 Vick 1983: 45.

129 Vick 1983:45–56.

130 Davydov 1977: 228.

131 Birket-Smith 1983: 38.

132 Larry Matfay, interview December 14, 1990, Alutiiq Museum oral history archive.

133 Larry Matfay, interview April 29, 1992, Alutiiq Museum oral history archive.

134 Sven Haakanson, Sr, interview August 6, 1987, Alutiiq Museum oral history archive.

135 Davydov 1977: 195–197.

136 Davydov 1977:186.

137 Village of Tatitlek and Alaska Department of Fish and Game 1999; Pratt Museum 1999.

138 Alutiiq Elders' Planning Conference for *Looking Both Ways*, 1997.

139 Russell 1991a, 1991b; Mulcahey 1988, 1993; Graham and Ouzinkie Botanical Society 1985.

140 Russell 1991b:37.

141 Russell 1991b:15.

142 Graham 1985:11–12.

143 Russell 1991a:48.

144 Birket Smith 1953:43.

145 Russel 1991b:41.

146 Russell 1991a:33

6

UKGWEPET—OUR BELIEFS[1]

Alutiiq Spiritual Life and Traditions

Aron L. Crowell and Jeff Leer

THE YEAR IS 1802. MEN, WOMEN, AND CHILDREN dressed in festive clothing and jewelry have gathered in a crowded *qasgiq* or ceremonial house at the settlement of Tangihnaq (Woody Island) in the Kodiak archipelago. Seal oil lamps cast a rich yellow light across the sacred space. Clean, dry grass is strewn on the floor and tied to the ceiling, and the fragrant smoke of angelica hangs in the air. Overhead, stuffed animal skins and models of boats dangle from a swaying framework of spears and arrows. People talk, eat, and laugh as young boys play and run away with unguarded bowls of food.

Then two men begin beating drums, and others sing and shake rattles made of seabird beaks. A pair of performers hold paddles and wear masks of bent sticks, through which their painted faces can be seen. Men in masks perch on platforms near the ceiling, and dancers on the floor below move like hunters in search for game. The performance ends, and another begins. This time, everyone joins in song as a single dancer leaps and shakes

180 Dancers with masks and puffin beak rattles. This scene represents a Kodiak Island hunting ceremony in the early- to mid-nineteenth century.

Illustration by Mark Matson, 1999.

and darts across the *qasgiq*. He wears a magnificent mask surrounded by a wooden hoop and ornamented with feathers and painted wood bangles. More dances follow into the night, performed by both women and men. Each portrays a different mask-spirit, whose legend is told in the words of its dance song.

This evening of dance, attended by Russian naval officer Gavriil Davydov on December 30, 1802, was part of an Alutiiq hunting festival held each winter to appeal to the spirit world for an abundant harvest of game.[2] The ceremony was one of many that took place in eighteenth- and nineteenth-century Alutiiq communities. Another old winter celebration, recalled in 1933 by Prince William Sound Elder Stepan Britskalov, was a festival similar to the Yup'ik Bladder Festival which honored the souls of animals that had been killed.[3] In the spring, Alutiiq people gathered to hear shamans forecast the success of hunting. In August, the Chugach of Prince William Sound held a Feast of the Dead to present food and gifts to ancestors.[4] During all months of the year, people throughout the Alutiiq region gathered to celebrate the completion of boats and houses and to mark life transitions such as a girl's first menstrual isolation or a young hunter's first kill. *Kassat*, or "wise men," led the major ceremonies on Kodiak Island, taught the oral traditions, and composed dances and songs. *Kaḻa'alek*, or shamans, consulted with spirits and healed the sick.

Ceremonies and feasts held social as well as religious meanings. Some were displays of wealth that resembled

189

Uganik *(Uganút)*, Kodiak Island, 1883
National Museum of Natural History, Smithsonian Institution
(NMNH 90438) Diameter 23 cm

*"The hunters . . . ring out their rattles in harmony with the music,
and all are singing happily with fair voice, changing the tune from
time to time as directed by the chief."*

—G. Davydov, Russian naval officer,
describing a dance on Kodiak Island, 1802

Hoop rattles hung with beaks, hooves, claws, and shells
were used by dancers and shamans over a wide area
of Alaska and the Northwest Coast of Canada.
This Kodiak Island rattle is made with beaks
from horned and tufted puffins (two varieties of seabirds), tied to a wooden frame
with sinew cords.

the famous potlatches of the Northwest Coast. Great quantities of food, furs, and gifts were given away to people of the village and to guests from other settlements. Hosts and guests engaged in spirited trade, and in matchmaking for the young people.

Changes came with the arrival of Russian fur trade companies in the late eighteenth century. Ceremonial life declined as epidemics and colonial exploitation depleted the wealth and social vitality of Alutiiq communities. Russian Orthodox monks established their first mission on Kodiak Island in 1794, and the influence of the church became widespread. Yet indigenous ceremonies and shamanism coexisted with the new faith for many decades, even after most Alutiit had received Christian baptism.

Over the course of two centuries in southern Alaska, the Russian Orthodox church has absorbed influences from Alutiiq culture. Celebrations still held in many villages around the time of Russian Christmas combine aspects of traditional masking, feasting, and dance with

Christian symbols and Russian folk traditions.[5] Other Alutiit adhere to non-Orthodox faiths, including Protestant denominations established in southern Alaska during the late nineteenth century as well as more recent evangelical movements.

Alutiiq Elders are proud of *ugkwepet*, "our beliefs," the rich and evolving spiritual heritage of the Alutiiq region. Discussions in this chapter are based on many sources, including oral history, archaeological studies, historical texts, and translations. Dominique Desson's analysis of Kodiak archipelago ritual in the late nineteenth century, based principally on the 1871–72 field notes of Alphonse Pinart, is a valuable resource. Contemporary Alutiiq perspectives were gathered at the 1997 Elders' Exhibition Planning Conference for *Looking Both Ways* in Kodiak and in Alutiiq language interviews conducted by linguist Jeff Leer, all used with permission. Leer writes about contemporary Russian Orthodoxy as a member of the church and long-time resident in Alutiiq communities.

The Spirit World

They say that one man was a hunter and that following the way of his fellow hunters, he ate and drank very little but could only kill a few animals. He thus asked for help and said: "Who will come to my help?" Then during the night he saw in a dream masks which the Koniags afterwards used as if they were alive and heard songs sung by some unknown voice. As soon as he awoke he began to sing these songs and went hunting and killed a great many animals. The other hunters asked him what talisman he possessed and he asked them to gather. He sang them the songs he had heard and told them that they had to sing them. Afterwards he made the different masks.

> —Kodiak Island story recorded by
> Alphonse Pinart in 1871–72[6]

IN THIS LEGEND, THE MASKS SEEN IN DREAMS ARE THE faces of spirits who bring success in hunting. Masked dances were dramas—called "plays" (*igrushki*) by the Russians—in which song, dance, and words dissolved the present into the mythical past, brought the mask-spirits to life, and granted access to their spiritual power. Who were these beings, and how were they represented in Alutiiq art and ritual?

Suk (Person)

> "Where are my big hands? Where is my big nose? Where is my big face?' Her husband was the bear, but now he had turned into a man.

> —From "The Woman Who Married a
> Bear," told by Stepan Britskalov,
> Prince William Sound Elder, 1933[7]

In Alutiiq, the word *suk* (person) has a rich variety of meanings.[8] In a spiritual sense, it refers to the personified consciousness of an animal, plant, place, thing, or natural force such as wind or fire. Anthropological literature generally refers to a different form of the same word, *sua*, meaning "its person."[9] Sally Ash of

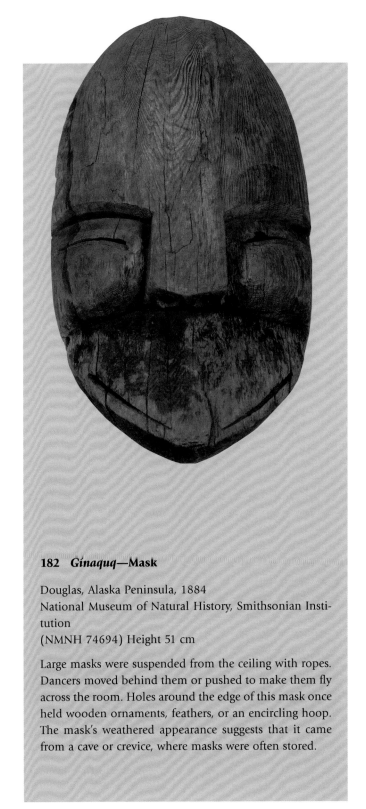

182 *Gínaquq*—Mask

Douglas, Alaska Peninsula, 1884
National Museum of Natural History, Smithsonian Institution
(NMNH 74694) Height 51 cm

Large masks were suspended from the ceiling with ropes. Dancers moved behind them or pushed to make them fly across the room. Holes around the edge of this mask once held wooden ornaments, feathers, or an encircling hoop. The mask's weathered appearance suggests that it came from a cave or crevice, where masks were often stored.

Nanwalek was told by her mother that *"Cacat nangluteng sungqehtut"*—"All things have [a] *suk,"*[10] describing a universe that is completely alive and in which every part of nature is conscious of human thought and action.

A *suk* spirit has, or can assume, individual human form, and the word refers as well to this kind of visible manifestation. Examples from the Alaska Peninsula include *ingngim súga,* a "mountain person," and *taitúm súga suuga,* a "fog person," small men who are still glimpsed occasionally in the wilderness. In Stepan Britskalov's tale from Prince William Sound, quoted above, the bear's transformation into a man is the animal's *suk* making itself visible. In other stories from the Alutiiq oral tradition, a bird opens its beak or an animal peels back its snout to reveal a human face inside. A *suk* that may otherwise appear completely human is sometimes revealed by a remnant tail or beak-shaped mouth, or because it gleams with a bright light. Encounters with such beings often take place in dreams or upon waking from sleep, a state that draws a person closer to the spirit world.[11]

Some tales tell of the opposite kind of change—human beings who turn into animals. In a 1933 narrative by Makari Chimovitski of Prince William Sound, a hunter follows the chief of the ground squirrels down into his burrow, and comes to a house where the squirrels all live. Here the chief squirrel removes his skin and appears as a man (*suk*). The hunter lives with the squirrels all winter, eating roots and berries. He gradually becomes a squirrel himself, unaware of his transformation until spring when he emerges from the burrow and discovers that his body is covered with fur.[12]

Prince William Sound Elders Stepan Britskalov and Makari Chimovitski spoke of three supremely important *suk* spirits. Lam Sua, who is still known to Elders from the entire Alutiiq area, was the "person of the universe," who could see and hear everything but was invisible to humans. When asked about the nature of Lam Sua, Elders tend to equate him with the God of Orthodox Chrisitianity, in Leer's experience. The second of the three described by Britskalov and Chimovitski was Imam Sua, the "female person" of all sea animals, who lived at the bottom of the sea. Chugach hunters prayed to her when they went hunting in kayaks, asking her to send game. The third was Nunam Sua, who dwelt in the forest and was the mistress of all land animals.[13]

Ceremonies, rituals, and the observance of proper behavior, from fasting to wearing clean and well-made clothing, communicated respect toward these sensitive

183 Ceremonial ermine cap

Ugashik *(Uggásaq)*, Alaska Peninsula, 1879–82
National Museum of Natural History, Smithsonian Institution (NMNH 72471) Length 20 cm

This hat was "worn by young men at dances and festivals," according to William J. Fisher. It is made from whole winter skins of ermine. The ermine heads have black beads for eyes and wear nose ornaments and necklaces. The central front part of the hat is made from iridescent cormorant breasts. The bottom band is red cloth with beaded designs.

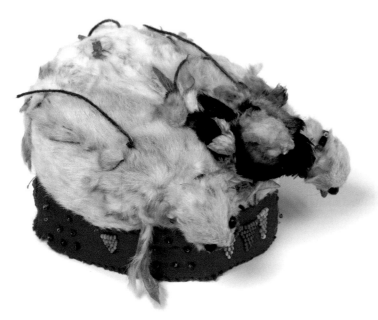

184 Kodiak Island mask collected by Alphonse Pinart in 1872, from the collection of the Château-Musée, Bulogne-sur-Mer, France. The face is encircled by a hoop and by circular and feather-like bangles of painted wood. The mask is backed by a tall painted plank trimmed with fur. It is 41 cm high.

Photograph courtesy Jean-Loup Rousselot.

spirits and appealed to their compassion for human needs. This relationship is illustrated in a story told by Stepan Britskalov. Once when he awoke from sleeping in the woods, he saw Nunam Sua, whose figure glowed with light. She was dressed in clothing made from all the animals in her domain. On the back of his hand she drew a circle, and inside he could see all of the animals. She promised that he would always be successful as a hunter if he followed her prescriptions—to wash himself before entering a house, never to speak of her when too many people were present, and to avoid all contact with women who were menstruating.[14]

Hands with circular holes, a motif in both Alutiiq and Yup'ik art, are an emblem of this dependence on the generosity of spirits who control the availability of game. Edward Nelson interpreted pierced hands on Yup'ik masks (which also lack thumbs) as symbolic of a mask-spirit's willingness to let animals escape its grasp and thus return to hunters on earth.[15] Anthropologist Ann Fienup-Riordan suggests that circles in Yup'ik art are passageways between worlds, traveled by animal souls, spirits, and shamans.[16]

Alutiiq masks never show an animal and its *suk* simultaneously, as many Yup'ik masks do. Some, however, are human faces with beak-like mouths, suggesting *suk* spirits that have only partially changed into human form. Rare masks show beings that are completely animal in appearance, while others depict fully human faces.

The Cycles of the Soul

Traditional Alutiiq belief distinguished between *suk* and another type of spiritual entity—the soul (*sugunha*) of a human or animal.[17] The soul survived death, returning to the world embodied in a new person or creature. Rituals aided these cycles of reincarnation, ensuring the return of new game animals and the regeneration of human communities.

In Prince William Sound, an animal's soul was envisioned as a small duplicate of itself, located in a certain part of the body. For example, a bear's soul was in its head, and the soul of a fish was found in its guts.[18] Alutiiq men and women were careful to return the soul-parts of animals back to the environment, so that they could be reborn. In Prince William Sound, sea otter bones and fish guts were thrown in the sea for this reason, and a dead bear's head was placed on the ground facing the mountains, where its soul would return. On the Alaska Peninsula today, bear hunters face a killed animal's head toward the east, the direction "that Christ is going to come," according to Virginia Aleck of Chignik Lake.[19] This may be a reinterpretation in Christian terms of the same concept of animal rebirth. Gideon noted that seal bladders, seal neck bones, and sea otter heads were stored in the sleeping rooms of nineteenth-century Kodiak Island houses "to commemorate the animals taken in the hunt," although no information on possible related rituals was collected.[20]

Alutiiq and Yup'ik beliefs about animal souls appear to be similar. According to Yup'ik Elder Paul John in 1994:

> They treat the seal's body as if it is their kayak. And when they catch it, its soul can go into its bladder. People said to themselves that the animal they caught was alive, saying its soul was in its bladder.[21]

In the Yup'ik Bladder Festival, inflated bladders of seals, walrus, whales, and polar bears were ritually fed before being returned to the sea through a hole in the ice.[22] The Chugach also held a Bladder Festival in December to honor animals that had been killed by hunters. The bladders were not actually returned to the water, however, but were placed in boxes and carried on hunting expeditions for luck.[23]

While it was important to restore an animal's soul to its environment, this alone was not enough to ensure that it would return to be hunted again. The collective personness of the animal, i.e. its *suk* spirit (or in Yup'ik, its *yuk*) also needed to be persuaded to release the individual animals' souls so that reincarnation could take place. Seeking this cooperation was the central focus of the midwinter Alutiiq Hunting Festival (described below) and the Yup'ik *Kelek*, also known as the *Agayuneq*, or Inviting-In Festival.[24] In these ceremonies, masks transformed dancers into animal-persons, and portrayed the spirit as having human, animal, or mixed features. The theme of physical transformation, so important in Alutiiq ceremonies, art, and oral tradition, emphasizes that humans and *suk* are also alike in consciousness, intelligence, even language.

Animal souls, in contrast, could not assume human shape or share human thought. Masks were notably absent from rituals that focused on animal souls, including both the Yup'ik and Chugach versions of the Bladder Festival.[25] Animal souls may, however, have been depicted in carvings used as hunting amulets or toys. Sea otter hunting amulets are engraved with spine and ribs, highlighting the skeletal location of the animal's soul (fig. 159).

Human Souls

In Prince William Sound, a person's soul was believed to reside in the breath. After death, it traveled to the sky where there were forests, mountains, and streams just as on earth.[26] At the Chugach Feast of the Dead, feasting and dancing ended with the burning of food and gifts, which rose in the smoke to these ancestors in the sky world.[27] In the Kodiak region, a human being was thought to have five lives. After his or her final death, a person's soul would travel to the lowest sky world, to live among the stars, moon, sun, and northern lights.[28]

Songs were sung to honor ancestors at the Kodiak winter ceremonies. Certain masks represented the dead, such as Kugukuak, the mask of a man who drowned and who came into the *qasgiq* covered with seaweed.[29]

Wooden dolls cared for by young girls were another link between the living and the dead. The dolls have been interpreted as souls that were waiting to be reborn when the girls became mothers.[30] A customary rule said that dolls could only be taken out of the house in spring.[31] In both Alutiiq and Yup'ik culture, the house represented a womb, and the doll's exit appears to have been a metaphor of birth. This could not take place until spring, the season of regeneration.[32]

Helping Spirits

In a story told in Prince William Sound, a man and his wife encounter a strange and frightening woman who asks them for food. They recognize her as a runaway from their village:

> The woman coming was sniffling. Her clothes were all worn along the bottom. When she got to them she said that she was hungry. Then they knew she was the woman who had run away. They realized that she had turned into a spirit. Her face was human, but the top of her head was pointed.[33]

Such was the fate of a person who was evil or insane, or who lived in isolation. He or she became a spirit with a long, pointed head, called a *kaḻa'aq* in the Chugach dialect of Prince William Sound Cook Inlet and an *íyaq*

185 Mask

Prince William Sound, 1875
National Museum of Natural History, Smithsonian Institution (NMNH 20265) Height 62 cm

This large mask has a whistling mouth and the pointed head of a *kaḻa'aq* spirit. It was one of seven taken from a cave in Prince William Sound by the Alaska Commercial Company in 1875, and sent to the Smithsonian Institution. The mask was repatriated to the Chugach Heritage Foundation in 2000.

in the Koniag dialect of Kodiak Island.[34] On Kodiak Island in the 1870s, Pinart was told that an *íyaq* (translated by Elders today as "devil") was the soul of an evil person that had flown away to the west after its fifth and final death.[35] In oral traditions from Prince William Sound, these spirits were hungry for meat or human flesh, and therefore dangerous. A *kala'aq* (or *íyaq*) could serve as a shaman's helping-spirit who transported him or her to other worlds and spied on distant events.[36] Holmberg learned from Kodiak Island Elder Arsenti Aminak that the "god" Ijak (*íyaq*) also listened to appeals from ordinary people, and that dead people who became "devils" brought luck.[37] Etymologically, *íyaq* (from earlier *íhaq*) means "one that is hidden."

A common form of Alutiiq mask is the human face with pointed head, which probably represents a *kala'aq* or *íyaq*. Many such masks have beak-like mouths, possibly related to the fact that helper-spirits often appeared in the guise of owls or cranes.[38] Others have puckered mouths which imitate the act of whistling. Whistling was the way that spirits spoke, which made it a dangerous thing for a person to do. Martha Demientieff said, "We had to be very careful, even how we played . . . don't whistle and things like that. . . . And somebody way up the Koyukuk River told me they have the same belief, that the spirits speak in whistling. Then they'll talk with words."[39]

Other Mask-Spirits

> From up there I descend, from the earthward side of those northern lights up there, from where I whirl around.
>
> —From the dance song of the spirit
> Shalgiiak, Kodiak Island, 1871–72 [40]

Other mask-spirits appeared at the winter ceremonies, traveling to the *qasgiq* from the sky worlds or from under the sea. Their identities are unclear; did they represent spirit persons (*suk*), helping spirits, ancestors, or other beings? Masks collected in the Kodiak archipelago by Pinart and discussed by Desson include Shalgaiak, "Hunter from the Aurora Borealis." The dancer's arms and the mouth of the mask were covered with blood. Unnuiaiuk ("night traveler") is a round mask, blackened and featureless on one side. The spirit's song and legend tell how its face was burned by glancing at an evil spectre. Another spirit was Chumugiiak ("one who has left his senses"), a shaman who changed himself into a mask and flew down from his house behind the sun. Paiulîk was a masked being who brought a bowl of plant foods to the Elders, and Iuilixia ("the voyager") promised game to hunters.[41]

For most masks, no songs or stories have survived, and the complexity and creativity of the dance ceremonies can only be appreciated in the imagination. Masks seem to have been based on traditional and perhaps very old designs, yet new ideas and visions must have constantly inspired their creation because no two surviving masks are exactly alike. Designs were probably conceived by the *kassat*, who composed and led the ceremonies. Alutiiq masks were often used in sets of two or three to tell stories, as in the Yup'ik tradition where each mask matched one verse of a song.[42]

Raven and Creatures of Myth

Raven is an important figure in Alutiiq mythology, with his own claim to being a creator and transformer of the world. He brings daylight by letting the sun out of a box, releases the moon and stars, and teaches people to make fire.[43] He is a powerful sky spirit who makes storms by

186 Rock painting of raven track at Tuxedni Bay, Cook Inlet.
de Laguna 1975: Plate 62b.

beating his wings and sending flashes of lightening from his angry eyes.[44] In one story, Raven plucks a whale from the sea in his talons.[45] However, Raven has a much less godlike—and much more human—side. He goes among people and tries to join village life, and especially to find a human wife. In such tales he is a clever, disgusting, and revengeful clown who uses tricks and magical powers to gain his ends. Yet he repulses everybody with his foul smell, and fails miserably as a hunter.[46] Similar stories about Raven are told by indigenous peoples of eastern Siberia, mainland Alaska, and the Northwest Coast, evidence of an ancient shared tradition. Although bird imagery is very common on Alutiiq ceremonial masks, it is not clear whether Raven is ever specifically represented.

Alutiiq folklore includes other extraordinary creatures and spirits, among them a monster that emerges from the sea to eat people[47] and a giant man-worm with many legs.[48] Best known are the "little people," *sungcút* or *inuwaqulút,* tiny but very strong men with loud voices. The *sungcút* had their own small villages and traveled in miniature boats.[49] Sometimes they helped people who were in trouble or brought good luck to hunters. Sven Haakanson, Sr., of Kodiak Island remembers an old custom of putting out scraps of food for them to eat.[50]

The Alutiiq Cosmos

Souls, spirits, and other beings all had dwelling places in the traditional Alutiiq conception of the universe. For Kodiak Islanders, the cosmos had five sky worlds, layered one above the other.[51] Lam Sua dwelt in the fifth and highest sky. Beings only slightly less pure and luminous lived in the fourth sky. In the third resided the *kassahpak* (literally, "chief *kassaq*"), a spirit who created all of the different birds and animals from a single "little man," (i.e., a *suk)*. He was also the ancestor and advisor

to human *kassat* on earth, who conducted the hunting festivals.[52] Through the *kassahpak,* the *kassat* learned about the wishes of Lam Sua. In this way, they must have understood what dances and songs were needed to ensure the success of the ceremonies.

The northern lights (aurora borealis), the moon, and the stars were located in the first sky, which is visible from earth. These celestial beings were *suk* spirits who appear in Alutiiq legends. The "star-men" lie face down on the tundra so that their single eyes—the stars—can shine down through holes in the sky onto the human world below. The moon is a man who puts on a different mask for each phase.[53]

The traditional Yup'ik cosmos also has five sky levels, depicted in the *ellanguaq* ("pretend universe"), concentric wooden hoops that hung from the ceiling of the men's house during ceremonies. The hoops represented the sky worlds and were decorated with feathers that stood for stars and snowflakes.[54] The sky worlds also are symbolized by hoops that encircle Yup'ik masks. Through the ritual of the dance, the mask-spirit in the center of the hoops is given power to see and travel through the layers of the cosmos that encircle it.

Hoops frame many Alutiiq masks, and the same meaning can be adduced. Concentric circles surround a face on the lid of a bentwood box from Karluk, representing the multilayered Alutiiq cosmos or a mask (fig. 187). The face in the center may be a *suk* spirit, poised to travel between worlds, or perhaps Lam Sua himself. Rays extending from the being's eyes suggest vision which penetrates through the layers of the universe, or beams of light. In Prince William Sound, Lam Sua was sometimes identified as the sun.[55]

The box lid drawing, painted about A.D. 1700, resembles Alutiiq rock art in the Kodiak archipelago, Cook Inlet, and Prince William Sound. These paintings were

187 Painted box panels

Karluk 1 site, Kodiak Island, A.D. 1400–1750
Alutiiq Museum, Koniag, Inc., Collection
(AM193-95-853) Width of larger panel 11 cm

These panels are from a small wooden box found at the Karluk
1 site, and are 250–600 years old. They are painted to represent the multiple sky worlds of the Alutiiq cosmos. Sky levels
were also symbolized by the rings that surrounded ceremonial masks. The face at the center may be L̲am Sua, the "person" of the universe.

probably also created during centuries just prior to Russian contact. Rock painting was part of whaling ritual
and also said to be the handiwork of shamans' helper-
spirits.[56]

Pinart was told that there were five underworlds as
well, but did not learn what beings might inhabit them.[57]
Dominique Desson suggests that *suk* spirits of animals
lived in these lower worlds, which were under the sea.
In Alutiiq mythology, the homes of fish, sea mammals,
and even bird spirits were reached by traveling through
water, and in one Kodiak story two brothers find a settlement under the sea where all the inhabitants wear dance
masks just like those used in the winter ceremonies.[58]

Traditional Ceremonies

CONTEMPORARY ALUTIIQ ELDERS GREW UP TWO generations or more after the last of the traditional winter hunting ceremonies were performed, and therefore did not witness them first-hand. Descriptions of the older rituals in the Kodiak archipelago survive, however, in the writings of colonial observers including Grigorii Shelikhov in 1784–86, Carl Heinrich Merck in 1790, Gavriil Davydov in 1802-03, Iurii Lisianskii in 1804–05, the Orthodox priest Gideon in 1804–07, naturalist Il'ia Voznesenskii in 1842–43, and French linguist Alphonse Pinart in 1871–72.[59] These included the masked Hunting Festival and the Doll Festival, both described below.

Prince William Sound Elders described Chugach beliefs and ceremonial life to anthropologists Kaj Birket-Smith and Frederica de Laguna in 1933.[60] Chugach ceremonies included a Bladder Festival and Great Feast of the Dead, both with close Yup'ik equivalents. Neither of these, however, is known to have been practiced on Kodiak or in the rest of the western Alutiiq region.

There is little information from any source for the Alaska Peninsula, Kenai Peninsula, and Cook Inlet, although some dance masks and clothing have been preserved. Smithsonian collector William J. Fisher bought headdresses and masks from Kodiak and the Alaska Peninsula in 1879–85. He never witnessed any masked ceremonies, although these were reportedly still practiced in some villages at that time. The traditional ceremonies of the Alutiiq people, described below, invite comparisons that extend across the northern world, including Alaska, Canada, Siberia, and Greenland. Ties are also evident with the Northwest Coast, where masks, body painting, puffin beak rattles, bird rattles and other aspects of ceremonial art and performance were similar.[61]

Bladder Festival

Stepan Britskalov told Birket-Smith about the Bladder Festival of Prince William Sound, and saw one of the ceremonies himself as a child in about 1882.[62] Participants wore fur headbands with feathers, and painted their faces in patterns that were different for each village. Hunters painted designs on the bladders of all the animals they had killed during the year and hung them from the ceiling, then danced and sang to tell the story of each hunt. They blew eagle down into the air so that it fell like snowflakes, gave away gifts, and played a game with inflated animal skins. After the ceremony, the bladders were stored away to be taken on hunting expeditions for good luck.

The practice of honoring animals killed during the year—or rather, the souls that resided in their bladders—was similar to the Yup'ik Bladder Festival of southwest Alaska and Nunivak Island.[63] Hunting hats and weapons were employed in the Yup'ik festival, which concluded with the return of bladders to the sea through a hole in the ice. The shaman then traveled underwater to visit the animal persons (*yuk*) and learn if they were pleased with the way that the festival had been conducted.

Hunting Festival

On Kodiak Island, masked dance ceremonies began in November after the end of salmon fishing, and continued through much of the winter. Davydov, Gideon, Voznesenskii, and Pinart all saw fairly similar performances at different dates and locations, suggesting that the dances were part of a single Hunting Festival that was repeated by different hosts and villages. The festival

had several parts and was probably performed over a period of days. The Chugach of Prince William Sound also held dances in the winter, but few details are known. As far as it can be reconstructed, the Alutiiq Hunting Festival was quite similar to the Yup'ik *Agayuyaraq* ceremony, also known as *Kelek*, or the "Inviting-In Feast," a midwinter masked dance ceremony.[64] Like the Alutiiq Hunting Festival, the Inviting-In Feast was "an appeal to the spirits represented by the masks...for future success in hunting."[65]

The Hunting Festival was part of the pattern of inter-village feasting and hospitality that characterized traditional ceremonial life. Arsenti Aminak remembered in 1851,

> Earlier, our people often celebrated games and dances, at which the guests were usually treated with food and gifts. To celebrate such feasts we sometimes traveled to Igat Bay; at other times the Igat inhabitants came to us, to Angyahtalek.[66]

188 Drummers at a winter ceremony on Kodiak Island, mid-nineteenth century.

Illustration by Mark Matson, 1999.

189 *Cauyaq*—Drum

Ugashik *(Uggásaq)*, Alaska Peninsula, 1879–82
National Museum of Natural History, Smithsonian Institution
(NMNH 72505) Diameter 49 cm

Drums are played to accompany song and dance. Traditionally, the drumhead was made from a seal hide, seal bladder, or halibut stomach. Some Alutiiq drums were painted with figures representing shamans' spirit helpers, while others had carved and painted handles.

An Alutiiq Mask Maker

Amy Steffian
Deputy Director, Alutiiq Museum

CEDAR AND PACIFIC YEW ARE NOT INDIGENOUS TO THE Kodiak archipelago, but they are raw materials that link carver Jerry Laktonen with his ancestors. Along the creeping boundary between Alaska's coastal rain forest and her windy seashore meadows, trees are relatively new. Spruce have just begun to colonize, marching gradually south in the past 800 years. For much of Kodiak's history, the sea provided the Alutiit with wood as it did fish and sea mammals. Carvers combed the beaches for exotic timber from Prince William Sound and southeast Alaska, carefully selecting the stock for household implements and ceremonial pieces. Jerry explores lumberyards for his wood, but he studies the color and density of each piece like his forefathers, searching for the grain that will best reveal the story he needs to tell.

At the Alutiiq Museum, Jerry pores over a drawer filled with wooden paddles from an archaeological site in Karluk—one of the communities that generations of his family called home. He carefully notes the marks left by beaver-tooth carving tools, seeking guidance from the past.

There are few traditional Alutiiq carvers and Jerry is self-taught. "I had no one to teach me so I have invented for myself the technique for interpreting what I found in books and museum photographs." Archaeological pieces have also provided inspiration, particularly paddles and masks. But as ancient objects are often incomplete, Jerry must reinvent them, combining twentieth-century materials and his own vision with classical forms. "I like to feel the flow of ancient characteristics pass through me and express to the world who we were and are."

Jerry's woodworking experience began with boats. As a commercial fisherman, he learned to repair skiffs with adzes, saws, and rasps. In 1989, he turned to his woodworking tools to cope with the personal crisis created by the *Exxon Valdez* oil spill. With fishing closed, Jerry cleaned crude-soiled beaches to feed his family. The devastating impacts to his economic well-being and the health of his homeland left him spiritually drained. Carving provided an outlet. "What could I do to make things better for all that I loved?"

His talent blossomed and in just ten years he has created a new career. He now owns his own studio and shows and sells his work nationally. But for Jerry, the sweetest payoff of commercial success is the perpetuation of Alutiiq tradition that it enables. "I feel a great responsibility in being on the forefront of a cultural reawakening. I . . . have as a goal the satisfaction of knowing that I have exposed Alutiiq art to the world, while keeping both my integrity and the spirit of the original artists." *Joe Hazelwood*, the mask loaned by Jerry for the *Looking Both Ways* exhibition, commemorates the oil spill and is a personal summary of his past ten years–a period of transformation and rediscovery. Fashioned from bass wood, and inspired by classical forms from Prince William Sound, it is also a tribute to cultural resilience—a metaphor for the many environmental, cultural, and personal disasters the Alutiiq people have endured.

190 "Joe Hazelwood": *Exxon Valdez* Ten-Year Commemorative Mask by Jerry Laktonen, 1999.
Courtesy of Jerry Laktonen.

191 *Nacaq*—**Man's dance cap**

Woody Island (Tangihnaq), Kodiak Island, 1879–82
National Museum of Natural History, Smithsonian Institution
(NMNH 72476) Height 25 cm

This beaded cap was a type "worn by men and dances and festivals," according to William J. Fisher. However, he also noted that such ceremonies had been discontinued at Woody Island and most other parts of Kodiak archipelago by the time this cap was acquired in 1879–82. It is likely that this and several other beaded garments in the Fisher Collection were made at his request and never worn (Crowell 1992). The shape of the cap and the absence of a long tail in back distinguishes the Alutiiq man's style from beaded headdresses worn by women (Hunt 2000). The cap is constructed on a lattice of leather strips and the beads are typical of the late nineteenth century, including "cornaline d'Aleppo" beads with white centers and various tubular and faceted types.

On Kodiak, a man who planned to hold a feast began by inviting others from his village to the *qasgiq*. He seated and served these Elders and advisers with great formality, each according to seniority and rank, and announced whom he wished to invite and what gifts would be given.[67] Arriving guests were greeted at the beach, and carried to the *qasgiq* from their boats on the backs of the hosts.[68] In the ceremonial house the guests ate *akutaq* made from berries and seal and whale fat, dried fish, and meats. The host tasted every dish first, before passing it to the most important guest.

Sven Haakanson, Sr., was told that a whole village would be invited to attend the ceremonies at another settlement, and that the gatherings involved trade and games such as hill races. The chief would plan the gathering, and consider the possibilities for marriage between young people of the different villages.[69]

During the Hunting Festival, the ceiling of the *qasgiq* was decorated with a hanging array of hunting weapons, boats, and stuffed animals. A man rocked this arrangement back and forth by pulling on it with a rope. The ceremonial house was fumigated with aromatic smoke, perhaps as a ritual of purification. The first dancers included girls dressed in parkas or gutskin *kanaglut*, nose pins, beads, and eagle feathers. They were accompanied by male dancers who wore face and body paint, feathers, and open headpieces made of bent sticks, through which their faces could be seen. Some carried paddles and puffin beak rattles. To the accompaniment of whistles, drums, and singing, the men mimicked the actions of hunting—paddling a kayak, throwing weapons, evading a stricken whale. A man playing the chief (perhaps the *kassaq*) narrated their actions, saying that the animals were coming. At the climax he called out "Here are the animals!" and the audience blew whistles and made loud cries that imitated animal voices.[70]

As Desson suggests, this first phase of the ceremony seems to have been a symbolic hunt, culminating in the arrival of the animals themselves, or perhaps their *suk* spirits. The whole community participated in the invitation and welcome of these beings. Whistles summoned the animal spirits, and represented their voices.

The second phase of the festival depicted visits by mask-spirits that were described in an earlier section. Dances followed one after another, each portraying a different being or group of beings. Both men and women

participated in these enactments. Women often danced without masks but sometimes wore special masks that framed, rather than covered, their faces.[71]

Some of the difficulties of interpreting these dances have been discussed. The words of dance songs appeal to "helping spirits"[72] for aid, and in turn promise them offerings of seals and other game. The exact meaning of the words is unclear, but they suggest the cycling of animals' souls between hunters and spirits that controlled their reincarnation. Some mask spirits were clearly thought to be dangerous. Stories recorded by Pinart tell of spirits so frightening that the stone lamp and grass on the floor of the *qasgiq* would retreat from them.[73] Davydov saw another part of the Hunting Festival in which men wearing masks were "devils" who deceived people, and who chased the women and children from the *qasgiq*.

192 *Naqugun*—Woman's dance belt

Ugashik *(Uggásaq)*, Alaska Peninsula, 1879–82
National Museum of Natural History, Smithsonian Institution (NMNH 72470) Length 118 cm

This belt was part of a "full set of bead ornaments worn by the Ugashak [Ugashik] belles" that William Fisher purchased in 1881. This set also included a beaded headdress, choker, heavy necklace (fig. 45), and earrings (fig. 46). The belt is made of soft caribou skin and is ornamented with glass trade beads and brass rifle cartridges. The stitching is of fine, braided sinew thread. The ties were for fastening the belt at the waist.

193 Young women dance at a midwinter ceremony in the nineteenth century.

Illustration by Mark Matson, 1999.

Gideon and Merck described women's dances that seem to have been part of the Hunting Festival (fig. 193).[74] A women's dance described by Gideon was to honor ancestors, and included light-hearted teasing between the sexes:

> Women and young girls always dance by themselves, without men. They solemnly line up in a row, tightly one behind another, and by slight, almost imperceptible movements, they crouch down, then straighten up in the same manner, now and then swaying to the right and then to the left. . . . As soon as those who beat the drums and sing begin to sing about their dead ancestors, mentioning the name and the death of a particular kinsmen, the women, immediately and in unison, turn their palms downward, toward the ground. During the women's dance, old men who are enjoying themselves make every possible effort to make some of them laugh, as according to their custom the father or husband of the woman who succumbs to teasing and laughs must pay a fine for the benefit of the old and the poor: it is enough for a wife or a daughter just to smile ever so slightly while dancing. [75]

At the end of the festival, masks and drums were broken or put away in caves.[76] Many old Alutiiq masks in museum collections are worn and weathered from storage in caves and rock crevices. Yup'ik people often burned their masks after ceremonies, and at least one Alutiiq mask in the Fisher Collection shows evidence of this practice (fig. 133).

194 Rock art images of drummers from Kodiak Island (Heizer 1956b) and Afognak Island (Clark 1970b).

Doll Festival

Davydov wrote, "In winter, at the end of the festival, the magicians [shamans] tell fortunes and forecast whether the hunting will be good or bad."[77] This may have occurred as part of the Hunting Festival itself, but was more likely to have been a separate ritual, in which the shaman consulted a spirit-helper in the form of a large wooden figurine. This ceremony, which was nearly identical to the Yup'ik Doll Festival,[78] was described by William Fisher:

> One of these images is kept in each native settlement. It is in [the] charge of the Shaman of the tribe. Once a year—in early spring—the image is brought forth by the shaman with great festivities. The shaman previously decks the image out with pieces of the skins of animals which the native hunt for their furs or meat—pieces of "Ukala" (*yukola,* dried fish)—berries—tobacco—tea—sugar—in fact appends samples of anything the native most desire, and according to the abundance or scarcity of the several articles in the coming year. After the conclusion of the festivities the image is returned by the Shaman to its hiding place—only known to him—to be reproduced after another year.[79]

Feast of the Dead

Yup'ik and Iñupiaq communities held a Feast of the Dead each winter, and a much larger Great Feast of the Dead at intervals of a decade of more. These complex and important ceremonies included rituals to provide food and clothing to ancestors for their use in the afterlife. Host villages demonstrated prosperity and gained prestige by giving away large quantities of food and furs.[80]

Birket-Smith reported that a Chugach Alutiiq Feast of the Dead was held each August in Prince William Sound, until about the 1880s. The wealthier villages of Nuchek, Palugvik, Montague, and Chenega took turns hosting the event, which was attended by guests from all of the surrounding settlements.[81] The Feast of the Dead was celebrated in addition to individual memorial feasts given forty days after death. Wealthy men received memorial feasts on Kodiak Island as well,[82] but there is no mention of a large annual ceremony. No Great Feast of the Dead is known for the Alutiiq area.

The Feast of the Dead in Prince William Sound began with a week or more of singing and dancing in the plank smokehouse. Comical dances were performed with masks. The musicians played large drums, and the dancers wore red paint around their eyes and on their chins.

At the lavish feast that followed, the hosts gave away furs, food, and other gifts to the poor, asking each recipient to remember the deceased. Other gifts were burned, sending them directly to the sky world where the ancestors lived. Masks used in the Feast of the Dead were placed in caves after the ceremony.

Rites of Passage

Other ceremonies gave public recognition to a young person's entry into adulthood. For a girl, this transition came with her first menstrual period. The change meant not only that she could potentially bear children, but also that she now was a source of blood which was spiritually powerful.

On nineteenth-century Kodiak Island, a girl who had her first period had to live alone in a small dwelling for six months. Her isolation was followed by a feast to celebrate her reentry into the community as an adult woman.[83] Lucille Antowak Davis remembers her own menstrual initiation at Karluk in the mid-1930s.[84] For fifteen days, she had to stay in one room of the house. She was not allowed to leave, and had her own food and eating utensils. The custom was very similar in Prince William Sound, where a girl cleansed herself at the end of her seclusion by diving five times into the sea or a fresh water pool.[85]

At the village of Ugashik on the Alaska Peninsula, a girl's family gave a feast before she began her menstrual isolation.[86] At this ceremony, the girl gave away her dolls and other toys, and her parents gifted all of their hunting and sewing implements. The girl chewed pieces of meat and gave them to young boys, who by eating them would become good hunters. Her hair was cut, and given to the shaman to wear on his or her parka. The girl dressed in a garment made from the skins of caribou calves, and her wrist, elbow, and other joints were tattooed and tied with braided strings of caribou sinew.

Another important tradition, practiced into the early decades of the twentieth century, was the ceremony held when a boy killed his first animal. In Prince William Sound, the boy fasted for three days, and all of the meat was given away. The family then provided a feast for the village, and two elderly women reenacted the hunt.[87] Elder Innokenty Inga said that his first seal was given to his mother at Old Harbor, and that during the New Year's festival in February there would be a dance when all the first-caught animals were presented by the parents of the novice hunters.[88] Wilfred Alexanderoff remembered that mothers danced holding their sons' first weasels and land otters at Russian Christmas.[89] Lucille Antowak Davis, whose father was a village leader at Karluk, linked the occasion of a chief's son's first kill with announcement of his future succession.

> "So, if I was a boy, his boy caught a first thing—if he caught the first seal, first fox in hunting, they celebrated. That's what it was all about.... They gathered together to let them know that their son caught his first seal and he's going to be going to teach him to be a chief."[90]

195 *Nacaq*—**Woman's beaded headdress**

Ugashik *(Uggásaq)*, Alaska Peninsula, 1883
National Museum of Natural History, Smithsonian Institution (NMNH 90453) Height 51 cm

Alaska Native peoples from the Yukon-Kuskokwim delta to southeastern Alaska made beaded headdresses. Fisher recorded that Alutiiq headdresses were "worn by women at dances and feasts." Alutiiq womens' headdresses had dangling pendants on the sides and long tails in the back. This headdress has a cap of small "seed" beads and a tail of heavier beads that widens at the bottom, an Alaska Peninsula style (Hunt 2000).
Photograph by Chip Clark, Smithsonian Institution.

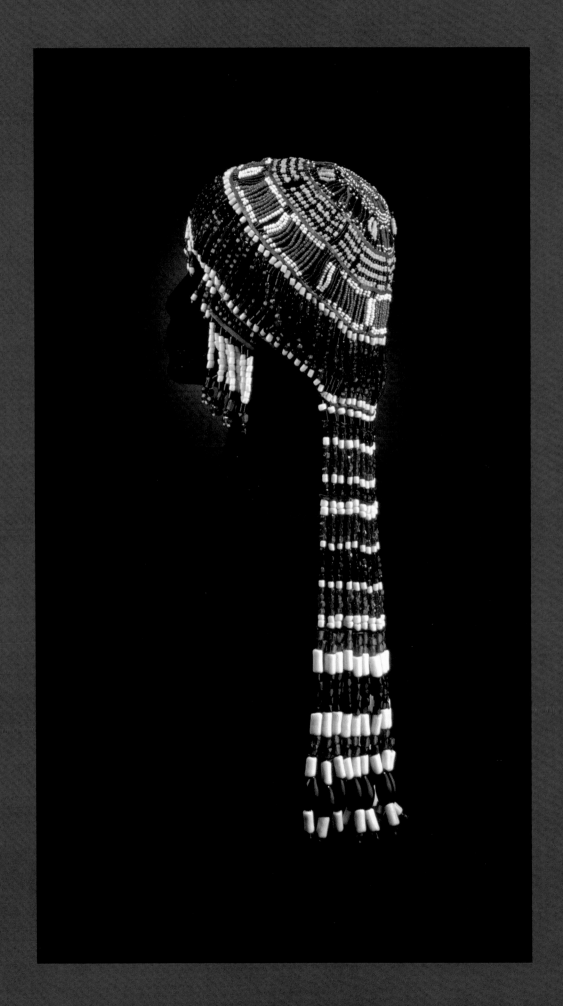

Shamans

MANY STORIES ARE TOLD ABOUT ALUTIIQ SHAMANS. They changed into animals, dove into the earth, and flew through the air.[91] It is said that shamans could cure the sick, quell storms, read minds, and see into the future. Others are remembered more for the evil magic they practiced. Shamans were active in some villages until the 1940s or even later, according to Sven Haakanson, Sr., Clyda Chistiansen, Lucille Antowak Davis, and other Kodiak area Elders.

The late Ignatius Kosbruk of Perryville narrated the legend of Pugla'allria, a famous shaman who lived in Katmai during the last years before the eruption in 1912.[92] Pugla'allria was turned into a shaman by his maternal uncle, who put the boy in a garbage pit for a whole winter. When the boy emerged unharmed in the spring, "He knew what was on everyone's minds. He knew how people would live in the future. He was a person who knew things. . . ." Among many other feats, Pugla'allria saved an entire fleet of sea otter hunters from a terrible storm by magically pulling the boats back to Katmai along a path of calm water.

The word *shaman* is from the Tungus language of eastern Siberia, and was introduced to southern Alaska during Russian times. In Alutiiq, the word has been modified to *samanaq*. The original Alutiiq term is *kala'alek*, or "one who has *kala'aq*" (a helping spirit, or supernatural power).

Both men and women could be shamans. Some sought this role by walking in wild, lonely places in hope of meeting spirits that would become their assistants. Sometimes initiation was involuntary. Kalushi, a Prince William Sound shaman who was also famous for stopping storms, acquired his power as a ten-year-old boy when a "little mask" saved him from drowning and became his helping spirit.[93] Others were turned toward the profession by their parents, who apprenticed them to master practitioners. Boys who had been raised as females were especially likely to follow a shaman's path.[94] In Prince William Sound, the role often passed down from parent to son or to sister's son.[95] Sven Haakanson, Sr., said that people who were blind or crippled frequently became shamans in order to serve their communities.[96]

As discussed earlier, a *kala'aq* or *íyaq*, the transformed soul of an evil person, could be employed by a shaman as a helping spirit. Other types of beings may also have served as supernatural assistants, including birds and animals. A novice was said to learn some secrets of the art directly from her first helping spirit, as well as the song she would use during healing and divining rituals.

196 Shaman's bird rattle

Ugashik (Uggásaq), Alaska Peninsula, 1885–86
National Museum of Natural History, Smithsonian Institution
(NMNH 127805) Length 25 cm

This rattle represents a bird with teeth inside its beak. Its eye is copper. Inside the rattle is a charm bundle—a crystal of quartz stone, a sliver of wood, a flake of shiny mica, and clippings of red and black hair, all wrapped in sinew thread. The meaning of these amulets is unknown.

197 Shaman's hat

Ugashik (Uggásaq), Alaska Peninsula, 1885–86
National Museum of Natural History, Smithsonian Institution
(NMNH 127804) Height 25 cm

This hat belonged to an Alaska Peninsula shaman and was part of a set of clothing and implements that included a charm belt hung with brown (grizzly) bear claws, a rattle (fig. 196), whistle (fig. 198), and bracelets (fig. 199). The front and back of the hat are black-painted skin stitched with caribou hair and colored thread. The side panels are white caribou skin, and the band around the bottom is seal with a short inset of caribou. Patches of grizzly bear hair are worked into the vertical seams.

198 Shaman's whistle

Ugashik *(Uggásaq)*, Alaska Peninsula, 1885–86
National Museum of Natural History, Smithsonian Institution
(NMNH 127807) Length 5 cm

*"We had to be very careful, even how we played . . . don't whistle
and things like that. . . . And somebody way up the Koyukok River
told me they have the same belief, that the spirits speak in whistling."*
  —Martha Demientieff, Alaska Peninsula Elder, 1997

Whistling was used by shamans to call the spirits and
maskalataq dancers blow whistles to imitate spirit voices. Parents caution children not to whistle, especially at night.

199 Shaman's bracelets

Ugashik *(Uggásaq)*, Alaska Peninsula, 1885–86
National Museum of Natural History, Smithsonian Institution
(NMNH 127803) Diameter 7 cm

The bracelets are made of the sewn-together snouts of river
otters, with bone or ivory pins inserted through the nose of
each animal. A beach pebble with a natural, waterworn hole—
one gray, one black—is attached to each bracelet.

Other familiar spirits were acquired through time. They
informed a shaman about events in distant places, transported her on journeys to other worlds, and helped or
harmed people according to her wishes.[97] The spirits
looked like balls of fire as they shot through the sky on
errands. Ephraim Agnot of Kodiak Island remembered a
tradition of shamans sending messages to other communities. "But then they said they had messengers. To
go from here to Old Harbor, or Karluk, or Larsen Bay.
And they travel as a ball of fire. They call them *keneq
íyaq* ("fire devils")."[98]

Shamans consulted their helping spirits during dra-
matic public seances. To the accompaniment of singing
and drumming, the shaman danced, sang, whirled, and
twisted his body in the throes of spirit possession, speaking a language that no one else could comprehend. Returning to his normal state, the shaman told what he
had learned.[99] He might predict the success of hunting,
or tell the whereabouts of a missing person. Shamans
could foresee their own deaths and when other people
would die. A blind Kodiak shaman named Lademka was

famous for this ability.[100] Shamans in Sven Haakanson,
Sr.'s, mother's generation predicted many changes such
as the coming of airplanes and electricity.[101]

Shamans performed naked in body paint and feathers, or dressed in wigs and backwards clothing. A set of
shaman's accessories from Ugashik, collected by William Fisher in 1885, included a peaked caribou-skin hat,
charm belt hung with bear claws and caribou teeth,
bracelets made from the snouts of river otters, whistle,
and bird-shaped rattle. Although the precise meanings
are unknown, it is notable that the Tlingit considered
the river (or land) otter to be the most potent shamanic
helper.[102] Chugach shamans wore masks during some
performances, and aprons decorated with puffin beaks.

One of the most important shamanic roles was healing. Evil spirits were thought to be the cause of some
sicknesses, and healing rituals were the only cure. It was
told that the Prince William Sound shaman Apuluq
cured patients by carrying them around a fire five times,
then diving into a spruce root basket with the patient
on his back.[103] Pinart described a performance on Kodiak

200 Stake dolls

Karluk 1 site, Kodiak Island, A.D. 1400–1750
Alutiiq Museum, Koniag, Inc., Collection
(UA85.193:4063 and UA85.193.3695) Height of both 16 cm

It was believed that shamans could put a spirit into a doll, then send it away to save people from danger—or to cause their deaths. Some dolls could speak, but only the shaman could hear their words. Spirit helpers also took the forms of owls and loons, whose calls meant the arrival of sickness.

Island by two masked men known as Axiashouk or Aĝiiashuk (possibly *agasúq* "cormorant"). In a dimly lit *qasgiq*, the masked shamans pretended to cut open a man with a large stone knife and to eat his intestines, then restore him to good health. The performance was made convincing by sleight of hand and hidden supplies of seal blood and intestines.[104]

Some shamans were also very knowledgeable about herbal medicines and medical treatment. Sven Haakanson, Sr., remembered a Kodiak Island shaman's treatment of an injured girl:

> A girl was out hunting sea gull eggs and she fell off the bluff and she was all smashed up. They brought her home; she's just screaming and crying. And the shaman went up the hill and come down and make some kind of roots and boiled them and let her drink the water. She calmed right down and she was even laughing while they were straightening her out so she could heal. So those shamans were real good. They studied their whole life to be shamans, to help their people. But later on, after Europeans came with all kinds of flu and diphtheria that killed a lot of people, the people didn't trust the shamans anymore.[105]

This account presents a positive view of shamans as healers. It refers, however, to a loss of trust that shamans suffered when their powers turned out to be ineffective against the new diseases. Shamans were probably always viewed with a mixture of respect and fear because their powers could be used to harm others.

An evil shaman would make a cloth or wooden image of his enemy, tied with strands of the victim's hair or a piece of his clothing. The shaman would cut the doll or stick it with pins to wound the intended victim. The dolls were placed near doorways and trails to harm a person as he or she walked past.[106] Lucille Antowak Davis remembers, "*Samanaqs* played games on you if they didn't like you, or if they were jealous of you. And if he didn't finish what he was trying to do to you, you would be that way. Maybe he did something to your mind and he didn't finish it and that's the way you would be the rest of your life. You would lose your mind."[107]

Alutiiq Russian Orthodoxy

The day we were baptized we were brought into the church and we'll go back to the same place when we depart. That's the way the baptism is, the way I understand it. And we must keep it up to keep our children, which are Orthodox, baptized the same way as our ancestors.

—Elder and church reader
Ignatius Kosbruk, 1997[108]

ALTHOUGH A FAIR-SIZED MINORITY OF ALUTIIT ARE NON-Orthodox Christians or are nonreligious, the majority currently belong to the Orthodox Church. And for most Alutiit, Orthodoxy is closely identified with traditional Alutiiq heritage. This is largely because of the history of the Orthodox Church in Alaska. After the United States bought Alaska from the Russians, the Alaska Orthodox church was no longer financially supported by the czarist government, and most of the Russian priests could or would not continue their work in the Alaska parishes without this support. As a result, the local churches became much more self-reliant. Native readers and laypeople took over the local leadership of the church, and in many places Alutiiq men entered the priesthood in order to provide their people with the fullness of the life of the church, including the Holy Eucharist (communion) and confession. Local Orthodox people also took charge of building and maintaining their churches.[109]

Furthermore, Euro-Americans have tended to regard the Orthodox Church as un-American, and this attitude was adopted by the U.S. government. This was manifested most strikingly during World War II, when the military built and manned non-Orthodox churches in

201 The Russian Orthodox cemetery and chapel at Karluk, on Kodiak Island. The chapel was built in 1888.
Photograph by Patrick Saltonstall, 1995.

202 *Cis̲laq*—**Russian Orthodox Peg Calendar**

Alaska Peninsula, 1883
National Museum of Natural History, Smithsonian Institution
(NMNH 90435) Width 17.5 cm

"The Elders at home, even when we got American calendars, they'd still use those wooden ones. Lots of holes. And they knew when all the holidays were, too."
—Clyda Christiansen, Kodiak Island Elder, 1997

Pegs were moved forward one hole each day on this household calendar of the Russian Orthodox year. One peg traveled the top row of seven holes for days of the week, with a cross for Sunday. Another moved through monthly rows of 30, 31, and 28 holes, starting with September, the beginning of the ecclesiastical year. Crosses, circles, and *x*'s mark major and minor feast days.

203 "Starring" at Chignik Lake, Alaska Peninsula, January 1992.

Photograph by Patricia Partnow.

traditionally Orthodox communities. The natural result was that Orthodox churches became even more closely identified with the Native people and their heritage, whereas non-Orthodox churches were identified with the Euro-American newcomers, together with their churches and government, which have historically sought to supplant the original Native peoples and superimpose their world view on them.

The focal point of the Orthodox Church year is the Feast of the Resurrection of Christ, that is, Easter. This service, together with the cycle of services leading up to and following from it, is celebrated in a very traditional fashion among Native Orthodox. During the Christmas cycle, on the other hand, Alutiit observe a number of more or less innovative practices and celebrations. Most of these clearly have their origins in the folk traditions of the Russian or Slavic Orthodox, although some may date to earlier times.

In the Alutiiq villages, The Feast of the Nativity of Our Lord God and Savior Jesus Christ ("Russian Christmas")

is celebrated on January 7 (which is December 25 on the Julian calendar). After church on that day and the two following days, the people go starring *(sláwihluteng)* from house to house. Starring *(Sláwiq)* is practiced by carrying a wooden star that is spun on a dowel at the top of the handle; attached to the front of the peg is an icon of the Nativity. At each house, the star-bearer spins the star while the people sing hymns and carols in Alutiiq and Russian, after which they partake of food and drink provided by the family of the house. The star is said to represent the star that the Magi followed to find the baby Jesus. In Nanwalek and Port Graham, it happens on rare occasions that a man will adopt the role of a devil *(íyaq)*, who mocks and pesters the procession. It is said that such a man will die soon after.[110]

Masking *(maskalataq)* is a custom that was once common to the entire Alutiiq region, but its practice has been minimized or abandoned in most villages, at least until the current revival in Native traditions and language. It appears to have its roots in Russia.[111] It is a folk tradition,

204   Russian Orthodox Christmas star

Alutiiq Museum
AM 407:1

Bands of singers follow bright, spinning stars through the village, stopping at each home to enjoy a feast of holiday foods including *akutaq* ("ice cream" made from fat, dried fish, and sugar or berries), cakes, and *piroq* (rice and salmon pie). Students at St. Innocent's Academy in Kodiak made this star for the exhibition.

Photograph by Patrick Saltonstall.

not associated with the church but not frowned upon. However, on the Eve of Theophany (Epiphany) people are supposed to cleanse themselves by taking a banya *(maqiq)* or, in the old days, by jumping into the ocean and then going to the church, still wet, to do penance. According to John Klashinoff of Nuchek, there was a saying:

> *Maskalátaḻet maqilahtut, qaqimaḻet naluwaluteng.*
> Those who have masked take banyas; those who have played the devil swim in the ocean.

"Playing the devil" is condoned neither by the church nor by the community. They say that in the old days those who impersonated devils used to dance on the red-hot stove. They also say that you should not go off with one who has not unmasked. This may be a devil in disguise, who will lead you into the woods where you will lose your way and perish unless you come to your senses.

The *maskalataq* tradition is strongest in the Kenai Peninsula villages of Nanwalek and Port Graham. Here *maskalataq* begins after the last round of *sláwiq* on the evening of January 9 and continues every evening until the Eve of Theophany on January 18, which marks the end of the Christmas season. The maskers *(maskalatalhít)* get dressed at home, or more commonly at the house of someone who has a lot of masking gear *(maskalatahsútet)*, dressing themselves with whatever they want and putting on masks. The whole body is supposed to be covered so that the masker is not identifiable on sight—but of course people usually recognize the dancers by their posture and mannerisms. Then the maskers go up to the community hall to dance. When they enter, they bow to the spectators and the band. The band plays guitars and when possible an accordion or organ; they used to play banjos and mandolins as well. There is a special set of tunes that are played at this time; such a tune is called a *Prazdnik (Prásenik)*. After dancing for a spell, the maskers usually go back to take a break and dress in a different costume, then return to dance again. Masking often goes on in this way until late at night.

On Russian New Year *(Núwikútaq,* January 14), these two communities each put on a pageant at their community hall. This pageant is called *Núwikútaq*. The performers belong to two factions. On one side are one or two sergeants-at-arms or MPs *(Sutiyaq/Sutiyak)*, the New Year *(Nuta'aq)*, and twelve women dressed in white gowns, representing the months *(Tanqit)*. On the other side are the Old Year *(Anguteq)* and the male clowns called the Old Ladies *(Ucinguhuat)*; unlike the New Year and his allies, they wear masks. The performers enter in this order, bow to the onlookers, circle the room, and leave. The New Year is dressed in white and carries a paddle; the Old Year is dressed in black, has a pack on his back made to look like a hunchback, and uses a cane. This is the first of twelve rounds. In each succeeding

round, things get a bit livelier. The New Year dances with each of the Months, as eventually do the Old Year and the Old Ladies. The Old Ladies begin to talk to the audience; these are the only performers allowed to speak, and they must speak only in Alutiiq. As the evening progresses, they get rowdier; they start teasing and flirting and pestering the New Year. When the MPs sound the whistle to go out, they refuse to leave with the others, so that the MPs have to hunt them down and eject them from the hall, sometimes more than once. The New Year rushes at the Old Year and hits him on the back with his paddle; when this happens, the MPs shoot their guns once all the performers are outside.

The final round ends at midnight, signaled with three gunshots. These signify the victory of the New Year over the Old Year. Then all the performers reenter the hall, and the Old Year and Old Ladies unmask themselves. Everyone faces the icons and prays the Lord's Prayer. After this, the band starts to play a waltz, and all the performers greet one another with a kiss and dance with one another in order, starting with the New and Old Years. After this, the audience is free to join in. In this way, the two factions are reconciled, and peace is restored to the community for the new year.

The *Núwikútaq* pageant is unique to the communities of Nanwalek and Port Graham. People from Kodiak remember that a similar but much less elaborate celebration used to be held on Russian New Year (fig. 205). The origin of this ceremony is not clear. It may be that it has its roots in Russian folk traditions, or that it continues in much revised form an ancient Alutiiq winter celebration. Or it may incorporate elements of the traditional Alutiiq ceremonies, reinterpreting them in terms of the Western conception of the New Year, much as the Western European Christmas holiday has incorporated elements of the pre-Christian ritual practices of the winter solstice, such as the Christmas tree and the Yuletide fire. During the ancient hunting festival, as described above, young women dressed in fine clothes danced with men, some of whom carried paddles. These call to mind the Months and the New Year of the *Núwikútaq* pageant, and the Old Year and Old Ladies are reminiscent of the men representing devils in the hunting festival. Whatever the history of the *Núwikútaq* pageant may be, it has evolved into a special celebration that is one of the highlights of the year for the Kenai Peninsula Alutiit and epitomizes the melding of cultures that has produced the modern Alutiiq way of life.

The Dance Continues

Jeff Leer
Alaska Native Language Center

IT IS THE SUMMER OF 1999. THE NIGHT IS DARK AT CAMP Dig Afognak, and it has been a long and full week. We are gathered in the communal tent, basking in the light and warmth, enjoying our impromptu celebration. Yet again, the Kodiak Elders ask Sperry Ash to dance for them. Sperry is a student of Alutiiq language and culture from the village of Nanwalek, and a founding member of the Nanwalek Dancers. As he struts his stuff, he encourages the others to join him, and explains to them the meaning of the dances.

The youth of Nanwalek have one foot planted in the modern world and the other in the life of the village. Because of this, they are able to compare these two lifestyles and perceive the actions and speech of the Elders that do not fit in with pan-American culture. They pay special attention to these aspects of village life, realizing that these are their links to the past. Sperry explains that the youth have observed very few examples of the original Alutiiq dance styles. But during the season of

maskalataq, the masking dances held between Russian Christmas and Theophany, each person has his or her unique dancing style. People pay close attention to these stylings, and note especially the characteristic movements of individual Elders. The Nanwalek Dancers purposefully used this knowledge to create new dances, asking themselves what this or that movement originally represented, perhaps the surfacing of a seal or the flight of a fowl. Therefore, although the dances are newly invented, they are built around the bits and pieces of traditional Alutiiq culture that the new generations have been able to mine from the tradition-bearers of the village.

In closing, Sperry exhorts the Kodiak Islanders not simply to copy these Nanwalek dances. Each community should rather evolve its own dance style according to its understanding of village tradition. So will they maintain the local diversity that has always been characteristic of the Alutiiq nation; so will they continue to be the many in one.

206 Dancers at the community barabara in Akhiok, Kodiak Island, 1989. From left to right: Connie Chya, Larry Matfay, Margaret Roberts.
Photograph courtesy of the Alutiiq Museum.

Chapter 6 notes

1 Advisor Lucille Antowak Davis suggested use of this term (*ukgwepet*, "our beliefs") in *Looking Both Ways* to refer inclusively to both traditional and contemporary spiritual views.

2 Davydov 1977:109–111.

3 Birket-Smith 1953:114.

4 Birker-Smith 1953:112–113.

5 Oleksa 1992; Partnow 1993.

6 Quoted in Desson (1995:33-34).

7 Birket-Smith 1953:15.

8 Meanings of *suk* include "person," "man" (implicitly male), "adult human being" (as opposed to child), "human being who knows how to behave as humans should" (as opposed to a foreigner or a person with insufficient social consciousness), "personified consciousness" (of a natural feature or inanimate object), "supernatural being" (associated with a natural feature), "head" (of a boil), and possibly others.

9 References to *sua* in English language texts are frequently awkward, as in the phrase "its *sua*," which literally means "its its person." Saying "its *suk*" is much more accurate from an Alutiiq speaker's perspective. *Sua* is comparable to *yua* in central Alaskan Yup'ik and *inua* in Iñupiaq (see Fitzhugh and Kaplan 1984 and Fienup-Riordan 1996).

10 Personal communication to Jeff Leer, 1999.

11 Birket-Smith 1953:120–125, 151–176; Golder 1903; Lantis 1938.

12 Birket-Smith 1953:156–157.

13 Desson 1995:46-49; Birket-Smith 1953:120–121; Holmberg 1985:61. According to Desson, Kodiak Island notes by Pinart (n.d.) and Chechenev (n.d.) refer to L̪am Sua as a single being. In his published discussion of Alutiiq religious beliefs, Pinart (1873:677) refers to multiple beings with the same name, all of whom live in the highest sky world.

14 Birket-Smith 1953:121–122.

15 Nelson 1983:395. A pierced hand design is painted on one of the masks collected by Pinart in the Kodiak archipelago (probably on Afognak Island), now housed at the Chateau Musée de Boulogne-sur-Mer (Desson 1995:81, 386 and Plate 17; Rousselot et. al 1991:318–319).

16 Fienup-Riordan 1990, 1994, 1996.

17 Birket-Smith (1953:123) discusses traditional beliefs about animal souls among the Chugach of Prince William Sound. Specific information on animal souls is not available for the western Alutiiq region, although concepts of human souls and reincarnation are explicit in Pinart's materials (Desson 1995; Pinart 1873).

18 Birket-Smith 1953:33, 38, 42,123.

19 Alutiiq Elders' Planning Conference for *Looking Both Ways*, 1997. Other Alaska Peninsula hunters orient the skull to the south or southeast in a gesture of thanks to family and ancestors for the success of the hunt (Fall and Hutchinson-Scarbrough 1996:10).

20 Gideon 1989:40.

21 Fienup-Riordan 1996:38.

22 Nelson 1983:382-393.

23 Birket-Smith 1953:114.

24 Fienup-Riordan 1996:40–41.

25 Bird masks and maskettes were worn during the Bladder Festival in some Yup'ik areas, but the purpose was to depict hunters' personal helping spirits (Fienup-Riordan 1996:97–98).

26 Birket-Smith 1953:119, 123.

27 Birket-Smith 1953:110–113.

28 Pinart 1873:677.

29 Desson 1995:255; Kugukuak is probably *kukukuaq*, "snipe.".

30 Ivanov 1949.

31 Lucille Antowak Davis, Alutiiq Elders' Planning Conference for *Looking Both Ways*, 1997.

32 Birket-Smith 1953:124; Fienup-Riordan 1990:61. Yupiit view birth as the return of someone who has died, and give that person's name to a newborn child. While Birket-Smith was told that this was not the custom in Prince William Sound, he also learned that ancestors whose names had been given to children were no longer sent offerings during the Feast of the Dead, implying that they now resided once again on earth.

33 Birket-Smith 1953:144–145.

34 Desson 1995:49–50: Birket-Smith 1953:124. Alutiiq terms in this section have been corrected by Leer.

35 Desson 1995:49–50.

36 Birket-Smith 1953:127–129.

37 Holmberg 1985:53, 61.

38 Birket-Smith 1953:126.

39 Alutiiq Elders' Planning Conference for *Looking Both Ways*, 1997.

40 Desson 1995:224. Translation from A. Pinart's field notes by Jeff Leer.

41 Desson 1995. Paiul̂ik may be Payulleq, possibly "that which was prepared for the journey." Iuilixia may be Iiwillria "the one who spins in circles.".

42 Desson 1995:188; Fienup-Riordan 1996:103-112.

43 Birket-Smith 1953:163–164; Golder 1903:85; Lisianskii 1968:197.

44 Pinart 1873.

45 Golder 1903:16–19.

46 Birket-Smith 1953; Golder 1903.

47 Golder 1909:15–16.

48 Desson 1995:53–54.

49 Birket-Smith 1953:125, 148–49; Desson 1995:52–53.

50 Interview August 6, 1987, Alutiiq Museum oral history archive.

51 Pinart 1872.

52 Davydov 1977:109; Desson 1995:136–137; Lisianskii 1968:208; Pinart 1873:677.

53 See "The Girl Who Married a Star" and "The Girl Who Married the Moon" in Golder 1903.

54 Fienup-Riordan 1996:125–131.

55 Birket-Smith 1953:121.

56 Birket-Smith 1953:34, 124.

57 Pinart 1873:678.

58 Desson 1995:59–61.

59 Shelikhov 1981; Merck 1980; Davydov 1977; Lisianskii 1968; Gideon 1989; Pinart 1873; Desson 1995; Lantis 1938.

60 Birket-Smith 1953.

61 Lantis 1938, 1947.

62 Birket-Smith 1953:114.

63 Lantis 1947; Nelson 1983:379-393.

64 Nelson 1983:358–359; Fienup-Riordan 1996.

65 Hawkes 1913.

66 Holmberg 1985:60.

67 Gideon 1989:44–45.

68 Shelikhov 1981:55.

69 Interview August 6, 1987, Alutiiq Museum oral history archive.

70 Davydov 1977:107–111; Desson 1995:126–270; Liapunova.

71 Crowell 1992.

72 The interpretation is difficult; the terms translated as "helping spirit" are no longer recognized by Alutiiq Elders, but may be based on the verb stem "-wiig," to go in a circle, perhaps to whirl around in dance.

73 Desson 1995:254.

74 Gideon 1989:45–46; Merck 1980:101.

75 Gideon 1989:46.

76 Shelikhov 1981:81.

77 Davydov 1977:170.

78 Nelson 1983:494.

79 Crowell 1992:27.

80 Fienup Riordan 1996; Lantis 1947; Nelson 1983:363–379.

81 Birket-Smith 1953:111–113.

82 Holmberg 1985:53.

83 Davydov 1977:171; Gideon 1989:51; Holmberg 1985:53.

84 Interview at Arctic Studies Center August 11, 1997.

85 Birket-Smith 1953:88.

86 Fisher 1882.

87 Birket-Smith 1953:87.

88 Interview January, 1962, Alutiiq Museum oral history archive.

89 Interview August 6, 1987, Alutiiq Museum oral history archive.

90 Alutiiq Elders' Planning Conference for *Looking Both Ways*, 1997.

91 Birket-Smith 1953:128–132; Desson 1995.

92 Partnow 1993:253-256.

93 Birket-Smith 1953:130.

94 Davydov 1977:166; Gideon 1989:60.

95 Birket-Smith 1953:126.

96 Interview June 29, 1991, Alutiiq Museum oral history archive.

97 Birket-Smith 1953:127–129.

98 Interview, August 1986, Alutiiq Museum oral history archive.

99 Desson 1995:142; Gideon 1989:59-60; Lisianskii 1968:207–208.

100 Interview with Ephraim Agnot, August 1987, Alutiiq Museum oral history archive.

101 Interview with Sven Haakanson, Sr., August 6, 1987, Alutiiq Museum oral history archive.

102 Crowell 1992; Jonaitis 1986:90.

103 Birket-Smith 1953:128.

104 Pinart 1872; Desson 1995:242–246 compares two different Pinart descriptions of this performance, which took place as part of the winter hunting festival.

105 Alutiiq Elders' Planning Conference for *Looking Both Ways*, 1997.

106 Knecht 1995:685; interview, Ephraim Agnot August 1987, Alutiiq Museum oral history archives.

107 Alutiiq Elders' Planning Conference for *Looking Both Ways*, 1997.

108 Alutiiq Elders' Planning Conference for *Looking Both Ways*, 1997.

109 See Oleksa (1992).

110 For a discussion of starring in Alaska Peninsula villages, see Partnow (1993).

111 Partnow (1993:305–310) suggests that *maskalataq* is "almost surely a combination of Russian and precontact Alutiiq custom," derived partially from traditional masked hunting ceremonies.

7

ALUTIIQ PATHS

Martha Demientieff, Olga Sam, Lucille Antowak Davis, Rena Peterson, Jennie Zeedar, Ignatius Kosbruk, Ed Gregorieff, Larry Matfay, and Roy Skonberg.
Edited by Shirley Mae Springer Staten

IN THIS CHAPTER, ALUTIIQ ELDERS FROM THE ALASKA Peninsula, Kodiak Island, and Prince William Sound share their thoughts on Alutiiq identity, values, and traditions. The selections are edited, with permission, from interviews provided at the Elders' Planning Conference for the *Looking Both Ways* exhibition in 1997. Interviews were conducted for the Arctic Studies Center and Alutiiq Museum by Maria Williams, Joe Kelley, Jean Anderson, and William Simeone. Additional comments by Edward Gregorieff are included from a 1997 interview in Tatitlek by William Simeone for the film *Alutiiq Pride: A Story of Subsistence*.

207   Child's boots

Probably the Alaska Peninsula, 1838–42
National Museum of Natural History, Smithsonian
   Institution
(NMNH 2129) Height 24 cm

"In the spring the man said to the bear: 'There is a lot of snow outside. We will have to make boots for the children, or they will get cold feet.'"
   —From "The Man Who Married a Bear,"
   traditional Prince William Sound story, 1931

Some traditional boots were plain, made of seal and sea lion skin. Others were beautifully decorated, like these caribou skin boots with neatly creased soles and seal-trimmed tops. The decorative bands are made from strips of dyed sea lion esophagus, embroidered with caribou hair.

Martha Demientieff

208 Martha Demientieff. In the photograph, Mrs. Demientieff wears temporary chin tattoos, a traditional women's style, to honor her grandmothers. The photograph was taken at the *Tamamta Katuhḻuta* heritage festival, Homer, Alaska, 1997.

Photograph by Lena Andersen.

MARTHA ROSE MCCOIN DEMIENTIEFF WAS BORN IN a *barabara*, a traditional sod-walled house, in the village of Kanatak on the Alaska Peninsula in 1933. She is the daughter of Katia Andrei of Chignik and William McCoin, a trapper and fisherman from Portland, Maine. Martha Demientieff grew up in the Bristol Bay area and received her early education at the Catholic mission school at Holy Cross on the Yukon River. Mrs. Demientieff holds a bachelor of arts degree from the University of Alaska Fairbanks in cross-cultural education. At the age of fifty, she began her graduate studies at Harvard University, where she received a master's degree in education. In 1949, she married Claude Demientieff. They have four children.

Mission School "At that time it was very easy to understand the objective of school, because it was to 'civilize' you. To civilize meant you had to speak English, you had to give up your Native ways and wear Western clothing and live in Western housing and be Christian. It was, you know, displace and replace. As a student I knew that I went there to learn white man's ways. There was no confusion about what I was supposed to learn. It was sad but it made me tough, and I had a classic education. I learned to read by reading the great authors, the great poets, the great artists. We never read Dick and Jane, and funny things like that. And part of our schooling was also practical—sewing, knitting, housekeeping, caring for children, gardening, gathering, preserving. The mission had to be self-supporting and that had to be done, so it was a way for us to learn it."

An Alutiiq Path "I can only talk about what it means to me to be Alutiiq. And what it means to me is that I have a path that I'm to follow, and I've been following that Alutiiq path all my life. I knew from the time I was a little child that I wanted to be a parent. I wanted to be a mom and I wanted to be like my Momma. When I look at the path of my life, there are the little infants at the beginning of the path, and when I was a girl I had to take care of my younger brothers and sisters. As I went along, as I got older, I was a little farther along on the path and it was clear to me that someone else was on that path before me. You might say they blazed the trail. Everybody is responsible for somebody else who is behind her. Everybody is supposed to help the younger ones.

"And that's so different from the way I've studied how people measure other people. We have that pyramid, too, but in ours, the Elders are at the top or at the end of that trail and the babies are at the bottom. We don't have a way to measure people that says 'middle-class,' 'upper middle class,' 'lower middle class,' and all that. We don't measure people by how much they have, their wealth. We measure them by their age, and that's why I see my life, my Aleut life, as a path. And I'm very aware of the responsibility I have to help everybody younger than me, to see that they're coming along okay.

"When I'm out berry picking, I have a picture in my mind of my ancestors, we don't know how many thousands of years back. I see their clothing and I see them picking the same kind of berries I'm picking, with the same feeling about how this is for my children, this is going to be so good. This is food for our bodies and for our souls. It's something that our grandmothers have done forever, we don't know how long.

"I know what I want to be as I get older. I want to be serene, I want to be gracious, I want to be kind. I'd like to be wise, and I'm very aware that every Elder is a teacher, and that's a big responsibility. The other wonderful reward on that path as I reach the Elder years is the love, being a beloved person. That's a reward.

"The clothes I wear now, the material things I have—I haven't lost them but they've shifted. Now, the masks are on the wall. The dress is only used for special occasions. The fur boots are my best clothes, which I wear only for big important events. Some of those Native clothes are still the most practical—big beaded fur mitts, and you know, parkys and ruffs and all that—but a lot of the other things have shifted from everyday use to being more for ceremonial use or celebration.

"And the material things now—I wouldn't wash clothes on a washboard like my mother did, or scrub my clothes on a rock in a creek. You couldn't force me to do that. I wouldn't give up my automatic washer and dryer. But it's only the material things that have either changed or shifted, the labor-saving things. The thing that the work does for me is still there. As I am washing the clothes I am sure I'm having the same feelings that my mother had about how she loved her children. The old people told me it's less important to say how you do something than to say what's happening inside of you. Like this one woman said, 'When I'm tanning furs, I'm looking at the beautiful world around me.'

"I still have the same values as my mother did. And some of those values are always to help, help anybody that needs help, to respect everybody and everything. I mean, I have to respect the trees, I have to respect the animals, I have to respect everything. I have to love work, and I always thought that if I were ever arrested the worst punishment they could give me would be to not let me work. Because I found out now that I'm older that when I'm working, it's my way of saying to my family or my friends or my relatives, 'I love you.'

"One of the things that is important to me now as an Aleut woman is to be happy. And that is kind of like a thread through everything. When we're sick, the Elders tell us, we have to be happy. Whereas Western medicine is mostly scientific and uses high technology, Native health practices always include the spiritual. And they say that part of your healing is to be happy. As a Native woman I have to love children and that's not a hard commandment, it's very easy. I have to be a lifelong learner. I'm here at this conference to learn as well as to teach. Using my mind and developing that mind is very important. Providing for the family. And that's just a small list of my social life as an Aleut woman.

"My spiritual life is even more intact than that. There's a belief in the One—the One who sees. And a great part of my upbringing was to always be aware that somebody sees us, so we have to act honorably even when we're alone. That was the most important lesson. The One who created us, the One who sees us. I believe that after death there is an afterlife, and that I will be with my loved ones again. How I act now will affect their well-being over there, and they can affect my well-being from there. A great part has to do with still having contact with my ancestors, my relatives who are dead. With that kind of spiritual belief I can feel safe. I don't have to keep worrying all the time. I know that I'm loved by the people who are living with me and by the people who are gone. They still love me. I've lost their bodies but I haven't lost their love."

Teaching and Learning "As a teacher, I've been trying to help non-Native teachers understand the importance of your tone of voice, and your expression and your choice of words. There's so much to say about the way we speak English that I've called it, in my classrooms, Our Heritage English. I resented the fact that they call it Village English, or somehow imply that it's a lesser form of English. But when you allow the children to write and speak that way, you get the most wonderful poems and beautiful things that you would never get otherwise.

"I try to teach my students formal English and when to use it without taking away their Native way of speaking. And there are real reasons for our way of speaking English. For instance, teachers often tell kids to correct a sentence such as 'I'm going store.' And as a Native teacher, that sounds right to me, because 'going' gives me a picture of forward motion, and 'to' gives me a picture of a forward motion, so 'to' is redundant. 'I'm going store' sounds perfect. So I try to teach my children to keep that, and also to use a more formal English depending on the situation. I think that's my task as far as language goes. The Native language that I know is my spirit language, my soul's language.

"In our Native education system, everybody succeeds. You choose what you want to learn and you pick your teacher. If I wanted to learn how to bead, I would know who is best at that and I'd go and do a service for that person. I would say, 'I wish I knew how.' And then they're free to teach me, or to not teach me. In the school system we have now, everyone takes the same thing, and you succeed or fail. In the system we had there was no failure because you chose your subject and you chose your teacher and you paid your teacher by doing them a service. And there was a place of honor for everybody."

Olga Sam

209 Olga Sam at Chignik Lake, 1981.
Courtesy of the Sam family.

OLGA PENA KUCHENOFF SAM WAS BORN IN 1945 IN Perryville on the Pacific coast of the Alaska Peninsula, to Natalia Alugak and Willie Kuchenoff. Perryville was established by Alutiiq refugees who were displaced from their home villages of Katmai and Douglas by the eruption of the Novarupta (Katmai) volcano in June 1912. The primary school at Perryville was run by the Bureau of Indian Affairs, and opened in 1927. As at other American schools in Alaska villages, students were forbidden to speak in their Native language. However, Olga's parents felt that it was imperative for their fifteen children to retain Native culture and language. Her parents spoke only Alutiiq in their home. On September 4, 1962, Olga married Mike Sam and together they led the effort to keep the Alutiiq language alive in the school district of Chignik Lagoon. They formed a team to teach the Alutiiq alphabet and Alutiiq songs to the students. Olga was married to Mike Sam for thirty-six years; he passed away in November 1999. Olga continues to share her language with her six children and grandchildren.

Growing Up on the Alaska Peninsula "My mom was born in Katmai. My dad was born in Sand Point. My mom is full-blooded Aleut; my dad was part Aleut and part Russian. My mom said she moved to Perryville after the eruption of the Katmai volcano. There were a lot of them who moved and some didn't make it. They had a hard time. She met my dad when he was fishing and used to go to Perryville from Sand Point on the boat.

"Then we came along! There were fifteen of us altogether. And all that's living now are three of us. I'm the oldest, my sister's next, and my brother's the youngest. I have one sister, one brother out of fifteen, because of that epidemic they had. In those days they didn't have doctors and nurses. I remember my oldest sister, who died of measles and pneumonia together. She was always helping my dad. She'd going hunting with him and trapping. When we were all sick she tried to help my

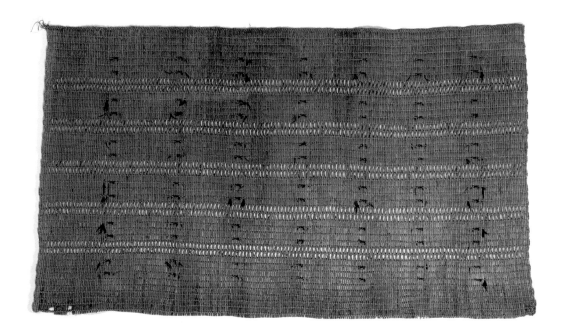

210 Grass mat

Nanwalek, Cook Inlet, 1883
National Museum of Natural History, Smithsonian Institution
(NMNH 90463) Length 128 cm

Grass mats served as bedding, door and wall coverings, household partitions, and kneeling pads in kayaks. The decorative feathers on this mat reflect the cultural value placed on quality and beauty in even everyday objects.

dad even though she was sick herself. She tried to help my mom and my dad.

"We used to go with my dad in wintertime to his trapping ground in Smoky Hollow. We used to have fun. He used to be our teacher too. He let us do our schoolwork and he'd play the violin. When we got lonesome he would sit us down and he would sing us old-time songs and play the violin. It was fun when he did that. And he was a preacher. My mom would wash clothes by hand. Before we'd go he'd have to get everything ready and then in the springtime we'd have to get ready too.

"We lived in a barabara, and we'd have to clean away all the old grass on the floor. They'd have stacked new ones, you know, and we'd always carry the grass in for my dad and he would put it on the floor. And we had

wooden beds and we put grass on the beds for mattresses. And canvas on the top of the grass. I used to always go walk the beach and I'd find arrowheads. My sister would say, 'How do you find them?' And I'd say, 'I don't know, I just walk and I see one and I pick it up!' And we used to have a *banya*, I remember that. We used to pile the rocks up, you know and make a fire, and pile them up. It was so neat, I always remember those days."

The Alutiiq (Aleut) Language   "I never want to forget my language. Now I have two grandsons that are small and I'm teaching them. The first time I taught one of them an Aleut word, he just laughed at me, just looked at me and laughed. Then he looked at me again and he said the same word and I looked at him, really surprised. I'm teaching him now, and he's been picking up a lot of words. My husband and I talk Aleut a lot at home.

"All we used to speak, you know, was Aleut. And if we tried to talk Native in school they would hit our hands with a ruler. And they would sit us down in a corner and let us write, 'I will not say this word,' about ten or twenty times. And then I'd just cry. I'd go home and tell my mom and dad, and my dad would go up and talk to the teacher. He'd tell them he didn't want them to do that to me because that's the first language I ever had in my life. And sometimes after I learned English, my mom would say something to me in Aleut, and if I didn't understand she'd get so mad. She'd say, 'You are not *Americaniq*, you're my Alutiiq!'

Lucille Antowak Davis

LUCILLE FEDOSIA ANTOWAK DAVIS WAS BORN IN 1926 at Karluk on Kodiak Island. Her parents were Fedosia and Matfay Antowak. Her godmother, Pelegia Alpiak, was influential in Lucille Davis' upbringing, and taught her to be a midwife. Among other childhood memories, Davis recalls the excitement of salmon fishing season at Karluk, when beach seine crews fished for the Alaska Packers Association. She had five children and is active as a storyteller, teacher, and advisor to Alutiiq heritage projects. She is also a member of the Russian Orthodox Church.

A Karluk Childhood "My godmother taught me a lot, through my faith especially. She took care of me and I spoke nothing but Alutiiq. I didn't understand anything about white people. My sister Elizabeth had already gone to school but I didn't pay attention to her. I was still talking in Aleut. They didn't have kindergarten at that time. They called it primer class, primer class! It was a big deal to go down to school. I'll never forget it. My first cousin and I were sitting in our little desks. We didn't know what we were going to do. But our teacher—it's funny, even though we didn't speak English, we were able to understand what they were telling us—she'd already written it down on the blackboard. We were not to talk our language, the Native language, around the school area. You know, only when we left the grounds and went home.... We couldn't keep our elbows on the desk, because here comes the teacher with the ruler. We couldn't sit like this (slumps); we had to sit like this (straightens). Or she'd hit us on top of our heads. So we learned English the hard way.

"Everything was homemade. In wintertime we had sleds made out of wood, really fancy. That was our

211 Lucille Antowak Davis.
Photograph by Carl C. Hansen, Smithsonian Institution.

RUSSIAN CHURCH AND GRAVE YARD. NATIVE HUTS & GOV'NT. SCHOOL HOUSE KARLUK ALASKA

Christmas present. . . . My skates, guess what they were? Evaporated milk cans! When they were empty we'd smash them down, and those were our skates. We'd hold our jackets out and let the wind sail us away.

"I began this morning with the Lord's Prayer. . . . This is what they did, at the beginning of everything, the beginning of hunting, the beginning of the season. Fishing season is what I liked most of all because it was from inside. It touched you. We'd be sitting in the grass and mama would have little blankets on us and we'd watch. The first thing they would do is blow the cannery whistle, three times. Even if we were sitting there we'd have to stand up. It was just like saluting the flag, okay? The American flag would come up and the guns were shooting. The church bell would ring on the side to wish the men a good season. The men were getting ready to go down with their boats, their fishing boats. With their

oars, they pushed out and that's when they would shoot three times. Boom! Boom! Boom! And then they made their haul. That was really special. The flag would come up, the American flag would come up, the church bells were ringing, everybody was happy. They didn't take that day for granted, no way.

"I'm so thankful and grateful that my papa taught me so many things. That's how I can outlive you all if we have to go out to the wilderness right now. I know how to provide!

"When I caught my first red fox in a trap, my papa said, 'I am not going to help you. You're going to kill that fox.' So I took this club, I'm walking around that thing, that poor thing was in the trap, you know! And I'm looking at it and it looks like a little puppy, so sad, looking at me like, 'What are you going to do now?' I'd say in Alutiiq, 'I'm not going to hurt you.' So, when it turned around I'd take the club and I'd go so far, and I'd say, 'No way, I can't hit that poor thing.' And it looked at me again, so sad. Papa said, 'We're running out of time, so here, go ahead.' Oh gee, here I go again. I said, 'Please turn around.' And that little thing did turn around. So I hit it on top of the head. . . . That was the first fur I ever caught.

"I could only hunt with him while I was young. I didn't know anything about menstruation. They never talked about it. But in the meantime he said, 'You can only go with me for so long.' We never asked questions, but my godmother taught me. She taught me all these things about me, as I'm growing up, what I'm going to turn out to be. You know, that I wouldn't be a little girl forever. I would be a woman one day, and I was going to be a wife. . . . And that's what he meant. 'Pretty soon when you hit your teens you're not going to go with me any more because you're going to dirty the ground where I trap. You will no longer be going along with me, when you get up to that age.' But he died before that. And so that's what it was about. That's what they believed, our ancestors did, that it's contaminating. They respected the land, the water, where we walk, and food."

Learning to Be a Midwife   "My godmother taught me how to deliver babies. . . . They did not waste anything that came out with the baby. In the hospitals now they throw the afterbirth away, and so forth. But in those days they did not. They took care of that afterbirth and buried it where people would not step on it. They respected that. . . . Babies are all born with a bag, to protect us. I would wash the baby and she would take care of that bag we're talking about. . . . They always embroidered the sign of the Russian Orthodox Church on there, because they were believers. The Orthodox people believed. And they would put that bag inside a piece of cloth and sew it around. As the baby grew older, days would go by, months would go by, and the baby would get uncomfortable. They would immediately put that around his or her neck. That would calm her down. If the baby was sick or uncomfortable, she was looking for her comfortable bag that she was inside. . .

"When I die I would like to leave them with good memories of me. I wish you all good luck, but never forget your ancestors. . . . I'm speaking to you, your generation, and your children. Don't let them forget where they came from. Be who you are and don't let anybody change you."

Jennie Zeedar

JENNIE ZEEDAR WAS BORN IN KARLUK IN 1930, TO Ephazinia Evan and Teacon Peterson. At the age of eight years she moved from Karluk to Akhiok. She became a healer by watching Elders in her community. During her teenage years, the Elders tried to impart their wisdom to the young people in her community.

Traditional Medicine   "The healer that she [Rena Peterson] was talking about [Oleanna Ashouwak]—she nursed me one time. When she needed her medication [wild plants] she went out and got it. In the summertime she would think about what she'd need in the wintertime. She would get what she might need and store it, but no one knew where it was. She would be the only one. She had to keep it in a secret place, or else it would not work.

"When my arthritis started, I was twenty-nine or thirty years old. She healed my aching bones, my arthritis. Forty years after, I started feeling my arthritis again, and I really, really thought about her. She had told me that if I needed to use that herb again, I had to do it by myself, where no one would see me. So when my niece called me to go and take a bath, a hot *banya*, I told her 'I'd like to take a steam bath by myself for a few minutes, just sit in there.' But I didn't tell her why. I remembered my healer and did what she told me, and I felt good. I took arthritis pills, which didn't help; the pain always came back. But after I took that one hot *banya* I felt good."

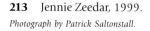

213   Jennie Zeedar, 1999.
Photograph by Patrick Saltonstall.

214 *Banya* in the village of Old Harbor, Kodiak Island.
Photograph by Richard Knecht.

215 *Qallúhun*—Water dipper

Katmai *(Qayihwik)*, Alaska Peninsula, 1883
National Museum of Natural History, Smithsonian Institution
(NMNH 90441) Length 19.5 cm

To create steam, water is ladled over hot rocks with a dipper.
This dipper is a traditional style, made from carved and bent
wood.

216 *Saqiyun*—Rock paddle

Karluk 1 site, Kodiak Island, 1400–1750
Alutiiq Museum, Koniag, Inc., Collection
(UA85.193:4816) Length 37 cm

"We believed that the bathhouse has a spirit called maqim
sungngua'a; *or 'person of the bathhouse.' If you heated rocks for
him, he made your hunt successful."*
                    —Bobby Stamp, Prince William Sound Elder, 1989

Hot rocks were carried with wooden paddles and tongs. Burn
marks are visible on this paddle from the Karluk 1 site.

Rena Peterson

217 Rena Peterson, 1999.

Photograph by Priscilla Russell.

RENA DONNA MELOVIDOV PETERSON WAS BORN IN Old Harbor, Kodiak Island, in 1941. She grew up in the village of Kaguyak. Her parents were Walter and Tulia Melovidov. Rena Melovidov was only two when her mother died. Rena Melovidov Peterson learned her healing practice from her foster mother and mentor, the well known traditional healer Oleanna Ashouwak. She practiced as a healer until after her first child was born, in 1959.

Healing "She [Oleanna Ashouwak] told me, 'I'll choose you to help me—start learning this so you'll keep it when I pass.' I didn't know anything. I'd just go along with her and she didn't explain what we were doing. They said we were helping people, that God wanted us to do this, to help people who were sick.

"We would hold their heads first and feel all their pressure places and check their hearts. Then we would tie a big, wide scarf around them and not let them move from the bed for about three days. She would put them on a diet, you know, and they couldn't eat certain foods. And they'd have to listen to her. She said, 'If you don't listen to me, I'm wasting my time, wasting my power on you. If you're going to listen to me I'll fix you, but if you're not going to listen, it's no use.'

"And then we would give them hot *banyas*, and we would hold them and everything. About the fifth day she would test them, make them walk really fast, half running, a long ways from the village along the beach. She would let them walk and come back. Then she would let them sit down and check their pulse again. And if it was good, she'd said, 'You're well, you can go home.' With some of them she'd have a hard time and have to work on them all over again. She wouldn't let them go until she knew that they were well, until she would get the right beat of their pulse. We used all these herbs from the land. We call them *táhiqs*. . . . We would go out on the tundra and pick them for medicine. Most of that we used in the *banya*."

Ignatius Kosbruk

218 Ignatius Kosbruk at Perryville, 1990.
Courtesy of Frieda Kosbruk.

IGNATIUS KOSBRUK WAS BORN ON DECEMBER 24, 1917, in Perryville, where he lived his entire life. He passed away in 1999. Young Kosbruk learned his Alutiiq culture and history from his father, George Kosbruk. George Kosbruk witnessed the Katmai eruption on Wednesday, June 12, 1912, at 2:30 A.M. He was one of the few refugees who spoke any English in 1912 and could translate the Katmai story. George was highly acclaimed as a storyteller and known as "Katmai Chief" in Perryville. Ignatius Kosbruk continued the work of his father. He cooperated with many writers and researchers through the years, sharing his knowledge of Alutiiq history, culture and language. He helped to compile an Alutiiq dictionary with linguists from the University of Alaska. Ignatius Kosbruk was also a hunter, fisherman, and trapper known for sharing generously with his family and friends. He always told his family "to feed anyone who is hungry, and to treat with kindness anyone who is angry." Mr. Kosbruk was an active member of the Russian Orthodox Church.

The Katmai Eruption, 1912 "My daddy talked to me and my grandparents talked to me. We were happy. They were telling me a story about when the volcano was going to blow up. People came to the village to prepare to salt fish when the salmon came in. They were all preparing to salt fish, and they were all getting ready. But there was one old man, he went up the hill and looked toward Katmai, and said that he saw the cloud that was coming out from the mountain. And he hollered, hollered to the people get plenty of water because when the ashes came down they would not have water to drink. They filled every container that they could find with water. And that old man, he knew where the spring was, and he found a pipe that must have been about eight or ten feet long, and he stuck that pipe into the spring water. He was the only one who saved them. When the ashes fell, and there was water running through that pipe, that's what saved them. The porpoises and the seals in the lagoon couldn't even dive anymore because they filled their nostrils with ashes.

"There was an old couple, there in Katmai.... They knew everything that was going to happen. And they told people way ahead of time, before the eruption, 'You people have to get away from Katmai, because the mountain's going to erupt soon.' They knew ahead of time. But the people didn't listen to them. So he just took his family and took that three-hole kayak and went into Shelikof Strait and rowed out. Before they reached across, the volcano erupted. They rowed out and rowed out, and kept on going. The stones started falling in the water and it was terrible, terrible! And still he kept going. They brought with them the icon and put it into their kayak. It was called the 'Mother of God'. It protected them from the volcano ashes. He put it in the bow of the kayak, and there was fire coming all over the place, and not one hit the kayak. The Savior saved them, our Mother of God."

Faith and the Future "I've seen a lot of changes. About the last ten years, the people are changing. But the old people used to tell me there would be change. Everything that the ancestors told me is coming true. But guys with a strong faith, they will never move. They will stay the way they are and they won't get hurt. With a strong mind and what knowledge they have.

"As you all know, religion is dying down for this young generation. But according to my mind, it will never, never fade away. We must keep it up. On the day we were baptized we were brought into the church, and we'll go back to the same place when we depart. That's the way the baptism is, the way I understand it. And we must keep it up, and keep our children, who are Orthodox, baptized the same way as our ancestors."

Ed Gregorieff

219 Ed Gregorieff.
Courtesy of Xenia Gregorieff.

EDWARD LARRY GREGORIEFF WAS BORN ON NOVEMBER 27, 1923, in the village of Ellamar in Prince Willam Sound. His father, Larry Gregorieff, was an orphan from Afognak. His mother was Natalia Malchoff from Nuchek. Edward's father later became a lay reader in the Russian Orthodox church. Edward's early childhood was spent in Valdez, where he attended school. In 1942, he joined the United States Army and served four years. Edward has lived for over seventy years in Prince William Sound, most of that time in the village of Tatitlek, and worked as a commercial fisherman and logger. He is highly knowledgeable about Alutiiq culture and history.

Segregated Schools "We were segregated, I guess you might say.... I went to school in Valdez, moved up there from Ellamar in 1927 and I started school a couple of years later in the 'government school.' That's what they called it. They didn't mean to teach us; they wanted to keep us downstairs. I can remember two or three years in a row when we had the same spelling book, the same reading book, primary grade books that never changed. I was getting old. If we tried to use the Aleut language, if we spoke a word of Aleut in the school during school hours we were punished. I spent a lot of time in the corner facing it for saying a word or two.

"I don't think the federal government wanted to teach us anything anyway. A year and a half before I got in the service—that was in 1942—the schoolteacher gave me a piece of paper that said I went through the eighth grade. That's as far as they taught in the government school, up to the eighth grade. What they called the "public school" was down the road from us. We couldn't go in there because we were Native."

Subsistence—Collecting Eggs "Eatable eggs, there aren't too many different kinds. There's goose eggs, seagull eggs, and arctic tern eggs. Duck eggs, they never did find them, seabird eggs once in a great while.... You cook them just like chicken eggs. You could boil them, and fry them. Seagull eggs make good tasty cakes. It's different. It's got a little stronger favor to it, real tasty.

"As long as you are on eggs, I'll tell you how to preserve them. We never did it here, my mother told me about it out in Nuchek. I heard stories from several other people that came here from Nuchek. They would take a *baidarka* [kayak] out around Cape Hinchinbrook and go out to the flats. The gravel bars were full of seagulls. They would fill those *baidarkas* from stem to stern—three, four, five *baidarkas* going out full of eggs. . . . They would do a lot of seal hunting and would melt the seal fat and make seal oil out of it and put it in barrels. When the eggs start to show, they would go out and get a bunch of them and share them with all the village. Put them raw into them fifteen- or twenty-gallon wooden barrels and fill them up to the top with seal oil. You can preserve all winter and whenever you need it—you could take them out and they would be fresh as the day they were picked.

"There was a Japanese woman who did it with arctic tern eggs. She was working for the BIA [Bureau of Indian Affairs]. She was living here for a while. She picked some of these arctic tern eggs. My mother and I were taking care of the kids. My mother asked if she would like some fresh eggs. We call them sea pigeons—the arctic tern. Evidently they did the same thing over there [in Japan] and that's where she learned to do it. She had these raw pigeon eggs in this jar and had it covered over with Wesson oil. Eggs have got these pores and unless you seal them up they spoil pretty fast."

Larry Matfay

220 Larry Matfay.
Courtesy of Florence Pestrikoff.

LARRY SAVA MATFAY WAS BORN ON MARCH 22, 1907, and was known as the last chief of Akhiok. Mr. Matfay used his Russian Orthodox Church name day, which was April 10, 1907, to celebrate the date of his birth. He was born to Pelagia Kejuk and Sava Matfay, both from Akhiok. On October 14, 1935, he married Martha Naumoff and they had two children, a son William, who died at age seven weeks, and a daughter Florence Pestrikoff who lives in Kodiak. There were many sides to Mr. Matfay's life. He was a culture bearer, a storyteller, a trapper, a reindeer herder, a commercial fisherman, and a family and community helper. His daughter Florence Pestrikoff remembers him as a "man of patience." He passed away in 1998.

Refurbishing a Kayak   "They'd take all the skin off, then invite the Grandpa from Momma's side, the only one who was living. He was kind of blind. They would turn the kayak upside down, and he would go around feeling with his hands, back and forth. He'd say, 'Sava, this is not good. . . . This is out a little bit.' That's what he said, and you'd look at it, sure enough, you could change that part back there, the keel. He knew what was right.

"And then after you'd get everything tied up, the ribs and all that, they'd lay seal skins in the middle of the barabara, all stretched out with lots of seal oil to soak them. It took about a week to sew the cover in a certain way. They'd take the seal skins and pin them on, coming from the bottom up, and sewing for a long time. They didn't do it in one or two days. It took a week or so, it took a little time because the seal skins were hard. They were dried quite a few times. The old ladies let the young girls sew the bow.

"Dad hunted the seals. I asked him, 'Can you get any kind of seal?' 'No, there's only a certain time when you get the seal skins for a kayak.' I said, 'How come?' 'They fight, bite each other, tear up the skin.' When they stretch the skin out, the big bites bust it up, and it has to be patched. My brother showed me how to sew these big holes and small holes."

221 Three-hatch *qayaq* on the beach at Chignik, 1909. *Courtesy of the Alaska State Library (PCA 24-99).*

222 Miniature work board

Karluk 1 site, Kodiak Island, A.D. 1400–1750
Alutiiq Museum, Koniag, Inc., Collection
(no catalog number) Length 15 cm

A sea otter swimming underwater, with trailing bubbles, is painted on this miniature example of a woman's work board for cutting skins. The artifact is probably a toy.

Sea Otter Hunting "My dad Sava Matfay went sea otter hunting. They'd go out to that island, way out there, in springtime, and they be out there, a bunch of them. Sometimes ten kayaks out there. Two people watched the weather, watched the stars. He said they got a lot of food out there, ducks and seals and all that.

"The old people would say in the morning, 'Tomorrow's going to be good day. You guys get ready and start early. There won't be much wind at all, the sea will be calm.' They'd go way out for sea otter hunting. The kelp patches, that's where sea otters live. You can find them along there. When the first guy saw a sea otter, he held his oar up—it was a sign, and the other people would see it.

"When the sea otter dove they made a circle. They'd see the bubbles as the sea otter dove down. When he floated up, the first guy would be in the middle, and he'd be the one with the first arrow, the first hit. After he hit it, somebody else would and somebody else. If the sea otter was not killed, then they could club it. . . . Two kayaks would get together to bring it up and club it. You'd see the arrows, cut them off, and holler 'Whose arrow is this?' 'That's mine!' Every one of them would get their tip, for their help, and so much for the sea otter. Whoever hit the tail would get a bigger tip. An otter can't move after you hit the tail.

"That's sea otter hunting, and he said he liked it. He had four or five sea otters right after he got married. He didn't tell us. He looked like a big, tall man. He spoke a little bit of Russian, a little bit of English, and Aleut. People came around buying sea otters in the fall of the year, and he sold four. I asked him, 'How come you're not going to sell this last one?' He said, 'I want to build a house. I want to buy lumber.' A guy said, 'Yeah, we'll get the lumber for you, in a schooner.' He didn't want logs, he wanted red cedar lumber for that house. Twenty foot, twenty by something. It wasn't too big—two rooms, little bedrooms. One sea otter! It only cost him one sea otter to build a house and put a stove in it. One sea otter. A lot of people don't believe it."

Roy Skonberg

223 Roy Skonberg, 2000.
Courtesy of Bristol Bay Native Corporation.

ROY HENRY SKONBERG WAS BORN ON DECEMBER 10, 1931, in Chignik Lagoon, on the "CWF side" (where Columbia Ward Fisheries was formerly located). His father was August Skonberg, a sailor from Sweden. His mother, Alice Anderson, was also born and raised in Chignik Lagoon. Roy's parents had fifteen children, including his twin brother Guy. Roy and his wife Minnie have five daughters. Roy's childhood was spent living a subsistence lifestyle, and his adult career has been in commercial fishing.

Village Life and Family "Years ago there was no running water, no electricity, no T.V. You were just out there chopping wood every day to keep the stove going. But now we've got everything back there in the villages that any place has. At night we used to get together and always have dances. I'm not much of a dancer now but when we were young we used to go out masking. You know, when you put masks on [*maskalataq*]? That was fun, you'd go from one house to the other, and you'd dance up a storm and nobody knew who you were. If you don't have a mask on you don't feel like dancing, you feel bashful. But you put a mask on and you grab someone and you say, 'Who are you?' And you find out you don't know, boy, you just clown off! And pretty soon you learned to dance—polkas, schottisches, waltzes, you know. . . . [I]t was nice.

"And then, back in '64, I got my own boat. I started running that. And my girls want to go fishing so if I can learn to pay my bills with the money I make I'll just give it to the girls because I can live off my pension. In the last few years the season hasn't been that good so they didn't make much, and I didn't make much, but we still make a good living, you know.

"When you're growing up, you take it for granted, you never think you're going to get old. You see your parents and you say, 'Gee, they're sixty-five!' Now I'm sixty-five and to me I still feel like I'm not old. . . . You just don't realize how much your parents mean to you till you lose them. I always tell the girls, 'I'm not trying to be mean to you—you can have anything you want. But when I say no, when you guys want to do something—how many times do I tell you guys no? Not many times, but when I do, you know there's a meaning behind it.' So they all listen, and I'm proud about that."

Glossary

Agasúq (Alutiiq)—Cormorant (Latin, *Phalacrocorax* spp.). A marine bird captured for food and for its iridescent feathers used in clothing.

Agayulqútaq (Alutiiq)—A mask.

Ahhuhsulek (Alutiiq)—A whaler; literally a "whale-hunting shaman."

Ahnaq (Alutiiq)—Sea otter (Latin, *Enhydra lutris*).

Ahnaucit (Alutiiq)—Transvestites; Alutiiq boys raised as girls who often became shamans.

Aklut (Alutiiq)—Clothing.

Akutaq (Alutiiq)—Dessert made from various combinations of berries, seal oil, salmon eggs, mashed potatoes, sugar and shortening.

Akkuilitaq (Alutiiq)—A kayak spray skirt fashioned from gut skin.

Alagnat (Alutiiq)—Salmonberries (Latin, *Rubus spectabilis*); large, red, juicy berries similar in appearance to raspberries.

Aleut (probably from the Koryak or Chukchi languages of eastern Siberia; Russianized plural **Aleuty**)—a general name applied by Russian fur traders to the Native peoples of the Aleutian Islands, Alaska Peninsula, Cook Inlet, Kenai Peninsula, Prince William Sound, and parts of Bristol Bay. It may have originally been derived from *Alut*, the name of a Koryak village on the Kamchatka Peninsula. The name **Aleut** (and its Sugtestun form **Alutiiq**) was adopted by Native peoples themselves during the Russian colonial period from the 1740s–1867. It is still commonly used today.

Alutiiq (Alutiiq)—the Sugtestun pronunciation of the Russian-introduced name **Aleut**. The plural (more than two people) is **Alutiit**. A commonly used self-designation in the Alutiiq region today. In the revised orthography the word would correctly be written **Alu'utíq**.

Angayuqaq (Alutiiq)—The inherited position of village headman or chief (Kodiak Island).

Angyaq (Alutiiq; pl. **Angyat**)—A large open skin boat used for traveling in groups, transporting quantities of goods, and waging warfare. Known also by the Russian term **baidara**.

Artel' (Russian; plural **arteli**) -Work stations established by Russian traders where Native people were conscripted to harvest resources.

Atsaq (Alutiiq)—Blueberry (Latin, *Vaccinium* spp.).

Átunaq (Alutiiq)—A leafy green vegetable known also as sourdock (Latin, *Rumex fenestratus*), wild rhubarb or wild spinach. Eaten boiled or added to pies, and used as a fever reducer and a purgative.

Augca'aq (Alutiiq)—Dart game where darts are thrown at a swinging whale or porpoise model by teams of players who kneel as if they are paddling a kayak.

Awihnaq (Alutiiq)—Spruce root hats woven like baskets and often heavily embellished with beads, *dentalium* shells and sea lion whiskers.

Baidara (Russian; pl. **baidary**)—A large open skin boat used for traveling in groups, transporting quantities of goods, and waging warfare. Known also by the Alutiiq term **angyaq**.

Baidarka (Russian)—A skin-covered kayak. Known in Alutiiq as a **qayak**.

Banya (Russian)—A steam bath created by splashing heated rock with water. Known in Alutiiq as a **maqiq**.

Barabara (Russian)—A semisubterranean house constructed of wood and covered with an insulating layer of sod. Known in Alutiiq as a **ciqluaq**.

Bidarkies (Alutiiq-Russian)—Derived from the Russian work **baidarka**, this term refers to the boat-like shape of an overturned chiton, **uhhítaq** in Alutiiq, a marine invertebrate that clings to tidal rocks. The animals are harvested for food.

Caguyaq (Alutiiq)—Bentwood hunting hat.

Cauyaq (Alutiiq)—Drum.

Chugach (possibly derived from the Alutiiq place name for Cook Inlet, *Cúngáciq*)—the Alutiiq people of Cook Inlet, the Kenai Peninsula and Prince William Sound; also the dialect of Alutiiq or Sugt̲estun that is spoken in these areas.

Ciqluaq (Alutiiq)—A semisubterranean house constructed of wood and covered with an insulating layer of sod. Known in Russian as a **barabara**.

Cisl̲aq (Alutiiq, Alaska Peninsula dialect; **cisl̲áq** on Kodiak Island; from Russian **cislo**)—Peg calendar used to keep track of Sundays, Russian Orthodox feast days, and other holy days.

Cíwaq (Alutiiq)—A fly.

Cúmil̲al̲het (Alutiiq)—"Our ancestors."

Ekgwiutaq (Alutiiq)—A hunting bag; a woman's sewing bag.

Ginaquq (Alutiiq)—A mask

Húwaq (Alutiiq)—Arrow, in the Koniag Alutiiq dialect.

Imam Sua (Alutiiq)—The female "person" of all sea animals, who lived at the bottom of the sea.

Inaqqamciq (Alutiiq)—The high bush cranberry or sourberry (Latin, *Viburnum edule*), harvested in fall for food, seasoning, and medicine.

Íngihsún (Alutiiq)—Snow goggles worn to protect the eye from glare.

Inuwaqul̲út (Alutiiq)—"Little People" from Alutiiq folklore; very strong tiny men with loud voices who occasionally helped those in trouble or brought good luck to hunters. Also known as **sungcút**.

Iqsak (Alutiiq)—Fish hook.

Iukola (Russian)—Dried fish.

Íyaq (Alutiiq; pl. **íyat**)—The spirit of an evil person, distinguished by its long pointed head. A devil. This word, from the Koniag Alutiiq dialect, translates literally as "one that is hidden." Known as a **kala'aq** (pl. **kala'at**) in the Chugach Alutiiq dialect.

Kadaq (Alutiiq)—Guessing game with marked sticks; traditionally played for wagers during winter festivals. Probably learned from Pomo or Miwok Indians at the Russian-American Company's Fort Ross in California when Alutiiq sea otter hunters were stationed there in the early 19th century.

Kakangaq (Alutiiq)—A game where discs are thrown at a target on a seal skin; literally a "gambling game."

Kakiwik (Alutiiq)—A decorated pouch for holding needles, thread and other sewing materials.

Kal̲a'alek (Alutiiq; pl. **kal̲a'alet**)—A shaman; literally, one who has a helping spirit.

Kal̲a'aq (Alutiiq; pl. **kal̲a'at**)—The spirit of an evil person, distinguished by its long pointed head. A "devil," also a shaman's helping spirit. From the Chugach Alutiiq dialect. Known as an **íyaq** in the Koniag Alutiiq dialect.

Kamleika (Russian)—A waterproof, hooded shirt sewn from animal intestines. Also known by the Alutiiq term **kanagl̲uk**.

Kanagl̲uk (Alutiiq)—A waterproof, hooded shirt fashioned from animal intestines. Also known by the Russian term **kamleika**.

Kappúset̲áhuaq (Alutiiq)—Sea lettuce (Latin, *Ulva* spp.), one of eight varieties of seaweeds harvested by the Alutiit.

Kassaq (Alutiiq; pl. **kassat**)—Elders on Kodiak Island who led major ceremonies, taught the oral traditions, and composed dances and songs.

Kenegtaq (Alutiiq)—The low bush cranberry or lingonberry *(Latin, Vaccinium vitis-idaea)*, harvested in fall for food, seasoning, and medicine.

Kepnehciq (Alutiiq)—The term for late winter (February), a period when subsistence foods are often in short supply and people rely on shellfish and the last pieces of dried fish in their stores; literally "cutting the dried fish into strips".

Kolosh (Russian)—Russian name for the Tlingit people of southeastern Alaska.

Koniag (Americanized version of the Unangan word **kanayis**)—people of Kodiak Island and the Alaska Peninsula. Koniag also refers to the dialect of the Alutiiq (Sugt̲estun) language that is spoken in these areas.

Lágaq (Alutiiq)—Chocolate Lilly (Latin, *Fritillaria camschatcensis*); a flowering herb with an edible rice-like root.

L̲am Sua (Alutiiq)—The Alutiiq supreme being.

Maskalataq (Alutiiq)—Masking; an Alutiiq tradition that follows **Sláwiq** (starring) during the celebration of Russian Christmas. Maskers (**maskalatalhít**) entertain by dancing in elaborate costumes (**maskalatahsútet**).

Maqiq (Alutiiq)—A steam bath created by splashing an iron stove and heated rocks with water, known in Russian as a **banya**.

Nacaq (Alutiiq)—Woman's beaded headdress.

Nasquluk (Alutiiq)—Bull kelp (Latin, *Nereocystis luetkeana*); a strong, supple seaweed used for line and to make pickles.

Naqugun (Alutiiq)—Woman's dance belt.

Neqlehtesútet (Alutiiq)—goose snares; literally "instruments for catching geese."

Nunam Sua (Alutiiq)—The female "person" of all land animals.

Nuqaq (Alutiiq)—Throwing board.

Odinochka (Russian)—A small Russian outpost and/or Native work crew, usually with a single Russian overseer.

Paitálek (Alutiiq)—A three person kayak developed for use during the Russian era.

Pakik (Alutiiq)—A crowberry (Latin, *Empetrum nigrum*), also known as a blackberry or a mossberry. A favorite addition to **akutaq**.

Pirok (Russian)—Rice and salmon pie; also **piruk**.

Pitrúsekáq (Alutiiq)—Beach lovage (Latin, *Ligusticum scoticum*), also known as wild parsley. A flavorful vegetable used to flavor soups, salads and fish.

Promyshlennik (Russian)—A Russian fur trader.

Puchki (Russian)—Cow Parsnip (Latin, *Heracleum lanatum*), known also by its Alutiiq name **ugsútet**. A wild vegetable that is eaten raw, used to flavor fish, and made into a soothing poultice for aches, pains, and infections.

Punehpak (Alutiiq)—Braided sinew line.

Qallúhun (Alutiiq)—Water dipper

Qanganaq (Alutiiq)—Man's ground squirrel parka.

Qasgiq (Alutiiq: pl. **qasgit**)—A ceremonial house, where winter festivals were conducted.

Qayanguaq (Alutiiq)—A single hatched kayak.

Qayahpak (Alutiiq)—A double hatched kayak.

Qayaq (Alutiiq; pl. **qayat**)—A kayak. Kayaks were made with one hatch (**qayanguaq**), two hatches (**qayahpak**), or three hatches (**paitálek**).

Qehuq (Alutiiq)—Arrow, in the Alaska Peninsula dialect.

Qikertaq (Alutiiq)—An island. The name "Kodiak" is believed to be derived from this Alutiiq word.

Qikertarmiut (Alutiiq)—The people of Kodiak Island.

Quliyanguat (Alutiiq)—Stories describing Alutiiq history.

Quyanásinaq (Alutiiq)—Thank you (**quyaná**) very much (**sinaq**).

Redut (Russian, plural **reduty**)—A Russian fort.

Saqiyun (Alutiiq)—Rock paddle for carrying heated stones into the steam bath.

Samanaq (Alutiiq)—A shaman. From the Tungus language of eastern Siberia, introduced to southern Alaska during Russian times. The original Alutiiq term for shaman is **kala'alek**, meaning one who has a helping spirit.

Sláwiq (Alutiiq)—Starring; a Christmas celebration in which carolers announce the birth of Christ with a brightly decorated star that is carried from house to house. **Sláwihluteng** (verb)—to go starring.

Sua (Alutiiq)—"It's person"; the human consciousness in all things—animals, plants, objects, places, and natural forces like the wind. The spirit of a thing. See **suk**.

Suqaq (Alutiiq)—Seal stomach container used to store food and oil.

Sugpiaq (Alutiiq; pl. **Sugpiat**)—"The real people"; term for the Alutiiq people in the Alutiiq language.

Sugunha (Alutiiq)—The soul of an animal perpetually reincarnated through ritual practice.

Súget (Alutiiq)—People (plural of **suk**).

Sugtestun (Alutiiq)—The Alutiiq language; literally "to speak like a person."

Súgucihpet (Alutiiq)—"Our way of living."

Suk (Alutiiq)—A person. Also the human consciousness in all things—animals, plants, objects, places, and natural forces like the wind. Anthropological literature often refers to a different form of the same word, **sua**, meaning "its person." The spirit of a thing.

Sungcút (Alutiiq)—"Little People" from Alutiiq folklore; very strong tiny men with loud voices who occasionally helped those in trouble or brought good luck to hunters. Also known by the Alutiiq term **inuwaqulút**.

Táhiteq (Alutiiq; pl. **táhitet**; also pronounced as **táhiqs**)—Bundle of lyme grass (Latin, *Elymus areharius*) roots used for scrubbing in the steam bath (**banya**).

Tammúq (Alutiiq)—Dried fish.

Toion (Russian)—A village headman of the Russian era.

Ugsútet (Alutiiq)—Cow Parsnip (Latin, *Heracleum lanatum*), known also by its Russian name **puchki**. A wild vegetable that is eaten raw, used to flavor fish, and made into a soothing poultice for aches, pains, and infections.

Ukgwepet (Alutiiq)—"Our beliefs."

Uhhítaq (Alutiiq)—A chiton, a small invertebrate collected from intertidal areas for food. Also known as a **bidarkie** in reference to its kayak-like shape.

Uhluwaq (Alutiiq)—Sinew-backed bow.

Ulukaq (Alutiiq, pl. **Ulukat**; also **uluaq**)—A semilunar knife of ground slate used for a variety of tasks from splitting fish to cooking.

Unegkuhmiut (Alutiiq)—The Alutiiq people of the Kenai Peninsula.

Unigkuat (Alutiiq)—Oral traditions about creation and ancient times.

Uyamilquat (Alutiiq)—Woman's necklace.

Wegguaq (Alutiiq)—Goose tongue (Latin,); a small grass-like plant eaten raw or boiled, and added to fish soup

References

Ackerman, R. E.

1992 Earliest Stone Industries on the North Pacific Coast of North America. *Arctic Anthropology* 29(2):18–27.

Alaska Federation of Natives

1989 *The AFN Report on the Status of Alaska Natives: A Call for Action.* Alaska. Alaska Federation of Natives, Anchorage.

Alaska Natives Commission

1994 *Final Report.* 3 vols. Joint Federal-State Commission on Policies and Programs Affecting Alaska Natives, Anchorage.

Alaska Native Review Commission.

1984 Transcript of Proceedings: Village Meeting. Volume 48, Kodiak. November 9, 1984.

Alaska Packers Association

1917 Petroglyphs on Kodiak Island. *American Anthropologist* 19:320–322.

Antonii, H.

1900a Report on the School Work of the Russian Orthodox Church in Alaska. *American Orthodox Messenger* 4(5):114–119.

1900b Report on the School Work of the Russian Orthodox Church in Alaska. *American Orthodox Messenger* 4(7):143–146.

Arndt, K.

1996 "Released to reside forever in the Colonies:" Founding of a Russian-American Company Retirement Settlement at Ninilchik, Alaska. In *Adventures Through Time: Readings in the Anthropology of Cook Inlet, Alaska,* edited by N.Y. Davis and W.E. Davis, pp. 235–250. Cook Inlet Historical Society, Anchorage.

Arteaga, I.

1779 Spanish Explorations of Alaska. Diary of the Arteaga Expedition. Unpublished translation by K. H. Moore. Katrina H. Moore Collection (Box 2, Folder 6), Alaska and Polar Regions Department, Elmer E. Rasmuson Library, University of Alaska Fairbanks.

Arutiunov, S. A., and W. W. Fitzhugh

1988 Prehistory of Siberia and the Bering Sea. In *Crossroads of Continents: Cultures of Siberia and Alaska,* edited by W. W. Fitzhugh and A. L. Crowell, pp. 117–129. Smithsonian Institution Press, Washington, D.C.

Beaglehole, J. C. (editor)

1967 *The Voyage of the Resolution and Discovery 1776–1780. The Journals of Captain James Cook on His Voyages of Discovery.* Hakluyt Society, Cambridge University Press, Cambridge.

Billings, J.

1980 Voyage of Mr. Billings from Okhotsk to Kamchatka; His Arrival There; Setting out for the American Islands: Return to Kamchatka: Second Sea Voyage to Those Islands from the North, Thence to Bering Strait and to Chukotskii Nos, 1789–1790–1791. In *Siberia and Northwestern America, 1788–1792. The Journal of Carl Heinrich Merck, Naturalist with the Russian Scientific Expedition Led by Captains Joseph Billings and Gavriil Sarychev,* pp. 199–210. Translated by F. Jaensch. Edited by R. A. Pierce. The Limestone Press, Kingston, Ontario.

Birket-Smith, K.

1941 *Early Collections from the Pacific Eskimo.* Nationalmuseets Skrifter, Etnografisk Række I–II. National Museum of Denmark, Copenhagen.

1953 *The Chugach Eskimo.* Nationalmuseets Skrifter, Etnografisk Række VI. National Museum of Denmark, Copenhagen.

Black, L. T.

1977 The Konyag (The Inhabitants of the Island of Kodiak) by Ioasaf [Bolotov] (1794–1799) and by Gideon (1804–1807). *Arctic Anthropology* 14(2):79–106).

1982 *Aleut Art: Unangam Aguqaadangin, Unangan of the Aleutian Archipelago.* Aleutian/Pribilof Island Association.

1987 Whaling in the Aleutians. *Études/Inuit/Studies* 11(2):7–50.

1988 The Story of Russian America. In *Crossroads of Continents: Cultures of Siberia and Alaska,* edited by W. W. Fitzhugh and A. L. Crowell, pp. 70–82. Smithsonian Institution Press, Washington, D.C.

1990 Creoles in Russian America. *Pacifica* 2(2):142–155.

1991 *Glory Remembered: Wooden Headgear of Alaska Sea Hunters.* Alaska State Museums, Juneau.

1992 The Russian Conquest of Kodiak. *Anthropological Papers of the University of Alaska* 24(1–2):165–182.

1994 Deciphering Aleut/Koniag Iconography. In *Anthropology of the North Pacific Rim,* edited by W. W. Fitzhugh and V. Chaussonnet, pps. 133–146. Smithsonian Institution Press, Washington, D.C.

Bray, T. L. and T. W. Killion (editors)

1994 *Reckoning with the Dead: The Larsen Bay Repatriation and the Smithsonian Institution.* Smithsonian Institution Press, Washington, D.C.

Clark, D. W.

1966a Perspectives on the Prehistory of Kodiak Island, Alaska. *American Antiquity* 31(3):358–371.

1966b Two Late Prehistoric Pottery-Bearing Sites on Kodiak Island, Alaska. *Arctic Anthropology* 3(2):157–184.

1970a The Late Kachemak Tradition at Three Saints Bay and Crag Point, Kodiak Island, Alaska. *Arctic Anthropology* 6(2):73–111.

1970b Petroglyphs on Afognak Island, Kodiak Group, Alaska. *Anthropological Papers of the University of Alaska* 15(1):284–293.

1974a *Contributions to the Later Prehistory of Kodiak Island, Alaska.* National Museum of Man Mercury Series, Archaeological Survey Paper 20. Ottawa.

1974b *Koniag Prehistory: Archaeological Investigations at Late Prehistoric Sites on Kodiak Island, Alaska.* Tübinger Monographien zur Urgeschichte. Kohlhamer, Stuttgart.

1979 Ocean Bay: An Early North Pacific Maritime Culture. *National Museum of Man Mercury Series, Archaeological Survey of Canada Paper* 86. Ottawa.

1982a An Example of Technological Change in Prehistory: The Origin of a Regional Ground Slate Industry in South-Central Coastal Alaska. *Arctic Anthropology* 19(1):103–126.

1982b From Just Beyond the Southern Fringe: A Comparison of Norton Culture and the Contemporary Kachemak Tradition of Kodiak Island. *Arctic Anthropology* 19(2):123–132.

1984a Prehistory of the Pacific Eskimo Region. In *Arctic,* edited by D. Damas, pp. 136–148. *Handbook of North American Indians,* vol. 5, W. C. Sturtevant, general editor. Smithsonian Institution, Washington, D.C.

1984b Pacific Eskimo: Historical Ethnography. In *Arctic,* edited by D. Damas, pp. 195–197. *Handbook of North American Indians,* vol. 5, W. C. Sturtevant, general editor. Smithsonian Institution, Washington, D.C.

1987   On a Misty Day You Can See Back to 1805: Ethnohistory and Historical Archaeology on the Southeastern Side of Kodiak Island, Alaska. *Anthropological Papers of the University of Alaska* 21(1–2):105–132.

1988   Pacific Eskimo Encoded Precontact History. In *Late Prehistoric Development of Alaska's Native People*, edited by R. D. Shaw, R. K. Harritt, and D. E. Dumond, pp. 211–223. Aurora: Monograph of the Alaska Anthropological Association No. 4. Anchorage.

1992   "Only a Skin Boat Load or Two": The Role of Migration in Kodiak Prehistory. *Arctic Anthropology* 29(1):2–17.

1994   Still a Big Story: The Prehistory of Kodiak Island. In *Reckoning with the Dead: The Larsen Bay Repatriation and the Smithsonian Institution*, edited by T. L. Bray and T. W. Killion, pps. 137–149. Smithsonian Institution Press, Washington, D.C.

1997   *The Early Kachemak Phase on Kodiak Island at Old Kiavak.* Mercury Series, Archaeological Survey of Canada Paper 155. Canadian Museum of Civilization, Hull, Quebec.

Clark, G. H.
1977   Archaeology of the Alaska Peninsula: The Coast of Shelikhov Strait 1963–65. *University of Oregon Anthropological Papers*, vol. 13. University of Oregon, Eugene.

Clifford, J.
1991   Four Northwest Coast Museums: Travel Reflections. In *Exhibiting Cultures: The Poetics and Politics of Museum Display*, edited by I. Karp and S. D. Lavine, pp. 212–254. Smithsonian Institution Press, Washington, D.C.

Cole, D.
1985   *Captured Heritage: The Scramble for Northwest Coast Artifacts.* University of Washington Press, Seattle.

Collins, H. B.
1937   *Archeology of St. Lawrence Island, Alaska.* Smithsonian Miscellaneous Collections 96(1). Smithsonian Institution, Washington, D.C.

1984   History of Research Before 1945. In *Arctic*, edited by D. Damas, pp. 8–22. *Handbook of North American Indians*, vol. 5, W. C. Sturtevant, general editor. Smithsonian Institution, Washington, D.C.

Coxe, W.
1780   *Account of the Russian Discoveries Between Asia and America to Which Are Added the Conquest of Siberia and the History of the Transactions and Commerce Between Russia and China.* T. Cadell, London.

Crowell, A. L.
1988   Prehistory of Alaska's Pacific Coast. In *Crossroads of Continents: Cultures of Siberia and Alaska*, edited by W. W. Fitzhugh and A. L. Crowell, pp. 130–140. Smithsonian Institution Press, Washington, D.C.

1992   Postcontact Koniag Ceremonialism on Kodiak Island and the Alaska Peninsula: Evidence from the Fisher Collection. *Arctic Anthropology* 29(1):18–37.

1994   Koniag Eskimo Poisoned-Dart Whaling. In *Anthropology of the North Pacific Rim*, edited by W. W. Fitzhugh and V. Chaussonnet, pp. 217–242. Smithsonian Institution Press, Washington, D.C.

1997   *Archaeology and the Capitalist World System: A Study from Russian America.* Plenum Press, New York.

2000   Maritime Cultures of the Gulf of Alaska. *Revista de Arqueologia Americana/Journal of American Archaeology* 16, in press.

Crowell, A. L., and D. H. Mann
1996   Human Populations, Sea Level Change, and the Archaeological Record of the Northern Gulf of Alaska Coastline. *Arctic Anthropology* 33(2):16–37.

1998   *Archaeology and Coastal Dynamics of Kenai Fjords National Park, Alaska.* National Park Service, Alaska Region, Anchorage.

Cruikshank, J.
1998   *The Social Life of Stories: Narrative and Knowledge in the Yukon Territory.* University of Nebraska Press, Lincoln.

Dall, W. H.
1877   *On Succession in the Shell-Heaps of the Aleutian Islands.* Part II, Contributions to North American Ethnology, Vol. I, pp. 41–92. Department of the Interior, U.S. Geographical and Geological Survey of the Rocky Mountain Region. Government Printing Office, Washington, D.C.

1878   *On the Remains of Later Pre-Historic Man Obtained from Caves in the Catherine Archipelago, Alaska Territory, and Especially from the Caves of the Aleutian Islands.* Smithsonian Contributions to Knowledge 318. Smithsonian Institution, Washington, D.C.

Damas, D.
1984   Introduction. In *Arctic*, edited by D. Damas, pp. 1–7. *Handbook of North American Indians*, vol. 5, W. C. Sturtevant, general editor. Smithsonian Institution, Washington, D.C.

Davis, N. Y.
1984   Contemporary Pacific Eskimo. In *Arctic*, edited by D. Damas, pp. 198–204. *Handbook of North American Indians*, vol. 5, W. C. Sturtevant, general editor. Smithsonian Institution, Washington, D.C.

Davis, S. D. (editor)
1989   *The Hidden Falls Site, Baranof Island, Alaska.* Aurora, Alaska Anthrpological Association Series No. 5, Anchorage.

Davydov, G. I.
1812   *Dvukratnoe puteshestvie v Ameriku Morskikh Ofitserov Khvostova i Davydova, pisannoe sim poslednim.* Vol. 2. Morskaia Tipografiia, St. Petersburg

1932-33 *Account of Two Voyages to America by the Naval Officers Khvostov and Davydov, with extracts from Davydov's Diary (1810–1812).* Translated by M.E. Affonin. MS at the Rasmuson Library, University of Alaska Fairbanks.

1977   *Two Voyages to Russian America, 1802-1807.* Translated by C. Bearne. Edited by R. Pierce. The Limestone Press, Kingston, Ontario.

de Laguna, F.
1956   *Chugach Prehistory: The Archaeology of Prince William Sound, Alaska.* University of Washington Publications in Anthropology, vol. 13. University of Washington Press, Seattle.

1975   *The Archaeology of Cook Inlet, Alaska.* 2nd ed. Alaska Historical Society, Anchorage.

Demidoff, R.
1962   Ah-hooh-shoo-lik (The Whaler). Collected by Irene Reed, Alaska Native Language Center, University of Alaska Fairbanks. Unpublished manuscript at the Alaska Native Language Center, University of Alaska Fairbanks.

Desson, D.
1995   *Masked Rituals of the Kodiak Archipelago.* Unpublished Ph. D. dissertation, University of Alaska Fairbanks.

Detterman, R. L.
1986   Glaciation of the Alaska Peninsula. In *Glaciation in Alaska: The Geological Record*, edited by T. D. Hamilton, K. M. Reed, and R. M. Thorson, pp. 151–170. The Alaska Geological Society, Anchorage.

Dixon, E. J.
1993   *Quest for the Origins of the First Americans.* University of New Mexico, Albuquerque.

Dixon, E. J., T. H. Heaton, T. E. Fifield, T. D. Hamilton, D. E. Putnam, and F. Grady

1997   Late Quaternary Regional Geoarchaeology of Southeast Alaska Karst: A Progress Report. *Geoarchaeology* 12:689–712.

Dixon, G.

1968   *A Voyage Round the World: But More Particularly to the North-West Coast of America: Performed in 1785, 1786, 1787, and 1788, in the King George and Queen Charlotte, Captains Portlock and Dixon.* Facsimile edition, Bibliotheca Australiana #37. N. Israel, Amsterdam and De Capo Press, New York.

Donta, C. L.

1993   Koniag Ceremonialism. Unpublished Ph. D. dissertation, , Bryn Mawr College, Bryn Mawr, PA.

Dumond, D. E.

1962   Prehistory in the Naknek Drainage: A Preliminary Statement. In *Research on Northwest Prehistory*, edited by L. S. Cressman and D. E. Dumond, pp. 7–54. Eugene: Department of Anthropology, University of Oregon.

1981   *Archaeology on the Alaska Peninsula: The Naknek Region 1960–1975.* University of Oregon Anthropological Papers 21. Eugene.

1987a   A Reexamination of Eskimo-Aleut Prehistory. *American Anthropologist* 89(1):32–56.

1987b   *The Eskimos and Aleuts.* Revised edition. Thames and Hudson, London.

1988   The Alaska Peninsula as Superhighway: A Comment. In *The Late Prehistoric Development of Alaska's Native People*, edited by R.D. Shaw, R.K. Harritt, and Don. E. Dumond, pp. 379–388. Aurora: Alaska Anthropological Associaton Monograph Series #4, Anchorage.

1994a   The Uyak Site in Prehistory. In *Reckoning with the Dead: The Larsen Bay Repatriation and the Smithsonian Institution*, edited by T. L. Bray and T. W. Killion, pp. 43–53. Smithsonian Institution, Washington, D.C.

1994b   A Reevaluation of Late Prehistoric Houses of the Naknek River region, Southwestern Alaska. *Arctic Anthropology* 31(2):108–118.

1998   Maritime Adaptation on the Northern Alaska Peninsula. *Arctic Anthropology* 35(1):187–203.

Dumond, D. E., and J. VanStone

1995   *Paugvik: A Nineteenth Century Native Village on the Naknek River, Alaska.* Fieldiana (n.s.) No. 24. Field Museum of Natural History, Chicago.

D'Wolf, J.

1968   *A Voyage to the North Pacific.* Ye Galleon Press, Fairfield, Washington.

Dybbroe, S.

1996   Questions of Identity and Issues of Self-Determination. *Etudes/Inuit/Studies* 20(2):39-53.

Dyson, G.

1986   *Baidarka.* Alaska Northwest Publishing Co., Edmonds, Washington.

Efimov, A. V.

1964   *Atlas Geografischeskikh Otkrytii v Sibirii i v Severo-Zapadnoi Amerike XVII – XVIII Vv.* Academiia Nauk SSSR Institut Etnografii, Moscow.

Erlandson, J. M., A. Crowell, C. Wooley, and J. Haggerty

1992   Spatial and Temporal Patterns in Alutiiq Paleodemography. *Arctic Anthropology* 29(2):42–62.

Exxon Valdez Oil Spill Trustee Council

1999   *Exxon Valdez Oil Spill Restoration Plan Update on Injured Resources and Services.* Exxon Valdez Oil Spill Trustee Council, Anchorage.

Fall, J. A.

1993   *An Overview of Subsistence Uses of the Northern Alaska Peninsula Herd by Communities of Game Management Units 9C and 9E Division of Subsistence, Alaska.* Alaska Department of Fish and Game, Juneau.

1999   Patterns of Subsistence Uses of Fish and Wildlife Resources in the Area of the *Exxon Valdez* Oil Spill. In *Evaluating and Communicating Subsistence Seafood Safety in a Cross-Cultural Context: Lessons Learned from the Exxon Valdez Oil Spill*, edited by L. J. Field, J. A. Fall, T. S. Nighswander, N. Peacock, and U. Varanasi, pp. 21–32. Society of Environmental Toxicology and Chemistry, Pensacola, FL.

Fall, J. A., and L. Hutchinson-Scarbrough

1996   *Subsistence Uses of Brown Bears in Communities of Game Management Unit 9E, Alaska Peninsula, Southwest Alaska.* Technical Paper No. 235, Alaska Department of Fish and Game, Division of Subsistence, Juneau.

Fedorova, S. G.

1973   *The Russian Population in Alaska and California, Late 18ᵗʰ Century-1867.* Translated and edited by R.A. Pierce and A. S. Donnelly. Materials for the Study of Alaska History No. 4. The Limestone Press, Kingston, Ontario.

Fidalgo, S.

1790   Report of Lieutenant Don Salvador Fidalgo, Commanding the Paquebot San Carlos, of the Results of His Mission to Explore Prince William Sound and the River of Cook. Translated by K. H. Moore. Ms. on file, Katrina H, Moore Collection (Box 1, Folder 10), Alaska and Polar Regions Department, Elmer E. Rasmuson Library, University of Alaska Fairbanks.

Fienup-Riordan, A.

1990   The Mask: Eye of the Dance. In *Eskimo Essays: Yup'ik Lives and How We See Them*, pp. 49–67. Rutgers University Press, New Brunswick.

1994   *Boundaries and Passages: Rule and Ritual in Central Yup'ik Oral Tradition.* University of Oklahoma Press, Norman.

1996   *The Living Tradition of Yup'ik Masks; Agayuliyararput, Our Way of Making Prayer.* University of Washington Press, Seattle.

Fisher, W. J.

1880   Kadiak Island. *Alaska Appeal* 1(20):2–3.

1882   Bureau of American Ethnology, Catalogue of Manuscripts, Ms. 305, December 1, 1882. "Two vocabularies: Ugashachmiut, Ugashak River, Bristol Bay, Alaska and Kageagemiut, Kaguiak, Kadiak Island" with ethnographic notes. National Anthropological Archives, Washington, DC.

1883   Catalogue of a Collection of Ethnological Specimens Obtained from the Ugashagmut Tribe, Ugashak River, Bristol Bay, Alaska. *Proceedings of the United States National Museum* 6(11):161–165.

Fitzhugh, J. B.

1996   The Evolution of Complex Hunter-Gatherers in the North Pacific: An Archaeological Case Study from Kodiak Island, Alaska. Unpublished Ph. D. dissertation, University of Michigan, Ann Arbor.

Fladmark, K. R.

1978   The Feasibility of the Northwest Coast as a Migration Route for Early Man. In *Early Man from a Circum-Pacific Perspective*, edited by A. L. Bryan, pp. 119–128. Occasional Papers No. 1, Department of Anthropology, University of Alberta, Edmunton.

Fortuine, R.

1989 *Chills and Fever. Health and Disease in the Early History of Alaska.* University of Alaska Press, Fairbanks.

Gibson, J. R.

1976 *Imperial Russia in Frontier America. The Changing Geography of Supply of Russian America, 1784–1867.* Oxford University Press, New York.

1987 Russian Dependence on the Natives of Alaska. In *Russia's American Colony*, edited by S.F. Starr, pp. 77–104. The Kennan Institute for Advanced Russian Studies of the Woodrow Wilson International Center for Scholars. Duke University Press, Durham.

Gideon

1989 *The Round the World Voyage of Hieromonk Gideon 1803–1809.* Translated, with an introduction and notes, by L. T. Black, edited by R. A. Pierce. The Limestone Press, Kingston, Ontario.

Golder, F. A.

1903 Tales from Kodiak Island. *Journal of American Folk-Lore* 16(60), Part I:16–31 and Part II:85–103.

1907 A Kadiak Island Story: The White-Faced Bear. *Journal of American Folk-Lore* 20(79):296–299.

1909 Eskimo and Aleut Stories from Alaska. *Journal of American Folk-lore* 22(83):2–16.

Golovin, P. N.

1979 *The End of Russian America. Captain P. N. Golovin's Last Report, 1862.* Translated with introduction and notes by B. Dmytryshyn and E.A.P. Crownhart-Vaughan. Oregon Historical Society, Portland.

Graham, F. K., and Ouzinkie Botanical Society

1985 Plantlore of an Alaskan Island. Alaska Northwest Publishing, Anchorage.

Griggs, R. F.

1922 *The Valley of Ten Thousand Smokes.* The National Geographic Society, Washington, D.C.

Hallowell, A. I.

1926 Bear Ceremonialism in the Northern Hemisphere. *American Anthropologist* 28(1):1–175.

Harritt, R. K.

1997 Problems in Prehistoric Ethnogenesis in Alaska: The Naknek Drainage and the Pacific Eskimo Area. *Arctic Anthropology* 34(2):45–73.

Hausler-Knecht, P.

1993 Early Prehistory of the Kodiak Archipelago. Paper presented at the International Seminar on the Origins, Development, and Spread of Prehistoric North Pacific-Bering Sea Maritime Cultures. National Science Foundation and the Japan Society for the Promotion of Science, Honolulu.

Hawkes, E. W.

1913 *The Inviting-In Feast of the Alaskan Eskimo.* Canada Geological Survey, Memoir 45, Anthropological Series 3.

Heizer, R. F.

1956a *Archaeology of the Uyak Site, Kodiak Island, Alaska.* University of California Anthropological Records 17(1). Berkeley.

1956b Petroglyphs of Southwestern Kodiak Island, Alaska. *Proceedings of the American Philosophical Society* 91:284–293.

Henn, W.

1978 *Archaeology on the Alaska Peninsula: The Ugashik Drainage, 1973–1975.* University of Oregon Anthropological Papers No. 14. Eugene.

Heusser, C. J.

1983 Holocene Vegetation History of the Price William Sound Region, South-Central Alaska. *Quaternary Research* 19:337–355.

Heusser, C. J., L. E. Heusser, and D. M. Peteet

1985 Late-Quaternary Climate Change on the American North Pacific Coast. *Nature* 315(6):486–487.

Hinsley, C. M.

1981 *The Smithsonian and the American Indian: Making a Moral Anthropology in Victorian America.* Smithsonian Institution Press, Washington, D.C.

Holm, B.

1988 Art and Culture at the Tlingit-Eskimo Border. In *Crossroads of Continents: Cultures of Siberia and Alaska*, edited by W. W. Fitzhugh and A. L. Crowell, pp. 281–293. Smithsonian Institution Press, Washington, D.C.

Holmberg, H. J.

1985 *Holmbergs's Ethnographic Sketches.* Translated by F. Jaensch, edited by M.W. Falk. The Rasmuson Library Historical Translation Series, Vol. 1. The University of Alaska Press, Fairbanks.

Hrdlička, A.

1930 *Anthropological Survey in Alaska.* U.S. Government Printing Office, Washington, D.C.

1944 *The Anthropology of Kodiak Island.* The Wistar Institute of Anatomy and Biology, Philadelphia.

Hunt, D. C.

2000 The Ethnohistory of Alutiiq Clothing: Comparative Analysis of the Smithsonian's Fisher Collection. Unpublished Master's thesis, San Francisco State University.

Hussey, J. A.

1971 *Embattled Katmai. A History of Katmai National Monument.* National Park Service, San Francisco.

Ivanov, S. V.

1930 Aleut Hunting Headgear and its Ornamentation. *Proceedings of the 23rd International Congress of Americanists*, 1928, New York, pp. 477–504.

1949 Sidiachie Chelovecheskiefigurki v Skul'pture Aleutov (Seated Human Figurines in Aleut Sculpture). *Sbornik Muzeia Antropologii I Etnografii* 12:195–212.

Jacobsen, J. A.

1977 *Alaskan Voyage 1881–1883: An Expedition to the Northwest Coast of America.* Tranlated by E. Gunther. University of Chicago Press, Chicago.

Jonaitis, A.

1986 *The Art of the Northern Tlingit.* University of Washington Press, Seattle.

Jordan, R. H.

1994 *Qasqiluteng*: Feasting and Ceremonialism among the Traditional Koniag of Kodiak Island, Alaska. In *Anthropology of the North Pacific Rim*, edited by W. W. Fitzhugh and V. Chaussonnet, pp. 147–174. Smithsonian Institution Press, Washington, D.C.

Jordan. R. H., and R. A. Knecht

1988 Archaeological Research on Western Kodiak Island, Alaska: The Development of Koniag Culture. In *Late Prehistoric Development of Alaska's Native People*, edited by R. D. Shaw, R. K. Harritt, and D. E. Dumond, pp. 225–306. Alaska Anthropological Association Monograph Series No. 4. Anchorage.

Kari, J.

1983 Kalifornsky, the Californian from Cook Inlet. *Alaska in Perspective* 5:1–11.

Kelley, J.

1996   The Alutiiq Kayak of Kodiak Island. *Sea Kayaker* 13(1):38–45 (April).

Khlebnikov, K. T.

1994   *Notes on Russian America. Parts II-V: Kadiak, Unalashka, Atka, the Pribilovs.* Compiled, with an introduction and commentaries, by R. G. Liapunova and S. G. Fedorova. Translated by M. Ramsay, edited by R. Pierce. The Limestone Press, Kingston, Ontario.

Klein, Janet R.

1996   *Archaeology of Kachemak Bay, Alaska.* Kachemak Country Publications, Homer.

Knecht, R. A.

1994   Working Together—Archaeology and Alutiiq Cultural Identity on Kodiak, Island. *Society for American Archaeology Bulletin* 12(5):8–10.

1995   The Late Prehistory of the Alutiiq People: Culture Change in the Kodiak Archipelago from 1200 – 1750 AD. Unpublished Ph. D. dissertation, Bryn Mawr College.

Knecht, R. A., and R. H. Jordan

1985   Nunakakhnak: An Historic Period Koniag Village in Karluk, Kodiak Island, Alaska. *Arctic Anthropology* 22(2):17–35.

Krauss, M. E.

1988   Many Tongues—Ancient Tales. In *Crossroads of Continents: Cultures of Siberia and Alaska,* edited by W. W. Fitzhugh and A. L. Crowell, pp. 144–150. Smithsonian Institution Press, Washington, D.C.

Krech, S. III

1989   *A Victorian Earl in the Arctic: The Travels and Collections of the Fifth Earl of Lonsdale 1888–89.* University of Washington Press, Seattle.

Langsdorff, G. H.

1993   *Remarks and Observations on a Voyage Around the World from 1803 to 1807.* 2 vols. Translated and annotated by V. J. Moessner. Edited by R. A. Pierce. The Limestone Press, Kingston, Ontario.

Lantis, M.

1938   The Mythology of Kodiak Island, Alaska. *Journal of American Folk-Lore* 51:123–172.

1947   *Alaskan Eskimo Ceremonialism.* Monographs of the American Ethnological Society, Vol. 11, edited by M. W. Smith. J. J. Augustin, New York.

1973   The Current Nativistic Movement in Alaska. In *Circumpolar Problems: Habitat, Economy, and Social Relationships in the Arctic,* edited by F. Berg, pp. 99–118. Pergamon Press, Oxford.

Laughlin, W. S.

1975   Aleuts: Ecosystem, Holocene History, and Siberian Origin. *Science* 189(4202):507–515.

Laughlin, W. S., and W. G. Reeder (editors)

1966   Studies in Aleut-Konyag Prehistory, Ecology, and Anthropology. *Arctic Anthropology* 3(2):1–240.

Ledyard, J.

1963   *John Ledyard's Journal of Captain Cook's Last Voyage.* Edited by J. K. Munford. Oregon State University Press, Corvallis, Oregon.

Leer, J.

1978   A Conversational Dictionary of Kodiak Alutiiq. Preliminary Edition. Alaska Native Language Center, University of Alaska Fairbanks.

1980   Kenai Peninsula Alutiiq Place Name List. Names given by Sergius Moonin, Joe Tanape, and Dan Anahonak. Unpublished ms. Alaska Native Language Center, University of Alaska Fairbanks.

1991   Evidence for a Northern Northwest Coast Language Area: Promiscuous Number Marking and Periphrastic Possessive Constructions in Haida, Eyak, and Aleut. *International Journal of American Linguistics* 37(2):158–93.

Lethcoe, J., and N. Lethcoe

1994   *History of Prince William Sound, Alaska.* Prince William Sound Books, Valdez.

Liapunova, R. G.

1987   Relations with the Natives of Russian America. In *Russia's American Colony,* edited by S.F. Starr, pp. 105–143. Duke University Press, Durham.

1994   Eskimo Masks from Kodiak Island in the Collections of the Peter the Great Museum of Anthropology and Ethnography in St. Petersburg. In *Anthropology of the North Pacific Rim,* edited by W. W. Fitzhugh and V. Chaussonnet, pp. 175–203. Smithsonian Institution Press, Washington, D.C.

Lisianskii [Lisiansky], U. [I]

1968   *Voyage Round the World in the Years 1803, 1804, 1805, and 1806.* Bibliotheca Australiana 42. N. Israel, Amsterdam and De Capo Press, New York.

Lobdell, J. E.

1980   Prehistoric Human Populations and Resource Utilization in Kachemak Bay, Gulf of Alaska. Unpublished Ph. D. dissertation, University of Tennessee, Knoxville.

López de Haro, G.

1788   Diary of the Voyage . . . [of the] First Pilot of the Royal Navy and Commander of His Majesty's Paquebot San Carlos . . . Don Gonzalo López de Haro. In The Voyage of the Princessa and the San Carlos to Prince William Sound, Kodiak, and Unalaska, March to October, 1788. Translated by K.H. Moore. Unpublished Ms., Katrina H, Moore Collection (Box 1, Folder 8), Alaska and Polar Regions Department, Elmer E. Rasmuson Library, University of Alaska Fairbanks.

Lührmann, S.

2000   *Alutiiq Villages Under Russian and U.S. Rule.* Unpublished Master's thesis, Johann Wolfgang Goethe University, Frankfurt.

Mason, O. K.

1998   The Contest between the Ipiutak, Old Bering Sea, and Birnirk Polities and the Origin of Whaling during the First Millennium A. D. along Bering Strait. *Journal of Anthropological Archaeology* 17:240–325.

Matfay, L.

1988   *Time to Dance: Life of an Alaska Native.* As told to Michael Rostad, Anchorage.

Matson, R. G., and G. Coupland

1995   *The Prehistory of the Northwest Coast.* Academic Press, New York.

Merck, C. H.

1980   *Siberia and Northwestern America, 1788 – 1792. The Journal of Carl Heinrich Merck, Naturalist with the Russian Scientific Expedition Led by Captains Joseph Billings and Gavriil Sarychev.* Translated by F. Jaensch, edited by R. A. Pierce. The Limestone Press, Kingston, Ontario.

Middleton-Moz, J.

1990   Cultural Depression in Native American Families. In *From Nightmare to Vision: A Training Manual for Native American Adult Children of Alcoholics,* edited by J. Middleton-Moz. Seattle Indian Health Board. Reprinted by the National Association for Native American Children of Alcoholics.

Middleton-Moz, J., and E. Fedrid

1987   The Many Faces of Grief: What Many Immigrants, Holocaust Survivors, Native Americans/Alaskans Have in Common with Adult Children of Alcoholics. *Changes*, July-August.

Mishler, C.

2001   *Black Ducks and Salmon Bellies: An Ethnography of Old Harbor and Ouzinkie, Alaska*. Technical Memorandum No. 7, Alaska Department of Fish and Game, Anchorage.

Mishler, C., and R. Mason

1996   Alutiiq Vikings: Kinship and Fishing in Old Harbor, Alaska. *Human Organization* 55(3):263–269.

Moonin, H.

1980   Killer Whales, Arllut. In *Allexandrovsk: English Bay in its Traditional Way*, pp. 75–76. Kenai Peninsula Borough School District. Alaska Printing Company, Anchorage.

Morseth, M.

1998   *Puyulek Pu'irtuq! The People of the Volcanoes*. Aniakchak National Monument and Preserve Ethnographic Overview & Assessment. National Park Service, Anchorage.

Moser, J. F.

1898   The Salmon and Salmon Fisheries of Alaska. Report of the Operations of the United States Fish Commission Steamer *Albatross* for the Year Ending June, 1898. *Bulletin of the United States Fish Commission* 18:1–178.

Moss, M.

1998   Northern Northwest Coast Regional Overview. *Arctic Anthropology* 35(1–2):88–111.

Moss, M. L., and J. M. Erlandson

1992   Forts, Refuge Rocks, and Defensive Sites: The Antiquity of Warfare along the North Pacific Coast of North America. *Arctic Anthropology* 29(2):73–90.

Moussalimas, S. A.

1990   Russian Orthodox Missionaries and Southern Alaskan Shamans: Interactions and Analysis. In *Russian in North America: Proceedings of the 2nd International Conference on Russian America, Sitka, Alaska, August 19–22, 1987*, edited by Richard A. Pierce, pp. 314–321. The Limestone Press, Kingston, Ontario.

Mulcahy, J. B.

1988   "Knowing Women": Narratives of Healing and Traditional Life from Kodiak Island, Alaska. Unpublished Ph. D. dissertation, University of Pennsylvania

1993   "How They Knew": Women's Talk about Healing on Kodiak Island, Alaska. In *Feminist Messages*, edited by J. N. Radner, pp. 183–202. University of Illinois Press.

2001   *Birth and Rebirth on an Alaskan Island: The Life of an Alutiiq Healer*. Foreword by Gordon L. Pullar. University of Georgia Press, Athens.

National Anthropological Archives

1882   Document 210, "Ugaschachmut and Kageagemut" (vocabularies and ethnographic notes by William J. Fisher). National Museum of Natural History, Washington, D.C.

National Geographic Society

1994   *Giant Bears of Kodiak Island* (video).

Nelson, E. W.

1983   The Eskimo About Bering Strait. *Bureau of American Ethnology Annual Report* 18:1–518, edited by W. W. Fitzhugh. Smithsonian Institution Press, Washington, D.C.

Okladnikova, E. A.

1987   Science and Education in Russian America. In *Russia's American Colony*, edited by S. F. Starr, pp. 218–248. Duke University Press, Durham.

Oleksa, M.

1992   *Orthodox Alaska: A Theology of Mission*. St. Vladimir's Seminary Press, Crestwood, N.J.

Oswalt, W. H.

1967   *Alaskan Eskimos*. Chandlar, San Francisco.

1979   *Eskimos and Explorers*. University of California Press, Los Angeles.

Parfit, M.

1981   Alaska Natives Are Bringing off the Biggest Corporate Takeover. *Smithsonian*. August:38.

Partlow, M.

1999   Vertebrate Fauna from the Zaimka Mound Site (KOD-013), Report on file Alutiiq Museum, Kodiak.

Partnow, P. H.

1993   *Alutiiq Ethnicity*. Unpublished Ph.D. dissertation, University of Alaska Fairbanks.

2001   *Making History: Alutiiq/Sugpiaq Life on the Alaska Peninsula*. University of Alaska Press, Fairbanks, in press.

Pearce, S.

1992   *Museums, Objects, and Collections: A Cultural Study*. Smithsonian Insitution Press, Washington, D.C.

Peterson, R.

1985   The Use of Certain Symbols in Connection with Greenlandic Identity. In *Native Power: The Quest for Autonomy and Nationhood of Indigenous People*, edited by J. Brøsted, J. Dahl, A. Gray, H.C. Gulløv, G. Henriksen, J.B. Jørgensen, and I. Keivan, pp. 294-300. Universitetsforlaget AS, Bergen, Oslo, Stavanger, Tromsø.

Petroff, I.

1884   *Report on the Population, Industries, and Resources of Alaska*. Department of the Interior, Census Office. Government Printing Office, Washington, D.C.

Pierce, R. (editor)

1978   *The Russian Orthodox Religious Mission in America, 1794–1837. with Materials Concerning the Life and Works of the Monk German, and Ethnographic Notes by the Hieromonk Gideon*. Translated by C. Bearne. The Limestone Press, Kingston, Ontario.

Pinart, A.

1872   *Catalog des Collections Rapportées de L'Amérique Russe, Ajourd'hui Territoire d'Alaska*. J. Claye, Paris.

1873   Eskimaux et Koloches: Idées Religieuses des Kaniagmioutes. *Revue d'Anthropologie* 2:673–680.

1875   *La Chasse aux Animals Marins et les Pêcheries Chez les Indigènes de la Côte Nord-Ouest d'Amérique*. Boulogne-Sur-Mer.

Pinney, D. S., and J. E. Begét

1991   Late Pleistocene Volcanic Deposits near the Valley of Ten Thousand Smokes, Katmai National Park, Alaska. *Short Notes on Alaska Geology, Alaska Depratment of Geological and Geophysical Surveys, Professional Report* 111, pp. 45–53.

Portlock, N.

1789   *A Voyage Round the World, But More Particularly to the North-West Coast of America: Performed in 1785, 1786, 1787, and 1788, in the King George and Queen Charlotte, Captains Portlock and Dixon*. John Stockdale, London. Facsimile edition, N. Israel (Amsterdam) and Da Capo Press (New York), 1968.

Pratt Museum

1999   *The Lore of Fishing and Maritime Harvesting in Kachemak Bay, Alaska* (video). Homer Society of Natural History, Homer, Alaska.

Pullar, G. L.

1992   Ethnic Identity, Cultural Pride, and Generations of Baggage: A Personal Experience. *Arctic Anthropology* 29(2):182–209.

1994 The Qikertarmiut and the Scientist: Fifty Years of Clashing World Views. In *Reckoning with the Dead: The Larsen Bay Repatriation and the Smithsonian Institution*, edited by T. L. Bray and K. W. Killion, pp. 15–25. Smithsonian Institution Press, Washington and London.

1996 Indigenous Identity on Kodiak Island," *Alaska Geographic: Native Cultures in Alaska*. Vol. 23(2):31–33.

Pullar, G. L., and R. A. Knecht

1995 Alutiiq. In *Crossroads Alaska: Native Cultures of Alaska and Siberia*, edited by V. Chaussonnet, pp. 14–15. Arctic Studies Center, Smithsonian Institution, Washington, D.C.

Reger, D. R.

1998 Archaeology of the Northern Kenai Peninsula and Upper Cook Inlet. *Arctic Anthropology* 35(1):160–171.

Roppel, P.

1987 *Salmon from Kodiak: An History of the Salmon Fisheries of Kodiak Island, Alaska*. Alaska Historical Commission, Anchorage.

Rousselot, J.-L., B. Abel, J. Pierre, and C. Bihl

1991 *Masques Eskimo d'Alaska*. Éditions Amez, Routelle, France.

Russell, P.

1991a *English Bay and Port Graham Alutiiq Plantlore*. Pratt Museum, Homer.

1991b *Kodiak Alutiiq Plantlore*. Ms. on file, Alutiiq Museum, Kodiak.

Saltonstall, P. G.

1997 Archaeology at Settlement Point, 1997 Preliminary Report. Report submitted to the Afognak Native Corporation, Kodiak.

Saltonstall, P. G., and A. F. Steffian

1999 Early Prehistoric Settlement in Chiniak Bay: A View from Zaimka Mound. Paper presented at the annual meeting of the Alaska Anthropological Association, Fairbanks.

Sarafian, W. L.

1970 *Russian-American Company Employee Policies and Practices, 1799–1867*. Ph.D. dissertation, University of California, Los Angeles.

Sarychev, G. A.

1826 *Atlas Severnoi Chasti Vostochnogo Oksana, Sostavlen v Cherteznoi Gosvdarstvennogo Admiralteiskogo Departmenta s Noveeshiikh Opisei i Kart pod Rukovodstvom Vitse-Admirala i Gidrografa Sarycheva*. Morskoi, St. Petersburg.

Sauer, M.

1802 *An Account of a Geographical and Astronomical Expedition to the Northern Parts of Russia*. A. Strahan, London.

Scott, G. R.

1991 Continuity or Replacement at the Uyak Site: A Physical Anthropological Analysis of Population Relationships. In *The Uyak Site on Kodiak Island: Its Place in Alaskan Prehistory*. University of Oregon Anthropological Papers No. 44. Eugene.

1992 Affinities of Prehistoric and Modern Kodiak Islanders and the Question of Kachemak-Koniag Biological Continuity. *Arctic Anthropology* 29(2):150–166.

1994 Teeth and Prehistory on Kodiak Island. In *Reckoning with the Dead: The Larsen Bay Repatriation and the Smithsonian Institution*, edited by T. L. Bray and T. W. Killion, pp. 67–74. Smithsonian Institution, Washington, D.C.

Shelikhov, G. I.

1981 *A Voyage to America 1783–1786*. Translated by Marina Ramsay. Edited, with an introduction, by Richard Pierce. The Limestone Press, Kingston, Ontario.

Shennan, S.

1989 Introduction: Archaeological Approaches to Cultural Identity. In *Archaeological Approaches to Cultural Identity*, edited by S. Shennan, pp. 1–32. Unwin Hyman, London.

Simeone, William E., and Rita A. Miraglia

2000 An Ethnography of Chenega Bay and Tatitlek, Alaska. Technical Memorandum No. 5, Alaska Department of Fish and Game, Anchorage.

Simon, J. J. K., and A. F. Steffian

1994 Cannibalism or Complex Mortuary Behavior? An Analysis of Patterned Variability in the Treatment of Human Remains from the Kachemak Tradition of Kodiak Island, Alaska. In, *Reckoning with the Dead: The Larsen Bay Repatriation and the Smithsonian Institution*, edited by T. Bray and T. Killion, pp. 75–100. Smithsonian Institution Press, Washington, D.C.

Smithsonian Institution Archives

1882–

1894 Record Unit 305 (United States National Museum, Registrar, 1834–1958.) Accession Records 12209, 14024, 15687, 18490, and 27806 (includes field catalogs and correspondence by William J. Fisher relating to his collections from southern Alaska). Washington, D.C.

Stanek, R.

1985 Patterns of Wild Resource Use in English Bay and Port Graham. *Alaska Department of Fish and Game, Division of Subsistence Technical Paper* 104. Alaska Department of Fish and Game, Juneau.

1999 Ethnographic Overview and Assessment for Nanwalek and Port Graham. Alaska Department of Fish and Game, Division of Subsistence, Anchorage.

Steffian, A. F.

1992a Archaeological Coal in the Gulf of Alaska: A View from Kodiak Island. *Arctic Anthropology* 29(2):111–129.

1992b Fifty Years After Hrdlička: Further Investigations at the Uyak Site, Kodiak Island, Alaska. In *Contributions to the Anthropology of Southcentral and Southwestern Alaska*, edited by R. H. Jordan, F. de Laguna, and A. F. Steffian. *Anthropological Papers of the University of Alaska* 24(1–2)141–164.

Steffian, A. F., and R. A. Knecht

1998 *Karluk One*. Pictures of Record, Weston, CT.

Steffian, A. F., E. B. Pontti, and P. G. Saltonstall

1998 *Archaeology of the Blisky Site, a Prehistoric Settlement on Near Island, Kodiak Archipelago, Alaska*. Report prepared for the Kodiak Island Borough. Alutiiq Museum, Kodiak.

Steffian, A. F., and P. G. Saltonstall

1995 Markers of Identity: Labrets and Social Evolution on Kodiak Island, Alaska. Paper presented at the 60th annual meeting of the Society for American Archaeology, Minneapolis.

Steller, G. W.

1988 *Journal of a Voyage with Bering, 1741–1742*. Translated by M. A. Engel and O. W. Frost, edited, with an introduction, by O. W. Frost. Stanford University Press, Stanford.

Street, S. R.

1994 Ales Hrdlička in Perspective: American Physical Anthropology and Bioarchaeology, with Reference to Alaska, the Aleutian Islands and the Kodiak Archipelago. Paper presented at the 21st Annual Meeting of the Alaska Anthropological Association, Juneau.

Tikhmenev, P. A.

1978 *A History of the Russian-American Company*. Translated and edited by R. A. Pierce and A. S. Donnelly. University of Washington Press, Seattle.

Townsend, J.

1980 Ranked Societies of the North Pacific Rim. In *Alaska Native Cultures and History*, edited by Y. Kotani and W. B. Workman, pp. 123–156. Senri Ethnological Series 4. National Museum of Ethnology, Osaka.

Turner, C. G. II

1988 Ancient Peoples of the North Pacific Rim. In *Crossroads of Continents: Cultures of Siberia and Alaska*, edited by W. W. Fitzhugh and A. L. Crowell, pp. 111–116. Smithsonian Institution Press, Washington, D.C.

Vancouver, G.

1801 *A Voyage of Discovery to the North Pacific Ocean and Around the World.* John Stockdale, London.

van Londen, S.

1996 Identity and Myth: The Case of the Orphan Boy. *Études/Inuit/Studies.* 20:2.

Varjola, P.

1990 *The Etholén Collection: The Ethnographic Collection of Adolf Etholén and His Contemporaries in the National Museum of Finland.* National Board of Antiquities of Finland, Helsinki.

Vick, A.

1983 *The Cama-I Book.* Anchor Books, Garden City, New York.

Village of Tatitlek and the Alaska Department of Fish and Game

1999 *Tatitlek, Changing Tides* (video). Taylor Productions, Anchorage.

Walker, A.

1982 *An Account of a Voyage to the North West Coast of America in 1785 and 1786*, edited by R. Fisher and J. M. Bumstead. University of Washington Press, Seattle.

West, F. H.

1996 *American Beginnings: The Prehistory and Paleoecology of Beringia.* The University of Chicago Press, Chicago.

Wiles, G. C., and P. E. Calkin

1990 Neoglaciation in the Southern Kenai Mountains, Alaska. *Annals of Glaciology* 14:319–322

Woodbury, A. C.

1984 Eskimo and Aleut Languages. In *Arctic*, edited by D. Damas, pp. 49–63. *Handbook of North American Indians*, vol. 5, W. C. Sturtevant, general editor. Smithsonian Institution, Washington, D.C.

Woodhouse-Beyer, K.

1998 Artels and Identities: Gender, Power and Russian America. In *Power, Gender and the Interpretation of Power in Archaeology*. Routledge Press, London.

Workman, W. B.

1980 Continuity and Change in the Prehistoric Record from Southern Alaska. In *Alaska Native Culture and History*, edited by Y. Kotani and W. B. Workman, pp. 49–101. Senri Ethnological Series No. 4, National Museum of Ethnology, Osaka.

1998 Archaeology of the Southern Kenai Peninsula. *Arctic Anthropology* 35(1):146–159.

Workman, W. B., and K. W. Workman

1988 The Last 1300 Years of Prehistory in Kachemak Bay: Where Later is Less. In *Late Prehistoric Development of Alaska's Native People,* edited by R. D. Shaw, R. K. Harritt, and D. E. Dumond, pp. 339–354. Aurora: Alaska Anthropological Association Monograph Series No. 4. Anchorage.

Workman, W. B., K. Workman, and D. R. Yesner

1997 Excavations at SEL-027: A Late Prehistoric Site at Port Graham, Kenai Peninsula, Alaska. Paper presented at the annual meeting of the Alaska Anthropological Association, Anchorage.

Wrangell, F. P. Von

1980 *Russian America: Statistical and Ethnographic Information.* Translated by M. Sadouski, edited by R. Pierce. The Limestone Press, Kingston, Ontario.

Yarborough, L. Finn, and M. R. Yarborough

1998 Prehistoric Maritime Adaptations of Prince William Sound and the Pacific Coast of the Kenai Peninsula. *Arctic Anthropology* 35(1):132–145.

Yesner, D. R.

1985 Cultural Boundaries and Ecological Frontiers in Coastal Regions: An Example from the Alaska Peninsula. In *The Archaeology of Frontiers and Boundaries*, edited by S. W. Green and S. M. Perlman, pp. 51–91. The Academic Press, Orlando.

1992 Evolution of Subsistence in the Kachemak Tradition: Evaluating the North Pacific Maritime Stability Model. *Arctic Anthropology* 29(2):167–181.

1998 Origins and Development of Maritime Adaptations in the Northwest Pacific Region of North America: A Zooarchaeological Perspective. *Arctic Anthropology* 35(1):204–222.

Zaikov, P.

1979 Journal of Navigator Potap Zaikov, on Ship Sv. Aleksandr Nevskii July 27–October 22, 1783 (Extract). In *A History of the Russian American Company*, vol. 2, edited by R. S. Pierce and A. S. Donnelly, pp. 1–6. Limestone Press, Kingston, Ontario.

Zimmerly, D. W.

1986 *Qajaq: Kayaks of Siberia and Alaska.* Alaska State Museum, Juneau.

Index

About the Editors

Aron L. Crowell, Ph.D., project director and curator for the *Looking Both Ways* exhibition, is Alaska regional director for the Arctic Studies Center, National Museum of Natural History, Smithsonian Institution. Crowell's research addresses the archaeology and ethnohistory of the Alutiiq region and the North Pacific, and his publications include *Archaeology and the Capitalist World System: A Study from Russian America* and *Crossroads of Continents: Cultures of Siberia and Alaska* (with William W. Fitzhugh). He teaches anthropology and museum studies at the University of Alaska Anchorage and works with Alaska Native museums and cultural centers on collaborative education and exhibition projects. His doctoral degree is from the University of California, Berkeley.

Amy F. Steffian, M.A., cocurator for the *Looking Both Ways* exhibition, is the deputy director of the Alutiiq Museum and Archaeological Repository in Kodiak, Alaska. An archaeologist who joined the museum's staff at its inception, Steffian works to design public education programs on Alutiiq culture and heritage. She is the creator of the museum's Alutiiq Word of the Week and Community Archaeology programs. Steffian teaches anthropology courses at the University of Alaska's Kodiak College and conducts research in Alutiiq prehistory. She is currently a Ph.D. candidate at the University of Michigan.

Gordon L. Pullar, Ph.D., is the director of the Department of Alaska Native and Rural Development in the College of Rural Alaska at the University of Alaska Fairbanks. He is the past president of the Kodiak Area Native Association and the current president of the Koniag Education Foundation and the Leisnoi Village Tribal Council. He also serves as chairman of the steering committee for the Arctic Studies Center, National Museum of Natural History, Smithsonian Institution. His publications have been on issues of Alutiiq identity, Native Americans and archaeology, repatriation, and cultural revitalization. He has conducted research on the organizational culture of Alaska Native organizations and the ethnohistory of Alutiiq villages. His doctorate is from the Union Institute.